WARMACHINE

PRIME
REMIX

Credits

Creators of the Iron Kingdoms
Brian Snöddy
Matt Wilson

Creative Director
Matt Wilson

Project Director
Bryan Cutler

Game Design
Matt Wilson

Lead Developer
Jason Soles

Art Director
James Davis

Development
Rob Stoddard

Writing
J. Michael Kilmartin
Douglas Seacat
Jason Soles
Bryan Steele
Matt Wilson

Continuity
Douglas Seacat
Jason Soles

Rules Editing
Steve Benton
Kevin Clark
Bryan Cutler
Andy Daniels
Gilles Reynaud
Jason Soles

Editing
Christopher Bodan
Bryan Cutler
Lauren Cutler
Andy Daniels

Cover Illustration
Matt Wilson

Illustrations
Abrar Ajmal
Daren Bader
Chippy
Matt Dixon
Jesper Ejsing
Andrew Hou
Imaginary Friends Studios
Lucio Parillo
Karl Richardson
Brian Snöddy
Mark Tedin
Eva Widermann
Matt Wilson

Concept Illustration
Matt Wilson

Cartography
Todd Gamble
Pierre-Alexandre Xavier

Graphic Design & Layout
Steve Angeles
Bryan Cutler
James Davis
Josh Manderville

Design Elements
Mike South

WARMACHINE Logo
Daniel Gelon

Miniatures Direction
Mike McVey

Sculpting
Gregory Clavilier
Christian Danckworth
Roy Eastland
Chaz Elliott
Will Hannah
Mike McVey
Jerzy Montwill
Paul Muller
Kevin White
John Winter

Miniatures Painting
Ron Kruzie
Mike McVey
Allison McVey
Dave Perrotta
Quentin Smith
Rob Stoddard

Terrain
Todd Gamble
Alfonso Falco
Mike McVey

Photography
Steve Angeles
Bryan Cutler
James Davis
Mike McVey

President
Sherry Yeary, PhD

Office Administrator
Marky Erhardt

Convention/Front Office Manager
Erik Breidenstein

Customer Support
Adam Johnson
Marc Verebely

Marketing Manager
Nathan Letsinger

NQM EIC
Nathan Letsinger

Licensing and Contract Manager
Brent Waldher

NQM Managing Editor
Eric Cagle

Press Gang Quartermaster
Dan Brandt

Assistant Quartermaster
Jamie Rarick

Production Manager
Mark Christensen

Technical Director
Kelly Yeager

Casting Manager
Douglas Colton

Shipping and Packing Manager
Kevin Clark

Production
Alex Badion
Trey Bindewald
Brandon Burton
Alex Chobot
Matt DiPietro
Joel Falkenhagen
Ryan Gatterman
Del Ivanov
Steve Kanick
Brad Lannon
Greg Lincoln
Craig Lowry
Joshua McDowell
Mike McIntosh
Justin Steurich
Ben Tracy
Clint Whiteside
Tom Williamson

Data Thrall
Don Ezra Cruz Plemons

RPG Line Director
Nathan Letsinger

Webmaster
James Kerr

Web and Forum Support
Peter Goublomme
Eric Lakin
David Ray

Infernals
David Bigley
Peter Goublomme
Isaiah Mitchell
Gilles Reynaud
John Simon

Playtesting
Alex Badion
Kayo Blackmoor
Scott Briggs
David Carl
Jessica Carl
Doug Carter
Kevin Clark
Cody Dupras
Jason Hill
Scott Hill
Rob Hinds
Chris Holt
Peter Jenisch
Jeremy Mueller
Adam Poirier
Adam Rosenblum
Bob Russel
Tim Simpson
David Sininger
Jason St. Pierre
Mark Thomas
Dan Tibbles
Kurtis Trimbo
Chris Vermeers
Dan Weber
Clint Whiteside
Eric Wilson

Proofreading
Chris Bodan
Dan Brandt
Kevin Clark
Bryan Cutler
Andy Daniels
Infernals
Doug Seacat
Johnny Servin
Jason Soles
Rob Stoddard
Marc Verebely
Brent Waldher

An extra super big dose of appreciation and thanks goes out to all our devoted players who have helped us shape WARMACHINE into the game it is today. Without your dedication to our beloved game, we would not have been able to see it grow and evolve over time. We also want to thank our infernals for all of their support. Not only do they assist us with answering questions on our forums, but they were an invaluable help with this book. We are lucky to have such a wonderful group of players and fans.

Table of Contents

Visit: www.privateerpress.com

Privateer Press, Inc.
13434 NE 16th St Suite 120 • Bellevue, WA 98005 • Tel (425) 643-5900 • Fax (425) 643-5902

For online customer service, email: frontdesk@privateerpress.com

PRIVATEER PRESS™

Foreword

To improve is to change; to be perfect is to change often. — Winston Churchill

A person can learn a thing or two in four years. What is the proper ratio of pizza to playtesters? How many cases of books do you really need to haul to a convention? If you're lucky, you might even learn how to do what you do a little better, and if you're smart, you do it.

Nearly four years ago, WARMACHINE released to an anxiously awaiting group of cutting edge early adopters. Since then WARMACHINE has garnered several awards, earned the respect of our peers, and become the cornerstone for a thriving game company populated by a crew of like-minded individuals who believe the best way to appreciate their loyal customers is to create quality products. What those early adopters might remember—and I'm talking about the people who found WARMACHINE that summer of 2002 before Prime, before cards, before we *really* had it all nailed down—was that the game of WARMACHINE was different.

At Gen Con 2002, Privateer Press had a small 10' x 20' booth situated in what one might politely refer to as B.F.E. With four small green felt demo stations, our tiny crew demonstrated the hell out of a brand new unreleased tabletop game about battle wizards and steam-powered robots. We sold early release miniatures hand-packed right there at the convention in brown craft paper boxes, and we took down each customer's name and address so that we could send them a free rulebook and stat cards once they were printed six months later. In the meantime, with each purchase we provided a plastic promotional ruler printed with 'cheat sheet' information and a folded photocopied flyer with the *original* quick start rules of WARMACHINE.

The funny thing about those original rules and that ruler is that they bear little resemblance to the game you have come to know as a veteran player or the one you are about to experience if you are new to the game. The fundamental concepts were there—warcasters commanded warjacks, pouring their focus into them to make them fight more capably while casting spells and mixing it up themselves—but the game system ran using action points, and the language found in those early rules was far from what we'd call 'bullet proof'. Nonetheless, WARMACHINE sparked something in the people who experienced it, and word of this new game spread quickly through the gaming community at large.

We were hiding a secret, though. WARMACHINE wasn't a completed game. Just a few weeks after what was otherwise a very successful convention for a tiny little startup company, we were tearing down the rules and building them up all over again. We knew the game could be better, faster, and stronger. We abandoned action points, stripped away rules, and refined language until what finally emerged was the game that would be printed in the six thousand original *WARMACHINE: Prime* rulebooks that shipped in April of 2003.

As those books arrived at the homes of our early adopters, readers quickly saw a drastic difference in how the game functioned. All of the attractive concepts that drew them into the game were still present, but the engine of the game had changed. It was better.

Prime Remix isn't as drastically different as *WARMACHINE: Prime* was from the original rules we distributed at Gen Con in 2002. The Remix is an attempt to get one step closer to perfection. Our goal has always been to make the absolute best tabletop miniatures game possible. The Remix cleans up small rules issues, makes minor adjustments to game balance, and most importantly, it puts all of the players of WARMACHINE on the same footing with a new volume that has been crafted with the wisdom of four years of experience. In that time we have had the opportunity to develop several expansions, observe countless tournaments, and find what works and what doesn't. This book is the culmination of our analysis and is meant to improve the overall gaming experience for WARMACHINE players. It boasts a few new tracks and some funky new beats, yet it is a sound comfortably familiar and excitingly fresh all at the same time.

This is not the last stop for WARMACHINE. We will always continue to move in the direction of perfection, learn from our experiences, and apply the lessons to the game. Maybe someday we'll even produce that perfect, final product, or at least figure out how much pizza you need to feed a roomful of gamers.

Warning: Not suitable for wussies!

Sissies, little girls, and nancy boys should go home now. This game is not for you.

If you cry when you lose, get lost 'cause you're going to lose. If it hurts your fragile sensibilities to see your favorite character get pounded unmercifully by a rapid succession of **no-holds-barred iron fury**, you'd better look the other way. If you've ever whined the words, "That's too powerful," then put the book down slowly and walk away before making eye contact with anyone, or they'll realize your voice hasn't changed yet.

This game is about aggression. This is the game of metal-on-metal combat. This is fuel-injected power hopped up on steroids. This is WARMACHINE—the battle game that kicks so much ass we have to use all capital letters.

We didn't set out to reinvent the wheel with this game. We just armor plated it, covered it in spikes, and **rolled it over your grandma's house.**

WARMACHINE is simple. It's easy to learn, has no reference charts, needs no heavy arithmetic, and doesn't require constant trips to the rulebook. At the same time, WARMACHINE possesses deep strategy. The ability to unlock combinations of abilities, spells, and maneuvers is practically limitless. For every perfect strategy, there is a foil. For every immovable object, **there is an unstoppable force.** Just when you think you've got it all worked out, you'll be blindsided by something you never saw before. The more you dig, the more you'll find.

WARMACHINE favors the aggressor. You've got to throw the first punch if you want to land on top! Too many other games set players up to be timid, and the battles drag out with little action because the game favors defensive strategies. Players park their soldiers behind walls like old ladies hiding from a loud noise. Not in WARMACHINE! If you wait for your opponent to come to you, you're going to get steamrolled. **You've got to have balls* to play this game!** You've got to charge your opponent and hang it all out there! You've got to break his formations. You've got to be relentless with your onslaught. You have to go for the jugular and latch on like a rabid dog that hasn't eaten in days. Anything less, and you'll be hamburger.

You're playing with power now. Don't be afraid! Few things are more satisfying than slamming your opponent's warjack into a unit of soldiers and watching them **fall like bowling pins!** (We call this 'jack bowling.) Try picking up an enemy warcaster (with a warjack, of course) and throwing it across the battlefield! It's almost more fun than you should be allowed to have with a miniatures game.

The miniatures of WARMACHINE deliver on every level the game does. These warjacks radiate power! We're pouring so much metal that we may soon deplete the world of tin. **These things were made for modeling.** The incredible detail and expert sculpting will create one of the most enjoyable painting experiences you've ever had.

You are now part of a new era in tabletop miniatures wargaming. This is a game made for you by people like you. It's not a load of sterilized mass market drek designed by a room full of corporate meatplows, and we've been proving it now for the past four years. **This is raw. This is brutal. This is WARMACHINE.**

So play like you've got a pair, or put down the metal and go join a quilting bee.

Metaphorically speaking, of course! Duh.

PLAY LIKE YOU'VE GOT A PAIR!

Frost and Thunder
Late Autumn 604 AR along the Khadoran and Llaelese border

Without warning the lead wagon burst into a ball of fire. The explosion sent splintered wood and twisted metal into the sky and tossed the dormant warjack it carried like a child's toy. The entire column collapsed in disarray as blue-clad soldiers tumbled to the side. Wildly swinging rifles sought targets as wide eyes scanned the snow-frosted tree line. The Trenchers at the fore recovered first and set up a firing line backed by the long gunners. The Stormblades to the rear did not flinch as debris bounced off their thick armor. They rushed forward to form a defensive line shielding the chief mechanik and his bodgers sitting on the second wagon. Proving his professionalism, the chief mechanik stoically ignored the debris and leapt down to the Ironclad thrown from the exploded wagon onto the snow-frosted road.

Commander Coleman Stryker stood out from the chaos, disruptor pistol in hand, and shouted orders to his men. "Sergeant Kilberge, get your long gunners under cover!" He pointed to a low line of rocks along the roadside to the right. "Sergeant Bridgely, stagger your Trenchers along that left gully and keep your eyes peeled. Lieutenant Kates, what's our damage?"

Lieutenant Jayne Kates had served as Stryker's journeyman warcaster for nearly a year on the northern front. She ran forward, hand cannon drawn, to consult with Chief Mechanik Jagins as he peered under the demolished wagon. She reported back to her commander. "A buried explosive in the road, sir." The gory carcasses of two of the forward draft horses lay seeping blood into the snow. The others had broken tethers and fled before anyone could grab them.

Not one to wait for orders, the third warcaster in the group—Captain Victoria Haley—advanced alongside the Trenchers. A Lancer warjack, its glowing eyes looking where she looked, accompanied her with shield and lance at the ready. She stood poised like a hunting hawk and sparked her vortex spear to life. From behind her goggles her sharp eyes searched the trees and hills for any sign of movement. Haley was a tall woman of slender frame even under the bulk of warcaster armor. "No enemies in sight, sir." She sounded vaguely disappointed.

Stryker's voice had the ring of a man comfortable with command as he addressed the group. "Everyone stay sharp. I don't want a word of chatter." He stepped up alongside Lieutenant Kates and the chief mechanik and sent his own escorting Charger to the fore of the column. Smoke poured from its stacks as it readied its double-barreled cannon.

They were escorting a large shipment of older heav[y] warjacks to the garrison at Redwall Fortress, taking a risk[y] but expedient path close to the Khadoran border. Keepin[g] only their light warjacks fired up and active reduced th[e] strain on the coal supply. The 'jack wagons were custo[m] built with heavy reinforced timber and iron straps, eac[h] designed to carry one inactive heavy 'jack or two light[s.] Stryker recognized the downed Ironclad, a 'jack he ha[d] nicknamed Ol' Rowdy, as an old favorite he had used sinc[e] his time as a captain. "How bad is it, chief?"

Jagins looked up and sighed. His face, uniform, an[d] gloves were covered in oil and grease. "Good thing it's a[n] Ironclad, sir, or it'd be spare parts. As it is we've got a ba[d] shear at the join between hips and lower torso. Need a sho[p] to do it right, but I can do a patch job." The chief mechani[k] saw one of his bodger assistants picking among the debri[s] and barked at him. "Don't just stand there. Get my twent[y] pound box-end spanner!" The gobber hastened to obey.

Lieutenant Kates stepped over to Stryker. The woma[n] had short, spiky blond hair and an athletic build, and th[e] commander had entrusted her with an old veteran Sentine[l.] Her 'jack boasted two decades of service and enough bad[ly] scratched paint and welded joins to speak to its time in battle[.] "I think we've been using this road too much the last fe[w] weeks, sir. They must have anticipated us. Though I'd recko[n] they weren't expecting to catch a wolf in this rabbit trap."

"Don't get overconfident, Lieutenant." Stryker warne[d] her. He had seen enough of the Khadorans to know the[y] were no fools. He turned to Chief Mechanik Jagins an[d] asked, "How long to patch that heap? We're going to nee[d] it to walk on its own with that wagon gone."

The red-faced man scowled back, "Could be a fe[w] minutes or an hour. I've seen worse, but the hip assembl[y] is clapped and all the pistons are crammed together. G[ot] to pry 'em loose."

Captain Haley returned to their position. She pulle[d] back her hood to reveal fine facial features and mid[-] length sandy blond hair. The row of badges on her sleev[e] designating service in numerous tours with the Third Arm[y] down south at Highgate marked her as an outsider amon[g] their force. "Sir, that explosion must have been heard fo[r] miles. Let me take a small force to scout ahead of the mai[n] column and check for ambush."

Commander Stryker disliked the idea of splittin[g] the force and frowned as he considered it. "We need t[o]

keep together." Stryker saw that Haley clearly did not like that answer, but she nodded. Despite his words Stryker's shoulders itched in a way that bothered him. After a pause he turned to the chief. "Fire up the Ironclad and offload the Defender. We're sitting ducks. You've got 20 minutes and not a second more to get that Ironclad on its feet." He walked away from the column to gain a better vantage.

Captain Haley came to join him. Her eyes suggested both a youthful enthusiasm and a hunger for battle dangerous for someone in her position. "Maybe we'll see some action, sir?"

The commander brooded. "Something is wrong. Khadoran movements have changed. The last few months we had skirmishes every few days and then not a single red and gold flag. Now this trap."

The captain remained silent, but Stryker sensed she did not understand. She reminded him of an unhooded hunting hawk poised to fly against its prey. Stryker knew more about Victoria Haley than she would have appreciated. He knew about the burned village of Ingrane, her murdered

family, and the talented sorceress bent on revenge standing before him. The last place she wanted to be was in the north watching the onset of winter.

Haley turned to the hills northwest of the road and her eyes narrowed. "Do you feel that?"

Stryker followed her line of sight and noted worse weather coming their way over the next ridge. His own Lancer and Charger turned their heads exactly as he did. "I don't see anything."

"I think I sense a warcaster nearby."

Stryker closed his eyes and found it at last. He felt an electric sensation and a slight tremble at the edge of his awareness. The fact that Haley had sensed it so easily confirmed the rumors he had heard of her arcane abilities.

There came a rumbling of steam engines and the heavy tread of warjacks. Haley's Lancer and Defender approached them. Stryker frowned at her impertinence, but she spoke in a rush before he could interject. "Let me investigate, sir. I can get a count on the enemy."

Stryker's eyes narrowed. His instinct told him it was a bad idea. Despite her youth, however, Victoria Haley was a veteran warcaster proven in many battles to the south. "Agreed, Captain. But don't engage. Determine their strength and get back."

"Yes, sir." She signaled the long gunners attached to her command, and alongside this escort and her two 'jacks, she hurried up the hill.

"Captain Haley!" Stryker called after her. She paused and looked over her shoulder. "Be careful. These aren't mindless thralls. They're Khadorans and they know our tactics."

The way her lips compressed suggested she did not share his concern. She offered a salute and continued on. Stryker sighed. It was always the same with officers from Highgate. Once they fought the Cryx they presumed they could handle anything.

Stryker jogged back to Lieutenant Kates. She snapped to attention and reported, "Trenchers are dug-in at the perimeter, and the long gunners have cover. Ready for your orders, Commander." She saw his frown. "Anything wrong, sir?"

He shook his head and his expression lost some of its tension. "Just another warcaster trying my patience."

"Warcasters can be like that, sir." Kates remarked with her face carefully blank.

"Morrow save me from stubborn women." He ignored her sour look and turned to the chief. "Is that thing ready yet, Jagins, or do you have a secret desire to learn Khadoran?"

"I've almost got it, Commander!" The Ironclad's engine was up and running, but Stryker could sense its legs remained inhibited.

Stryker gathered his Stormblades and ordered the Trenchers to heed Lieutenant Kates in getting the group ready to move. Every instinct he had told him something bad was coming like the first blizzard of winter.

* * *

Captain Haley felt a keen desire to prove herself to this commander. His understated condescension was getting under her skin. She had learned to fight against waves of Cryxian raiders on the southern coasts, so she had no fear of lumbering Khadorans and their clumsy machines.

She sent her senses through the Lancer as the nimble warjack ran ahead and managed to spot the enemy. Through the machine's eyes she identified a Destroyer up on a hill across a short valley of rough, snowy ground. A heavy fog threatening snow settled across the area. The fog made it difficult to discern details, but Haley could see movement across the valley to the west. A surprisingly large force was making its way directly toward where the explosion had halted the Cygnaran column. She estimated troops were closing in from two directions and the one to the west would soon come upon the road. If she went back to tell the commander now, she would only arrive in time to be surrounded and attacked from both sides.

Haley did not casually disobey orders, but her warcaster training told her to trust her instincts. Her Defender's heavy barrel cannon would have range on the Destroyer and she could pick it apart from a distance. If she could divert this force and draw fire it might buy time for the soldiers on the road. The sound of battle here would serve as a better warning than marching back with her slow Defender in tow. She silently signaled the long gunners to circle to the right and keep to the trees.

She saw the shape of what could only be a Juggernaut emerge from the fog ahead and begin advancing across the intervening ground. This disabused her of the notion she could catch the enemy by surprise. Clearly her Khadoran counterpart had sensed Haley's approach. The valley between the Lancer and the Khadoran 'jack was filled with thorny brambles and snow covered rocks which Haley knew would keep the Juggernaut mired. She looked through her Defender's eyes and raised its heavy barrel. Its eyes blazed as she instilled it with arcane energy. The cannon fired with a loud *thump*, and the Defender shuddered as its chassis absorbed the recoil. The shell flew true, trailed smoke as it hurtled into the advancing warjack, and impacted with the sound of tearing metal.

Haley directed the Lancer, running on agile metal legs, to cross below the long gunners. She hoped to evade the Juggernaut and rush the arc node nearer to the real threat of the Destroyer. She signaled her long gunners to take their shot. They raised rifles in a smooth line followed by the satisfying crackle of repeating long guns laying down a hail of concentrated fire. Bullets tore through exposed piping, gears, and armored plates, but still the Juggernaut plodded forward without slowing.

A sudden noise made her turn just in time to witness several long gunners, including Sergeant Kilberge, drop almost soundlessly to the snow. The rolling echo of rifle fire reached them an instant later. White snow blossomed with shockingly red blood. Haley and the surviving men hunkered down, and she caught sight of huddled forms down the next slope. They looked like Khadorans in dark leathers almost hidden among the trees with long rifles in hand.

Haley snapped to full battle awareness. Looking through the Lancer's eyes, she drew a clear line to the nearest Widowmaker as he chambered another cartridge into his hunting rifle. She unleashed lightning and poured arcane strength into the attack. A torrent of pure electrical power channeled through the Lancer with a crackle and boom of thunder. It leapt from one Khadoran to the next, and they burned and fell, smoking and twitching. Haley found it a grimly satisfying sight.

A surge of movement to her left made her turn back. The Juggernaut—which had been plodding through the broken ground—was charging forward at impossible speed. The nine-ton warjack waded through the field of rocks and brambles as if they were no impediment. The edge of the massive axe glowed blue with mechanika and glittered like ice as the 'jack raised the weapon to strike.

The axe fell with the force of an avalanche. It clove through the Lancer's heavy shield and left arm before sinking deep into its frame and shattering armored plates. The Lancer suddenly frosted over and became encased in ice. While the smaller warjack stood frozen and helpless the Juggernaut hacked once more straight into the exposed engine casing and reduced it to a pile of smoking wreckage. Haley felt its engine's heartfire die and heard a thump as the boiler exploded from the steam pressure. The Juggernaut turned to look straight at Captain Haley with glowing eyes, and she realized too late that she might have made a tactical mistake.

* * *

Just as Chief Jagins declared the Ironclad ready, Commander Stryker heard the distinct thump of a Defender's cannon followed by sporadic rifle fire. He cursed and ordered his men into motion. "Everyone move! Double time!" He ran with his pistol in one hand and Quicksilver in the other. He urged all of his warjacks forward as fast as their steam-driven legs could push them. Each stride of the hulking machines sunk through the snow to the hardened ground beneath.

Stryker turned to his Stormblades, and a ring of glowing runes circled his wrist as he instilled their glaives with sorcerous power that extended the reach of their lightning blasts. From the battle ahead came a sound reminiscent of a locomotive thrown off its tracks, and he recognized the distinctive music of one warjack tearing another apart. A nightmare image came to Commander Stryker, and he rushed ahead heedless of outpacing his force.

* * *

Haley knew she was still in the battle despite the troubling loss of her Lancer. Retreat was a poor option given the Khadoran warcaster had the ability to speed warjacks across difficult terrain. She yelled "Fire!" to the

long gunners, and they unleashed another mass volley. She still had her Defender, and she urged it to step up and interpose its bulk between her and the enemy. Its cannon fired again. The heavy shell blasted into Khadoran armor with a screech of protesting metal. She could not believe the thing was still standing. It just kept coming despite torn armor and broken pipes venting steam. It was as relentless as an enraged bear.

She looked past the Juggernaut and blood drained from her face. It was not just the sight of the Khadoran warcaster charging down the hill as if borne by the wind itself nor even the *two* Destroyers following after launching shells in whistling arcs. What unnerved her was the horde of red-uniformed soldiers pouring from the forest. She saw what looked like an entire Winter Guard company, a squad of Iron Fang Pikemen, and—as if that were not enough—Man-O-War in heavy steam-powered armor. She had sought to draw the attention of the Khadorans, and she had succeeded.

Haley surrounded herself in a shell of magical protection as bombard shells exploded around her and rocked the earth. One impacted directly on her Defender and nearly tore off its heavy barrel in the blast. She shielded her face against a spray of heavy debris that her armor's power field and arcane defenses barely deflected. The other shell prompted screams of pain and anguish when it landed among the long gunners. Those surviving turned and routed heedless of her shouts. The enemy warcaster advanced and reached the Juggernaut's side in a few long strides. The stern woman in red armor held a wicked mechanikal polearm.

Haley sent forth a ripple of power to dilate time itself. Through sheer arcane skill she forced her enemies to walk through this distortion while her allies remained untouched. Anyone unaffected saw those trapped by this power move with ponderous deliberation and exaggerate their every motion.

It helped, but even slowed the enemy advanced unrelentingly. Soldiers, a warcaster, and no less than three warjacks closed in on all sides. The red-armored warcaster bore an expression as hard as stone and cold blue eyes that seemed to pick her enemy apart and dismiss her. Haley sensed this was a woman who had fought and killed many Cygnarans.

There was a moment of frisson and the air itself crystallized in a blast of cold so intense it knocked the breath from Haley's lungs. A white ripple spread through the air and turned it suddenly and unnaturally clear. Haley discovered she could no longer move. Everything was completely frozen. Through her connection to the Defender's cortex she sensed its alarm as its engine fire banked and its limbs refused to respond. Paralyzed alongside her warjack Haley was helpless. She could do nothing but pray to Morrow and force all of her will into the power field shimmering around her.

* * *

Stryker heard more explosions and the rifle fire peter out. *A bad sign*, he thought. He topped the rise and saw the horrific tableau of what looked like a major Khadoran force crossing the intervening valley. "Trenchers advance! Lay down smoke and cover the captain! Kates, get that Sentinel into position. Stormblades, to Haley!" He knew the barrier reducing their charge to a slow dance would not hold. As if hearing Stryker's thought, Haley's barrier faded and the Khadorans rushed forward like hounds let off their leashes.

There was only one hope. In a tremendous surge of arcane power Stryker reached out across the field of battle. His body became surrounded by circles of shimmering runes that mirrored in a brief flash around all his men and Captain Haley.

It came just in time, as the enemy Destroyers advanced to fire bombards. One shell landed squarely on Captain Haley. Though still frozen she staggered as the blast washed over an invisible shell a few inches from her skin. Her overboosted power field and Stryker's protections proved just enough to deflect the blast.

Stryker ran as fast as he could but was still too far away when the female Khadoran charged forward and swung her scythe in a tremendous sweeping blow that leveraged all of her momentum straight into Captain Haley's side. Thanks to Stryker's efforts and Haley's other layered protections it was like hitting an impervious stone. The Khadoran's strike bounced off with nothing but a ripple of shimmering blue in the air. The enemy warcaster followed with two more blows with similar effect before Stryker's impelled Lancer managed to run straight into her from the flank. The 'jack battered her with the flat of its shield and sent her flying ten yards back and sliding along the ground.

Stryker extended his will to his Charger and felt its dual cannon as if it were in his own hands. Ideally he would have fired on the downed warcaster, but she had slid out of range. He targeted the Juggernaut instead as it approached the captain with its axe raised. A long shot, he judged, but just in range. The cannon fired with a paired sequence of low thuds, and the shells impacted the battered Juggernaut with loud pings. The light warjack's cannon was not built to penetrate a Khadoran heavy, and the only sign of the shots were two smoking holes in its red armor.

"All attacks on the Juggernaut! Fire storm glaives!" Stormblade Sergeant Keller Mackler shouted as his men came alongside the Charger. They extended their glowing blades and the air darkened and thickened with the smell of ozone. Forks of lightning surged forth. Thunder rolled across the valley as energy consumed the Juggernaut and tore through its hull to shred the fragile gearworks beneath. With a grinding noise the smoking husk of the machine finally halted.

The Khadoran warcaster scrambled quickly to her feet and backed away a few paces with a cold rage in her eyes, and Stryker felt a moment's satisfaction. He doubted she had realized she faced more than one enemy warcaster until this moment.

Stryker had no time to exchange insults with his enemy. His awareness spread across the battlefield. He could feel Ol' Rowdy coming from behind, and he stressed its pressured boilers to the limit as he urged it to accelerate. Lieutenant Kates's Sentinel laid down suppressing fire with its spinning chain gun. Bullets flew across the valley to tear through the Winter Guard's lightly armored uniforms. Those hit tumbled to the snow in plumes of blood, but there were still too many. Trencher smoke began to obscure the Cygnarans but not before they endured a massive barrage of blunderbuss fire. Shots whizzed through the air, but Stryker's protections kept his men safe for the moment. He knew it would not last.

Stryker had the lives of his men foremost on his mind. He conceived and dismissed a dozen plans of attack knowing the cost would be too high. He grabbed Haley's arm to pull her back from the front and felt her start to thaw from paralysis. His Lancer was in position. He recognized the signs of a larger Khadoran force behind this vanguard in the black smoke of 'jack furnaces over the next rise and what looked like more soldiers moving between the trees.

Stryker timed it carefully. He sent Ol' Rowdy past him and extended his power through the Lancer. Runes again circled his outstretched fingers as he sent an eruption of arcane power centered on the heavily armored Man-O-War in the Khadoran line. The earth heaved and split apart. The ground dropped below the advancing soldiers and slammed upward to topple the entire front. The Ironclad strode like a giant into the center of the Iron Fangs and sent them sprawling when it hammered the ground with its quake hammer.

The Destroyers fired explosive rounds as they advanced, but Captain Haley raised her hand alongside Stryker's. Pointing directly at the nearest Destroyer, she sent a confusing surge of bewildering power to scramble the matrix of the 'jack's artificial mind. It swayed and lurched off to the side, temporarily neutralized. For a moment Stryker caught the eye of the Khadoran warcaster. He could see the torment in her eyes as she considered attacking despite everything. Even knowing that her line was tripped up and that she faced two warcasters now with only one of her warjacks responding to her will, she still longed to press the attack. Cursing in Khadoran she gathered a swirling wind around her, stirring snow and fog, and retreated.

Commander Stryker yelled out to his men. "Fall back! Fall back! Sergeant Bridgely keep that smoke up. Stormblades cover the Trenchers. Back to the column!"

They withdrew with each warcaster firing hand cannons until the wall of smoke obscured the enemy. Captain Haley spoke over the continuing shrieks of incoming blind Destroyer fire. "I'm sorry I didn't withdraw, sir. I spotted a force heading toward our column, so I took the opportunity to divert them."

Apparently uncertain of the size of the Cygnaran force, the Khadorans slowed their pursuit and fired a last volley. The Cygnaran warjacks kept toward the rear. Kates' Sentinel and Stryker's Charger fired to discourage the enemy advance. "That was foolish, Captain," Stryker said. "You have no right to take unnecessary risks with the lives of *my* men, especially when you are under my command." Haley lowered her eyes with a troubled expression at this reminder of the fallen long gunners. "If we shake these Khadorans we'll come back for the dead. They will get a proper burial. I'll make sure of that."

"Thank you, sir." Haley's voice was small. For a moment she seemed extremely young. *Far too young for bloodshed like this*, Stryker thought. He quickly dismissed the notion. Cygnar needed every warcaster they had right now. Winter was coming, and who knew how many of them would live long enough to see the spring?

He barked orders to organize their return to the caravan, anxious to get word to the generals about Khadoran troop movements. They cleared the trees and looked down on the road where the wagons had halted. A barrage of Khadoran artillery had pummeled the snow-covered road and left a series of smoking black craters. He was relieved to see the chief engineer and his crew alive sheltering on the side of the road. Stryker lifted his goggles and exposed battle weary, soot-rimmed eyes. Both warcasters considered how many would be dead if they had remained with the caravan. His voice was only audible to Haley, and he nodded his head toward the craters below. "Sometimes you have to trust your instincts."

The Iron Kingdoms
Forging a world in blood and metal

From the journals of Rhupert Carvolo, the Ordic Piper of Sorrows

Evening of Solesh the 28th, 601 AR

I am a traveler. I call no land my home, and my sore feet have crossed the length of these kingdoms. I earn my coin in battle and move constantly from one field of strife to another. I have only a few spare hours between to note my thoughts and to rest and recover my strength. Though Ordic born I have no living family and few ties to that land. I must confess I feel more comfortable anywhere but there, as those hills remind me of tragedies I have tried to forget. Now I sit in one of many pubs in western Caspia, City of Walls. It is a maze city where the view is choked on all sides by mighty bulwarks rising to the sky. How many bloody wars have unfolded beyond these great gates? How many swords and spears have torn human flesh to purchase another few yards of land? It was here that our ancestors forged the enormous colossals, the giant war machines which fought off the Orgoth invaders. Many look no further back than that as if our history began in those days. Their narrow view ignores the deeper roots of the people of this region.

For an era long beyond reckoning mankind roamed Immoren in wild and savage tribes, incapable of recording their deeds. Menoth, our Creator, left us in this state to test our strength. After a time we caught His eye when we put forward the rudiments of culture. The first priests rose, chosen by The Lawgiver to bind us together, and taught us law. Some call it a gift and others a curse. Menoth was our first and eldest god, the Shaper of Man, and our form resembles Him that made us.

I am a tale-spinner. I chronicle man's endless appetites for destruction and strife, and his search to redeem bloodshed through heroics, in song and melody. Some distinguish between fact and legend, but I insist the two are inseparable. That Menoth once strode Caen is a fact to me as solid as the count of those who fell at the Boarsgate Massacre. Menoth's priests shaped our earliest villages and farming communities into true towns and cities. Some of our buildings today stand on the bones of ancient structures. Take this city, for example. I do not visit it often. I find it oppressive and over-crowded, but even a simple tale-spinner from Ord can recognize Caspia as one of the grandest and eldest of man's works still standing. One can walk through these ancient streets and mark the entire course of our history brick by brick. Still, these accomplishments—great cities, statues of ancient kings, libraries with marbled floors—pale before man's inexhaustible thirst for war. In the ancient Warlord Era our communities fought endless battles. I am inclined

to believe it was Menoth's will, for he saw strength as an essential quality in both ruler and ruled.

Even in the face of vast cycles of history, some events are so significant they forever change the shape of the world. The rise of the Twins was one such moment. Many consider their arrival the birth of modern thought. They see it as the first attempt to discern the world by philosophy rather than blind obedience to the priest caste. These two great figures shattered the way mankind saw his place in the world among its people.

The Twins were mortals who transcended their flesh to become gods. They cut their own paths in a time that considered free thinking blasphemy, and they stood above the teeming masses as intellectual giants. They left their footprints across Immoren and drew thousands of followers to learn from their example. We always speak of Morrow before his sister, as her legacy is as dark as his is bright, but their destinies were joined. One need not be a theologian to appreciate the rich complexity of the philosophies arising in their wake. Their ideas shook the foundations of civilization.

Morrow taught there was more to life than battle and blind obedience to law. He claimed a good man must think of others before himself. Thousands followed his example and looked inward for answers. Morrow said that leading a good life required the will to promote the well-being of others, to right injustice, to fight honorably in war, and leave a noble legacy to the next generation. Morrow was a warrior-philosopher such as the world has yet to see again. No wonder his religion spread faster than the Menites could contain it.

Nor do I forget the darkly beautiful Thamar. Selfish as her brother was selfless and as fascinated by the darkness as he the light, Thamar did not heed her brother but paved her own path. She felt true power came from placing the one before the many and compromising nothing in the pursuit of individual strength and power. She taught that a person should not allow morality to limit his or her freedom. Thamar delved into forgotten occult lore and profane secrets. She ascended by freeing her mind from the shackles of conscience. Priests describe Thamar as depraved as her brother was enlightened, and she transformed into the dark mirror of her brother, a goddess of temptation, indulgence, dark magic, and deception. The rise of these gods marked the beginning of the Thousand Cities Era.

Like a stained-glass window fallen from its casing to shatter on the ground, the map of western Immoren fractured. City-states of various sizes arose, each with its own warlord or petty king. Pub-born treaties and back-alley allegiances lasted only long enough to muster men-at-arms for countless murderous excursions. Bloody raids to pillage our neighbors extended beyond our own species. We battled trollkin and ogrun tribes, and we foolishly encroached on the ancient, secluded lands ruled by the dwarves of Rhul and the inscrutable elves of Ios. Our efforts resulted in defeat after bloody defeat. The dwarves would not budge from lines drawn in the rocky soil of Rhul, and every force sent into Ios simply vanished.

Though the warfare never ceased, the fractured map began to consolidate as strong kings seized the lands of their rivals and brought more people under their heels. Caspia expanded. Thuria rose and Tordor consumed it. The Midlunds unified. The vast Khardic Empire stretched from the north to consume the Kos, Skirov, Umbrean, and

> # Even in the face of vast cycles of histori some events are so significant they fore change the shape of the world.

Ryn peoples. Caspia experienced a flowering of thought and reason including the construction of the Archcourt Cathedral in the Sancteum. Khardic engineers invented the steam engine and began to realize its potential. Ships fueled by coal plied the rivers without relying on currents or winds. Among my ancestors the dirgenmast captains of Tordor formed an armada stronger than the world had ever seen, and the sails of a thousand ships spread across the ocean from horizon to horizon. Who can say what heights we might have reached had we been able to capitalize on these achievements? Such was not to be. Across the ocean came a nightmare given form in a fleet of black longboats landing on our shores.

The arrival of the Orgoth would eclipse even the ascension of the Twins and leave an indelible stain across our history.

The Orgoth arrived with a rapacious hunger for slaughter and enslavement. They seemed human enough but proved more cruel and calculating than our ancestors. Where we were warlike, the Orgoth embraced slaughter and cruelty with complete enthusiasm. The Tordoran Armada sailed to meet the Orgoth ship to ship, but they sent our proud vessels to the deep and spawned the Sea of a Thousand Souls. Countless longboats spilled cruel warriors onto the beaches of Immoren. The once-warring tribes and towns of the Thousand Cities fought valiantly together for the first time, but the disorganized resistance failed to stop them.

The Orgoth consorted with dark powers. They boasted fell magic and wielded weapons terrible beyond reckoning. In that time we had not invented the firearm or the colossal, nor had we any wizards among us. Menite war priests and Morrowan battle chaplains brought the power of their gods and fought as best they could, but we were undone. The Orgoth pacified us through rivers of our own blood although it took nearly two centuries.

The Orgoth did not seek to destroy Immoren. No. They subjugated and enslaved us instead. Camps of starving men and women lashed on by whip and the threat of torture pounded out the fine roads we still use today. Thousands of stone-torn hands erected the basalt fortresses and towers

The arrival of the Orgoth would eclipse even the ascension of the Twins and leave an indelible stain across our history.

of our conquerors. Our forefathers died realizing the vision that the Orgoth sculpted of our primal clay, and much of that blood-soaked stone and marble foundation holds up our world. Caspia alone held them at bay, but only their towering walls kept the Caspians safe. The Caspian armies were defeated every time they marched from their walls to test the Orgoth. For four centuries the Orgoth occupied our lands uncontested, crushed us underfoot, extinguished generations of progress, and plunged us into a dark period best forgotten.

Neither quick nor easy, our eventual defiance and overthrow of the Orgoth proved a painful and excruciating process that consumed us for two hundred years. My poet's soul finds it somehow fitting that just as it took two hundred years to pacify us, we required two hundred more to break the chains binding us. After six centuries of abuse, a rising tide of resentment swept up our ancestors and put fire back in their eyes. The spark of resistance returned to their spirits, yet spirit alone was not enough. Every rebellion requires weapons and a cost paid in blood. The dark goddess

Thamar played a part by giving us our first taste of magic with the "Gift of Sorcery". From this one spark of formerly forbidden power the Rebellion sustained itself and innovated new weapons even after suffering setback and defeat. Once the blaze of rebellion ignited no efforts by the Orgoth, no matter how brutal their reprisals, could extinguish this slim hope of eventual freedom.

The rebels earned key victories not by simple courage but by the inventive application of new skills and lore combined with engineering principles predating the Orgoth. Sorcery alone was too blunt an instrument. The tyrants had their own warwitches and fiendish weapons to tear a man's soul from his flesh. We invented the firearm from alchemy developed when survivors of the Battle of the Hundred Wizards fled east, but even guns could not turn the Orgoth aside. It was the effort of other inventors to integrate the new science of mechanika with old principles of engineering, such as the Khardic steam engine, which provided the key. These brilliant minds conceived the first colossal as a steam-driven, war-ready construct of gears, iron, and smoke standing fifty feet tall or more. It only remained to find the means to build these iron monsters without detection at a time when the Orgoth still controlled so much of the region.

Man's commitment and resourcefulness so impressed the dwarves of Rhul that they pledged their aid. They would not fight directly but their assistance with supplies and labor brought the colossals from a dream on an engineer's drafting table to a towering reality. This heralded a new age of mechanika which has touched every corner of our lives since.

We earned small gains in earlier great battles by freeing Leryn and later Korsk, but our situation remained tenuous until the colossals strode from the bowels of Caspia to march on Orgoth fortresses. The greatest gains of the Rebellion came in a few short years once we unleashed the giant constructs. The Orgoth Empire toppled as every giant footstep pushed the black-hearted invaders west. They fled by boat but did not go quietly. The Orgoth razed cities as they retreated, poisoned wells, salted fields, and defiled the lands in an act called the 'Scourge'.

We rediscovered what it meant to govern ourselves when the leaders of the victorious armies, called the 'Council of Ten', met in Corvis, Cygnar's City of Ghosts. This council hammered out the new Iron Kingdoms on their political anvils. Deliberations lasted for weeks. Blood is thick, and these hard-nosed men came from lineages once longtime enemies. The negotiations resulted in the Corvis Treaties that drew the borderlines for the newly formed territories and created the kingdoms of Cygnar, Khador, Ord, and Llael.

Midmorning, Glaceus the 24th, 602 AR

Western Immoren stretches from the sandstorm-ridden Bloodstone Marches and the secret confines of Ios to the long, unending waters of Meredius in the west. The dark lands of necromantic Cryx sprawl across the Scharde Islands and form the southwestern edge of Immoren while the northern tundra of savage, snow-covered glacial plains, inhabited by the territorial Nyss, cap this realm in the north. The last four centuries have known much strife with no end in sight: wars waged and peace shattered, sovereigns elevated and torn down, old kingdoms devoured and new ones born, borders bent and rewritten, and crowns acquired by ruse, poison, or blade.

The elven homeland of Ios lies nestled in a vast forest valley between barrier mountains which prevent the encroachment of the Bloodstone Marches. Ios has sealed off their borders for decades, and what we know of Ios is mostly rumor and fabrication. Foolish trespassers who venture under their trees uninvited never return. A long shadow of superstition extends from their borders, and some whisper of dark machinations growing within.

Rhul is the mountain nation of dwarves and the ogrun welcomed into their cities. Rhulfolk are honorable, stoic, and robust people boasting a culture that has changed little in thousands of years. They pride themselves on their mastery of stone crafting, but do not believe foolish rumors that dwarves live only below the soil. They have erected tremendous castles, vaulted halls, and towers that scrape the sky, and their industrious nature is one we could do worse than emulate. Rhulfolk trace their heritage back to the original thirteen clans who founded their nation and appear to revere the clan fathers as gods. As Menite priests once ruled the land by the dictates of the 'True Law' the Rhulfolk obey the 'Codex' which serves as both a holy text and a summary of their confusing laws.

Dwarves, unlike Iosans, enjoy the company of mankind. They trade large quantities of manufactured goods and mined materials to Khador and Cygnar in exchange for food, timber, and other materials difficult to find in their rocky homeland. Every passing generation pays greater mind to happenings abroad, and many venture south to make their fortunes.

Evening of Casteus the 10th, 602 AR

Today I pen a few words on the smaller kingdoms often overlooked by the great powers: Llael and Ord. The tiny kingdom of Llael boasts a bevy of nobles consumed by politics and trade arrangements. Ord, the land of my birth, brings me both happiness and sorrow in equal measure.

Llael sits nestled at the easternmost corner of Immoren betwixt Rhul, Ios, Khador, and Cygnar. Their western border has been in constant flux since the Corvis Treaties as border wars with Khadorans provoke adjustments bought in blood. Llael has seen kings come and go, but their last passed without a clear heir. Now they flounder without a king. Profusion, not lack, of progeny caused the confusion. A wave of assassinations and backstabbing followed before the governorship fell to their wicked and self-serving prime minister. Llael relies on its alliance to Cygnar and lets its army wither. As a man who has seen a lifetime of bloodshed I consider this foolish. Cygnar has its own borders to look to, and the prime minister is no friend of Cygnar's king.

When I speak of Ord I like to compare my homeland to a walnut: a tough exterior, difficult to crack, with nourishing meat at its center. My land is a moody realm of foggy bogs, wet marshes, and difficult farmland and lacks the resources of some great kingdoms. Land-owning castellans maintain themselves on herds of cattle and horses aloof from the masses struggling to put food on the table. We are a tough people not easily discomfited. We find diversion in song, gambling, or ale rather than dwelling on life's inequities.

Ord's coastal cities are a sailor's paradise, and we boast the best mariners of our continent. The ocean has brought a bounty of riches the peat bogs lack, but the sea is a harsh mistress filled with Cryxian pirates and other hazards. The Ordic Royal Navy is counted a peer among the powers of western Immoren. Our army does not have similar acclaim, but make no mistake those men are tough as trollkin and have courage to spare. Talk to the men serving at Highgate or the fortresses watching Khador and you will find soldiers the equal of any. Despite our resolve, however, Ord lacks for modern weapons and engineering to contest with our neighbors. Khador has often come snapping at Ord's heels like a wolf after a famished deer, but we have held. We lost territory in the old border wars but gave as good as we got. Many dead Khadorans underestimated our border guard. I hope my kingdom can maintain its neutrality in the days ahead and stand apart from larger wars, but I fear the rabid northern beast will come to consume us.

Day of Markus, Evening of Trineus the 3rd, 602 AR

Every year if possible I return to Midfast on the Day of Markus. I look north and consider the rugged and cruel men who dominate the expanse called Khador. Here at Midfast the people of Ord beat them back in 305 AR. From these walls our tired soldiers witnessed the ascension of Markus to join Morrow. He sacrificed his life to buy time for reinforcements to reach the city and proved that the few can defend against the many if courage holds.

I will not deceive. I loathe the descendants of the Khardic Empire and find in them little to praise. Such men ruined my family, and the blood they have spilled in their unrelenting thirst for conquest spots the pages of history. I prize truth and scorn those guilty of overblown rhetoric, so I will restrain my natural loathing and attempt to write of the northerners with what measure of fairness they warrant.

Without question Khador's people are tough, irascible, weathered, and proud. They learned well from those ancient days when man endured through strength and cruelty. The north keeps deep and ancient customs derived from when barbaric horselords roamed and ruled the Khardic Empire with their pompous, gold-laden Menite priests. The Khadorans took to Morrow's message later but heeded only select words of the old philosopher-warrior. They laud his advice on nobility in battle and ignore his condemnation of rampant aggression.

If one is to understand these steel-eyed northerners consider that much of Khador is frozen five months out of the year. Strong winds snap trees in half, and sudden snows sweep in so fast that entire wagon trains have vanished in mere seconds. Many are never seen again. Only the strong survive in such a harsh place. Khador's military personifies this strength with huge warjacks thundering along next to hearty men and women armed to the teeth with axe and gun.

Perhaps in such a frozen place the concept of freedom becomes meaningless. Khador has conscripted its soldiers since the time of the old empire. Every adult male and any female who wishes and is not with child serves the so-called 'Motherland' for at least one period of service. Their mastery of durable mechanika is nearly the equal of their southern rival. Even I who loathe them will admit there are many Khadorans as shrewd and cunning as they are implacable.

The Old Faith, a branch of Menoth worship, is stronger in the north than anywhere outside the Protectorate of Menoth. Morrowans form the majority, but not an overwhelming one as in Cygnar, Ord, and Llael. Whether Menite or Morrowan, however, they love their queen above all. The Khadorans are as patriotic a people as you will ever find, and it is part of what makes them obnoxious to outsiders.

Khador has never rested comfortably with the compromises made in the Corvis Treaties, for they remember the glory of their old Khardic Empire. Every generation a new imperialist rises from their nobility to declare the time ripe for border wars to 'reclaim' lands 'stolen' in past generations from their rightful inhabitants. It is unfortunate the old northern tribes of Kossites and Skirov do not remember they once had their own pride separate from the Khards. Now they are all alike in their blind devotion to the rebirth of the old empire and heedless of the consequences of their warlike savagery.

Khador's strongest adversary remains Cygnar. They are known for coming to the aid of their Llaelese allies and even supporting Ord in a few wars over the centuries. Three post-Rebellion wars have erupted between Cygnar and Khador, but this gives no sense of the state of constant tension and animosity simmering in times of 'peace'. Every few years bring battle between the two sides along the borders. There is no word in the Khadoran root language of Khurzic for 'surrender,' but they have a dozen synonyms for 'vengeance'.

Afternoon of Cinten the 11th, 602 AR

At the center of the Iron Kingdoms lies Cygnar, and I often find myself here for one reason or another. Cygnar emerged strongest and wealthiest from the Corvis Treaties. It united the diverse and powerful peoples of the ancient lands of Caspia, the sweeping Midlund farmlands, and the heart of ancient Thuria combined with the Thornwood Forest and its wily Morridanes. Cygnar has no lack of iron, gold, timber, food, gems, quarries, or any other resource a modern nation requires. Coming as I do from the poorer lands of Ord, I view these people as overly fortunate and know they do not appreciate the advantages given them by dint of birth. Cygnar's technology and alchemy is superb and improving every day, yet it is their mechanikal engineering that gives them the edge. Their warjacks boast inventive armaments and bow to the will of their warcasters.

Cygnar's borders touch all of the true Iron Kingdoms formed by the Council of Ten: Ord to the northwest, Khador to the north, and Llael in the northeast. The Bloodstone Marches made up their entire eastern border until the Cygnaran Civil War. The end of that war resulted in the Protectorate of Menoth becoming their newest eastern neighbor and enemy.

I have mixed feelings about Cygnar. They are far better than Khadorans and Ord has reason to appreciate their support, but they enjoy putting their head into the bear's mouth and riling up enemies with little concern to the future. I wonder if the rivalry between Khador and Cygnar will consume all lesser nations in a funerary pyre. Would it not be better if these two powers focused on the threat of Cryx in the southwest? It is my opinion that Cygnar has been short sighted about the enemy off their western shore. Furthermore, every Cygnaran king since the Civil War has also ignored tensions with the Protectorate. Each has left that problem as an inheritance to his successor.

Cygnar endured tragedy in recent times when the current sovereign, King Leto 'the Younger' Raelthorne, ousted his older brother King Vinter IV, 'the Elder.' Vinter, a paranoid tyrant, managed to escape but recently returned from the Bloodstone Marches with strange allies. He attempted to seize Corvis, but the city's defenders pushed him back into the storm-ridden wastes. It has never been easy to wear the Cygnaran crown. Still, I feel little pity as many of their rulers have purchased their sorrows with coin of their own minting.

Early Morning, Octesh the 15th, 602 AR

I am not a comfortable guest here in Sul, and they watch me with mistrust. Still, a mercenary can find employment here, and I have friends among the alleyways. From my room's balcony I overlook a solemn procession in the street below. It is impossible not to be reminded of the strength of faith in this place. Faith is the tie that binds here.

For years historians and politicians both have pretended the Protectorate was not a nation of its own because the agreements that ended the Civil War left them tentatively beholden to Cygnar. That is a farce, and most admit the

Protectorate is the youngest Iron Kingdom. The tale of the Cygnaran Civil War is for a different time. Suffice to say this religious schism opened a wound that has never healed. Any who delude themselves by thinking the Protectorate is a part of Cygnar have not seen the battle lines along the Black River or the periodic clashes of fire, spear, lightning, and sword.

Caspia divided after the Civil War to create Sul and placed two cities where one had stood before. It put bitter enemies at close proximity like a powder keg waiting for the right spark. The rest of the Protectorate stretches east and southeast into an arid and resource-poor region adjacent to the dangerous Bloodstone Marches.

Sul-Menites practice a strict form of worship and believe endless punishment awaits them in the afterlife if they do not obey the True Law. Priests instill a terror of the clergy from an early age, and they teach the people to obey without question and to expect the lash for expressing the slightest doubt. Nowhere except the Protectorate is the old god obeyed exclusively and unflinchingly harkening back to the time of the priest-kings of old.

There are Menites abroad who, eager to return to the old ways, occasionally send aid to the Protectorate. I have heard of secret factories and armories along with tremendous hidden weapons stashes to arm the entire nation at a moment's notice. When the hierarch gives the call, I hope Cygnar is ready for war. No man should underestimate the resolve of these fanatics. They care not if they are outnumbered or outgunned and will fight to the last in the name of their uncompromising god. I intend not to be here when that day comes.

Somewhere off the Gulf of Cygnar, late 602 AR

I write from the hold of a northbound steamer crossing the heaving waters on a perilous journey. From the crow's nest I have seen the slender watchtower called Hell's Hook on the eastern tip of the island once called Scharde—now the heart of the island empire of the Cryx. Few outsiders, myself included, have walked the black soil amidst the undying hordes and necro-mechanikal constructs that call this place home. Steaming so close to it now invites our destruction. I only hope our captain knows his course.

The feverish and malignant Scharde Islands off the Broken Coast of southern Cygnar are also named Cryx, the Nightmare Empire. Skell is its capital, and I fear that place more than the hellish wilds of Urcaen. There Lord Toruk landed to claim the islands as His own. He is the father of all dragons, and He rules without question. Toruk's ancient talons have ground entire towns to dust, and thousands feel the lash of His lich lord generals. Still more fail to escape the call to war even in death.

Cryxians sail from their island home in search of plunder and spill thousands of bloodthirsty pirates, marauders, bonejacks, and helljacks onto the shores of the mainland. Some slaves end up forcibly enlisted in the armies of Cryx as undead thralls fused with mechanika. Through necromancy Lord Toruk boasts an eternal army that grows with each victory.

Dawn of Cinten the 19th, 603 AR

I look out over the storm-blown sands of the Bloodstone Marches and wonder that any would willingly traverse its fierce expanse. I avoid this region as a general rule but felt compelled to visit the small mining town of Ternon Crag at the fringes of this bleak expanse.

The Bloodstone Marches represent a sun-scorched and windswept wasteland. Beyond the howling winds, mirages, and indigenous beasts lies a blasted expanse called the Stormlands. It is a withered realm shattered by constant lightning strikes and thunder. If one discounts the

Protectorate capital of Imer, the only human settlement abutting the Marches is this hovel of Ternon Crag. The miners of the Crag make a perilous living digging gold and coal from the mountains ringing the marches and have learned to stay out of that void to the east.

In recent times one man of note has flown in the face of such danger. Vinter Raelthorne IV, 'the Exile' was hurled into the east while riding an imperfect balloon intended to soar above the ground and vanished in 594. Inexplicably he returned in 603 AR and brought terrifying allies never seen before in the west: the skorne.

I know little about these skorne except that they are powerful warriors with a cruel temperament. The skorne march to battle alongside great beasts and wield their own firearms and cannons. Skorne beasts and warriors bested Cygnar's Corvis garrison when the Elder's invasion force attacked. Some claim Corvis received aid through direct divine intervention from the very hand of Morrow. I wonder what the appearance of these new invaders heralds and whether it presages the decent of another dark era to test man's strength. We know the Exile survived the battle of Corvis, and I expect his tale is not ended. At times like this I am glad to be but a simple mercenary and leave the fates of nations in sager hands. They say King Leto does not rest easily. I for one do not envy the crown upon his brow.

Dusk of Octesh the 1st, 603 AR

Mankind is a destructive lot, and war is always around us. I hear the echo of ship cannons not far from my balcony in Five Fingers. I find it strange that I no longer flinch at the sound. Where once soldiers wielded sword and spear they now launch cannon shot from massive guns and deadly rounds from hand cannons while mechaniks put their skills to work arming volatile, smoke-spewing warjacks.

We stand in the uneasy calm before the storm. Our finest hours have often come in the tumult of battle. I have found that Immoren's—maybe even Caen's as a whole—heartfire is stoked by the wars and skirmishes around and within it.

War has become my meat and drink. As the storm comes I feel a stirring in my soul like drums calling soldiers to the line in morning fog. Each of us must choose a side, raise a weapon, and lift our banner to join in the strife to come. Better to fall in heroic charge than to waste away nursing sullen regrets. We who fight will sign our names on the pages of eternity with our blood. If I should live I will tell tales of glory and triumph that endures even past the shroud of death.

The Game

Rules Basics
General Knowledge for Combat in WARMACHINE

Game Overview

In WARMACHINE, the very earth shakes during fierce confrontations where six-ton constructs of tempered iron and steel slam into each other with the destructive force of a locomotive, where lead-spewing cannons chew through armor plating as easily as flesh, and where a tempest of arcane magic sets the battlefield ablaze with such Armageddon-like proportion that the gods themselves fear to tread such tormented ground.

WARMACHINE is a fast-paced and aggressive 30mm tabletop miniatures battle game set in the steam-powered fantasy world of the Iron Kingdoms. Players take on the role of elite soldier-sorcerers known as *warcasters*. Though warcasters are formidable combatants on their own, their true strength lies in their magical ability to control and coordinate mighty *warjacks*—massive steam-powered combat automatons that are the pinnacle of military might in the Iron Kingdoms. Players collect, assemble, and paint fantastically detailed models representing the varied men, machines, and creatures in their army. This book provides rules for using those models in swift and brutal conflict. This is steam-powered miniatures combat, and your tabletop will never be the same!

A WARMACHINE army is built around a warcaster and his *battlegroup* of warjacks. Squads of soldiers and support teams may be fielded to bolster a battlegroup's combat capability further. Sometimes huge armies with multiple battlegroups and legions of soldiers take the field to crush their enemies with the combined might of muscle and iron.

Warjacks, called *'jacks* for short, are specialized fighting machines. They are hulking iron giants powered by a fusion of steam technology and arcane science and are controlled with deadly precision by a warcaster. Warjacks can be outfitted with a plethora of wicked melee or ranged weaponry and equipment. Specialized 'jacks, known as *channelers*, are equipped with a device called an *arc node* that lets the warcaster project a spell through the warjack itself.

A warcaster is in constant telepathic contact with the 'jacks in his battlegroup. During the course of a confrontation, warcasters continually draw on a magical energy called *focus*. A warcaster's focus points may be used to boost his own combat abilities, boost those of his warjacks in his *control area*, or cast powerful spells.

The warcaster is the tie binding the battlegroup together but is also its weakest link. If the warcaster falls, his 'jacks become little more than iron shells.

The outcome of a battle depends on your ability to think quickly, use sound tactics, and decisively employ your forces. A crucial component of your strategy will be the management of your warcaster's focus points and how you use them to boost your warjacks' abilities. Focus points can be used to enhance a 'jack's already impressive combat power significantly. Properly allocated, they can make an entire battlegroup a nigh-unstoppable instrument of destruction!

Victory favors the bold! So bring it on, if you've got the metal.

Summary of Play

Before a battle begins, players agree on an encounter level and a scenario to be played, and then they create their armies based on those guidelines. Next, determine the turn order. It will not change throughout the game. Players then deploy their forces and prepare for the battle to begin.

Battles are conducted in a series of *game rounds*. Each game round, every player receives one turn to command his army. During his turn, a player activates all the models in his force, one after the other. When activated, a model may move and then perform one of a variety of actions such as attacking, repairing a 'jack, or casting spells. Once all players have taken their turns, the current game round ends and a new one begins starting again with the first player. Game rounds continue until one side wins either by

---

WHAT YOU NEED FOR WARMACHINE

IN ADDITION TO THIS BOOK AND YOUR ARMY OF WARMACHINE MODELS, YOU WILL ALSO NEED A FEW BASIC ITEMS TO PLAY:

- A TABLE OR PLAYING SURFACE WHERE YOU CAN CONDUCT YOUR BATTLES (TYPICALLY 4' X 4').

- A TAPE MEASURE OR RULER MARKED IN INCHES AND FRACTIONS THEREOF TO MEASURE MOVEMENT AND ATTACK DISTANCES.

- A FEW SIX-SIDED DICE. FOUR WILL BE PLENTY.

- A HANDFUL OF TOKENS TO INDICATE FOCUS POINTS, SPELL EFFECTS, ETC.

- THE APPROPRIATE STAT CARDS INCLUDED WITH EACH MODEL. WE SUGGEST YOU PUT THEM IN CARD SLEEVES AND USE A DRY ERASE MARKER TO MARK DAMAGE.

- THE MARKERS AND TEMPLATES FOUND ON PAGE 256 AT THE BACK OF THIS BOOK. YOU MAY PHOTOCOPY THEM FOR PERSONAL USE.

destroying all opposition, meeting scenario objectives, or accepting the surrender of all his opponents.

Dice and Rounding

WARMACHINE uses six-sided dice, abbreviated d6, to determine the success of attacks and other actions. Most events, such as attacks, require rolling two dice (abbreviated 2d6). Other events typically require rolling from one to four dice. Die rolls often have modifiers, which are expressed as + or − some quantity after the die roll notation. For example, melee attack rolls are described as "2d6+MAT." This means 'roll two six-sided dice and add the attacking model's MAT to the result.'

Some events call for rolling a d3. To do so, roll a d6, divide the result by two, and round up.

Some instances call for a model's stat or a die roll to be divided in half. With the exception of distance measurements, always round a fractional result to the next highest whole number.

General Guidelines

This section covers how WARMACHINE handles game terms, the relationship between standard and special rules, sportsmanship between players, and the procedures for resolving rules disputes.

Game Terms

When these rules introduce a game term in a definitive fashion, its name appears in **bold**. If the rules reference a term from another section, its first appearance in that section will be in *italics*. For ease of reference, game terms are defined in the Glossary.

For the sake of brevity, the phrase "model with the _____ ability" is sometimes replaced with the ability's name. For example, a model with the 'Jack Marshal ability may be referred to simply as a 'jack marshal, and a model with the Spell Caster ability is referred to as a spell caster. Similarly, the phrases "attack with the _____ weapon" and "attack granted by the _____ ability" are replaced by the expression "_____ attack." For instance, Caine's Maelstrom feat allows him to make several attacks with his Spellstorm Pistols. These attacks are referred to as "Spellstorm Pistol attacks" in the text of Maelstrom. In the same way, the extra attacks granted by the Strafe ability of a Cygnar Sentinel's Chain Gun are referred to as "Strafe attacks" and the attacks a trampling warjack makes against models that it moved over are called "trample attacks."

Rule Priority

WARMACHINE is a complex game providing a multitude of options, but its rules are actually intuitive and easy to learn. The standard rules lay the foundation upon which the game is built and provide all the typical mechanics used in play. Additional special rules apply to specific models and modify the standard rules in certain circumstances. When they apply, special rules take precedence.

Unless otherwise specified, multiple instances of the same effect are not cumulative. However, different effects

---

WHAT'S A D6? HOW ABOUT A D3?

A SIX-SIDED DIE IS REFERRED TO AS A D6. TWO SIX-SIDED DICE ARE ABBREVIATED AS 2D6, THREE DICE AS 3D6, AND SO ON.

A D3 IS A QUICK WAY TO SAY, "ROLL A D6, DIVIDE BY 2, AND ROUND UP." QUITE A MOUTHFUL! HERE'S HOW TO READ THE RESULTS OF A D3 ROLL QUICKLY:

1 OR 2 = 1

3 OR 4 = 2

5 OR 6 = 3

Rules Basics

are cumulative with each other, even if they have the same net effect on a model. For example, a warjack only suffers −2 MAT and RAT due to being in a Burning Ash cloud regardless of the number of clouds affecting it. The warjack does, however, suffer a further −2 to both MAT and RAT if it is also affected by Fell Call. Multiple instances of the same effect are not cumulative even when the effect comes from different sources. For example, a Dark Shroud spell would not be cumulative with the Dark Shroud ability of Bane Thralls.

Sportsmanship & Sharing Information

Although WARMACHINE simulates violent battles between mammoth forces, you should still strive to be a good sportsman in all aspects of the game. Remember, this is a game meant to provide entertainment and friendly competition. Whether winning or losing, you should still be having lots of fun.

From time to time, your opponent may wish to see your records to verify a model's stats or see how much damage a particular warjack has taken. Always represent this information honestly and share your records and information without hesitation.

Resolving Rules Issues

These rules have been carefully designed to provide as much guidance as possible in all aspects of play. However, you may encounter situations where the proper course of action is not immediately obvious. For instance, players may disagree on whether or not a model has *line of sight* to its intended target.

During a game, try to resolve the issue quickly in the interest of keeping the game flowing. After the game you will have plenty of time to decide the best answer, and it can then be incorporated into future games.

If a situation arises in which all players cannot agree on a solution, quickly discuss the matter and reference this rulebook for an answer, but do not spend so much time doing so that you slow the game. In striving to resolve an issue, common sense and the precedents set by the rules should be your guides.

If the dispute cannot be solved quickly, have one player from each side roll a d6—the highest roller gets to decide the outcome. Re-roll any ties. In the interest of fairness, once a ruling has been made for a specific issue, it applies for all similar circumstances for the rest of the game. After the game ends, you can take the time to reference the rules

and thoroughly discuss the issue to decide how best to handle that same situation in the future.

Measuring Distances

When measuring the distance from a model, measure from the edge of the model's base. Similarly, when measuring the distance to a model, measure to the edge of that model's base. Thus, a model is *within* a given distance when the nearest edge of its base is within that distance, or equivalently, when any part of its base is within the given distance.

A model is *completely within* a given distance when its entire base is within that distance. Equivalently, a model is completely within a given distance when the farthest edge of its base is within that distance.

When determining the effects of a spell or ability that affects other models within a specified number of inches of a model, unless the spell or ability says otherwise, that model is not considered to be within the distance. For example, when an Ironclad uses its Tremor special attack, it affects all models within two inches of itself, but Tremor does not affect the Ironclad.

Within vs. Completely Within

Bile Thrall A does not have any portion of its base in the shaded area, so it is not within *the shaded area. Bile Thralls B and C do have a portion of their bases in the shaded area, so they are* within *it. Bile Thralls D and E are* completely within *the shaded area because each of their bases is entirely within the shaded area.*

Models—The Dogs of War
Model Types, Stats, and Damage Capacity

Each WARMACHINE combatant is represented on the tabletop by a highly detailed and dramatically posed miniature figurine referred to as a **model**. There are several basic **model types**: *warcasters*, *warjacks*, *troopers*, and *solos*. Warcasters, troopers, and solos are collectively referred to as **warriors**. Non-warjack models are **living models** unless otherwise noted.

Independent Models

Independent models are those that activate individually. Warcasters, warjacks, and solos are independent models. A **battlegroup** includes a warcaster and the warjacks he controls. A warcaster can allocate focus points to or channel spells through only the warjacks in his battlegroup.

Warcaster

A **warcaster** is a tremendously powerful sorcerer, warpriest, or battlemage with the ability to control a group of warjacks telepathically. A warcaster is a deadly opponent highly skilled in both physical combat and arcane spell casting.

During battle, a warcaster commands his *battlegroup* of warjacks in an effort to complete his objectives. A warcaster may use his *focus points* to enhance his combat abilities and cast spells, or he may assign them to individual warjacks to increase their fighting abilities. A warcaster may also channel spells through 'jacks equipped with *arc nodes*, effectively extending the range of his magical powers.

Warcasters are *independent models*.

Warjacks

A **steamjack** is a mechanikal construct given the ability to reason by a magical brain, known as a **cortex**, housed within its hull. A steamjack does not possess high cognitive powers, but it can execute simple commands and make logical decisions to complete its assigned tasks. Steamjacks are used throughout the Iron Kingdoms for a variety of heavy or dangerous tasks that would be impossible for a human to perform.

A **warjack** is a steamjack built expressly to wage war. Armed with the most fearsome ranged and close-combat weaponry yet devised, a warjack is more than a match for a dozen men. Though able to think and operate independently, a warjack reaches its full destructive potential only when controlled by a warcaster. The warcaster forms a telepathic link to each of the warjacks in his battlegroup. This link lets the warcaster give his warjacks commands and use focus to *boost* their abilities with just a thought. Through focus, a warcaster can make his warjacks' attacks more accurate and powerful. A well-controlled warjack can even perform amazing *power attacks*, such as slamming its opponents into buildings, grappling their weapons, or even throwing them.

The telepathic link binding a warcaster to his warjacks is fragile. If a warjack's cortex is disabled, it can no longer be allocated focus points. Even worse, should a warcaster become incapacitated, the telepathic links to his 'jacks will be severed. The accompanying feedback of uncontrolled magical energies overloads and shorts out his warjacks' cortexes and causes the 'jacks to cease functioning.

Warjacks are classified according to base size: Generally speaking, a **light warjack** has a medium base (40 mm), and a **heavy warjack** has a large base (50 mm). Even though it is assigned to a specific battlegroup, each warjack is an *independent model*.

Solos

Solos are individuals such as assassins and snipers that operate alone. Solos are *independent models*.

Units

A **unit** is a group of similarly trained and equipped trooper models operating together as a single force. A unit usually contains one leader and two or more additional troopers.

Troopers

Troopers are models such as swordsmen, riflemen, and mechaniks that operate together in groups called **units**. A unit always operates as a single coherent force. Troopers in a unit generally share identical attributes and carry the same weapons.

Some special rules and spells affect entire units. When any trooper in a unit is affected by a special rule such as terror or a unit-affecting spell, every member of that unit is affected. Special rules and spells that affect units are noted in their descriptions.

Leaders

Usually one trooper in a unit is trained as a **leader** and can give his unit *orders*. It is generally represented by a model with a different stat profile and possibly different

Models

Iron Lich Asphyxious: Warcaster

Ironclad: Heavy Warjack

Temple Flameguard: Unit

Manhunter: Solo

weaponry. A leader generally has a higher Command (CMD) stat than the other troopers in his unit, and a unit uses its leader's CMD stat for all command checks while its leader is in play. Additionally, a unit leader can attempt to *rally* the members of his unit if they are fleeing.

Model Profiles

Every model and unit has a unique profile that translates its combat abilities into game terms. WARMACHINE uses a series of *stats* to quantify and scale the attributes fundamental to game play. In addition, a model may have *special rules* that further enhance its performance. The faction section provides all the game information required for your army to battle across the tabletop.

A model or unit's **stat card** provides a quick in-game reference for its profile and special rules. The card's front has model and weapon stats, a special rules list, and a damage track or damage grid if applicable. Field allowance, point cost, unit composition, victory points, and summarized special rule descriptions appear on the card's back. Warcasters have an additional stat card used to explain their spells and feats. Refer to this and other WARMACHINE books for the complete text of special rules and spells; they take precedence over the abridged version on the stat cards.

Model Statistics

Model **statistics**, or **stats**, provide a numerical representation of a model's basic combat qualities—the higher the number,

the better the stat. These stats are used for various die rolls throughout the game. A **stat bar** presents model statistics in an easy-to-reference format.

The model statistics and their definitions follow:

STRYKER				CMD 9	
SPD	STR	MAT	RAT	DEF	ARM
6	6	6	6	16	15

Commander Coleman Stryker

Speed (SPD) — A model's normal movement rate. A model moves its SPD in inches when *advancing*.

Strength (STR) — A model's physical strength. STR is used to calculate damage, grab onto or break free from a model, or determine how far a model is thrown.

Melee Attack (MAT) — A model's skill with melee weapons such as swords and hammers or natural weapons like fists and teeth. Add a model's MAT to its *melee attack* rolls.

Ranged Attack (RAT) — A model's accuracy with ranged weapons such as guns and crossbows or thrown items like spears and knives. Add a model's RAT to its *ranged attack* rolls.

Defense (DEF) — A model's ability to avoid being hit by an attack. A model's size, quickness, skill, and even magical protection can all contribute to its DEF. An *attack roll* must be equal to or greater than the target model's DEF to score a hit against it.

Armor (ARM) — A model's ability to resist being damaged. This resistance may come from natural resilience, worn armor, or even magical benefits. A model takes one *damage point* for every point that a *damage roll* exceeds its ARM.

Command (CMD) — A model's willpower, leadership, and self-discipline. To pass a *command check*, a model must roll equal to or less than its CMD on 2d6. Command also determines the *command range* of a model with the *Commander* ability, such as a warcaster, and the marshaling range of a 'jack marshal.

Focus (FOC) — A model's arcane power. Only models with the *Focus Manipulation* ability, such as warcasters, have a FOC stat. Focus determines a model's *control area* and *focus points*. Add the model's FOC stat to its *magic attack* rolls.

Some special rules change a model's **base stat** to a specific value. Apply this change before applying any other modifiers to the stat. For example, stationary targets have a base DEF of 5, so a stationary model behind cover has a net DEF of 9 (base DEF 5 +4 DEF for cover).

Weapon Statistics

Each of a model's weapons has its own stat bar. A sword icon denotes a melee weapon, a pistol icon denotes a ranged weapon, and a horseshoe icon denotes a mount. A weapon's stat bar only lists the stats that apply to its use.

	DISRUPTOR PISTOL		
RNG	**ROF**	**AOE**	**POW**
10	1	—	10

Sample ranged weapon stat bar

QUICKSILVER		
SPECIAL	**POW**	**P+S**
Disrupt	7	13

Sample melee weapon stat bar

MOUNT		
SPECIAL	**POW**	**P+S**
—	10	—

Sample mount weapon stat bar

Range (RNG) — The maximum distance in inches a model can make ranged attacks with this weapon. Measure range from the nearest edge of the attacking model's base to the nearest edge of the target model's base.

Rate of Fire (ROF) — The maximum number of times a model can make ranged attacks with this weapon during its activation. Reloading time limits most ranged weapons to only one attack per activation.

Area-of-Effect (AOE) — The diameter in inches of the template an *area-of-effect* (AOE) weapon uses for damage effects. When using an AOE weapon, center the template on the determined *point of impact*. All models covered by the template, even partially, potentially suffer the attack's effects. See page 48 for detailed rules on AOE weapons. Templates for AOEs can be found on page 256.

Power (POW) — The base amount of damage a weapon inflicts. Add the weapon's POW to its damage roll.

Special Rules — In addition to their normal damage, many weapons have unique advantages or produce extraordinary effects explained by their special rules. A weapon with more than one such rule has "Multi" in its stat bar and gives the complete list of effects in the special rules section for the model. Note that a ranged weapon's stat bar does not list its special rules. Be sure to check the model's army list entry or stat card for any special rules that the weapon might have.

Power plus Strength (P+S) — Melee weapons add both the weapon's POW and the model's STR to the damage roll. For quick reference, the P+S value provides the sum of these two stats.

Location — A warjack's weapon stat bars indicate where its weapons are located such as left arm (L), right arm (R), or head (H). When all of the *system boxes* for a location have been damaged, all weapons in that location are no longer functional (see Disabling Systems, pg. 55). These weapon locations are also used when resolving *head and arm locks* (pg. 40).

Special Rules

Most WARMACHINE combatants are highly specialized and trained to fill unique roles on the battlefield. To represent this, certain models have **special rules** that take precedence over the standard rules. Depending on their use, special rules are categorized as *abilities*, *feats*, *special actions*, *special attacks*, or *orders*.

The back of a model's stat card summarizes its special rules whereas the army list entry has the complete text for the special rules. In addition, Combat (pg. 38) and Warcasters and Focus (pg. 64) detail many special rules common to all warcasters and warjacks that do not appear on their stat cards or in their army list entries.

Models

Abilities — An ability typically gives a benefit or capability that modifies how the standard rules apply to the model. Abilities are always in effect and apply every time a game situation warrants their use.

Feats — Each warcaster has a unique feat that can be used once per game. A warcaster can use this feat freely at any time during his activation in addition to moving and performing an action.

Special Actions (★Action) — A special action lets a model perform an action normally unavailable to other models. A model can perform a special action instead of its combat action if it meets the specific requirements for its use.

Special Attacks (★Attack) — A special attack gives a model an attack option normally unavailable to other models. Warjacks may also make a variety of punishing special attacks called *power attacks* described on page 40. A model may make one special attack instead of making initial melee or ranged attacks during its combat action if it meets the specific requirements of the attack.

Orders — An order lets a unit perform a specialized combat maneuver during its activation. A unit may be given an order by a model with the Commander ability prior to the unit's activation or by its leader at the beginning of its activation.

Damage Capacity and Damage Grids

A model's **damage capacity** determines how many damage points it can suffer before being *destroyed*. Most *troopers* do not have a damage capacity; they are destroyed and removed from the table as soon as they suffer one damage point. The army list entry for a more resilient model gives the total amount of damage it can suffer before being destroyed. Its stat card provides a row of **damage boxes** for tracking the damage it receives. Unmarked damage boxes are sometimes called **wounds**. A warjack's damage boxes are arranged in a **damage grid**.

Every time one of these models suffers damage, mark one damage box for each damage point taken. A model with damage capacity is **destroyed** once all its damage boxes are marked. However, a warjack may lose *systems* or become *disabled* before its damage grid is completely filled. Some of a warjack's damage boxes are **system boxes**. These are labeled with a letter denoting the component of the model they represent. When all system boxes for a specific system have been marked, the warjack loses the use of that system. Mark the appropriate **system status box** to show that it is *disabled*. See Damage (pg. 54) in the Combat section for detailed rules on recording damage and its effects.

Base Size and Facing

The physical model itself has a couple of properties important to game play: *base size* and *facing*.

Base Size

The physical size and mass of a model are reflected by its **base size**. There are three base sizes: **small base** (30mm), **medium base** (40mm), and **large base** (50mm). Generally speaking, most human-sized warrior models have small bases, larger creatures and light warjacks have medium bases, and very large creatures and heavy warjacks have large bases. A model's army list entry states its base size.

Facing

A model's **facing** is the direction indicated by its head's orientation. The 180° arc centered on the direction its head faces defines the model's **front arc**; the opposite 180° defines its **back arc**. You may want to make two small marks on either side of each of your models' bases to indicate where the front arc ends and the back arc begins.

A model's front arc determines its perspective of the battlefield. A model typically directs its *actions*, determines *line of sight*, and makes attacks through this arc. Likewise, a model is usually more vulnerable to attacks from its back arc due to a lack of awareness in that direction.

Sample Damage Grid

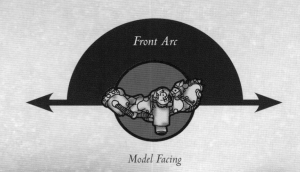

Model Facing

Preparing for War
Building an Army Suitable for Crushing Your Opponent

Creating an Army

A warcaster and his warjacks form the central fighting group of every WARMACHINE force. Units and solos with a variety of abilities further support the warcaster and his warjacks. In larger battles, you can even field multiple warcasters for greater might.

To create an army, first decide on an *encounter level*, and then spend the allotted *army points* to purchase models and units from your chosen faction's army list and from mercenaries that will work for that faction. Although mercenaries are not a faction per se, you may field an all-mercenary army by choosing a *contract* (pg. 61) that determines which mercenary models and units you can include in your army. Every army list entry and stat card provides the model's or unit's *point cost* and *field allowance* values to which you must adhere when designing your force. Specific *scenarios* may modify the standard army creation rules. Generally at least one warcaster must be included in every army.

Encounter Levels

WARMACHINE battles are played at different encounter levels to allow for a diversity of army sizes, strategies, and game experiences. Each encounter level gives the maximum number of **army points** each player can spend when designing an army. You need not spend every point available, but your army cannot exceed the maximum number of points allowed by the selected level.

Each encounter level also limits the number of warcasters available to each player.

Duel

Max Warcasters: 1   **Army Points: 350**
Est. Play Time: 30 Minutes

A duel occurs when two warcasters cross paths. Sometimes they are on special assignments, but other times they are out to settle vicious rivalries. Duels include only individual warcasters and their personal warjacks. A duel is the perfect match for playing with the contents of a Battlegroup Box.

Rumble

Max Warcasters: 1   **Army Points: 500**
Est. Play Time: 60 Minutes

A rumble is an encounter that includes a single warcaster and his warjacks supported by a small retinue of units and solos. Rumbles can occur over such things as routine border patrols or elite surgical missions.

Grand Melee

Max Warcasters: 1   **Army Points: 750**
Est. Play Time: 90 Minutes

As warfare rages across the land, escalating hostilities rage unchecked and out of control. Each faction races to bring its most devastating engines of war to the battlefield to ensure total victory. Everywhere warcasters command armies to march to battle.

Battle Royale

Max Warcasters: 2   **Army Points: 1000**
Est. Play Time: 2 hours

Battles decide the pivotal events in the course of a military campaign. With two warcasters in an army, you can fully realize the opportunities for army customization and heavy firepower.

War

Max Warcasters: 3   **Army Points: 1500**
Est. Play Time: 3 hours

When objectives can no longer be achieved by deploying small forces and when both sides refuse to yield, nothing less than war can resolve the differences. This huge game, in which each side fields up to three warcasters, allows your forces enough breadth and depth to inflict and recover from staggering blows as the fight swings back and forth.

Apocalypse

Max Warcasters: 4+   **Army Points: 2000+**
Est. Play Time: 4+ hours

When a conflict rages so bitterly that war itself cannot resolve it, the final reckoning has arrived. You have summoned the apocalypse. An apocalypse is a massive game employing four or more warcasters in each force. Although this vast endeavor should never be undertaken lightly, it yields game experiences that can be found in no other arena. One warcaster may be added to an army for each additional increment of 500 points.

Battlegroups

Each warcaster in an army controls a group of warjacks. A warcaster and his assigned warjacks are collectively referred to as a **battlegroup**. There is no limit to the number of

Sample Army

We built the following army to illustrate WARMACHINE's force creation concepts. This army is designed for the Battle Royale encounter level, meaning a player can spend a maximum of 1,000 army points and field up to two warcasters.

WARCASTER—COMMANDER STRYKER	64
STRYKER'S BATTLEGROUP	
1 IRONCLAD HEAVY WARJACK	103
2 LANCER LIGHT WARJACKS	152 (76 EA.)
WARCASTER—CAPTAIN HALEY	58
HALEY'S BATTLEGROUP	
1 DEFENDER HEAVY WARJACK	122
1 CHARGER LIGHT WARJACK	75
1 LANCER LIGHT WARJACK	76
SUPPORT	
1 LONG GUNNER SQUAD (FA:2)	
WITH 1 ADDITIONAL TROOPER	74 (64 + 10)
3 STORMBLADE SQUADS (FA: 2)	252 (84 EACH)
1 FIELD MECHANIK UNIT (FA: 3)	
WITH 2 ADDITIONAL BODGERS	20 (16+2+2)
TOTAL	**996 POINTS**

THE CHOSEN WARCASTERS ARE COMMANDER STRYKER AND CAPTAIN HALEY, AVOIDING DUPLICATION SINCE THEY ARE NAMED CHARACTERS. THE SIX WARJACKS IN THE ARMY ARE ASSIGNED TO SPECIFIC BATTLEGROUPS. THE UNIT OF LONG GUNNERS HAS AN ADDITIONAL TROOPER, AS ALLOWED BY THE UNIT OPTIONS. WE INCLUDED THREE UNITS OF STORMBLADES AS WELL. WITH AN FA: 2 AND TWO WARCASTERS, THIS ARMY COULD HAVE A TOTAL OF FOUR SUCH UNITS. FINALLY, WE ADD TWO ADDITIONAL BODGERS TO THE MECHANIK UNIT. THIS BRINGS THE TOTAL ARMY POINTS SPENT TO 996. SINCE THE MECHANIK UNIT IS AT MAXIMUM SIZE AND NOTHING ELSE IS AVAILABLE FOR 4 POINTS OR LESS, THOSE POINTS REMAIN UNSPENT.

warjacks that may be fielded in each warcaster's battlegroup. All warjacks must begin the game assigned to a battlegroup or controlled by a 'jack marshal (pg. 58).

A warcaster can allocate focus points only to warjacks in his battlegroup. If an army has multiple battlegroups, it is important to distinguish which warjacks are controlled by each warcaster.

Since warcasters and warjacks are *independent models*, each model in a battlegroup can move freely about the battlefield separate from the rest of the group. Although warjacks usually benefit from remaining within their warcaster's *control area*, they are not required to do so.

Characters

Some models represent unique individuals from the Iron Kingdoms. These personalities receive proper names and are identified as **characters**. Characters follow the rules for their basic model type.

Unique units and units that include named characters are designated as **character units**. They remain character units even after the named characters in them have been eliminated from play. For example, Boomhowler & Co. is a character unit and thus an invalid target for Deneghra's Dark Seduction spell even if Boomhowler himself is no longer on the table.

An army may include only one model of each named character and only one of each character unit. For instance, you can never have two Commander Coleman Strykers in the same army. However, two rival Cygnar players could each field Stryker. How can this be?

In the chaos and tumult now engulfing war-torn Immoren, pretenders and imposters abound. Thus, you may find yourself fielding one or more warcasters who impossibly face their apparent counterparts across the field of battle. Who is the *real* Commander Coleman Stryker or Butcher of Khardov? Victory alone can determine the answer.

Point Costs

A model's **point cost** indicates how many *army points* you must spend to include one of these models (or in the case of units, one basic unit) in your army. Some entries also include options to spend additional points for upgrades typically in the form of adding more troopers to a unit.

Field Allowance

Field allowance (FA) is the maximum number of models or units of a given type that may be included for each warcaster in an army. For example, Cygnar Trenchers have FA 2, indicating that an army may have up to two Trencher units for each warcaster. An army with two warcasters could have up to four Trencher units.

A field allowance of "U" means an unlimited number of these models or units may be fielded in an army. A field allowance of "C" means the model or unit is a character; only one model of each named character and only one of each character unit is allowed per army regardless of the number of warcasters.

Field allowance is not faction-specific. If an army includes both faction and mercenary warcasters, count all of the warcasters in the army when determining field allowance limits for both faction and mercenary models and units. For example, if a Cygnar army contains both a Cygnar warcaster and a mercenary warcaster, that army may include up to four Trencher units just as if it had two Cygnar warcasters.

Setup, Deployment, and Victory Conditions

WARMACHINE games can be played in a variety of ways. The primary influences on a game's setup are its encounter level, number of players, and victory conditions. Players may also agree to play a specific scenario or even design one of their own.

Two-Player Games

In a typical WARMACHINE game, two players match forces across a 4' x 4' playing surface. After setting up the battlefield according to Terrain (pg. 77), players make a **starting roll**: each player rolls a d6. The highest roller chooses any player, including himself, to be the **first player**. Once established, the **turn order** remains the same for the rest of the game.

Players then deploy their armies starting with the first player. The first player may choose any edge of the playing surface and deploy all his forces completely within 10" of that edge. This area is that player's **deployment zone**. Deploy units so that all of their troopers are *in formation*. The second player then deploys his forces on the opposite side of the playing surface following the same guidelines.

Multiplayer Games

When playing multiplayer games of WARMACHINE, players can choose to play either a team game or a free-for-all game. After agreeing on the type of game to be played, set up the battlefield and use the following guidelines to determine the game's turn order.

Team Games

Before beginning a team game, the players must split into two opposing sides. Decide the composition of the teams. Teams should be made up exclusively of models from the same faction and the mercenaries that will work for that faction. If a team wishes to field an all-mercenary force, all the members of the team must use the same *contract* (pg. 61). Each team may only include one of any *character*

model. To begin, have one player from each team roll a d6 to establish the turn order. The team that rolls highest gets to choose which team goes first, and the first team chooses which of its players will be the first player. Once the first player is determined, the opposing team chooses which of its players will go next. The first team then nominates one of its players to be third, followed again by the opposing team. This continues until all players have a place in the turn order and ensures the turn order will alternate between players of opposing teams.

Force deployment should be done in turn order following the above guidelines, with teammates sharing the same deployment zone across the battlefield from their opponents' deployment zone.

Free-for-all Games

You can also choose to play a multiplayer game in which each player fights independently in a free-for-all game. To establish turn order, each player rolls a d6. Starting with the highest roller and working to the lowest, each player chooses any available position in the turn order. Re-roll ties as they occur with the highest re-roller winning his choice of position, followed by the next highest re-roller, and so on. For example, Matt, Jason, Mike, and Steve roll 6, 5, 5, and 3 respectively for turn order. Matt chooses his position first. Then Jason and Mike re-roll their tie, getting a 4 and a 2. Jason chooses next, followed by Mike. As the lowest roller, Steve gets the remaining position in the turn order.

Use your best judgment to establish deployment zones based on the number of players and the size and shape of your playing surface. Deployment zones should be spaced such that no player gets a significant advantage or disadvantage—unless mutually agreed upon. As a starting point, for games with three or four players on a 4' x 4' playing surface, consider deploying forces completely within 10" of any corner of the playing area to ensure adequate separation.

Scenarios

If all players agree, you can set up the game according to a specific scenario. Scenarios add an extra layer of excitement by incorporating special circumstances and unique rules. A player wins a scenario by achieving its objectives, not necessarily by eliminating his opponent's forces. Certain scenarios have specific guidelines for playing-area size, terrain setup, deployment zones, and turn order. See Scenarios (pg. 81) for the scenario descriptions. If you feel

Preparing for War

particularly daring, you can randomly determine which scenario to play.

As long as all players agree, you can even design your own scenarios to create a unique battle experience. Just be sure to allow a minimum of 28" between rival deployment zones. Feel free to be creative when setting up your games. For instance, if you have three players, one player could set up in the middle of the table as a defender and the other two could attack from opposite edges. Furthermore, you could have a four-player team game with teammates deploying across from each other on opposite edges of the battlefield meaning everyone will have enemies on either side. Your imagination is the only limit.

Victory Conditions

Establish victory conditions before deploying forces. Typically victory goes to the player or team who eliminates the opposition or accepts their surrender. A scenario defines specific objectives for each side. You can also use *victory points* to determine a game's winner.

Victory Points

Every model and unit is worth a set number of victory points. A player or team scores victory points for each of its opponents' models that have been destroyed or removed from play regardless of which player controls the model at the time it leaves the table.

Award victory points for models destroyed or removed from play when the models leave the table. All other victory points for eliminating models are awarded at the end of the game. In particular, victory points for disabled and inert enemy warjacks are not awarded until the end of the game. If a player accidentally or intentionally eliminates a friendly model or unit, award its victory points to his opponent. Once a player has been awarded victory points for eliminating a model or unit, these points are never lost even if the model subsequently returns to play. If returned models are later eliminated, award victory points for them again.

In a team game, victory points for eliminating models are awarded to an entire team instead of its individual players. When there are more than two opposing sides, be they teams or individual players, only the side that was responsible for the elimination of a model or unit is awarded the victory points for it. However, should a player eliminate a friendly model, whether his own or a teammate's, award its victory points to all of his opponents. In the case of a disabled or inert warjack, the side that last caused the warjack to become disabled or inert will receive the victory points for it unless that was the side which controls the warjack, in which case all opponents receive the victory points.

Decide how victory points will be used, if at all, before starting the game. One option is to end the game after a chosen number of *game rounds*. Victory goes to the player or team with the most victory points at the end of the last game round. Another option is to end the game once any player or team accumulates a minimum number of victory points. Once a player or team reaches the victory point goal, the game will end at the conclusion of the current game round, and victory goes to the player or team with the most victory points at that time. If you run out of time while playing a game with other victory conditions, you may use victory points to determine the winner.

Starting the Game

After establishing victory conditions and deploying forces, the first *game round* begins. Every warcaster and other model with the *Focus Manipulation* ability begins the game with a number of *focus points* equal to its FOC stat. Starting with the first player, each player takes a turn in turn order. Game rounds continue until one side achieves its victory conditions and wins the game.

A WARMACHINE battlefield
before a battle commences

Gameplay—the Rules of Engagement
Turn Sequence, Movement, and Actions

The Game Round

WARMACHINE battles are fought in a series of **game rounds**. Each game round, every player takes a turn in the order established during setup. Once the last player in the turn order completes his turn, the current game round ends. A new game round then begins starting again with the first player. Game rounds continue until one side wins the game.

For game effects, a **round** is measured from the current player's turn to the beginning of that player's next turn regardless of his location in the turn order. When put in play, a game effect with a duration of one round expires at the beginning of the current player's next turn. This means every player will take one turn while the effect is in play.

The Player Turn

A player's turn has three phases: *Maintenance, Control,* and *Activation.*

Maintenance Phase

During the Maintenance Phase, perform the following steps in order:

1) Remove any effects that expire at the beginning of your turn.

2) Remove all focus points from your models.

3) Resolve any non-fleeing compulsory effects on your models. These effects may require you to activate those models now. If a model is affected by contradictory compulsory effects, it will activate but do nothing.

4) Check for expiration of *continuous effects* on any models you control and apply those that remain in play.

5) Activate *fleeing* models and fleeing units under your control. A fleeing model or unit may attempt to *rally* at the end of this activation. See Command (pg. 74) for detailed rules on fleeing and rallying.

Control Phase

During the Control Phase, perform the following steps in order:

1) Each of your models with the Focus Manipulation ability, like warcasters, replenishes his focus and receives a number of focus points equal to his current Focus stat (FOC).

2) Each warcaster may then allocate focus points to his battlegroup's warjacks within his control area and spend focus points to maintain his *upkeep spells* in play. If a warcaster does not spend focus points to maintain a spell requiring upkeep, it expires and its effects end immediately.

3) Resolve any other effects that occur during the Control Phase.

Activation Phase

The Activation Phase is the major portion of a player's turn. All models you control must be activated once per turn. This is usually done during the Activation Phase, but models may activate earlier in the turn due to fleeing or other effects. Units and independent models are activated one at a time in an order of your choosing. A model cannot forfeit its activation unless allowed to do so by a special rule. A model must be on the table to activate.

An active model first moves (see Movement pg. 33) or forfeits its movement, and then it may perform one *action* (see Actions pg. 36) allowed by the movement option chosen.

Activating Models

Always completely resolve the active model or unit's movement before it performs any actions.

Activating Independent Models

Independent models activate individually. Only one independent model can activate at a time. The active model must complete its movement and completely resolve its action before another model or unit can be activated.

Activating Units

Troopers do not activate individually. Instead, the entire unit activates at once. When a unit activates, every trooper in the unit must complete or forfeit its movement before any actions can be performed. After completing the entire unit's movement, each

---

WHAT DOES A MODEL DO WHEN ACTIVATED?

AN ACTIVE MODEL FIRST MOVES OR FORFEITS ITS MOVEMENT. DEPENDING ON THE MOVEMENT OPTION CHOSEN, THE MODEL MAY BE ABLE TO PERFORM EITHER A COMBAT ACTION OR A SPECIAL ACTION. A COMBAT ACTION LETS A MODEL MAKE ATTACKS. A SPECIAL ACTION LETS A MODEL PERFORM A UNIQUE BATTLEFIELD FUNCTION SUCH AS DIGGING IN OR CREATING SCRAP THRALLS.

Gameplay

trooper may then perform an action, one trooper at a time. However, when part of a unit is *fleeing* (Command, p. 74), the fleeing troopers activate during the Maintenance Phase and the rest of the unit activates during the Activation Phase.

Units require strong leadership and guidance to be effective on the battlefield. Since a unit operates as one body, it functions best when all members are in formation. A unit must receive an order from its leader or a nearby model with the Commander ability to run, charge, or perform a specialized combat maneuver. Additionally, a unit must end its movement with all members *in formation*.

Line of Sight

Many game situations such as charging, ranged attacks, and most magic attacks require a model to have **line of sight (LOS)** to its intended target. A model has line of sight to a target if you can draw a straight, unobstructed line from the center of its base at head height through

Warrior held weapon: no line of sight

Clear line of sight

Warjack weapon: clear line of sight

its front arc to any part of the target model, including its base, unless its base is completely obscured by *intervening models*. Warrior models present a slight exception to this rule. Unlike warjack models, items held in the hands of warrior models—such as their weapons or banner poles—do not count as part of the model for determining line of sight. For example, a Khadoran Widowmaker does not have line of sight to a Protectorate Temple Flameguard if all he can see is the tip of a spear poking out from behind a wall.

LOS and Targeting

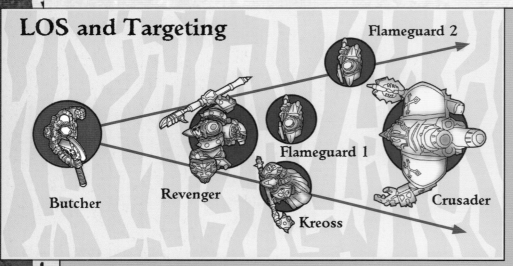

Flameguard 2

Butcher

Revenger

Flameguard 1

Kreoss

Crusader

LOS to Flameguard 1 since he cannot draw a line to its base that does not cross the Revenger's base. Because they have smaller bases than the Crusader, the Revenger and the two Flameguard do not block LOS to the Crusader. The Butcher can draw a line of sight to the Crusader as if those models were not there.

The Revenger is an intervening model for Kreoss, and the Butcher has LOS to Kreoss since his base is not completely obscured, just like Flameguard 2. The difference is that Kreoss is within 1" of an intervening model with an equal or larger-sized base, so he gains +2 DEF against the Butcher's ranged and magic attacks because he is screened by the Revenger.

This diagram highlights the LOS rules. The Butcher has LOS to the Revenger. Since the Revenger has a medium base, it blocks LOS to other models with medium and small bases. The Butcher has LOS to Flameguard 2 because he can draw a line of sight to it that does not cross the Revenger's base. On the other hand, the Butcher does not have

If the Butcher were on higher elevation than the Protectorate models, he would have LOS to Flameguard 1 though Flameguard 1 would still be screened by the Revenger because he is within 1" of the Revenger.

Simply put, having line of sight means that the model can see its target. If a model's line of sight is questionable, it may be easiest for a player to position himself to see the table from his model's perspective. A laser pointer may also come in handy when determining line of sight.

Intervening Models

A model blocks line of sight to models that have equal or smaller-sized bases. If any line between the center of the attacking model's base at head height and the target passes over another model's base, that model is an **intervening model**. You cannot draw a line of sight across an intervening model's base to models that have equal or smaller-sized bases if the target's base is completely obscured by the intervening model's base. You can draw a line of sight to the target if its base is not completely obscured by the intervening model's base.

An intervening model does not block line of sight to models that have larger bases, so ignore it when drawing line of sight.

Screening

A **screening model** is an intervening model that has an equal or larger-sized base than the target model and is within 1" of it. The target model is **screened** by a screening model and gains +2 DEF against ranged and magic attacks. The target does not gain this bonus if the intervening model has a smaller base, if the attacker's line of sight to the screening model is completely obstructed by terrain, or if the target's base is more than 1" away from the screening model's base regardless of base size. The screening bonus is only applied once regardless of the number of screening models.

Elevation and LOS

When drawing line of sight from a model on a higher elevation than its target, ignore all intervening models on lower elevation than the attacking model except those that would normally screen the target. Additionally, you can draw a line of sight through screening models that have equal or smaller-sized bases than the attacking model, but the target still gets +2 DEF for being screened.

When drawing line of sight from a model on a lower elevation than its target, ignore all intervening models on a lower elevation than the target. A model on higher elevation than its attacker gains +2 DEF against ranged and magic attacks from that opponent. Models on lower elevations than the target do not provide *screening*.

Movement

The first part of a model's activation is movement. A model must use or forfeit its movement before performing any action. When moving a model, first declare the type of movement the model will perform, and then measure the distance. Make all movement measurements from the front of a model's base. Determine the distance a model moves by measuring how far the front of its base travels. The distance moved is absolute; we suggest using a flexible measuring device to keep accurate track of a model's movement.

A moving model's base may not pass over another model's base. It can move between models only if enough room exists for its base to pass between the other models' bases without touching them.

A model can voluntarily forfeit its movement by not changing its position or facing. If it does so, the model can perform one action and gains an aiming bonus for any ranged attacks made during its activation.

A model unable to move cannot change its position or facing. It may or may not be able to perform an action depending on the effect preventing its movement. A model that cannot move cannot forfeit its movement and therefore does not receive the aiming bonus for doing so. Sometimes models are placed in a new location as a result of an ability or spell. When a model is placed it is not considered to have moved and cannot be targeted by free strikes.

There are three basic types of movement: advancing, running, and charging.

The term *normal movement* refers to the movement a model makes during the movement portion of its activation, not to any movement due to other effects such as spells or being slammed. Terrain, spells, and other effects can reduce a model's movement or prevent it completely. Penalties

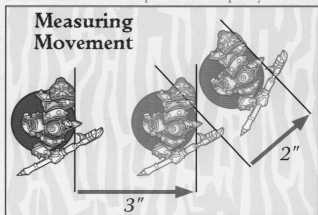

Measuring Movement

3"

2"

Gameplay

to movement are cumulative, but a model allowed to make its normal movement can always move at least 1". See Terrain (pg. 77) for full details on terrain features and how they affect movement.

Advancing

An advancing model may move up to its current speed (SPD) in inches. An advancing model always faces its direction of movement, but it may change facing freely while moving and may face any direction after moving. After a model advances, it may perform one action.

Running

A running model may move up to twice its current speed (SPD) in inches. Declare that a model or unit will run when you activate it. A running model always faces its direction of movement, but it may change facing freely while moving and may face any direction after moving. A model that runs cannot perform an action, cast spells, or use feats this turn. A running model's activation ends at the completion of its movement. A model that was knocked down but forfeited its action to stand this activation cannot run.

Some models must meet special requirements to run:

- A warcaster or solo may always run instead of advancing.
- A warjack must spend a focus point to run.
- A trooper must receive a run order to run.
- An out-of-formation trooper may attempt to regain formation by running.

Though a model cannot perform an action if it runs, it does not have to be able to perform an action in order to run.

Charging

A charging model rushes into melee range with an opponent and takes advantage of its momentum to make a more powerful strike. A charge combines a model's movement and combat action. A model suffering a penalty to its SPD or movement for any reason, regardless of offsetting bonuses, or that is denied its movement or action cannot charge. A model without a melee range cannot charge.

A model may attempt to charge any other model, friendly or enemy, in line of sight at the beginning of its normal movement. Declare a charge and its target before

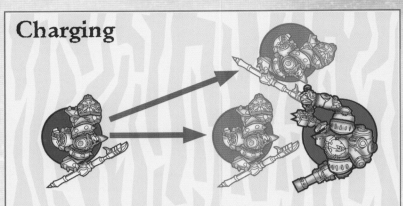

Charging

Either of these charge moves is legal for this model. After charging, the attacking model must turn to face the center of its target's base.

moving the model. After declaring a charge, the charging model turns to face in any direction which, ignoring terrain and other models, will bring the charging model to within its melee range of its target. The charging model then moves its current SPD plus 3" in that direction in a straight line and must stop while its target is in melee range, but it may end this movement at any point its target is in its melee range. It must stop if it moves into contact with another model, an obstacle, an obstruction, or rough terrain. At the completion of its movement, the charging model turns to face the center of its target's base.

Some effects require a model to charge. A model required to charge must charge a model in line of sight. If there are no models in line of sight, the model activates but must forfeit its movement and action.

A charging model that ends its movement with its intended target in melee range performs a combat action. If the charging model moved at least 3", its first attack must target the model charged and is a **charge attack**. This is not an extra attack in addition to a model's regular attack. Rather, it is simply the model's first attack after its charge movement. The attack roll is made normally and may be boosted. If the charge attack hits, add an additional die to the first damage roll. This damage roll cannot be boosted. After the charge attack, the charging model makes the rest of its melee attacks normally and may spend focus points to make additional melee attacks. A model cannot make *power attacks* or ranged attacks after charging.

If a charging model moved less than 3", it performs its combat action and attacks normally, but its first attack is not a charge attack because the model did not move far or fast enough to add sufficient momentum to its strike.

A charging model's activation ends if it comes into contact with a terrain feature that obstructs or slows its movement or if its intended target is not in melee range at the end of movement. Some models must meet special requirements to charge:

- A warcaster or solo may always charge instead of advancing.
- A warjack must spend a focus point to charge. A warjack cannot make a power attack after charging, but it may make other special attacks.
- A trooper must receive the charge order to charge. When a trooper receives a charge order, it must either run or charge. Troopers may charge the same target or multiple targets but must be in formation at the end of the unit's movement.

Cavalry models have additional rules governing charges. See Cavalry, pg. 58.

When the charging model performs its combat action, if the intended target of the charge is no longer in melee range, as is the case when another model in a charging unit destroys the intended target, the charging model may make melee attacks against other eligible targets but does not make a charge attack.

Unit Formation

An army's soldiers and support personnel are organized into units. Every member of a unit is similarly equipped and trained to fulfill a certain battlefield role. Some units specialize in melee combat, others excel with ranged weapons, and some provide critical or highly specialized capabilities. Regardless of their duties, one thing is certain: a unit is most effective when all of its members are in formation. A unit's controller may measure the distance between the models in a unit anytime during that unit's activation.

A unit must operate as a single coherent force, but its formation may be of any size or shape. Troopers up to 3" apart are in **skirmish formation**.

Troopers up to 1" apart are in **open formation**. Troopers in open formation are close enough to coordinate attacks and provide each other mutual support.

Troopers that form up in ranks are in **tight formation**. A rank is a row of troopers in base-to-base contact, or as close as the actual models allow, all facing in the same direction perpendicular to the row of models. A tight formation may consist of any number of ranks, but each rank must be at least two troopers wide. Each rank after the front-most must be parallel to it and have at least one trooper in base-to-base contact with a trooper in the rank

ahead of it, or as close as the actual models allow. Troopers in contact with the rank ahead must be lined up directly behind the trooper ahead of them.

Cavalry troopers (pg. 58) have an additional formation option available to them. Cavalry troopers up to 5" apart are in **cavalry formation**.

Formations are not mutually exclusive. Troopers in tight formation are also in open and skirmish formation. Likewise, troopers in open formation are also in skirmish formation.

Some special rules require a group of troopers to be in a specific formation. This does not require every model in the unit to be in the specified formation, but only those models in that formation will gain the special rule's benefits. A group of troopers is in the specified formation when every model in the group can be connected by a chain of models also in the group and in the specified formation. For example, in the illustration on the following page, troopers B and C form a group in open formation as do troopers D and E, but all four of them do not form a single open-formation group.

Out of Formation

A unit must begin the game in formation. A unit's leader is always **in formation**. The status of other troopers is based on their relationship to the unit's leader. The group of troopers in skirmish formation with the leader is in formation, while all others are **out of formation**. If the unit has no leader or its leader is no longer in play, then the largest group of troopers in skirmish formation is in formation. If two or more groups have the largest number of troopers, their controller chooses which group is in formation. A lone surviving trooper of a unit is always in formation whether he is the leader or not. When determining whether a cavalry trooper is in formation or not, use cavalry formation instead of skirmish formation.

At the beginning of a unit's activation, determine if any troopers are out of formation. Those who are will not receive any order given to their unit. An out-of-formation trooper must attempt to regain formation, but the desire to stay alive tempers this mandate. The trooper can advance or run in an effort to regain formation, but he must move by the most direct route that does not take him through a damaging effect or let enemies engage him. If enemy models obstruct a trooper's only path back to his unit, he must engage and attack them unless he has a ranged weapon. An out-of-formation trooper in this situation

Models Out of Formation

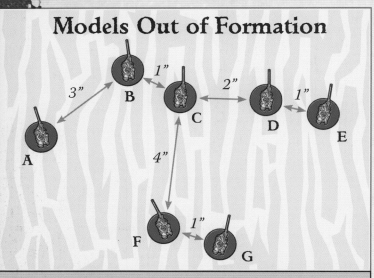

Long Gunner A is in skirmish formation with B. B and C are in open formation with each other. D is within 3" of C so is in skirmish formation with C. E is within 1" of D, so those two troopers are in open formation with each other. F and G are in skirmish formation with each other. However, they are more than 3" away from the rest of the unit, so not every model in the unit will be in formation. If the unit's leader is one of the models A through E, then those models are in formation while F and G are not. If the leader is either F or G, then only F and G are in formation, and the rest of the unit is out of formation. Finally, if the unit's leader is no longer on the table, then models A through E are in formation but F and G are not because A through E form the largest skirmish-formation group of the unit.

formation trooper makes this command check individually. If he fails the check, he does not cause the entire unit to flee. An out-of-formation trooper in command range of a friendly model with the Commander ability may use that model's command (CMD) stat for the check instead of his own. See Command (pg. 74) for detailed rules on command checks and fleeing.

Moving Units

When you activate a unit, you are simulating that its members' movement and actions occur simultaneously even though each model moves and acts individually. A unit required to make a command check as a result of its movement, other than from Massive Casualties (pg. 74), does not do so until after every trooper has completed its movement. Troopers can move in any order, but they must be in formation after all troopers have completed their movement.

Actions

An active model may be entitled to perform one action depending on the type of movement it made. There are two broad action types: combat and special. A combat action lets a model make one or more attacks. A special action lets a model perform a specialized function. A model forfeits its action if it does not use it during its activation. A model cannot move after performing any action unless a special rule specifically allows it to do so.

Combat Actions

A model can perform a combat action after advancing, charging, or forfeiting its movement. A combat action lets

can stop moving once in range and make ranged attacks against those opponents. An out of formation trooper that begins his activation engaged by an enemy model may advance and attack that model instead of disengaging.

At the end of a unit's activation, every out-of-formation trooper must make a command check or flee. Unlike most other command checks made by troopers, an out-of-

These cavalry models are on large bases, so they are actually further apart than they appear. Each model can be up to 5 inches apart.

Storm Lances in Cavalry Formation

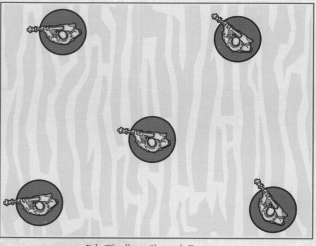

Bile Thralls in Skirmish Formation

a model make *attacks*. A model performing a combat action can choose one of the following options:

- A model can make one *melee attack* with each of its melee weapons in melee range. These attacks are called **initial attacks**. A model making more than one attack may divide them among any eligible targets.

- A model not *in melee* that did not charge can make one *ranged attack* with each of its ranged weapons. These attacks are called **initial attacks**. A model making more than one attack may divide them among any eligible targets. Each ranged weapon only makes one initial attack regardless of its ROF.

- A model can make one special attack (★Attack) allowed by its special rules instead of making initial attacks.

- A warjack that did not charge can spend a focus point to make one power attack instead of making initial attacks. A power attack is considered a melee attack.

After resolving these attacks, a warcaster or warjack may spend focus points to make **additional attacks**, one per focus point spent. Each additional attack may be made with any appropriate weapons the model possesses, including multiple attacks with the same weapon. However, a ranged weapon cannot exceed its rate of fire (ROF) during a model's activation. Completely resolve each additional attack before spending another focus point to make another additional attack.

Unless noted otherwise, a model cannot make both melee and ranged attacks in the same combat action. Additional attacks must be of the same type (melee or ranged) as the model's original attack. A model may make

additional attacks after a special attack or power attack, but they too must correspond to the basic nature (either melee or ranged) of the original attack made. Some special attacks are neither melee attacks nor ranged attacks. The rules for these special attacks indicate the nature of any additional attacks that may be made afterwards. A model cannot make a special attack or a power attack as an additional attack.

See Combat (pg. 38) for detailed rules on making attacks and determining their results.

Special Actions

Some models can perform a special action instead of a combat action. Unless otherwise noted, a model can perform a special action only after advancing or forfeiting its movement. A special action's description details its requirements and results.

Skill Checks

Some special actions appear with a **skill value** following their names. When the model performs one of these special actions, make a **skill check** to determine its success. Roll 2d6. If the result is equal to or less than the skill value, the model passes its skill check and its results are applied immediately. If the roll is greater than the model's skill value, the special action fails. Typically nothing happens if a model fails a skill check. However, some special actions may impose negative consequences for a failed skill check.

For example, the Cygnar Field Mechanik has the special action *Repair[9]*. The Mechanik's repair special action will succeed on a 2d6 roll of 9 or less.

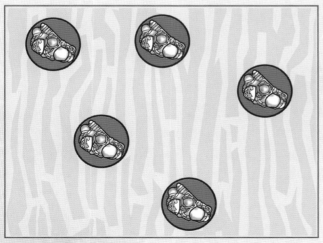

Winter Guard in Open Formation

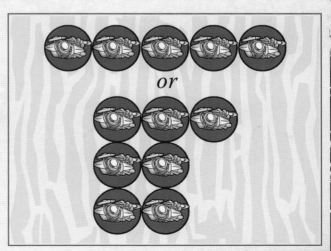

Temple Flameguard in Tight Formation

Combat—Throwing Down
Melee attacks, Ranged Attacks, and Damage

Combat Overview

A model's combat action allows it to make attacks. An attack roll determines if an attack successfully hits its target. After a successful attack, a damage roll determines how much damage, if any, the target suffers.

Unless stated otherwise, an attack can be made against any model, friendly or enemy, and against certain terrain features.

There are two broad categories of combat: melee combat and ranged combat. A model can only make attacks of the same type during its combat action. A model cannot make a ranged attack after making a melee attack, and it cannot make a melee attack after making a ranged attack.

Melee Combat

A model using its combat action for **melee attacks** can make one initial attack with each of its melee weapons. Some models have special rules that allow additional melee attacks. Warcasters and warjacks may spend focus points to make additional melee attacks, for example. Each additional melee attack may be made with any melee weapon the model possesses with no limit to the number of attacks made per weapon.

A melee attack can be made against any target in melee range of the weapon being used. A model cannot make a melee attack over another model's base, regardless of base size. A model making more than one melee attack may divide its attacks among any eligible targets.

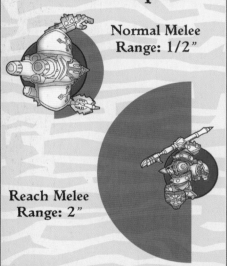

Melee Range, Engaged Models, and Reach Weapons

Normal Melee Range: 1/2"

Reach Melee Range: 2"

If a model is in melee range, it has engaged its opponent in melee combat. When opposing models are in each other's melee range, they are both engaged. However, a model with a reach weapon can take advantage of its greater melee range to engage an opponent with only normal melee range weapons without becoming engaged itself. While both models are considered to be in melee, a model is engaged only if it is in its opponent's melee range!

Melee Weapons

Melee weapons include such implements as spears, swords, hammers, flails, saws, and axes. A warjack can also use its body as a melee weapon for attacks such as bashes, head-butts, and slams.

A melee weapon's damage roll is 2d6+POW+STR.

Melee Range

A model can make melee attacks against any target in melee range. A weapon's melee range extends 1/2" beyond the model's front arc for any type of melee attack. A reach weapon has a melee range of 2". Some effects and special rules may even increase a weapon's melee range beyond this. A model's melee range is the longest melee range of its usable melee weapons. A model possessing a reach weapon and another melee weapon can engage and attack an opponent up to 2" away with its reach weapon, but its other weapons can only be used to attack models within their normal 1/2" melee range. Non-warjack models with no melee weapons have no melee range. Warjacks always have 1/2" melee range. A model cannot target another model with a melee attack if the attacking model's LOS to the target model is completely obstructed by terrain.

Engaged Models and Models in Melee

When a model is within an enemy model's melee range, it is **engaged** in combat and primarily concerned with fighting its nearest threat. Both the engaged and engaging models are considered to be **in melee** and cannot make ranged attacks. An engaged model can move freely as long as it stays inside its opponent's melee range.

A model can **disengage** from melee by moving out of its enemy's melee range, but doing so is risky. A model disengaging from melee combat is subject to a *free strike* by the enemy model.

Free Strikes

When a model moves out of an enemy's melee range, the enemy model may immediately make a **free strike** against it just before it leaves melee range. The model makes one melee attack with any melee weapon that has sufficient melee range to reach the moving model and gains a +2 bonus to its melee attack roll. If the attack succeeds, add an additional die to the damage roll. A free strike's attack and damage rolls cannot be boosted.

A model may make one free strike against each enemy that moves out of its melee range.

Melee Attack Rolls

Determine a melee attack's success by making a melee attack roll. Roll 2d6 and add the attacking model's melee attack (MAT). Boosted attack rolls add an additional die to this roll. Special rules and certain circumstances may modify the attack roll as well.

Melee Attack Roll = 2d6+MAT

A target is *directly hit* by an attack if the attack roll equals or exceeds the target's defense (DEF). If the attack roll is less than the target's DEF, the attack misses. A roll of all 1's on the dice is a miss. A roll of all 6's is a direct hit unless you are rolling only one die, regardless of the attacker's MAT or his target's DEF. Sometimes a special rule causes an attack to hit automatically. Such automatic hits are also direct hits.

Melee Attack Modifiers

The most common modifiers affecting a model's melee attack roll are summarized here for easy reference. Where necessary, additional detail can be found on the pages listed.

- *Back strike* (pg. 51): A melee attack against a target's back arc from a model that began its activation in the target's back arc gains a +2 bonus to the attack roll.

- *Free strike* (above): A melee attack against a disengaging model gains a +2 bonus to the attack roll and adds an additional die to the damage roll.

- *Intervening Terrain:* A model with any portion of its base obscured from its attacker by an obstacle or an obstruction gains +2 DEF against melee attacks.

- *Stationary Target* (pg. 54): A melee attack against a stationary target hits automatically.

Warjack Melee Attack Options

Warjacks have melee attack options unavailable to other model types. Unless otherwise noted, a warjack can use any of the following attack options that its weaponry and functional systems allow.

Bash Attacks

A warjack with no functioning melee weapons may use its body as a weapon to bash its opponent. This is not an optimum attack, but it may be the last resort for a warjack whose melee weapons have all been *disabled*. A bash attack suffers a –2 penalty to the attack roll. A hit causes a damage roll with a POW equal to the attacker's current STR.

A warjack that makes a bash attack can do nothing else during its combat action. Only one bash attack can be made during a single combat action, and focus points cannot be used for additional attacks afterward. A warjack held by an arm lock or headlock cannot make a bash attack.

Open Fists

Some warjacks have Open Fists that can be used to manipulate objects. A warjack may use its Open Fist to make normal melee attacks, but its Open Fist also allows the warjack to make certain *power attacks*. A warjack with a usable Open Fist may make arm lock, headlock, and throw power attacks; a warjack with two usable Open Fists may also perform a double-hand throw.

Combat

Shields and Bucklers

A warjack with a shield or buckler has two Armor (ARM) stats. While its shield is usable, the warjack uses the ARM stat indicated by the shield icon against any damage that does not originate in its back arc. If its shield is unusable (because the arm on which it is located has been disabled or is being held in an arm lock, for example), the warjack's ARM reverts to the stat listed in its stat bar. Attacks and damage originating in the warjack's back arc do not trigger special abilities of its shield. For example, a warjack attacking a Lancer from the Lancer's back arc will not suffer an automatic point of cortex damage after the attack is resolved (see Origin of Damage, pg. 53).

While a warjack's shield is a weapon in its own right, a buckler is attached to one of the warjack's melee weapons. The presence of a buckler will be noted in the special rules for the weapon. In all other respects, a buckler functions in the same way as a shield.

Sample warjack stat bar with a shield.

SPD	STR	MAT	RAT	DEF	ARM
6	8	5	5	13	16
					18

Power Attacks

Power attacks are special attacks that may be made by warjacks. A warjack must spend a focus point to make a power attack. Unlike other special attacks, a warjack cannot make a power attack after charging. A warjack may make additional melee attacks after a power attack, but it must spend focus points to do so. Power attacks are melee attacks with a 1/2" melee range.

Arm Lock/Headlock

As its combat action, a warjack with at least one usable Open Fist may spend a focus point to use it to seize another warjack's arm system or head and prevent its use. Declare what the warjack is attempting to lock and which open fist it is using for the attempt before making a melee attack roll. Locks can be attempted and maintained against a disabled system. A knocked down model cannot be locked. A hit locks the named component, but it does

not cause any damage. A locked system is treated as if it were disabled but does not count toward the number of disabled systems required to disable the warjack being held unless that system is also disabled by damage. In particular, none of the weapons located on the locked system may be used until the lock is broken. A warjack being held in an arm lock or headlock may not make bash attacks or special attacks.

Once involved in a lock, the attacker cannot use the Open Fist with which it made the lock attempt, nor can it use any other weapon in the same location. The attacker and the defender are free to attack with any of their other melee weapons.

For example, Rob's Juggernaut successfully locks the head of Erik's Slayer with its Open Fist. The Slayer cannot make head-butt attacks or tusk attacks, and the Juggernaut cannot make attacks with its Open Fist until the headlock is broken or released.

During its activation, a warjack suffering an arm lock or headlock must attempt to break the lock by performing a combat action. During this combat action, for each arm lock and headlock it suffers, both models involved in the lock roll a d6 and add their STR. If the locked model's total exceeds that of the model holding it in the lock, the lock is broken. The locked warjack may also make normal melee attacks with any usable melee weapons. After resolving these attacks and attempts to break free, a warjack may spend focus points to make more attempts to break a lock, one attempt per focus point spent, or to make additional attacks with usable weapons. Once a lock is broken, the warjack may use the weapons that were locked. It may not make initial attacks with those weapons during that combat action, but it may spend focus points to make additional melee attacks with them.

A warjack may release a lock it is holding at any time during its own activation. Neither model may move while involved in a lock. Any effect that causes either model to move, places either model, knocks down the defender, or causes the attacker to become stationary automatically breaks the lock. If the system on which the weapon being used to maintain the lock becomes disabled due to damage, the lock is automatically released. A lock is also broken once either model is disabled, destroyed, or removed from play. A successful lock against a warjack that is already locking another model does not break the existing lock.

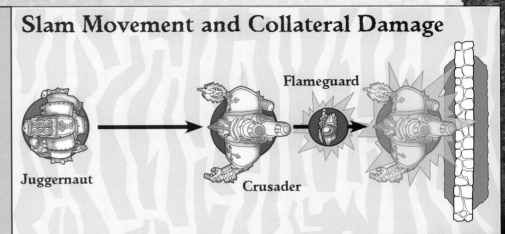

Slam Movement and Collateral Damage

A Juggernaut declares a slam attack against a Crusader. Because it moved more than 3" to make contact with the Crusader, the Juggernaut will be able to slam its target. The attack succeeds, and the Crusader is knocked back d6". The roll comes up a 6, but the Crusader stops when it hits the wall 5" behind it. During the slam, the Crusader passes over a Temple Flameguard, and the Flameguard suffers collateral damage. In addition, because the Crusader was slammed into a wall, it suffers a damage roll of 3d6 plus the STR of the Juggernaut (2d6 plus an extra die for colliding with a solid terrain feature).

Head-butt

As its combat action, a warjack may spend a focus point to head-butt a model and drive it to the ground. The attacking model makes a melee attack roll which suffers a −2 penalty against a target with an equal or smaller-sized base and a −4 penalty against a target with a larger base. A hit causes a damage roll with a POW equal to the attacker's current STR and knocks the target model down.

A warjack cannot make a head-butt if held in a headlock.

Push

As its combat action, a warjack may spend a focus point to push another model. Both models roll a d6 and add their STR. If the defender's total is greater, it resists being pushed. If the attacker's total equals or exceeds the defender's, the defending model suffers no damage but is moved one full inch directly away from the attacker.

A pushed model moves at half rate through rough terrain, suffers the effects of any hazards, and stops if it comes in contact with an obstacle, obstruction, or another model. A pushed model cannot be targeted by free strikes during this movement.

A pushed model falls off elevated terrain if it ends its push movement with less than 1" of ground under its base. See Falling (pg. 52) for detailed rules on determining damage from a fall.

After a successful push, the attacker may immediately make a follow-up move directly toward the pushed model up to the distance the pushed model was moved.

Slam

A warjack may spend a focus point to slam a model by ramming it with the full force of its body to send it flying backward and knock it to the ground. A slam combines a warjack's movement and combat action. A warjack suffering a penalty to its SPD or movement for any reason, regardless of offsetting bonuses, or that is denied its movement or action cannot attempt a slam.

A warjack may attempt to slam any other model, friendly or enemy, in line of sight at the beginning of its normal movement. Declare the slam attempt and its target before moving the warjack. A knocked down model cannot be slammed. After declaring a slam, the warjack turns to face the center of its target's base. The warjack then moves its full SPD plus 3" directly toward the center of its target's base, stopping short at any point within 1/2" of its target. It must stop if it contacts another model, an obstacle, an obstruction, or rough terrain. The slamming model cannot change its facing during or after this movement.

A warjack attempting a slam that ends its movement within 1/2" of its intended target and moved at least 3" performs a slam attack as its combat action. The attacking model makes a melee attack roll which suffers a −2 penalty against a target with an equal or smaller-sized base and a −4 penalty against a target with a larger base. If the slam attack hits, the target is slammed directly away from its attacker and is knocked down, and then it suffers damage as detailed under *Slam Damage*.

If a warjack attempting a slam attack moved less than 3", it has not moved fast enough to get its full weight and power into the blow. The attack roll suffers a −2 penalty regardless of the target's base size. A hit does not move the

Combat

target model, but it does cause the target to suffer damage as detailed under Slam Damage.

A slamming warjack's activation ends if it contacts a terrain feature that obstructs or slows its movement or if it is not within 1/2" of its intended target after moving. It may not perform an action during this activation.

Being Slammed

A slammed model is moved d6 inches directly away from its attacker and is then knocked down. Halve the slam distance if the target has a larger base than the attacker. A slammed model moves at half rate through rough terrain, suffers any damaging effects through which it passes, and stops if it contacts an obstacle, obstruction, or a model with an equal or larger-sized base. A slammed model cannot be targeted by free strikes during this movement.

A slammed model moves through a model with a smaller base. If its slam movement ends up on top of a smaller model, the smaller model's controller pushes it back to make room for the slammed model.

A slammed model falls off elevated terrain if it ends its slam movement with less than 1" of ground under its base. See Falling (pg. 52) for detailed rules on determining damage from a fall. Resolve the falling damage, if any, before resolving slam damage.

Slam Damage

Determine slam damage after moving the slammed model. A slammed model suffers a damage roll with a POW equal to the attacker's current STR. Add an additional die to the damage roll if the slammed model contacts an obstacle, obstruction, or a model with an equal or larger-sized base. Slam damage may be boosted.

Collateral Damage

If a slammed model contacts or moves through a model with an equal or smaller-sized base, that model is knocked down and suffers collateral damage. A model taking collateral damage suffers a damage roll with a POW equal to the attacker's current STR. Collateral damage cannot be boosted. A model with a larger-sized base than the slammed model does not suffer collateral damage. Collateral damage is simultaneous with slam damage.

Super Slam!!!

A WARJACK THAT SLAMS ITS TARGET INTO A SOLID TERRAIN FEATURE OR A MODEL WITH AN EQUAL OR LARGER-SIZED BASE ADDS AN ADDITIONAL DIE TO ITS DAMAGE ROLL FOR A TOTAL OF THREE DICE. THE WARJACK MAY SPEND A FOCUS POINT TO BOOST THIS DAMAGE ROLL AND ADD ANOTHER DIE FOR A TOTAL OF FOUR DICE!

Throw

As its combat action, a warjack with a usable Open Fist may spend a focus point to pick up and throw a model with an equal or smaller-sized base. The attacking model makes a melee attack roll which suffers a −2 penalty. If the attack hits, both models roll a d6 and add their current STR. If the target's total is greater, it breaks free without taking any damage and avoids being thrown. If the attacker's total equals or exceeds the target's, the target model gets thrown, is knocked down, and then suffers damage as detailed in Throw Damage.

Being Thrown

After a successful throw attack, the attacker throws the target. Measure a distance from the target equal to half the attacker's current STR in inches in a direction chosen by the attacker's controller away from the throwing model. A large-based model throwing a small-based model adds 1" to this distance. From that point, determine where the thrown model actually lands by rolling for deviation. Referencing the deviation rules (pg. 49), roll a d6 for direction and a d3 for distance in inches. The thrown model is moved directly from its current location in a straight line to the determined point of impact, ending centered on that point. The thrown model is then knocked down.

Rough terrain and obstacles do not affect this movement, but the thrown model stops if it contacts an obstruction, table edge, or a model with an equal or larger-sized base. A thrown model cannot be targeted by free strikes during this movement.

A thrown model moves over a model with a smaller base without contacting it. If its impact point ends up on top of a smaller model, the smaller model is contacted and its controller pushes it back to make room for the thrown model.

A thrown model falls off elevated terrain if it ends its throw movement with less than 1" of ground under its base. See Falling (pg. 52) for detailed rules on determining damage from a fall. Resolve the falling damage, if any, before resolving throw damage. Thrown models travel over wrecks.

Throw Damage

Determine throw damage after moving the thrown model. A thrown model suffers a damage roll with a POW equal to the attacker's current STR. Add an additional die to the damage roll if the thrown model contacts an

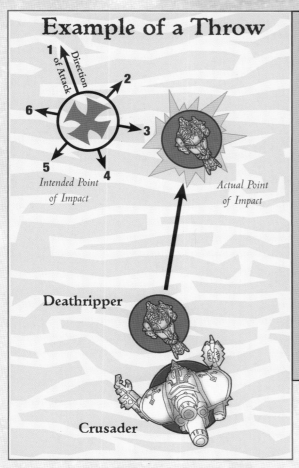

Example of a Throw

1 — Direction of Attack
2
6
3
5
4

Intended Point of Impact

Actual Point of Impact

Deathripper

Crusader

A Crusader throws a bonejack. Since the Crusader has a STR of 11, measure 5½" from the thrown model to determine the intended point of impact and determine deviation from that point. The Crusader rolls a 3 for deviation direction and a 6 for distance. On a d3, that comes to 3" of deviation, reduced to 2¾" because the deviation cannot exceed half of the throw distance. Measure the deviation distance in the direction indicated by the deviation diagram to determine the actual point of impact. The bonejack moves from its current position directly toward the point of impact and ends its movement centered on that point.

obstruction or a model with an equal or larger-sized base. Throw damage may be boosted.

Collateral Damage

If a thrown model contacts a model with an equal or smaller-sized base, that model is knocked down and suffers collateral damage. A model taking collateral damage suffers a damage roll with a POW equal to the attacker's current STR. Collateral damage cannot be boosted. A model with a larger-sized base than the thrown model does not suffer collateral damage. Collateral damage is simultaneous with throw damage.

Double-Hand Throw

As its combat action, a warjack with two usable Open Fists may spend a focus point to pick up and throw a model with an equal or smaller-sized base. The attacking model makes a melee attack roll. If the attack hits, the target rolls a d6 and adds its current STR. The attacker rolls 2d6 and adds its current STR. If the target's total is greater, it breaks free without taking any damage and avoids being thrown. If the attacker's total equals or exceeds the target's, the

target model gets thrown, is knocked down, and then suffers damage as detailed in Throw Damage. Follow the guidelines in Being Thrown above for resolving a double-hand throw.

Instead of throwing its target in a general direction after a successful double-hand throw attack, the attacker may throw it at another model within LOS. Ignore the model being thrown when selecting the target model. If this new target model is within the throw distance as described above, the attacker makes a ranged attack roll against it. On a hit, the thrown model is moved directly from its current location in a straight line toward the center of the base of the ranged attack roll's target. It ends this movement in base-to-base contact with the target and collides with it unless the movement is stopped by an obstruction or another model. A double-hand throw at a specific target is not a ranged or melee attack, but it is still an attack.

If the attack roll fails, determine the thrown model's point of impact by rolling deviation from the center of the target model's base. If the target model is beyond the throw distance, determine deviation from a point on the line to the target equal to the throw distance. Referencing the deviation rules (pg. 49), roll a d6 for the direction and a d3 for distance in inches. The thrown model moves directly from its current location in a straight line to the determined point of impact, ending centered on that point.

Rough terrain and obstacles do not affect a thrown model's movement, but the model stops if it contacts an obstruction or a model with an equal or larger-sized base. A thrown model cannot be targeted by free strikes during this movement.

A thrown model moves over a model with a smaller base without contacting it. If its impact point ends up on top of a smaller model, the smaller model is contacted and its controller pushes it back to make room for the thrown model.

After moving the thrown model, it is knocked down and then suffers damage as detailed in Throw Damage. If

Combat

a thrown model contacts another model with an equal or smaller-sized base, that model is knocked down and suffers damage as detailed in Collateral Damage.

Trample

A heavy warjack may spend a focus point to trample over small-based models in its path. Trampling combines a warjack's movement and combat action. A warjack that suffers a penalty to its SPD or movement for any reason, regardless of offsetting bonuses, or is denied its movement or action cannot make a trample power attack. Any effects that prevent charging also prevent a model from making a trample power attack.

Declare a trample attack at the beginning of the warjack's movement. Choose a direction in which you wish to trample, and turn the model to face that direction. The warjack then moves up to its current SPD +3" in a straight line. It may move through any small-based model in its path, and there must be room for the trampling model's base at the end of this movement. During trample movement, the warjack cannot move over terrain across which it could not also charge, and it cannot change its facing during or after. Do not resolve free strikes against the trampling warjack during this movement.

After the warjack has finished its movement, it makes a melee attack against each small-based model through which it moved during this movement in the order it moved through them. Resolve each trample attack as if it took place where the trampling model contacted the small-based model during its trample movement. Completely resolve each attack individually and apply the targets' special rules immediately as each attack is resolved. Models hit cannot perform free strikes against the trampling warjack and suffer a damage roll with a POW equal to the current STR of the attacker. Resolve all free strikes against the trampling warjack after resolving trample attacks. Resolve each free strike as if it took place where the trampling model disengaged from the model making the free strike.

After making all of its trample attacks, a warjack may spend focus points to make additional melee attacks against any models in melee range.

Ranged Combat

Many would argue there is no honor in defeating an enemy without being close enough to look him in the eyes. However, when a soul-burning helljack with two fists full of iron-shredding claws bears down on you faster than a charging destrier, it is a good plan to keep your distance and consider your ranged attack options.

A model using its combat action for **ranged attacks** makes one initial attack with each of its ranged weapons. Some models have special rules that allow additional ranged attacks. Warcasters and warjacks may spend focus points to make additional ranged attacks. Each additional attack may be made with any ranged weapon the model possesses, but a ranged weapon can never make more attacks in a single activation than its rate of fire (ROF).

A ranged attack can be declared against any target in line of sight subject to the targeting rules. A model making more than one ranged attack may divide its attacks among any eligible targets. A model in melee cannot make ranged attacks.

Some spells and special rules let certain models make magic attacks. Magic attacks are similar to ranged attacks and follow most of the same rules. However, magic attacks are not affected by a rule that only affects ranged attacks. See Casting Spells (pg. 66) for full details on magic attacks.

Ranged Weapons

Ranged weapons include bows, rifles, flamethrowers, crossbows, harpoon guns, and mortars. A ranged weapon's damage roll is 2d6+POW.

Declaring a Target

A ranged or magic attack can be declared against any target in the attacker's line of sight subject to the targeting rules. The attack must be declared before measuring the range to the intended target. Unless a model's special rules say otherwise, it can make ranged and magic attacks only through its front arc.

Targeting

A ranged or magic attack must be declared against a model or an object on the battlefield within LOS that can normally be damaged. See Line of Sight (pg. 32) for full details. Neither attack type can target open ground or a permanent terrain feature. A ranged attack need not target the nearest enemy model, but intervening models may prevent a model further away from being targeted.

Certain rules and effects create situations that specifically prevent a model from being targeted. A model that cannot be targeted by an attack still suffers its effects if inside the attack's area-of-effect. Other rules and effects, such as Stealth, only cause an attack to miss automatically. They do not prevent the model from being targeted by the attack.

Measuring Range

A ranged or magic attack must be declared against a legal target prior to measuring range. After declaring the attack, use a measuring device to see if the target is within Range (RNG) of the attack. Range is measured from the nearest edge of the attacking model's base to the nearest edge of the target model's base. If the target is in range, make a *ranged attack roll* or *magic attack roll*, as applicable. If the target is beyond maximum range, the attack automatically misses. If a ranged attack has an area-of-effect (AOE) and the attack's target is out of range, it automatically misses, and its *point of impact* will deviate from the point on the line to its declared target at a distance equal to its RNG. See Area-of-Effect Attacks (pg. 48) for full details on these attacks and deviation.

Rate of Fire

A weapon's rate of fire (ROF) indicates the maximum number of ranged attacks it may make in an activation. Reloading time prevents most ranged weapons from being used more than once per activation. Some ranged weapons reload faster and may make multiple attacks if a model is able to make additional attacks. However, a ranged weapon may not make more attacks per activation than its rate of fire regardless of the number of additional attacks a model is entitled to make.

Ranged Attack Rolls

Determine a ranged attack's success by making a ranged attack roll. Roll 2d6 and add the attacking model's Ranged Attack (RAT). A boosted attack roll adds an additional die to this roll. Special rules and certain circumstances may modify the attack roll as well.

Ranged Attack Roll = 2d6+RAT

A target is *directly hit* by an attack if the attack roll equals or exceeds the target's Defense (DEF). If the attack roll is less than the target's DEF, the attack misses. A roll of all 1's on the dice is a miss. A roll of all 6's is a direct hit unless you are rolling only one die, regardless of the attacker's RAT or his target's DEF.

Sometimes a special rule causes an attack to hit automatically. Such automatic hits are also direct hits.

Ranged Attack Modifiers

The most common modifiers affecting a model's ranged attack roll are summarized here for easy reference. Where necessary, additional detail can be found on the pages listed.

- *Aiming*: A model that voluntarily forfeits its movement by not changing its position or facing gains a +2 bonus to every ranged attack roll it makes that turn. If a model moves that turn, it loses the bonus for aiming. A magic attack does not get the aiming bonus.

- *Back Strike* (pg. 51): A ranged or magic attack against target model's back arc from a model that began its activation in the target's back arc gains a +2 bonus to the attack roll.

Combat

- *Cloud Effect* (pg. 57): A model inside a cloud effect gains +2 DEF against all ranged and magic attacks.
- *Concealment*: A model with concealment in relation to its attacker gains +2 DEF against ranged and magic attacks.
- *Cover*: A model with cover in relation to its attacker gains +4 DEF against ranged and magic attacks.
- *Elevated Target*: When drawing line of sight from a model on a lower elevation than its target, ignore all intervening models on a lower elevation than the target. A model on higher elevation than its attacker gains +2 DEF against ranged and magic attacks. Models on lower elevations than the target do not provide *screening*.
- *Elevated Attacker*: When drawing line of sight from a model on a higher elevation than its target, ignore all intervening models on lower elevation than the attacking model except those that would normally screen the target. Additionally, you can draw a line of sight through screening models that have equal or smaller-sized bases than the attacking model, but the target still gets +2 DEF for being screened.
- *Stationary Target* (pg. 54): A stationary target has a base DEF of 5.
- *Screened Target* (pg 33): A screened target gains +2 DEF against ranged and magic attacks.
- *Target in Melee* (pg. 47): A ranged or magic attack against a target in melee suffers a −4 penalty to the attack roll. If the attack misses its target, it may hit a nearby model instead.

Concealment and Cover

Terrain features, spells, and other effects may make it more difficult to hit a model with a ranged or magic attack. A model within 1" of a terrain feature that obscures any portion of its base from an attacker may gain either a concealment or cover bonus, depending on the type of terrain, to its DEF against ranged or magic attacks. Concealment and cover bonuses are not cumulative with themselves or each other, but they are cumulative with other effects that modify a model's DEF. See Terrain (pg. 77) for full details on terrain features and how they provide concealment or cover.

Some terrain features and special effects grant a model **concealment** by making it more difficult to be seen, but they are not actually dense enough to block an attack. Examples include low hedges or bushes. A model within 1" of a concealing terrain feature that obscures any portion of its base from an attacker gains +2 DEF against ranged and magic attacks. Concealment provides no benefit against spray attacks.

Other terrain features and special effects grant a model **cover** by being physically solid enough to block an attack against it. Examples include stone walls, giant boulders, and buildings. A model within 1" of a covering terrain feature that obscures any portion of its base from an attacker gains +4 DEF against ranged and magic attacks. Cover provides no benefit against spray attacks.

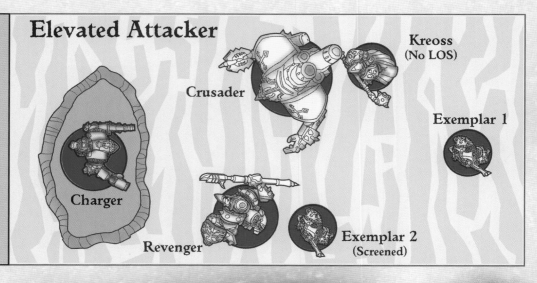

A Charger standing on top of a hill is choosing his target for a Dual Cannon ranged attack. Because the Crusader has a larger base than the Charger and Kreoss is close enough to be screened by it, it blocks LOS to Kreoss. However, the Charger can draw line of sight to all the other models because an elevated attacker ignores intervening models of equal or smaller base size on lower elevation. Effectively the Charger can see over the Revenger to target Exemplar 2. Even though the Charger has LOS to him, Exemplar 2 still receives +2 DEF for being screened.

Elevated Attacker

Kreoss (No LOS)

Crusader

Exemplar 1

Charger

Revenger

Exemplar 2 (Screened)

Examples of Concealment and Cover

Cover: +4 DEF

Concealment: +2 DEF

Cover: +4 DEF

Targeting a Model in Melee

A model making a ranged or magic attack against a target *in melee* risks hitting another model participating in the combat, including friendly models. The standard targeting rules, including line of sight and screening, must be observed when targeting a model that is in melee. *Combined ranged attacks* cannot target a model in melee; it is impossible to concentrate such firepower against a single target in a swirling fight.

In addition to any other attack modifiers, a ranged attack against a target in melee suffers a –4 penalty to the attack roll. All of the target's special rules and effects in play on it still apply. For instance, an attack targeting a model with the Stealth ability from greater than 5" away still automatically misses, and a ranged attack against a model affected by Severius' Death Sentence spell still automatically hits.

If the attack against the intended target misses and the target was in range, it may hit another combatant. The attacker must immediately re-roll his attack against another model in that combat. Randomly determine which other model in the combat (not including the intended target) becomes the new target. When determining the attack's new target, only the models that are in melee with the attack's original target and any other models in melee with those models are considered to be in the same combat. Every model meeting these criteria is eligible to become the new target, regardless of line of sight, with two exceptions: a model is ineligible to become the new target if it has a special rule preventing it from being targeted or if the attacker's line of sight to it is completely blocked by obstructing terrain. If multiple models in the combat are eligible targets, randomly determine which model becomes the new target.

For example, using a d6, if there are three other models in the combat, the first model will become the new target on a 1 or 2, the second on a 3 or 4, and the third on a 5 or 6. However, if the attacker cannot draw a line of sight

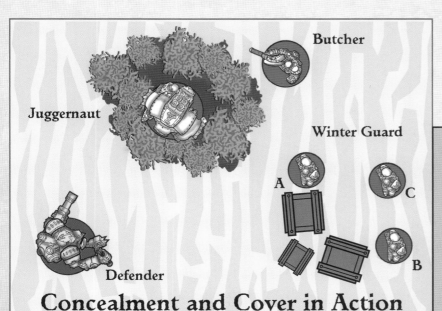

Concealment and Cover in Action

Butcher

Juggernaut

Winter Guard

A

C

B

Defender

It may appear at first that the Defender has several targets from which to choose, but many of them are actually well defended. The forest grants concealment (+2 DEF) to the Juggernaut, and the crates grant cover (+4 DEF) to Winter Guard A and Winter Guard B. Because there is a forest between it and the Butcher, the Defender cannot draw LOS to the Butcher at all. Winter Guard C is behind the crates, but because he is more than 1" from the crates, he does not benefit from the cover bonus.

Combat

to one of those models due to an obstruction (e.g., it's around a corner), ignore that model and randomize the attack between the other two: it targets the first on a 1 through 3 or the second on a 4 through 6. If one of those two models cannot be targeted for some reason (such as being under the protection of a Safe Passage battle hymn), then only one model is an eligible target and a random roll is not necessary.

When re-rolling the attack against the new target, all modifiers affecting the attacker still apply such as boosting the attack roll, the aiming bonus, spell effects, and the −4 penalty for targeting a model in melee. All modifiers affecting the newly targeted model also apply, but ignore those that only applied to the intended target. If the attack against the new target misses, it misses completely without targeting any more models.

For instance, Stryker is in melee with a Revenger affected by the Protection of Menoth spell. A Charger forfeits its movement, aims, targets the Revenger with its dual cannon, and spends a focus point to boost its attack roll. The Charger's attack roll gains an additional die for boosting the attack roll and the aiming bonus and suffers the penalty for targeting a model in melee. In addition, the Revenger's DEF against this attack is enhanced due to the spell affecting it. If the attack misses, the Charger re-rolls the attack, this time targeting Stryker. It still includes the additional die for boosting the attack roll, aiming bonus, and the penalty for targeting a model in melee. If Stryker is behind cover in relation to the Charger, then he gains +4 DEF against this attack.

As a second example (see diagram), Stryker is in melee with Deneghra and a Deathripper. A Long Gunner enters the fight from the side to engage Deneghra but not the Deathripper. A Charger makes a ranged attack against the Deathripper and misses. Since Stryker is in melee with the Deathripper and Deneghra is in melee with Stryker, they are both in the same combat as the intended target. The Long Gunner is not included because he is not in melee with the intended target (the Deathripper) or with another model in melee with the intended target (Stryker). He is far enough from the intended target not to be attacked accidentally. A random die roll determines that Deneghra is the new target. Unfortunately, since the Charger is more than 5" away from Deneghra, her Stealth ability makes the attack automatically miss without even rolling. Even though Stealth prevents Deneghra from being hit, she can still be targeted. Since the attack missed both its intended target and the new target, it misses completely with no further chance of hitting Stryker or the Long Gunner.

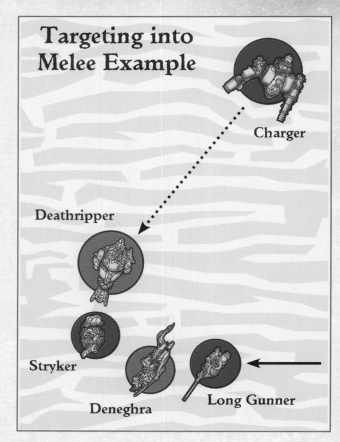

Targeting into Melee Example

Charger

Deathripper

Stryker

Deneghra

Long Gunner

An area-of-effect attack that misses a target in melee deviates normally instead of following these rules.

Area-of-Effect Attacks

An attack with an area-of-effect is sometimes referred to as an AOE attack. A ranged attack with an AOE is a ranged attack. A magic attack with an AOE is a magic attack. A melee attack with an AOE is a melee attack. An area-of-effect attack, such as from an explosive spell or a gas cloud, affects every model in an area centered on its point of impact. The attack covers an area with a diameter equal to its area-of-effect (AOE). Templates for AOEs can be found on page 256.

An AOE attack follows all normal targeting restrictions. A successful attack roll indicates a **direct hit** on the intended target, which suffers a direct hit damage roll of 2d6+POW. Center the AOE template over the point of impact—in the case of a direct hit, the center of the targeted model's base. Every other model with any part of its base covered by the AOE template is automatically hit by the attack and suffers a **blast damage** roll of 2d6+1/2 POW. Make separate damage rolls against each model in the AOE; each roll must be boosted individually. Every model caught in an attack's area-of-effect is subject to its special effects.

An AOE attack that misses its target deviates a random direction and distance. An area-of-effect attack declared against a target out of range (RNG) automatically misses, and its point of impact deviates from the point on the line to its declared target at a distance equal to its RNG. An area-of-effect attack that misses a target in range deviates from the point directly over its intended target.

An area-of-effect attack's point of impact determines the origin of the damage and effects for models not directly hit by the attack. For instance, suppose an AOE ranged attack targets a trooper in the second rank of a shield wall formation from the trooper's front arc. If the attack is successful, the target trooper will benefit from the shield wall, as will other troopers in the same rank, but troopers in the rank in front of his will not because the points of impact of the AOE attack is in their rear arc. Should the attack miss and deviate long, the target trooper would not benefit from being in the shield wall either since the attack's point of impact is now in his rear arc.

Deviation

When an AOE attack misses its target, determine its actual point of impact by rolling deviation. Referencing the deviation template (pg. 256), roll a d6 to determine the direction the attack deviates. For example, a roll of 1 means the attack goes long and a roll of 4 means the attack lands short. Roll another d6 to determine the deviation distance in inches. Determine the missed attack's point of impact by measuring the rolled distance from the center of the original target in the direction determined by the deviation roll. If the deviated point of impact would be off the table, reduce the deviation distance so that the point of impact is on the edge of the table instead. If the intended target is beyond the weapon's RNG, determine deviation from the point on the line to its declared target at a distance equal to its RNG.

An attack will not deviate further than half the distance from the attacker to its intended target. Use the exact value for this maximum—do not round it. For instance, an attack made at a target 5" away from the attacker will deviate a maximum of 2.5" even if the attacker rolls a 3, 4, 5, or 6 for deviation distance.

Terrain features, models, or other effects do not block deviating AOE attacks. They always take effect at the determined point of impact.

Center the AOE template over the point of impact. Every model with any part of its base covered by the AOE template is automatically hit by the attack and takes a blast damage roll of 2d6+1/2 POW. Make separate damage rolls against each model in the area-of-effect; each roll must be boosted individually. Every model caught in an attack's area-of-effect is subject to its special effects.

Deviating area-of-effect attacks never cause direct hits even if the point of impact is on top of a model.

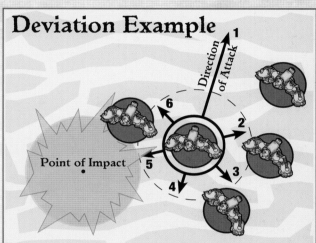

Deviation Example

Direction of Attack

Point of Impact

Mechanithralls

Redeemer

A Redeemer makes a ranged attack with its Skyhammer rocket targeting the Mechanithrall in the middle of the unit 11" away. If the target is hit, the Skyhammer will catch four Mechanithralls under the template! The Redeemer's ranged attack roll is unsuccessful however, and since the attack is an area-of-effect, the Redeemer's controller must roll deviation to determine the attack's point of impact. The roll is a 5 for direction and a 4 for 4" of deviation. Measure this distance in the deviation direction from the center of its original target to locate the point of impact. Models under the template suffer blast damage and are subject to the attack's special effects. The Redeemer does not hit as many Mechanithralls as it wanted, but it still catches one under the template.

Examples of Spray Attacks

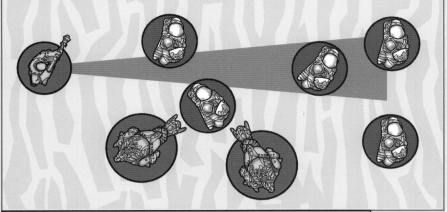

A Bile Thrall makes a spray attack against a group of Winter Guard. The Cryx player centers the spray template laterally over an eligible target. The player chooses the centermost Winter Guard because that trooper's comrades are too far away to be intervening models. Targeting that trooper also lets the player cover the greatest number of Winter Guard without covering his own nearby bonejacks. He rolls a ranged attack against each of the four Winter Guard in the spray. Per the "Targeting a Model in Melee" rules, if the attack against the Winter Guard in melee with the bonejacks misses, it will potentially hit one of the bonejacks instead even though they are not actually under the spray template!

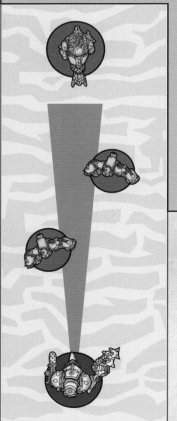

A pair of Mechanithralls has advanced to within a Repenter's Flame Thrower range. The Cryx player has been careful to place them far enough apart so that a spray attack targeted against either one of them will not catch the other under the template. Unfortunately he has not taken the Deathripper behind them into account. The Repenter has line of sight to the Deathripper so can target it with its Flame Thrower even though it is out of range. By doing so, both Mechanithralls will be covered by the spray template.

Spray Attacks

An attack using the spray template is sometimes referred to as a spray attack. Some weapons and spells, such as flamethrowers and Deneghra's Venom spell, make spray attacks. This devastating short-ranged attack can potentially hit several models. A spray attack has a RNG of "SP" and uses the spray template. The spray template can be found on page 256.

When making a spray attack, center the spray template laterally over an eligible target in the attacker's front arc with the narrow end of the template touching the nearest edge of the attacker's base. This target need not itself be under the template. The targeting rules apply when selecting the attack's primary target. Every model with any part of its base covered by the spray template may be hit by the attack.

Make separate ranged attack rolls against each model under the template; each roll must be boosted individually. A model under the spray template does not receive any benefit from concealment, cover, or intervening models because the attack comes over, around, or in some cases through its protection.

A spray attack against a model in melee suffers a –4 penalty to its attack roll against those models. An attack that misses has the potential to hit another model in the combat, including those already affected by the spray and models that are not under the template at all. See Targeting a Model in Melee (pg. 47) for full details on resolving this situation.

Terrain that obstructs LOS blocks spray attacks. A model under the spray template cannot be hit by the attack if the attacker's LOS is completely blocked by terrain.

Every model hit by a spray attack suffers a *direct hit* and is subject to its special effects. Make separate damage rolls against each model hit; each roll must be boosted individually.

Special Combat Situations

The chaos of a battlefield is constantly producing the unexpected. Although several situations can arise as a result of unique circumstances or a model's special rules, these rules should enable a smooth resolution. Savvy players will use these rules to their best advantage.

Attacks that Hit or Miss Automatically

Some special rules cause attacks to hit automatically or miss automatically. If a special rule will cause an attack to hit automatically, you do not have to make an attack roll. If you do make a roll (for example, because you want to try for a critical hit), the attack will no longer hit automatically. If the attack roll fails, the attack misses.

Similarly, if a special rule will cause an attack to miss automatically, you do not have to make an attack roll unless there's a possibility that the attacker will suffer a detrimental effect because of the die roll. If you do make an attack roll, the attack will miss regardless of the result of the roll. For example, a ranged attack against Deneghra from over 5" away does not usually require a die roll because her Stealth ability causes the attack to miss automatically. However, a Deliverer making a Skyhammer attack against her from the same distance must make an attack roll because the Skyhammer's Misfire rule causes an explosion on a roll of all 1s.

In cases of conflicting special rules, one causing an attack to hit automatically takes precedence over one causing an attack to miss automatically. For instance, Severius' Death Sentence spell allows attacks to hit automatically, which overrides special rules such as Stealth that would otherwise cause an attack to miss automatically. In such a case, you do not have to make an attack roll even if there is a possible detriment to the attacker because of the roll. The rules for automatic hits take precedence over the rules for automatic misses.

Back Strikes

A **back strike** grants a +2 bonus to the attack roll of any melee, ranged, or magic attack made against a model from its back arc. To receive the back strike bonus, the attacking model must spend its entire activation up to the moment of its attack in the target's rear arc. If any portion of the attacking model's base enters the target's front arc, the attacker does not receive this bonus. However, when channeling an offensive spell, the warcaster's location is irrelevant. In this case, the attack receives the back strike bonus if the channeler is in the target's rear arc. A model only receives a back strike bonus during its activation.

Combined Melee Attacks

Two or more troopers in the same unit with this ability in melee range of the same target may combine their attacks. In order to participate in a combined melee attack, a trooper must be able to declare a melee attack against the intended target. The trooper with the highest MAT in the attacking group makes one melee attack roll for the group, adding +1 to the attack and damage rolls for each model, including himself, participating in the attack. If multiple troopers participating in the attack have the same MAT, declare which model is the primary attacker. All other bonuses and penalties to the attack and damage rolls, such as the bonus for intervening terrain, are based on the primary attacker. If the target of a combined melee attack has a special rule or effect in play that affects its attackers, only the primary attacker—the model making the attack roll—suffers those effects.

A unit's melee attacks may be grouped in any manner, including multiple combined melee attacks. Troopers capable of multiple melee attacks can divide them among eligible targets and participate in multiple combined melee attacks.

Example: Four members of a Protectorate Temple Flameguard unit, including their captain, make a combined melee attack against a Cygnar Defender. Since the captain has the highest MAT, he makes one melee attack for the group, adding +4 to his attack and damage rolls since there are four models participating in the attack. Two other troopers in the same Flameguard unit make a combined melee attack against a nearby Sentinel. The trooper declared as the primary attacker makes one melee attack and adds +2 to its attack and damage rolls.

Cannot make a back strike

May make a back strike

Front Arc

Back Strikes

Combat

Combined Ranged Attacks

Two or more troopers in the same unit with this ability may combine their ranged attacks against the same target. In order to participate in a combined ranged attack, a trooper must be able to declare a ranged attack against the intended target and be in a single open formation group with the other participants. The trooper with the highest RAT in the attacking group makes one ranged attack roll for the group, gaining +1 to the attack and damage rolls for each model, including himself, participating in the attack. If multiple troopers participating in the attack have the same RAT, declare which model is the primary attacker.

Combined ranged attacks cannot target a model in melee.

If the target of a combined attack can claim concealment or cover in relation to any member of the attacking group, it gets the appropriate bonus against the attack. All other bonuses and penalties are based on the primary attacker. If the target of a combined ranged attack has a special rule or effect in play that affects its attackers, only the primary attacker—the model making the attack roll—suffers those effects.

After measuring range, any models found to be out of range of the target do not contribute to the attack and damage roll bonus, but they are still considered to have made a ranged attack. If the primary attacker is out of range, the entire combined attack automatically misses regardless of bonuses. Similarly, models found to be more than 5" away from a target with the Stealth ability do not contribute, and the entire combined attack automatically misses if the primary attacker is more than 5" away from the target.

A unit's ranged attacks may be grouped in any manner, including multiple combined ranged attacks. Troopers capable of multiple ranged attacks can divide them among eligible targets and participate in multiple combined ranged attacks.

Example: Four members of a Cygnar Long Gunner unit, including its sergeant, are in an open formation group and declare a combined ranged attack against a Khador Juggernaut. When measuring range, the player discovers one trooper is out of range and cannot participate in the attack. Since the sergeant has the highest RAT, he makes one ranged attack for the group, adding +3 to his attack and damage rolls since only three of the four models participating in the attack contribute to it. Two other troopers in the same Long Gunner unit could not participate in the combined attack because they are not in the same open formation as the others. They declare individual ranged attacks against two Iron Fang Pikemen nearby.

Corpse Tokens

Some models can claim a model's corpse, represented by a **corpse token**, when it is destroyed. Living and some undead models generate corpse tokens. A model's special ability that allows it to claim corpse tokens will specify which undead models' corpses it may claim. A model only has one corpse. If more than one model is eligible to claim its corpse, the model nearest the destroyed model receives the token. Refer to a model's special rules for how it utilizes corpse tokens. Models removed from play but not also destroyed do not generate corpse tokens.

Effects with Simultaneous Timing

If multiple special rules with contradictory effects are triggered at the same time, the attacker's special rule takes precedence.

Falling

A model slammed, thrown, pushed, or that otherwise moves off of an elevated surface greater than 1" high is knocked down and suffers a damage roll. A fall of up to 3" causes a POW 10 damage roll. Add an additional die to the damage roll for every additional increment of three inches the model falls, rounded up.

For example, a model falling 7" suffers a damage roll of 4d6+10!

If a falling model lands on top of a smaller model, the smaller model's controller pushes it back to make room for the falling model.

If a falling model contacts a model with an equal or smaller-sized base, that model is knocked down and suffers the same damage roll as the falling model. A model with a larger-sized base than the falling model, however, does not suffer damage and is not knocked down. All damage resulting from the fall is simultaneous.

Knockdown

Some attacks and special rules cause a model to be **knocked down**. Mark a knocked down model with a token. A knocked down model is *stationary* and obeys those rules until it stands up. A knocked down model does not count as an intervening model and therefore it does not block LOS or provide screening. It may be ignored for targeting purposes. A knocked down model has no facing and no back arc; its front arc extends 360°. A knocked down model cannot be slammed or locked, but it can be pushed.

A knocked down model may stand up at the start of its next activation before doing anything else. However, if a model is knocked down during its controller's turn, it may not stand up until that player's next turn even if it has not been yet activated this turn.

To stand up, a model must forfeit either its movement or its action for that activation. A model may face any direction when it stands up. A model that forfeits its movement to

stand can perform an action as if it had advanced, but it cannot make attacks involving movement such as a slam. A model that forfeits its action to stand can advance but cannot run or charge.

Leaving the Play Area

A model that flees off the table is removed from play. A model that would leave the table for any other reason (such as being thrown or slammed) will stop at the table edge and remain in play. The table edge does not count as an obstacle; models do not take additional damage for stopping there.

Origin of Damage

Damage that is the direct result of an attack originates from the origin of the attack, that is, either the attacking or channeling model. This is also the origin of the damage for a spray attack or a Strafe attack. Some abilities, such as Skarre's Sacrificial Strike, allow a model to damage another directly without making an attack. The origin of the damage in this case is again the effect's origin. The origin of damage for a *direct hit* with an AOE attack is the attack's origin, but the origin of damage for any other damage caused by an AOE attack is the attack's point of impact. Finally, some non-AOE attacks, such as Ashes to Ashes and Chain Lightning, have special rules that allow

them to damage other models besides the attack's target. The origin of damage in those cases is the model or point from which you measure the range to other affected models. For example, the origin of damage for the target of Ashes to Ashes is the spell's origin, but the origin of damage for the other models affected by the spell is the target model. Similarly, when Chain Lightning arcs to another model, the previous model hit by the spell is the origin of that damage.

Replacing Models

When replacing one model with another, place the new model so that the area covered by the smaller of the bases is completely within the area covered by the larger. If the two bases are the same size, place the new model in the same location as the one being replaced.

Soul Tokens

Certain models can claim a model's soul, represented by a **soul token**, when it is destroyed. Only living models generate soul tokens. A model only has one soul. If more than one model is eligible to claim a soul, the model nearest the destroyed model receives the token. Refer to a model's special rules for how it utilizes soul tokens. Models removed from play but not also destroyed do not generate soul tokens.

Combat

Special Attacks

Certain models have special rules allowing them to make special attacks. A model may make one special attack instead of making its initial melee or ranged attacks during its combat action if it meets the specific requirements for its use. Resolve the special attack following the rules for melee combat or ranged combat as applicable. Models may spend focus points to make additional attacks after a special attack, but they may only be normal melee or ranged attacks and must correspond to the nature of the special attack made.

Power attacks are a unique type of special attack. Unlike other special attacks, power attacks cannot be made after charging.

Stationary Models

A **stationary model** is one that has been knocked down or immobilized. A stationary model cannot move, perform actions, make attacks, cast spells, use animi, use feats, or give orders. A stationary model does not have a melee range. A model is never in melee with a stationary model. A stationary model does not engage other models nor does a model engage a stationary model.

A melee attack against a stationary model automatically hits it directly. A stationary model has a base DEF of 5.

ANIMI? WHAT ARE ANIMI?
ANIMI ARE THE SPELL-LIKE ABILITIES UTILIZED BY WARBEASTS IN HORDES, WARMACHINE's FERAL TWIN.

Damage

Warcasters, warjacks, and some other models can take a tremendous amount of damage before they fall in combat. What may be an incapacitating or mortal wound to a regular trooper will just dent a warjack's hull or be deflected by a warcaster's arcane protections.

Damage Rolls

Determine how much damage a successful attack causes by making a **damage roll**. Roll 2d6 and add the attack's Power (POW). Melee attacks also add the attacker's STR. A boosted damage roll adds an additional die to this roll. Special rules for certain circumstances may modify the damage roll as well.

Damage roll = 2d6 + POW (+STR if applicable)

Compare this total against the target's Armor (ARM) stat. The target takes one **damage point** for every point that the damage roll exceeds its ARM.

Attacks that generate multiple attack and/or damage rolls do so simultaneously. Completely resolve all of the attack and damage rolls before applying any of the target's special rules that are triggered by suffering damage, being destroyed, or being removed from play. For example, suppose a Repenter makes a Flame Thrower spray attack against some Scrap Thralls. Scrap Thralls destroyed by the attack do not explode due to their Thrall Bomb ability until after all of the attack and damage rolls generated by the spray attack have been resolved.

As a second example, Captain Haley targets a member of a unit of Knights Exemplar with her Chain Lightning spell and hits three additional Knights. Haley's controller resolves the damage rolls for the 4 Knights Exemplar hit by Chain Lightning before any of the Knights Exemplar gain their benefits from Bond of Brotherhood.

Some attacks, such as the Sentinel's Strafe and the Vanquisher's Circular Strike abilities, are not resolved simultaneously. Attacks that are not simultaneous will state, "Completely resolve each attack individually and apply the targets' special rules immediately as each attack is resolved."

Recording Damage

A model's army list entry gives the total amount of damage it can suffer before being *destroyed*. Most models are destroyed after taking one damage point. A model resilient enough to take more than one point of damage will have a row of **damage boxes** on its stat card for tracking damage it receives. Record its damage left to right by marking one damage box for each damage point taken. A model is destroyed once all of its damage boxes have been marked. Every fifth damage box is colored for ease of counting. Unmarked damage boxes are often called **wounds**.

A warjack has a **damage grid** consisting of six columns of damage boxes labeled with the numbers 1 through 6. Different warjacks' damage grids may be slightly different in shape and number of damage boxes, but they function the same. When a warjack suffers damage, roll a d6 to determine which column takes the damage. Starting with the uppermost empty box in that column and working down, mark one damage box per damage point taken. Once a column is full, continue recording damage in the next column to the right that contains unmarked damage boxes. If all the damage boxes in column 6 are marked, continue recording damage in column 1 or the next column that contains unmarked damage boxes. Continue shifting columns as required until every damage point taken has been recorded.

Disabling Systems

When a warjack suffers damage, individual systems critical to its combat performance may be damaged and disabled. A warjack's blank damage boxes represent its **hull**. Beneath the hull are the model's vital systems indicated by system boxes. Each system uses a different letter to label its system boxes. When recording damage, mark both blank boxes and system boxes. A system becomes disabled when all its system boxes are marked. Mark the appropriate system status box to show this. The effects of disabled systems are as follows:

Disabled Arc Node: A warcaster cannot channel spells through a warjack with a disabled arc node.

Disabled Cortex: A warjack with a disabled cortex loses any unused focus points and cannot be allocated focus points. It cannot use focus points for any reason.

Disabled Hull: Disabling a warjack's hull has no direct effect, so no system status box is provided. However, a disabled hull counts toward the disabled systems limit for disabling the entire warjack.

Disabled Movement: A warjack with disabled movement has its base Speed (SPD) changed to 1 and its base Defense (DEF) changed to 7. Disabled movement prevents a warjack from charging or making slam power attacks.

Disabled Arm or Weapon System: A disabled arm or weapon system cannot be used to make attacks. The warjack cannot use special rules that require the use of this system. When a warjack's arm that contains a shield or buckler is disabled, the warjack loses its use, and the warjack's Armor (ARM) reverts to the value listed in its stat bar.

Disabling a Warjack

A warjack is completely disabled and can no longer function once three of its systems are disabled. Though not technically a system, a warjack's hull counts as such for purposes of disabling it. Thus, a warjack will be disabled if all its hull damage boxes are marked and it already has two other disabled systems.

Replace a disabled warjack model with a disabled warjack wreck marker corresponding to its base size. A disabled warjack wreck marker counts as rough terrain for movement and provides cover to models within 1" whose bases are partially obscured from the attacker by the wreck. Models at least partially within the area of the wreck also gain cover. Models can stand on and move through warjack wrecks. A disabled warjack has no facing, loses all special abilities, cannot receive focus, and does not gain an ARM bonus for still-functional shields or bucklers. A disabled warjack wreck marker is still a warjack and is therefore also a model. It may be attacked as a stationary target, and effects, spells, and animi on it remain in play. A disabled warjack may return to operation if enough of its damage boxes are repaired.

Warjack wreck markers, both disabled and totaled, are never intervening models and do not provide screening.

Combat

Melee attacks may be made across warjack wreck markers. Warjack wreck markers cannot be slammed, thrown, pushed, or moved.

Be sure to keep track of exactly which model a marker represents. We suggest numbering your wreck markers or even making a specific wreck marker for each warjack in your army.

Destroying a Warjack

A warjack is destroyed or totaled when all of its damage boxes are marked. Remove a totaled warjack from the table and replace it with a totaled warjack wreck marker corresponding to its base size. A totaled warjack wreck marker counts as rough terrain for movement and provides cover to models within 1" whose bases are partially obscured from the attacker by the wreck. Models at least partially within the area of the wreck also gain cover. Any effects, spells, and animi on a warjack instantly expire when it is totaled. A totaled warjack cannot be repaired.

Destroyed vs. Removed From Play

When a model suffers sufficient damage to be eliminated from play, it is **destroyed**. A model without damage capacity is destroyed as soon as it takes one *damage point*. Models with damage boxes are destroyed when all their damage boxes have been filled. Destroyed models are cleared from the play area and set aside. It is possible for destroyed models to return to play.

Occasionally models will be outright **removed from play**, sometimes instead of being destroyed, at other times in addition to being destroyed. A model removed from play cannot return to the table for any reason. When a model is both destroyed and removed from play, effects triggered by its destruction still occur.

Warcaster Death

Should a warcaster be unfortunate enough to fall in combat, his entire army will suffer from the harsh blow. All upkeep spells cast by this warcaster immediately expire. Every warjack in the warcaster's battlegroup instantly becomes inert and suffers the penalties of being stationary. An **inert** warjack has no facing, loses all special abilities, and does not gain an ARM bonus for functioning shields or bucklers.

In many cases, the death of a warcaster heralds the end of the battle. However, if an army contains other warcasters or 'jack marshals, they may reactivate the inert warjacks and add them to their respective battlegroups.

Reactivating Warjacks

A warcaster or 'jack marshal that ends its movement in base-to-base contact with an inert warjack may reactivate it. To reactivate the warjack, the model must forfeit its action this turn but may still cast spells, use its feat, and use special abilities. The warjack must forfeit its activation and cannot channel spells on the turn it is reactivated, but it functions normally next turn.

Special Effects

Many attacks cause special effects in addition to causing damage. Each special effect is unique in its application. There are four categories of special effects: automatic effects, critical effects, continuous effects, and cloud effects. A special effect may belong to more than one category, and its category may change depending on the weapon. For instance, one weapon may cause fire automatically on a successful hit, but another may require a critical hit to cause fire.

Pay close attention to the exact wording for each model's special effects. Even though the effect may be the same for different models with the same weapon or ability, it may require different conditions to function. Some models' special effects function if the target is hit, others require the target to take damage, and critical effects require a *critical hit* on the attack roll.

Automatic Effects

Apply an automatic effect every time it meets the conditions required to function.

Critical Effects

Apply a critical effect if any two dice in the attack roll show the same number and the attack hits—this is a **critical hit**. The target model suffers the special effect even if it takes no damage from the damage roll unless the specific effect requires that it do so. An *area-of-effect attack's* critical effect only functions with a *direct hit*, but every model under the template will suffer the critical effect.

A weapon with a critical effect has the label "Critical" to distinguish it from an automatic damage effect.

Continuous Effects

Continuous effects remain on a model and have the potential to damage or affect it some other way on subsequent turns. A model can have multiple continuous effects on it at once, but it can have only one of each continuous effect type on it at a time.

Resolve continuous effects on models you control during the Maintenance Phase of your turn. Roll a d6—if the result is a 1 or 2, the continuous effect immediately expires without further effect. On a 3 through 6, it remains in play and the model immediately suffers its effects.

Continuous effects do not require focus points for *upkeep* and cannot be removed voluntarily. Remove a continuous effect only when it expires, a special situation causes it to end, or the affected model is removed from the table.

For example, a Crusader attacks a Defender with its Inferno Mace and rolls a critical hit. The Defender is now on fire. It takes no damage from the fire at this point. During its controller's next Maintenance Phase, the Defender's controller rolls a d6. The result is a 5, so the Defender suffers a POW 12 damage roll from the fire. The Crusader attacks it again on its turn and rolls another critical hit, but since the Defender is already on fire, there is no further effect from the critical hit. When the Defender's controller's Maintenance Phase comes around again, he rolls another d6 for the fire. This time the result is a 1, so the fire goes out without doing any more damage to the Defender.

Cloud Effects

A cloud effect produces an area of dense smoke, magical darkness, gas, etc. that remains in play at its *point of impact*. Use an area-of-effect template of the appropriate diameter to represent the cloud. Consider every model with any part of its base covered by the cloud's template to be inside the cloud and susceptible to its effects.

In addition to being affected by a cloud's special rules, a model inside a cloud effect gains +2 DEF against ranged and magic attacks, which is cumulative with *concealment* or *cover*. A model in a cloud effect may target models outside of it normally. For a model outside of it, the cloud effect completely obstructs line of sight to anything beyond it. Thus, a model can see into or out of a cloud effect but not through one. A cloud effect provides no protection from melee attacks.

A model that enters an existing cloud effect suffers its effects immediately. A model that begins its activation inside an existing cloud effect and does not move out of it suffers its effects at the end of its activation.

Remove a cloud effect when it expires or if a special situation causes it to end.

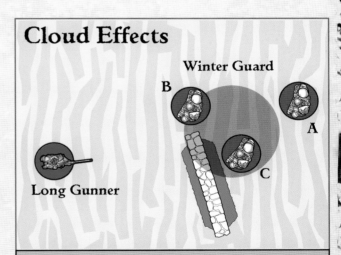

Cloud Effects

The Long Gunner has LOS to Winter Guard B and C, but they both gain +2 DEF against any ranged or magic attacks from the Long Gunner for being in the cloud effect. The Long Gunner's LOS to Winter Guard C crosses a solid terrain feature, so Winter Guard C also gains +4 DEF from cover for a total of +6 DEF against the Long Gunner's attacks. The Long Gunner and Winter Guard A do not have LOS to each other since LOS cannot be drawn through a cloud effect.

Winter Guard B and C can make ranged or magic attacks against the Long Gunner at no penalty. However, Winter Guard B and C do gain +2 DEF against attacks from each other.

Best of the Rest
Marshalling, Cavalry, and Mercenary Contracts

'Jack Marshals

Warcasters are elite military leaders representing a combination of mage and warrior rare in the Iron Kingdoms. Supporting their armies are capable soldiers specially trained to command warjacks without the benefit of magical skills. These specialists, called 'jack marshals, can control warjacks using gestures and commands shouted across the battlefield. Though not as efficient as using focus, the 'jack marshal can guide a warjack to perform maneuvers it normally would not be able to on its own. They are not warcasters, but 'jack marshals may begin the game controlling one or more faction warjacks. These warjacks are not part of any warcaster's battlegroup. Mercenary 'jack marshals can only control mercenary warjacks and cannot control warjacks belonging to a faction.

The number of warjacks a 'jack marshal can control is listed in parentheses beside the 'Jack Marshal special ability in the model's description. For example, a model with 'Jack Marshal (2) in its special rules may control up to two warjacks. Each 'jack marshal has a **marshaling range** equal to his Command (CMD) stat in inches. A controlled warjack within marshaling range of its controlling 'jack marshal may run, charge, or boost one attack or damage roll once per activation. A warjack gains these benefits even if its controlling 'jack marshal is stationary.

If a 'jack marshal is destroyed or removed from play, his warjacks become **autonomous** but do not become inert. Autonomous warjacks remain active but do not have a controller. An autonomous warjack acts normally but may not be marshaled or have focus allocated to it, though it may receive focus from other sources. A warjack must have a controller at the start of the game. It may not begin the game autonomous.

A 'jack marshal may reactivate one inert friendly faction warjack per turn in the same manner as a warcaster (pg. 56). Mercenary 'jack marshals may only reactivate mercenary warjacks. The reactivated warjack comes under the 'jack marshal's control unless he already controls his limit of warjacks. If the 'jack marshal already controls his limit, the reactivated warjack becomes autonomous. Likewise, if an opposing player takes control of a 'jack marshal, with the use of the Convert or Dark Seduction spell for example, a warjack controlled by the 'jack marshal remains under the control of its original player and becomes autonomous.

If control of the 'jack marshal is returned to his original player, the 'jack marshal resumes control of the warjack unless some other model has already taken control of it.

A warcaster or 'jack marshal who does not already control his limit of warjacks may take control of an autonomous friendly faction warjack. To take control of the warjack, the warcaster or 'jack marshal must be in base-to-base contact with the warjack and forfeit his action, but he may still cast spells, use his feat, and use special abilities. The warjack must forfeit its activation and cannot channel spells on the turn it becomes controlled. Beginning with the next turn, it may be marshaled or allocated focus.

Attachments

Attachments are made up of one or more models that may be added to a unit specified in the attachment's description. They may only be fielded as part of a unit. Attachments may not be added to weapon crews. There are different types of attachments such as **unit attachments** and **special weapon attachments**. A unit may have several attachments, but only one of each type of attachment may be added to a unit. An attachment may increase the victory point value of the unit to which it is added by an amount detailed in its description.

A model with the **Officer** special ability in a unit attachment becomes the unit's leader. The normal unit leader remains part of the unit but loses the Leader ability while the officer is on the table. The normal unit leader cannot issue orders without the Leader ability but may use all of its other abilities.

Cavalry

Slamming into the enemy with incredible force with weapons drawn makes cavalry ideally suited for breaking or disintegrating enemy lines. Mounted forces are renowned for their terrifying charges that couple tremendous speed with great weight. Even troops who can avoid being cut down by lance or saber are still vulnerable to being crushed underfoot. It is little wonder that the cavalry charge has remained a valid military tactic since its inception thousands of years before the arrival of the Orgoth.

Certain WARMACHINE models and units are designated as cavalry. In addition to all of the standard rules for models of their types, cavalry models have the following additional set of rules in common:

Cavalry Formation

Cavalry troopers have an additional formation available to them. Troopers in a cavalry unit that are up to 5" apart are in **cavalry formation**. Determine whether a cavalry trooper is in formation or not using cavalry formation groups instead of skirmish formation groups.

Tall In the Saddle

Cavalry models ignore intervening models with smaller bases than their own when making melee attacks.

Ride-By Attack

A cavalry model may combine its movement and action in a **ride-by attack**. Declare that the model is doing so at the beginning of its movement. The model advances and interrupts its movement at any point to perform its combat action. After completing its combat action, the model may then resume its movement. A cavalry trooper making a ride-by attack must complete both its movement and combat action before the next model is moved.

Some models must meet special requirements to make ride-by attacks:

- A cavalry solo may always make a ride-by attack instead of advancing.
- A cavalry trooper must receive an order to make a ride-by attack. This order may be issued by the unit leader or a model with the Commander ability, such as a warcaster.

Mount

A cavalry model's mount not only provides transportation but is also a weapon in its own right. Mounts are indicated by a distinctive horseshoe icon in their stat bars. A mount has a 1/2" melee range. Attacks made with a mount are melee attacks and are resolved normally except that the damage roll is only 2d6 plus the POW of the mount. Do not add the cavalry model's STR to mount damage rolls. Mount attack and damage rolls cannot be boosted.

Normally a model may only use its mount to make *impact attacks* (see Cavalry Charge below). However, expert riders on well-trained mounts are able to attack with their mounts at other times as well. Such models will have special rules that describe when they are able to do so.

Cavalry Charge

A charge performed by a cavalry model differs in several ways from a standard charge. When drawing line of sight for a cavalry charge, ignore intervening models with the same base size as the target or smaller.

If a charging cavalry model contacts another model during its movement and has moved at least 3", it stops and makes **impact attacks** with its mount (see Mount above) against all models in the mount's melee range. Completely resolve each impact attack individually and apply the targets' special rules immediately as each impact attack is resolved. Abilities that modify charge attack rolls also affect impact attacks. After resolving the impact attacks, the charging model may continue moving until it contacts another model, an obstacle, an obstruction, or rough terrain. It may not make further impact attacks during this charge. If the charging cavalry model did not move at least 3" before contacting the other model, it does not make any impact attacks and must stop its movement at that point. If the cavalry model's target is not in melee at the end of the charge movement, the charge fails and the model's activation immediately ends.

Best of the Rest

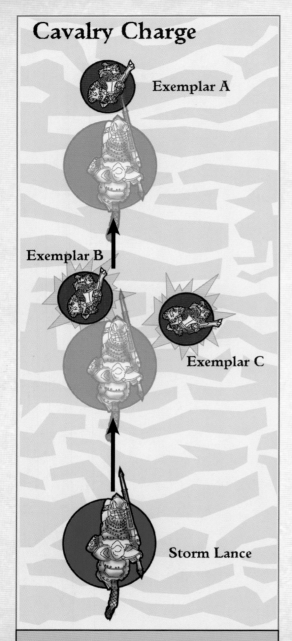

Cavalry Charge

Exemplar A

Exemplar B

Exemplar C

Storm Lance

The Storm Lance declares a charge targeting Exemplar A. He ignores Exemplars B and C for the purposes of LOS when declaring the charge because they have the same base size as the target of the charge.

The Storm Lance then moves in a straight line toward his target. After moving 4", he stops short when he moves into base-to-base contact with Exemplar B. He then makes impact attacks targeting Exemplars B and C since both models are in his mount's melee range.

After hitting and destroying Exemplars B and C, the Storm Lance continues his charge movement to Exemplar A.

A cavalry model gains +2 to charge attack rolls. Impact attacks do not receive this bonus.

Dragoons

Dragoons are cavalry models that begin the game mounted but may become dismounted during play. For some dragoons the ability to be dismounted is optional. Adding this ability to the dragoon increases its point cost and total damage capacity.

While mounted, a dragoon is subject to all cavalry rules above. Once the dragoon has become dismounted, it is no longer a cavalry model and loses all cavalry abilities. Additionally, the dragoon loses all mounted dragoon abilities and may no longer use his mount and its abilities. Some dragoons have stats with two different base values. Use the first value while the dragoon is mounted and the second once the dragoon has become dismounted.

When a mounted dragoon suffers damage, apply the damage to its mounted dragoon damage boxes. When all of these damage boxes have been marked, the dragoon is destroyed if it does not have the ability to become dismounted. If the dragoon does have this ability, it becomes dismounted instead of being destroyed. Damage points in excess of the mounted dragoon's wounds are lost. If this occurs during the dragoon's activation, its activation ends immediately. Remove the mounted dragoon model from the table and replace it with the dismounted dragoon model. Effects, spells, and animi on the mounted dragoon are applied to the dismounted dragoon. Apply any further damage suffered by the dragoon to its dismounted dragoon damage boxes. The model is destroyed when all of its dismounted dragoon damage boxes have been marked.

Mercenary Warcasters and Warjacks

A mercenary warcaster counts toward the maximum number of warcasters allowed in an army. Only mercenaries may be included in an army if the only warcasters are mercenaries. Field allowance is not faction-specific. If an army includes both faction and mercenary warcasters, count all of the warcasters in the army when determining field allowance limits for both faction and mercenary models and units.

A mercenary warcaster (or other mercenary with the Commander ability) may only give orders to friendly mercenary units and may rally only friendly mercenary models. Only friendly mercenaries may use his CMD when making command checks.

Mercenary warjacks may only be controlled and reactivated by mercenary warcasters and 'jack marshals. By the same token, a mercenary warcaster or 'jack marshal may only control and reactivate mercenary warjacks.

Unique Warjacks

Unique warjacks are character warjacks representing the pinnacle of each faction's mechanikal development. Due to their experimental or unpredictable nature, unique warjacks cannot bond (pg. 69). Likewise, unique warjacks cannot begin a game under the control of a 'jack marshal.

Weapon Crews

Weapon crews are small units that operate large or cumbersome weapons. Weapon crews are made up of a gunner and one or more crewmen. Unlike other units, weapon crews do not have leaders. Weapon crews may not have attachments. A weapon crew cannot run or charge. The gunner gains +2" of movement for each crewman from his own unit in base-to-base contact with him when he begins his activation. If the gunner is destroyed or removed from play, a crewman in the same unit within 1" can take the destroyed gunner's place immediately and become the new gunner. Remove the crewman from the table instead of the gunner. Effects, spells, and animi on the damaged gunner expire. Effects, spells, and animi on the removed crewman are applied to the new gunner.

A gunner is generally treated as a small-based model unless its rules say otherwise.

Mercenary Contracts

Whether for a private war or to supplement the forces of a kingdom, mercenary contracts provide powerful and wealthy patrons with a means to quickly build an army. Though most patrons prefer to hire larger contingents, in a pinch smaller bands may be combined to form a force large enough for the task. Though they are a diverse lot, the mercenaries of the Iron Kingdoms can be relied upon to set aside their petty differences for the right price. After all, few loyalties are as solid as gold, and with enough coin one can buy an army—or at least rent one for a time. On the other hand, even though each man has his price, not every mercenary is willing to serve any master.

Mercenary contracts allow players to field armies made up entirely of mercenary models. These contracts detail the background of the mercenaries' employers, the history of the contract, and rules for constructing an army. Some players may choose to represent a new contract each time they play. Others might dedicate themselves to playing a particular mercenary contract, painting and modeling their forces to reflect the flavor or color scheme of a specific army.

Building a Mercenary Army

To field a mercenary army, you must choose a mercenary contract. Each contract includes the rules to be followed when building an army according to that contract. Otherwise, follow all of the normal army compositions rules.

Mercenary warjacks may only be included in a battlegroup controlled by a mercenary warcaster or assigned to a mercenary with the 'jack marshal ability. Some mercenary warjacks, such as custom or Rhulic warjacks, are further restricted by their special rules to the battlegroups of particular warcasters. For example, the Renegade and Mangler are both custom warjacks and may only be included in a battlegroup controlled by Magnus the Traitor or epic warcaster Magnus the Warlord. In addition to the guidelines presented in a contract, mercenary armies follow all the normal army composition rules.

Some mercenary contracts include special rules unrelated to army composition.

Contracts

The Four Star Syndicate

A shadowy organization notorious even among the pirates and cutthroats in the back streets of Five Fingers, the Four Star Syndicate (or simply the Syndicate) fills its own pockets through daring raids overland and at sea. As the Mercarian League has learned at great expense, no target seems to lie beyond the reach of this exceptionally well-funded confederacy of mercenaries, thieves, and desperate men. Backed by warjacks controlled by freelance warcasters, the Syndicate acts brazenly, openly targeting rail yards, small fleets, and even Cygnaran military supply trains. Land-based raids along the shores of the Dragon's Tongue have captured several shipments of armaments, explosives, and even warjacks that the Syndicate then quietly sold on the black market for outrageous profits. However, for reasons hitherto unknown, the Syndicate seldom operates within Ordic waters.

Few know anything of the Syndicate's inner workings. Only the organization's internal documents, signed only

Best of the Rest

with four black stars in a diamond pattern, provide a clue to the identities of the hidden benefactors who fund the Syndicate. A favorite target of these operations, the Mercarian League has spent no small fortune to uncover the secrets of the organization but with disappointing results. Syndicate loyalties are bought with gold coin and bound with iron promises of retribution.

The success enjoyed by the Syndicate has drawn much attention to the organization. Profit is the purest motive a mercenary has, and those who know a way into the mercenary market in Five Fingers can easily find a way onto the writ of the Four Star Syndicate. Even those who might not regularly serve beside treacherous villains often find a way to compromise their values. The Syndicate pays well, and in Five Fingers a full purse can even buy a clear conscience.

Four Star Syndicate Contract Army Composition

- An army constructed under the Four Star Syndicate contract may include any mercenary models that will work for Cryx or Khador.
- The army may also include the Ordic mercenaries Captain Sam MacHorne & the Devil Dogs and Rupert Carvolo, Piper of Ord.

The Highborn Covenant

Note: The following description refers to events described in *WARMACHINE: Escalation*.

Many of Llael's exiled nobles have turned to mercenaries to fight the Khadorans occupying their nation. The Highborn Covenant Mercenary Contract represents the most coherent of these efforts. With considerable backing from émigré nobles and certain merchant concerns, the Highborn Covenant has assembled a formidable army that may not care much about Llaelese land but has a great interest in Llaelese coin.

Rumors hold that the free chapters of the Order of the Golden Crucible also sponsor the Highborn Covenant, but they have kept their involvement secret to maintain the lives of any brethren held in service to the Khadoran crown.

While the Highborn Covenant has lofty and somewhat long-term goals of liberating Llael from its Khadoran invaders, it also serves to help the exiled nobility maintain some legitimacy. Without this mercenary army, the exiles' claims on land, title, and station would be tenuous at best. The Highborn Covenant ensures that they maintain some grip on authority in Llael, even if only in appearance.

The Highborn Covenant was drafted only days after news of the fall of Merywyn reached Corvis, shortly after Cygnar pulled most of its forces out of Llael. By the end of Rowen 605 AR, the Highborn Covenant had begun actively seeking mercenary interests that had previously demonstrated hostility towards Khador.

Mercenary forces under the Highborn Covenant serve six to eight months with extensions offered to individuals and mercenary companies that prove trustworthy and reliable. Due to conflicts of interest with kriels that have maintained mercenary operations against Rynnish interests in the past, the Covenant turns away any company with trollkin members even if they have previously fought for Llael or against Khador.

Highborn Covenant Contract Army Composition

- An army constructed under the Highborn Covenant contract may include any mercenary models/units that will work for Cygnar.
- Due to a long-standing animosity between the Rynnish nobility and the trollkin, a Highborn Covenant contract army cannot include Greygore Boomhowler & Co. or other trollkin models/units.
- **Spies:** One solo in the army gains Advance Deployment. Place models with Advance Deployment after normal deployment up to 12" beyond the established deployment zone.

The Searforge Commission

Fighting in the south has given valuable combat experience to the dwarves of the Hammerfall Fortress and others who have joined them, and it has allowed the Rhulfolk to keep apprised of the ongoing struggles across the countryside. No matter who wins the southern wars, the clans of Rhul are determined to keep trade lanes open. The Searforge Commission takes a sometimes more brutal and direct approach than others to getting business done and has no fear of shedding human blood to protect its interests

After the invasion of Llael, Clan Searforge, one of Rhul's most wealthy mercantile clans, came to the realization that it could be caught in a bad situation if it did not act. Clan Searforge had taken a controlling interest in the trade of several clans who shipped weapons, alloys, and steamjack parts south to dwarven enclaves in the lands of man, including Khador and Cygnar now embroiled in bitter war.

In 605 AR they founded the Searforge Commission to band together mercenaries working outside the kingdom and deployed them wherever necessary to keep trade flowing. The commission primarily serves the interests of Clan Searforge, but it has accepted contracts that benefit other mercantile Rhulic clans such as Clan Ghordson, Clan Grundback, Clan Serric, and even Stone House Dhurg which controls the Hammerfall Fortress.

This group exists to protect vital weapon, steamjack, and alloy trades. To that end they coordinate the actions of mercenary groups and send forces to escort trade shipments through hostile territory. They even made proactive strikes against battles in action to clear the way for their shipments. If Cygnar and Khador are engaged in a fight along their trade lanes, the commission will send their forces in to 'neutralize' the problem, one way or the other, and open the roads or railways again.

The hard-edged commission is determined to ensure that outsiders do not underestimate the risks of interfering with dwarven business. Though the nation of Rhul may prefer its neutral stance and avoids stepping on toes, the Searforge Commission is ready to load double-barreled rifles and lay down fire. People have learned not to mess with agents bearing the sigil of the commission unless they want to deal with a nine-foot tall ogrun and his war cleaver. These highly effective mixed forces consider themselves the equal of any regular army, and they have no fear of engaging in all-out war if pushed.

Searforge Commission Army Composition

- An army constructed under the Searforge Commission contract may include Rhulic and Ogrun mercenary models/units.
- The army may also include Herne & Jonne.
- Increase the FA of all non-character Rhulic and Ogrun mercenary models/units included in the army by one.
- Hammerfall High Shield Gun Corps models included in a Searforge Commission army gain Advance Deployment. Place models with Advance Deployment after normal deployment, up to 12" beyond the established deployment zone.

Magnus' Agenda

Note: The following description refers to events described in *WARMACHINE: Superiority*.

Asheth Magnus is not part of any company, and while he expects reimbursement for his services, the coin is only a resource to him. It is a commodity useful for buying weapons and equipment and for repairing his warjacks.

Magnus is a man who hires and employs other mercenaries to do his bidding. He does not pretend neutrality or detached professionalism. Those who fight alongside him know that he has his own agenda, and his every action furthers his cause.

For years only a few suspected his true purpose. Most thought Magnus to be a simple creature of revenge. He has fought against both the nation that labeled him a traitor and Coleman Stryker who humiliated him and left him maimed, but they are only a small part of the larger agenda motivating Magnus to wage continual war against his enemies with no nation to back him and no friends he can trust. Magnus is in fact a loyal and devoted vassal of the former king of Cygnar, Vinter Raelthorne IV. He fought beside Vinter during the coup, and his dedication to the ex-king has never wavered. He has been in communication with his liege across the great distance of the Bloodstone Marches, and he awaits Vinter's return. He will do his part to prepare by hiring his services to undermine Cygnar at every opportunity.

Magnus does not work alone, for he has found a number of willing allies including many mercenaries who, like himself, are marked as criminals and exiles of Cygnar. This includes the notorious cutthroat Jarok Croe as well as the premiere sniper Kell Bailoch. Magnus has further recruited Boomhowler and his trollkin into his schemes as well as others. He has even managed to persuade 'loyalist' soldiers to desert Cygnar's army and join his fight, men who believe they will be better rewarded by King Vinter than King Leto.

Magnus' Agenda Contract Army Composition

- An army constructed under the Magnus' Agenda contract must include either Magnus the Traitor or epic warcaster Magnus the Warlord and his battlegroup.
- The army may also include Boomhowler & Co., Croe's Cutthroats, Gorman di Wulfe, Kell Bailoch, and Steelhead Halberdiers.
- A single unit of Cygnar Trenchers or a single unit of Cygnar Long Gunners may be included in the army. This unit cannot be a weapon crew, nor can it include attachments. The troopers in the unit are deserters. They are considered mercenary models instead of Cygnar models.

Warcasters and Focus—True Power
Special Rules, Managing Focus Points, and Casting Spells

The warcaster is the single most important model in a player's army. In large games, you can employ multiple warcasters, but each should be considered significant and essential to the success of any battle.

Warcasters are the most powerful models represented in WARMACHINE. They are highly trained combat wizards as effective in martial combat as when wielding arcane forces. However, a warcaster's greatest function on the battlefield is controlling his warjacks, whether he's ordering them to attack or defend, head for an objective, or channel a spell.

Battles are won or lost purely by how well a warcaster manages his focus—the magical energy that lets him control warjacks and cast spells. Often, a warcaster must decide between casting a spell and *boosting* a warjack's attack, and choosing well or poorly usually means the difference between victory and defeat.

Warcaster Special Rules

All warcasters have the following special rules in common:

Battlegroup Commander

Each warcaster controls a group of warjacks. A warcaster and his assigned 'jacks are collectively referred to as a battlegroup. A warcaster can allocate focus points only to warjacks in his battlegroup and may only channel spells through channelers in his battlegroup.

Commander

A friendly model or unit in the warcaster's *command range* may use the warcaster's Command (CMD) stat for any *command checks*. A warcaster can attempt to *rally* any *fleeing* friendly units in his command range. A warcaster can *give orders* to one friendly unit in his command range during his activation. See Command (pg. 74) for full details on command checks, fleeing, and giving orders. A mercenary warcaster may only rally or give orders to mercenaries.

Fearless

A warcaster never flees.

Feats

Each warcaster has a unique feat that can turn the tide of battle if used at the right time. A warcaster may use his feat before or after moving, but not in the middle of his movement. Likewise, he may use his feat before and after each attack, but he cannot interrupt an unresolved attack, nor can he use his feat between the movement and attack portions of a charge. Feats may be used prior to initiating an attack or after completely resolving an attack, including determining hits, damage, and special effects. A warcaster cannot use his feat if he runs.

A warcaster's feat can only be used once per game.

Focus Manipulation

Warcasters have a Focus (FOC) stat. During each of his controller's Control Phases, each warcaster **replenishes** his focus points, receiving a number of them equal to his current FOC. Focus points can be used for spell casting or to boost the combat abilities of the warcaster and his warjacks.

Power Field

Warcaster armor is perhaps the most sophisticated blend of magic and mechanics to be found anywhere. Besides its seemingly impossible strength, this armor creates a magical field that surrounds and protects the warcaster from damage that would rend a normal man to pieces.

A warcaster's damage capacity is largely a result of his power field's protection. The warcaster can use focus points to regenerate damage done to the power field. A warcaster's unspent focus points overboost his power field and give him increased protection.

Spell Caster

A warcaster may cast a spell before or after moving, but not in the middle of his movement. Likewise, he may cast a spell before and after each attack, but he cannot interrupt an unresolved attack, nor can he cast a spell between the movement and attack portions of a charge. Spells may be cast prior to initiating an attack or after completely resolving an attack, including determining hits, damage, and special effects. A warcaster cannot cast spells if he runs.

Focus Points

A warcaster's greatest resource is the magical energy known as *focus*. Each warcaster begins the game with a number of focus points equal to his Focus (FOC) stat. During your Control Phase, each of your warcasters and other models with the Focus Manipulation ability replenish those focus points and receive a number equal to their current FOC. A warcaster may *allocate* focus points to eligible warjacks in his control area and to his spells that require upkeep, or he can keep them to enhance his own abilities and cast spells.

Remove unused focus points from all models you control during your Maintenance Phase.

Control Area

A warcaster's **control area** extends out from the warcaster in all directions for a distance equal to twice his current Focus

(FOC) stat in inches. Measure this distance from the edge of the warcaster's base. A warcaster is always considered to be in his own control area. When a special rule changes a warcaster's FOC stat, his control area changes accordingly. Some spells and feats use the warcaster's control area as their *area of effect*.

A warjack must be within its warcaster's control area to receive focus points from the warcaster or to *channel* spells, but it does not have to be within line of sight.

Measuring Control Areas

A player may measure his warcaster's control area at any time for any reason. While measuring a warcaster's control area, the controller may determine the proximity of other models to his warcaster. Specifically, a player may measure the distance from his warcaster to any point within the warcaster's control area at any time.

For control area effects against opposing models, a player does not have to measure his warcaster's control area until after the enemy model commits to its movement or action. For example, say a warcaster casts a spell that turns his control area into rough terrain. That warcaster's controller does not have to measure his control area prior to an enemy model entering it. The opposing player will have to adjust his model's position after completing its movement if it entered the warcaster's control area and had its movement reduced by the spell's effect.

Allocating Focus Points

During your Control Phase, each warcaster in your army may **allocate** his focus points to warjacks in his own battlegroup. Take care to remember which warjacks belong

> ### Focus? Why, he doesn't even know us!
> Players should use coins, colored beads, or tokens to represent focus points. During a player's control phase, place a number of tokens equal to the warcaster's current FOC next to the model. These tokens may be allocated to eligible warjacks in that warcaster's battlegroup by moving them next to those models. Remove focus point tokens from the table as they are used. Each of a warcaster's unspent focus points next to the warcaster gives him a +1 ARM bonus until the focus points are no longer on the table.

> ### Control Area
> A warcaster's control area is a circular area centered on the warcaster with a radius that extends out from the edge of his base a number of inches equal to twice his current Focus (FOC) stat.

to which battlegroup. A warcaster cannot allocate focus points to warjacks in another warcaster's battlegroup even if they are both part of the same army.

To receive focus points allocated from its controlling warcaster, a warjack must be within its warcaster's control area, but it need not be in line of sight. If a warjack's cortex is disabled, it can no longer be allocated focus points. A warcaster can divide his focus points between himself and as many of his warjacks as desired. However, a warjack cannot be allocated more than three focus points per turn.

The Rule of Three

A warjack can be allocated up to three focus points per turn. A warjack cannot receive more than this unless a special rule specifically allows it.

Using Focus Points

A warcaster has many powerful uses for the focus points at his disposal. The real trick is knowing which use is best depending on what dire circumstances his army faces. Some of these uses are available to any model with focus points while others can only be used by specific model types.

A warjack can only spend the focus points it has received, and a warcaster can only spend the focus points he did not allocate to other models. A model's unused focus points cannot be reallocated or spent by other models. Unless otherwise stated, a model may spend a focus point any time during its activation for any of the following effects:

Additional Attack

A warcaster or warjack may spend a focus point to make an additional melee or ranged attack as part of his combat action. The model may make one additional attack for each focus point it spends. A model using focus to make additional ranged attacks cannot exceed a weapon's *rate of fire* (ROF). A model cannot spend focus points to make additional special attacks.

Boosting Attack & Damage Rolls

A model may spend a focus point to add one die to any attack roll or damage roll. This is commonly called **boosting**. Boosting must be declared before rolling any dice. Each attack or damage roll can only be boosted once, but a model can boost multiple rolls during its activation. When an attack affects several models, the attack and damage rolls against each individual model must be boosted separately.

Cast Spell

In addition to his movement and action, a warcaster may cast spells during his activation by simply spending the appropriate number of focus points and immediately resolving their effects. A warcaster may cast any number of spells during his activation provided he has enough focus points to do so. See Casting Spells below.

Overboost Power Field

Each of a warcaster's unspent focus points gives him + 1 Armor (ARM) against all attacks. This bonus stays in effect until the focus points are no longer on the warcaster.

Regenerate Power Field

A warcaster may spend focus points to regenerate his power field. Each focus point spent in this manner removes one damage point from him.

Run, Charge, Power Attacks

A warjack must spend a focus point to run, charge, or make a power attack.

Casting Spells

Warcasters have the ability to cast spells. A warcaster may cast spells during his activation by spending a number of focus points equal to the spell's focus cost. Resolve the spell's effects immediately. Unless noted otherwise, spells that target a model other than where the spell originates require line of sight to their targets. Warcasters cannot target themselves with offensive spells. Any spell, including offensive spells, may be cast while the warcaster is in melee. Resolve the spell's effects immediately. A warcaster may cast as many spells during his activation for which he can pay the focus cost. The same spell may be cast multiple times during the warcaster's activation.

A warcaster may cast spells before or after moving, but not in the middle of his movement. Likewise, he may cast spells before and after each attack, but he cannot interrupt an unresolved attack, nor can he cast spells between the movement and attack portions of a charge. Spells may be cast prior to initiating an attack or after completely resolving an attack, including determining hits, damage, and special effects. A warcaster cannot cast any spells if he runs during his activation.

For example, a warcaster could cast a spell, move, use his combat action to make a melee attack, cast two more spells and then spend another focus point to make an additional melee attack.

Offensive Spells & Magic Attacks

An **offensive spell** requires that the model casting the spell succeed in a magic attack roll to put its effects in play. Magic attacks are similar to *ranged attacks* and follow most of the same rules. Determine a magic attack's success by making a **magic attack roll**. Roll 2d6 and add the attacking model's current FOC. A *boosted* attack roll adds an additional die to this roll. Special rules and certain circumstances may modify the attack roll as well.

Magic Attack Roll = 2d6 + FOC

A target is directly hit by a magic attack if the attack roll equals or exceeds the target's DEF. If the attack roll is less than the target's DEF, the attack misses. A roll of all 1s on the dice causes an automatic miss. A roll of all 6s causes an automatic hit regardless of the attacker's FOC or his target's DEF, unless you are rolling only one die. Sometimes a special rule causes an attack to hit automatically. Such automatic hits are also direct hits.

Unless stated otherwise, a model making a magic attack must obey the *targeting* rules when declaring a target. A model may not target itself with an offensive spell. A magic attack's target may benefit from such modifiers as *concealment* and *cover*, but magic attacks are not affected by rules that only apply to ranged attacks. A model does not benefit from *aiming* when making a magic attack.

A magic attack does not suffer the *target in melee* attack roll penalty when the attacker is in melee with the target. However, if such an attack misses and there are multiple models in the combat, the attack may still hit another random model in the combat, excluding the attacker and the original target. Resolve these situations per the *Targeting a Model in Melee* rules on page 47 and the Spell Targeting rules below. A spell with an AOE is sometimes referred to as an AOE spell. An AOE spell that misses in this situation will deviate normally.

Spell Targeting

Many spells can only be cast on certain types of models such as warjacks or enemy troopers. Such restrictions are noted in a spell's description. A shorthand is commonly used to denote these targeting restrictions. When a spell's description mentions an effect against a "target something,"

the spell may only be cast on that type of model. Some spells mention two or more target types. These spells may be cast on models that match any of the designated types. For example, Skarre's Fly's Kiss spell states that a "target living model destroyed by Fly's Kiss explodes in a 3" AOE," therefore, this spell may only target a living model. When attacking a *structure* with an offensive spell, ignore the spell's targeting restrictions.

Note that this shorthand for targeting restrictions only applies to spells. Even if a weapon's special rules describe an effect that affects only certain types of models, attacks with that weapon may target any type of model. So for instance, a Defender is free to attack any model with its Shock Hammer, but only warjacks will be affected by Critical Cortex Damage.

When an offensive spell targeting a model *in melee* misses, ignore its targeting restrictions when determining which model in the combat might be hit instead. If the new target is an invalid one for the spell, the magic attack has no further effect. (See Targeting a Model in Melee, pg. 47, and Offensive Spells & Magic Attacks, above, for details on resolving a magic attack against a model in melee.) An *area-of-effect* spell that misses will deviate normally instead.

For example, Skarre attempts to cast Fly's Kiss on a Protectorate Temple Flameguard trooper in melee with one of her Deathrippers, itself in melee with two other Flameguard troopers. Thus, there are four models in the combat. If she misses, determine which of the other three models might be hit by the spell instead as usual. If one of the other Flameguard troopers is chosen, make another attack roll and resolve the attack normally. If, on the other hand, the Deathripper is chosen, do not make another attack roll. The spell simply fizzles with no effect at all.

Upkeep Spells

Upkeep spells can be maintained for more than one round. During the Control Phase, your warcasters may spend focus points to keep them in play. Each upkeep spell requires one focus point. A warcaster can maintain an upkeep spell even if the spell's effects are outside his control area. If a focus point is not spent to maintain an upkeep spell at this time, it immediately expires and its effects end.

A warcaster may only have one of each specific upkeep spell in play at a time, but he can maintain any number of different upkeep spells simultaneously if he spends enough

Channeling 101

CHANNELING A SPELL DOES NOT REQUIRE THE WARCASTER TO HAVE LINE OF SIGHT TO EITHER THE CHANNELER OR THE SPELL'S TARGET. HOWEVER, THE CHANNELING WARJACK MUST HAVE LINE OF SIGHT TO THE SPELL'S TARGET.

A WARCASTER CAN ONLY CHANNEL A SPELL THROUGH A SINGLE CHANNELER AT A TIME. SPELLS CANNOT BE RELAYED FROM ONE CHANNELER TO ANOTHER.

THE WARCASTER CASTS THE SPELL, AND THE CHANNELING WARJACK IS THE SPELL'S POINT OF ORIGIN. IF THE CHANNELING WARJACK IS IN THE TARGET'S REAR ARC, THE MAGIC ATTACK IS A BACK STRIKE.

A WARJACK CANNOT BE THE TARGET OF AN OFFENSIVE SPELL IT CHANNELS.

focus points to do so. A model or unit may only have one friendly and one enemy upkeep spell in play on it at one time. If another upkeep spell is cast on a model that already has one from the same side—friendly or enemy—the old upkeep spell expires and is replaced by the newly cast one.

A warcaster may recast any of his upkeep spells already in play. When a warcaster does so, the spell's previous casting immediately expires and its effects end.

For example, a unit of Khador Iron Fang Pikemen currently has the Iron Flesh spell in play on it. The Khador player decides it would be more beneficial to have the Fury spell cast on the unit instead, which immediately removes the Iron Flesh spell once cast. During the Cryx player's turn, Deneghra casts Crippling Grasp on the unit. This does not remove the Fury spell because an enemy upkeep spell does not replace a friendly one. Pay particular attention to this restriction when casting upkeep spells with a target of 'Self'. If Severius has Eye of Menoth active, casting Vision would cause Eye of Menoth to expire.

Multiple Spell Effects

Although it is not possible to have more than one upkeep spell on a model or unit, it is possible for a model or unit to be affected by more than one spell or animus at a time. For example, Haley casts Deadeye on a unit of Arcane Tempest Gun Mages already under the effects of Arcane Shield. Arcane Shield does not expire when Deadeye is cast because Deadeye is not an upkeep spell. As long as a model or unit is under the effects of no more than one friendly and one enemy upkeep spell, it can be affected by any number of non-upkeep spells and up to one animus effect at the same time.

Channeling

Specialized warjacks, known as **channelers,** are equipped with devices called **arc nodes** that act as passive relays for a warcaster's spells and extend the warcaster's effective spell range. A warcaster may cast spells through any channeler in his battlegroup that is also within his control area. The warcaster is still the attacker, but the channeler becomes the spell's point of origin and is considered the attacker for the purpose of determining LOS for the channeled spell. Determine eligible targets and measure the spell's range from the channeling warjack. Channeling a spell does not require the warcaster to have line of sight to either the channeler or the spell's target. However, the channeling warjack must have line of sight to the spell's target. There is no additional focus cost for channeling a spell.

A channeler engaged by an enemy model cannot channel spells. A stationary channeler can channel spells, but one that is knocked down cannot. A channeler can

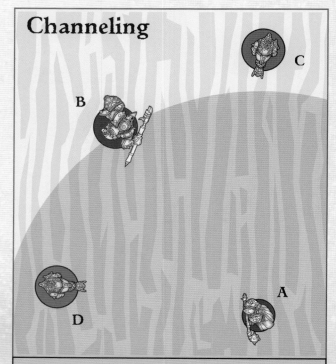

Channeling

With a FOC of 7, High Exemplar Kreoss' control area, represented by the shaded area, measures 14" out from his base. Kreoss (A) may channel spells through his Revenger warjack (B) as long as the Revenger is within his control area.

A warjack must have line of sight to a target to be able to channel spells at it. Therefore the Revenger can channel spells at Bonejack C, but it cannot channel spells at Bonejack D even though Kreoss himself has line of sight to it.

be the target of a non-offensive spell it channels, but a spell with a Range (RNG) of "Self" cannot be channeled. A channeler cannot be the target of an offensive spell channeled through it.

Make a magic attack for a channeled offensive spell normally. The warcaster may spend focus points to boost die rolls or otherwise enhance the spell normally. If the channeler is in the target's rear arc when the spell is cast, it is a *back strike*.

Remember, the channeler is just a relay. Channeling a spell is a passive effect that occurs during a warcaster's activation and has no impact on the channeling model's own activation. Focus points allocated to a channeler may not be used to affect the channeled spell in any way.

Spell Statistics

A spell is defined by the following six statistics:

- **Cost:** The number of focus points that must be spent to cast the spell.
- **Range (RNG):** The maximum distance in inches that a spell can be used against a target. Range is measured from the nearest edge of the casting model's base to the nearest edge of the target model's base. A RNG of "Self" indicates that the spell can only be cast on the model casting it.
- **Power (POW):** The base amount of damage a spell inflicts. Add a spell's POW to its damage roll.
- **Area-of-Effect (AOE):** The diameter in inches of the template an area-of-effect spell uses for damage effects. When casting an AOE spell, center the template on the determined point of impact. Models covered by the template potentially suffer the spell's effects. See Combat (pg. 38) for detailed rules on AOE attacks. Templates for AOEs can be found on page 256. A spell with an AOE of "CTRL" is centered on the warcaster and affects models in his control area.
- **Upkeep (UP):** An upkeep spell remains in play if the warcaster who cast it spends a focus point to maintain it during his controller's Control Phase.
- **Offensive (OFF):** An offensive spell requires a successful magic attack roll to take effect. If the attack roll fails, the attack misses and the spell has no effect. A failed attack roll for a spell with an area of effect deviates according to those rules instead.

Warjack Bonding

The potent connection shared between a warcaster and his warjacks may evolve into powerful bonds over time. Bonding awakens a warjack's cortex, opens it more fully to its controller, and infects it with limited self-awareness. As this connection grows stronger, the warjack begins to develop a rudimentary personality drawing on the characteristics of its warcaster. In essence, the personality of the warcaster is imprinted on the warjack's cortex.

RANGE: CASTER
SOME OLDER RULES AND STAT CARDS HAVE "CASTER" AS THE RANGE OF SOME SPELLS OR REFER TO SPELLS WITH A RANGE OF "CASTER." TREAT THEM ALL AS IF THEY SAID "SELF" INSTEAD.

Since this imprinting tends to take place in moments of extreme emotional duress such as in the heat of battle, the effects of bonding are unpredictable. While one bonded warjack may become protective of its warcaster or act like a faithful hound, another may take on darker aspects of its controller's personality like relishing in the suffering of others.

Through continuous contact a warcaster learns the subtle intricacies of the warjack's unique cortex, allowing him to enhance his control over the machine. An open conduit, the bonded warjack is able to receive greater amounts of focus from its controller.

Bonds require time to establish. Bonding is an optional rule best suited to campaign or league play. However, if all players agree each may begin a game with one or more bonded warjacks. Bonding does not affect the point cost of a warjack.

Forging a Bond

After a player completes a campaign or league game, he may make a roll to determine if a bond forms between each warcaster who participated and survived the battle and each of the warjacks in his battlegroup that were not destroyed or removed from play during the battle. Warcasters that were destroyed or removed from play during the battle may not make bonding checks, but their existing bonds are unaffected.

The longer a particular warjack has served in a warcaster's battlegroup, the greater the chance a bond will be established after each game. During league or

Warcasters and Focus

campaign play, a player should keep track of the number of consecutive battles in which an unbonded warjack has not been destroyed or removed from play and has been part of the same warcaster's battlegroup.

When determining if a bond is formed, roll a d6 and add one to the roll for each consecutive battle, including the one just completed, in which the warjack served in that warcaster's battlegroup. A bond is formed on a roll of seven (7) or greater.

For example, after finishing a campaign battle James rolls to see if The High Reclaimer's unbonded Crusader bonds to him. Since this was its third game under his control without being destroyed or removed from play, the bond forms on a roll of 4 or more.

A warcaster may bond to more than one warjack, but each warjack can only bond to a single warcaster. Furthermore, if a bond already exists for a warjack, do not roll to see if another is forged. Once a warjack is bonded, it remains bonded to the warcaster until the bonded warjack is destroyed or removed from play. While not under the control of the warcaster to whom it is bonded, a warjack loses all benefits from its bond, but the bond itself is not broken.

Breaking a Bond

If a bonded warjack ends a game destroyed or removed from play, the bond is broken. A player may also choose to remove a bond from a warjack before any game. The warjack's controlling warcaster has had the warjack's cortex reinitialized. Its bond is broken and the current game is counted as the first consecutive game for the warjack's bonding roll bonus.

Effects of Bonding

A warcaster may allocate one additional focus point to a warjack bonded to him. For example, a warcaster who could allocate up to three focus points to a warjack in his battlegroup can now allocate up to four focus points to this warjack when bonded.

Bonding also affects each warjack in a unique way as its personality develops. When a bond is established, roll 2d6 plus the warcaster's CMD and consult the corresponding faction table at the end of this section to determine the effects of the bonding. The player may add one to or subtract one from his die roll when determining the effects of a bond.

Remember that a bonded warjack loses all benefits from its bond while not under the control of the warcaster to whom it is bonded.

Epic Warcasters

Constant exposure to the carnage of the battlefield and the tumultuous nature of combat takes its toll. The warriors of western Immoren are locked in world-shaping conflict and must continually push themselves to the limits of their capabilities. The rigors of war affect the most stalwart men, and not even the mightiest of warcasters can weather them unchanged.

Epic warcasters are variations of warcaster models with fresh abilities, strengths, and weaknesses. Epic warcasters are not more powerful versions of the original warcasters, but instead they reflect character growth and changes set about in major story arcs. If these models were simply improvements on older warcasters, the older models would quickly become obsolete. Epic warcasters do not replace the original 'casters upon which they were based; they instead offer players the opportunity to play whichever version they prefer.

In story terms, these characters have not lost their older abilities but have instead adapted to the demands of war by adopting new tactics, equipment, and spells as necessary. Though an epic warcaster's spells may differ from his earlier incarnation, the character has not truly lost the ability to cast the old spells. He has simply chosen to utilize a new repertoire of spells to suit his current needs.

Because all versions of a warcaster are considered the same character, an army or team may include only one version of a warcaster. Just as a player cannot field two Eiryss, Mage Hunter of Ios models in the same army, he cannot field both Commander Coleman Stryker and epic warcaster Lord Commander Stryker at the same time.

To reflect the nature of epic warcasters and to preserve game balance, an epic warcaster may not be included in games with an army point limit smaller than 750 points. Only one more epic warcaster may be added to the army for each additional increment of 750 points.

For example, Jason and Rob play a Battle Royale, which has an army point limit of 1000 points. Each player may field two warcasters, but only one of these warcasters can be an epic warcaster. If they were instead playing a War with a limit of 1500 points, each could field three warcasters, but only two of them could be epic.

Epic Warcaster Warjack Bonds

Some epic warcasters have the Warjack Bond ability representing an exceptionally powerful connection between the warcaster and some of his warjacks. This ability allows the epic warcaster to start a game bonded to a number of warjacks in his battlegroup. These bonds follow the rules given in Warjack Bonds (pg. 69) except as noted here. Do not roll on the bond effect tables for these bonds. Their effects are described in the epic warcaster's special rules.

The epic warcaster's controller must designate which warjacks are bonded to the warcaster before each battle in which he is used. The warcaster does not need to bond with the same warjacks from battle to battle. These bonds are in addition to any other bonds the warcaster has formed during play (Warjack Bonding, pg. 69). A warjack can only be bonded once, however. If an epic warcaster's Warjack Bond ability is applied to a warjack that is already bonded to a warcaster, including himself, the previous bond is broken and its effects are lost. After the battle, do not make a bonding check for a warjack affected by the Warjack Bond ability: it is already bonded to the warcaster.

Elite Cadres

Many epic warcasters have a great deal of influence over the military forces of their factions and may handpick their own troops. If an epic warcaster possesses an Elite Cadre, all units of a particular type dictated by the warcaster's special rules included in an army with the warcaster gain the benefits of Elite Cadre. These models gain +1 MAT, RAT, and CMD and an additional ability determined by the particular warcaster.

Cryx Bonds

2D6 + CMD	RESULT
10 OR LESS	BANEFUL — While the warjack's controlling warcaster is engaged, the warjack may charge without spending a focus point and gains +2 to melee attack and melee damage rolls. At the start of its activation, if the warjack has LOS to one or more enemy models engaging its warcaster, it must charge one of the enemy models.
11	BLOODTHIRSTY — Anytime the warjack destroys another model in melee, it must immediately make one melee attack against another model in melee range, friendly or enemy.
12	BELLICOSE — The warjack gains +2 to attack and damage rolls targeting warjacks and warbeasts. A friendly model attacking an enemy model engaged by this warjack suffers −2 to attack rolls.
13	STALWART — The warjack is not disabled until it has lost at least four systems.
14	APPETITE FOR DESTRUCTION — The warjack may make power attacks without spending a focus point and rolls an additional damage die on successful power attacks. The warjack's first melee attack each turn must be a power attack. If the warjack cannot make a power attack, it may make normal melee attacks.
15	RIGHTEOUS INDIGNATION — When a model in the warjack's battlegroup is targeted by an enemy attack, the warjack gains +2 to attack and damage rolls for one round.
16	PREDATOR — The bonding awakens murderous tendencies within the cortex of the warjack. During its activation, the warjack must move directly toward the nearest living enemy model in LOS and within its current SPD in inches, stopping short only when it engages the enemy model. It may advance, charge, or slam during this movement. The warjack gains +2 to all attack rolls against living models. Additionally, the warjack rolls an additional damage die on back strikes.
17	GLORY HOG — The warjack gains +2" movement and may run, charge, or slam without spending a focus point. The warjack must be the first model its controlling player activates each turn.
18	MAGNATE — The warjack gains +2 to melee attack rolls. If it misses with a melee attack roll, its activation ends immediately.
19	IMITATION — When attacking a model that was previously targeted with an attack by the warjack's controlling warcaster in the same turn, the warjack gains +2 to its attack and damage rolls.
20 OR MORE	HEIGHTENED AWARENESS — The warjack may change its facing at the start of its activation before moving or declaring a charge or slam against a target.

Warcasters and Focus

Cygnar Bonds

2d6 + CMD	Result
10 OR LESS	CRAVEN — The warjack gains +2" movement and +2 DEF and may run without spending a focus point. During its activation the warjack cannot slam or move into an enemy model's melee range.
11	GLORY HOG — The warjack gains +2" movement and may run, charge, or slam without spending a focus point. The warjack must be the first model its controlling player activates each turn.
12	STALWART — The warjack is not disabled until it has lost at least four systems.
13	OVERLY PROTECTIVE — During any round in which its controlling warcaster was damaged by an enemy model, the warjack gains +2" movement and boosted attack and damage rolls against any model within 6" of its warcaster.
14	BELLICOSE — The warjack gains +2 to attack and damage rolls targeting warjacks and warbeasts. A friendly model attacking an enemy model engaged by this warjack suffers −2 to all attack rolls.
15	HIP SHOOTER — The warjack gains an aiming bonus even when it moves.
16	MAGNATE — The warjack gains +2 to melee attack rolls. If it misses with a melee attack roll, its activation ends immediately.
17	NEEDY — The warjack may spend one focus point to boost both its attack roll and damage roll. The warjack must forfeit its movement during any turn it was not allocated focus.
18	RIGHTEOUS INDIGNATION — When a model in the warjack's battlegroup is targeted by an enemy attack, the warjack gains +2 to attack and damage rolls for one round.
19	HEIGHTENED AWARENESS — The warjack may change its facing at the start of its activation before moving or declaring a charge or slam against a target.
20 OR MORE	IMITATION — When attacking a model that was previously targeted with an attack by the warjack's controlling warcaster in the same turn, the warjack gains +2 to its attack and damage rolls.

Protectorate Bonds

2d6 + CMD	Result
10 OR LESS	APPETITE FOR DESTRUCTION — The warjack may make power attacks without spending a focus point and gains an additional damage die on successful power attacks. The warjack's first melee attack each turn must be a power attack. If the warjack cannot make a power attack, it may make normal melee attacks.
11	STALWART — The warjack is not disabled until it has lost at least four systems.
12	BANEFUL — While the warjack's controlling warcaster is engaged, the warjack may charge without spending a focus point and gains +2 to all melee attack and melee damage rolls. At the start of its activation, if the warjack has LOS to one or more enemy models engaging its warcaster, it must charge one of the enemy models.
13	GLORY HOG — The warjack gains +2" movement and may run, charge, or slam without spending a focus point. The warjack must be the first model its controlling player activates each turn.
14	OVERLY PROTECTIVE — During any round in which its controlling warcaster was damaged by an enemy model, the warjack gains +2" movement and boosted attack and damage rolls against any model within 6" of its warcaster.
15	BODYGUARD — The first time the warjack's controlling warcaster is directly hit by a ranged attack during an opponent's turn, it must move to intercept the attack. The warjack must be within 2" of its warcaster and be able to position itself as an intervening model between the warcaster and the attacker using its normal movement. The warjack then moves, is hit automatically by the attack, and suffers full damage and effects. If the warjack uses Bodyguard, it may not use it again until after its controlling player's next turn. If the warjack is denied its full normal movement for any reason it cannot use Bodyguard.
16	IMITATION — When attacking a model that was previously targeted with an attack by the warjack's controlling warcaster in the same turn, the warjack gains +2 to its attack and damage rolls.
17	NEEDY — The warjack may spend one focus point to boost both its attack roll and damage roll. The warjack must forfeit its movement during any turn it was not allocated focus.
18	BELLICOSE — The warjack gains +2 to attack and damage rolls targeting warjacks and warbeasts. A friendly model attacking an enemy model engaged by this warjack suffers −2 to all attack rolls.
19	MAGNATE — The warjack gains +2 to melee attack rolls. If it misses with a melee attack roll, its activation ends immediately.
20 OR MORE	RIGHTEOUS INDIGNATION — When any model in the warjack's battlegroup is targeted by an enemy attack, the warjack gains +2 to all attack and damage rolls for one round.

Khador Bonds

2D6 + CMD	RESULT
10 OR LESS	BLOODTHIRSTY — Anytime the warjack destroys another model in melee, it must immediately make one melee attack against another model in melee range, friendly or enemy.
11	BELLICOSE — The warjack gains +2 to attack and damage rolls targeting warjacks and warbeasts. A friendly model attacking an enemy model engaged by this warjack suffers −2 on all attack rolls.
12	NEEDY — The warjack may spend one focus point to boost both its attack roll and damage roll. The warjack must forfeit its movement during any turn it was not allocated focus.
13	STALWART — The warjack is not disabled until it has lost at least four systems.
14	AGGRESSIVE — While in its warcaster's control area, this warjack may charge without spending a focus point and gains +2 to melee attack rolls.
15	APPETITE FOR DESTRUCTION — The warjack may make power attacks without spending a focus point and gains an additional damage die on successful power attacks. The warjack's first melee attack each turn must be a power attack. If the warjack cannot make a power attack, it may make normal melee attacks.
16	MAGNATE — The warjack gains +2 to melee attack rolls. If it misses with a melee attack roll, its activation ends immediately.
17	IRRESISTIBLE FORCE — The warjack may slam without spending a focus point and gains a +2 to the slam attack roll. At the start of its activation, if the warjack has LOS and an unobstructed path to an enemy model, it must slam the enemy model.
18	IMITATION — When attacking a model that was previously targeted with an attack by the warjack's controlling warcaster in the same turn, the warjack gains +2 to its attack and damage rolls.
19	GLORY HOG — The warjack gains +2" movement and may run, charge, or slam without spending a focus point. The warjack must be the first model its controlling player activates each turn.
20 OR MORE	OVERLY PROTECTIVE — During any round in which its controlling warcaster was damaged by an enemy model, the warjack gains +2" movement and boosted attack and damage rolls against any model within 6" of its warcaster.

Mercenary Bonds

2D6 + CMD	RESULT
10 OR LESS	APPETITE FOR DESTRUCTION — The warjack may make power attacks without spending a focus point and gains an additional damage die on successful power attacks. The warjack's first melee attack each turn must be a power attack. If the warjack cannot make a power attack, it may make normal melee attacks.
11	BLOODTHIRSTY — Anytime the warjack destroys another model in melee, it must immediately make one melee attack against another model in melee range, friendly or enemy.
12	BELLICOSE — The warjack gains +2 to attack and damage rolls targeting warjacks and warbeasts. A friendly model attacking an enemy model engaged by this warjack suffers −2 to attack rolls.
13	GLORY HOG — The warjack gains +2" movement and may run, charge, or slam without spending a focus point. The warjack must be the first model its controlling player activates each turn.
14	MAGNATE — The warjack gains +2 to melee attack rolls. If it misses with a melee attack roll, its activation ends immediately.
15	PLAYIN' POSSUM — The warjack has developed a base level of guile and is adept at dramatically venting smoke and playing dead when the need arises. While knocked down or stationary, the warjack cannot be targeted by ranged or magic attacks.
16	BANEFUL — While the warjack's controlling warcaster is engaged, the warjack may charge without spending a focus point and gains +2 on melee attack and melee damage rolls. At the start of its activation, if the warjack has LOS to one or more enemy models engaging its warcaster, it must charge one of the enemy models.
17	STALWART — The warjack is not disabled until it has lost at least four systems.
18	NEEDY — The warjack may spend one focus point to boost both its attack roll and damage roll. The warjack must forfeit its movement during any turn it was not allocated focus.
19	IMITATION — When attacking a model that was previously targeted with an attack by the warjack's controlling warcaster in the same turn, the warjack gains +2 to its attack and damage rolls.
20 OR MORE	CRAVEN — The warjack gains +2" movement and +2 DEF and may run without spending a focus point. During its activation the warjack cannot slam or move into an enemy model's melee range.

Command—Of Mice and Men
Command Checks, Fleeing, and Orders

Regardless of a soldier's skill at arms, his real worth is measured by his will to fight. Warriors may break and flee after suffering massive casualties or when confronted by terrifying entities while manipulative spells can warp the minds of the weak-willed and cause them to attack their allies. The inspiring presence of a nearby warcaster or a unit's leader can steel the nerves of warriors faced with these mental assaults and even rally them before their panic becomes a full-blown rout. Command checks determine the outcome of these game situations that test a combatant's discipline or mental resolve.

Command Checks

There are several different circumstances that require a model or unit to make a command check: *massive casualties*, *terrifying entities*, and a spell or other attack's special rules.

Massive Casualties

A unit suffers massive casualties when it loses 50% or more of the models in it at the beginning of the current turn. The unit must immediately pass a command check or flee. A unit will only make up to one command check a turn due to massive casualties.

Terrifying Entity

A terrifying entity is one with either the Terror or Abomination special ability. A model/unit in *melee range* of an enemy model with Terror, a model/unit with an enemy model with Terror in its melee range, or a model/unit within 3" of an abomination—friendly or enemy—must pass a command check or flee. Make this command check after the active model or unit completes its movement but before it performs any actions. If a model or unit encounters a terrifying entity at some other time, such as when an enemy model gains the Terror ability or a terrifying entity is placed near the model or unit, make the command check immediately after resolving the attack or effect that caused the encounter.

For instance, if the Iron Lich Asphyxious moves into melee with a Temple Flameguard, the Flameguard's unit makes a command check as soon as Asphyxious ends his movement. However, if a Flameguard moves into melee with Asphyxious, make a command check for his unit after every trooper in the unit finishes moving. In either case, make the command check before any model performs an action.

A model or unit that passes a command check caused by its proximity to a terrifying entity does not make further command checks as a result of proximity to that entity as long as it remains inside the range that triggered the effect. If these models become separated and encounter each other again later, another command check will be required. A unit that consists of terrifying entities counts as a single terrifying entity for the purpose of these rules. A model/unit need only make a single command check for encountering the unit regardless of how many of its troopers it actually encounters.

Special Rules

Some spells and other attacks cause an individual model or an entire unit to make a command check. Reference the specific description to determine the attack's eligible targets and effects. Though fleeing is the most common outcome of a failed command check, some spells and effects have more sinister effects.

When one of these situations requires a model or unit to make a command check, roll 2d6. If the result is equal to or less than its Command (CMD) stat, it passes the check. In most cases, this means the model or unit continues to function normally or rallies if it was fleeing. If the roll is greater than its CMD, the check fails and the model or unit suffers the consequences. When a unit fails a command check, every trooper in that unit suffers the effects, including out-of-formation troopers.

For example, a Khadoran Manhunter has a CMD of 9. The Manhunter passes a command check on a 2d6 roll of 9 or less.

A model or unit that fails a command check against massive casualties or terrifying entities immediately flees; one that fails a command check against a spell suffers the associated effect.

An independent model makes a command check on an individual basis using its own CMD. It may use the CMD of a friendly faction model with the Commander ability instead of its own if it is in that model's command range.

In most cases, troopers make command checks at the unit level. Some exceptions include troopers that end their activations out of formation and spells that specifically target single models. Make one command check for the entire unit using the unit leader's CMD if he is still in play, and apply its results to every trooper in that unit unless stated otherwise. If the unit has no leader, use the highest CMD of the troopers that are in formation for

the command check. A unit making a command check within command range of a friendly faction model with the Commander ability may use that model's CMD stat instead. A trooper making an individual command check may use his leader's CMD if he is in formation or the CMD of a friendly faction model with the Commander ability if he is within that model's command range.

Command Range

A model with the **Commander** ability, such as a warcaster, has a command range equal to its CMD in inches. A friendly model or unit in such a model's command range may use that model's CMD when making a command check, but it is not required to do so. Only one model in a unit must be in the commander's command range for the entire unit to be considered in command range.

A unit leader can *rally* and *give orders* only to his troopers in formation, but a model with the Commander ability can rally any friendly model or unit and give orders to any friendly unit in his command range. A trooper out of formation cannot be rallied by his unit leader or receive any orders. A trooper making an individual command check may use his leader's CMD if he is in formation or the CMD of a friendly model with the Commander ability if he is within its command range.

A mercenary model with the Commander ability may only rally and give orders to mercenaries. Only friendly mercenaries may use the CMD of a mercenary model with the Commander ability if they are within its command range.

Fleeing

A model or unit that fails a command check against fleeing flees. Some special rules may even cause a model to flee without making a command check at all. When a model **flees**, it immediately turns to face directly away from the threat that caused it to flee. If this occurs during the model or unit's activation, its activation immediately ends. Other than changing facing, the fleeing model does not move until its next activation. A fleeing model will not flee again, nor does it make command checks against fleeing. For example, if the Butcher of Khardov, a terrifying entity, moves within melee range of a fleeing model, it does not make a command check against fleeing.

A fleeing model activates during its controller's Maintenance Phase. All fleeing models in a unit activate at the same time. If there are also models in the unit that are not fleeing, those other models will activate normally

Command

during the Activation Phase. A fleeing model automatically runs away from its nearest threat toward its deployment edge using the most direct route that does not take it through a damaging effect or allows enemies to engage it. When playing games without defined deployment edges, fleeing models run toward the nearest table edge. Fleeing troopers are not required to remain in formation. A fleeing model cannot perform any actions. A fleeing model that leaves the battlefield is *removed from play*. A fleeing model with no escape route will cower in its current position and forfeit its activation. Models engaged at the time they flee will incur free strikes normally when they disengage.

At the end of its activation, a fleeing model may have an opportunity to *rally* (see Rallying, below).

Rallying

A fleeing model can make a command check at the end of its activation in the Maintenance Phase if it is in formation with its unit leader or if it is within the command range of a friendly faction model with the Commander ability. If all of the troopers in a unit are fleeing and either the unit's leader is still on the table or a model in the unit is within the command range of a friendly faction model with the Commander ability, make a single unit-level command check instead of individual checks for each of the troopers. Each trooper in the unit will be affected by the result of this command check regardless of his in-formation status.

If it passes the command check, the model or unit rallies and turns to face its nearest enemies. This ends its activation and the model cannot activate again this turn, but it may function normally next turn. If the fleeing model or unit fails the command check, it continues to flee and will activate again during its controller's next Maintenance Phase.

Fearless Models

A model with the **fearless** special ability never flees. However, the model is still subject to command checks that have penalties other than fleeing. Fleeing models that become Fearless immediately rally.

Issuing Orders

An order lets a model make a specialized combat maneuver during its activation. Unlike other warrior models, troopers cannot automatically choose to run or charge; they must receive an order to do so.

Similarly, a cavalry trooper must receive an order to make a *ride-by attack* (Cavalry, pg. 58). A unit may receive an order from a friendly model with the Commander ability prior to its activation or from its leader at the beginning of its activation. Alternatively, the unit's leader may issue an order granted by his special rules such as a Trencher Sergeant giving a bayonet charge order. A unit whose leader is no longer in play cannot use its leader's unique orders.

A unit can receive only one order per activation. Every trooper in formation receives the order and must obey it. An out-of-formation trooper cannot receive an order and does not perform the task or gain its benefits. A unit not given a specific order can advance and perform its actions normally. A unit must be given new orders for each activation. Orders do not carry over from one activation to another.

At any time during its activation, a model with the Commander ability can give a run, charge, or ride-by attack order to one friendly unit in its command range, but if the unit has already activated, the order expires at the end of the turn.

Terrain—Your Best Friend
The Battlefield, Hazards, and Structures

The lay of the land has a tremendous impact on an army's ability to maneuver. The most cunning commanders use the terrain conditions to their best advantage. These terrain rules provide guidelines for establishing the effects and restrictions a battlefield's objects and environment can have on a game. Players should discuss the terrain prior to a game and agree on the characteristics for different terrain features. Covering the rules for every possible terrain type would be an endless task, so players themselves must determine the exact nature of each terrain feature on the battlefield before the game begins.

Battlefield Setup

Use the amount of terrain that suits the type of game you wish to play. A table with few terrain features favors ranged attacks and swift movement while having more terrain features shifts the emphasis toward melee combat.

Give consideration to model base sizes when placing terrain features close together since a model can move between terrain features only if its base will fit between them. With careful placement, you can create narrow passages that can be accessed only by models with smaller bases.

All players should agree upon terrain setup. When placing terrain, strive for a visually appealing and tactically challenging battlefield. These qualities provide the most exciting and memorable games. Battlefield setup and terrain placement is not a competitive portion of the game—players should not strategically place terrain features in a manner that unfairly aids or penalizes a specific army. However, a published or homemade scenario might dictate doing so to represent, for example, an overmatched force defending a village or mountain pass. In such a scenario, giving the defending army a strong defensive position would be one way to make up for being outclassed by its opponent.

If all players are involved with the battlefield setup, or if an impartial third party sets up the terrain, establish turn order and deploy forces normally. If only one player or team sets up the battlefield, then the opposing player or team chooses on which table edge to deploy his forces before determining turn order.

Before the game begins, all players should agree on each terrain feature's game effects.

Terrain

A model's movement can be penalized depending on the type of ground over which it moves. In WARMACHINE, terrain falls into one of three categories: *open, rough,* and *impassable*.

Open terrain is mostly smooth, even ground. Examples include grassy plains, barren fields, flat rooftops, dirt roads, elevated walkways, and paved surfaces. A model moves across open terrain without penalty.

Rough terrain can be traversed but at a significantly slower pace than open terrain. Examples include thick brush, rocky areas, murky bogs, shallow water, and deep snow. As long as any part of its base is in rough terrain, a model moves at 1/2 normal movement rate. Therefore, a model in rough terrain actually moves only 1/2" for every 1" of its movement used.

Impassable terrain is natural terrain that completely prohibits movement. This includes terrain such as cliff faces and lava. A model cannot move across impassable terrain.

Terrain Features

Natural and man-made objects on the battlefield are terrain features. Each terrain feature is unique, so you must decide its exact qualities before staring the game. Terrain features are virtually limitless in their variety, but you can quantify each by how it affects movement, the type of protection it affords, and any adverse effects it causes.

In addition to hindering movement, terrain features can also provide protection against ranged and magic attacks. A terrain feature such as a hedge or a mesh fence grants a model *concealment* by making it more difficult to be seen even though it is not dense enough actually to block an attack. A terrain feature such as a stone wall, a giant boulder, or a building grants a model *cover* by being physically solid enough to block an attack.

Obstacles & Obstructions

Obstacles and obstructions are terrain features that affect a model's movement, provide protection from ranged and magic attacks, and serve as *intervening terrain* during melee combat.

An **obstacle** is any terrain feature up to 1" tall. Obstacles are low enough that they can be climbed upon or, in some

Terrain

cases, easily crossed. A model can climb atop and stand on an obstacle at least 1" thick such as a raised platform or the sides of a ziggurat.

An advancing or running model can climb atop an obstacle by using 2" of its movement. A model cannot climb an obstacle if it does not have at least 2" of movement remaining. Place a model that climbs an obstacle atop it with the front of the model's base making only 1" of forward progress. Once atop an obstacle, the model may continue with the remainder of its movement. A charging model may not climb an obstacle and ends its movement as soon as it contacts the obstacle.

Realize that a model on a medium or large base may have trouble balancing atop an obstacle if it does not continue moving after initially climbing it. With only 1" of forward progress, the back of the model's base will hang off the back end of the obstacle. This is fine—just prop up the model with some extra dice until it can move again.

A moving model can descend an obstacle without penalty.

A **linear obstacle** is an obstacle up to 1" tall but less than 1" thick such as a wall or hedge. An advancing or running model can cross a linear obstacle at no penalty as long as the model has enough movement remaining to end its move with its base completely clear of the obstacle. If it does not, the model must stop short of the linear obstacle. A model cannot partially cross or stand atop a linear obstacle. A charging model cannot cross a linear obstacle.

In some rare cases, a model may be posed with its head so low that it has no line of sight over an obstacle. If this model's base touches an obstacle or if it is as close as its pose allows, assume the model is standing in a manner allowing it to see and attack over the obstacle. When this occurs, determine the model's *line of sight* from a point directly over the center of its base at the height of the wall. However, enemy models that have line of sight to that point may attack this model as well.

An **obstruction** is a terrain feature greater than 1" tall such as a high wall, a building, or a gigantic boulder. Treat obstructions as *impassable terrain*.

Forest

A typical **forest** has many trees and dense underbrush, but any terrain feature that hinders movement and makes a model inside it difficult to see can also follow these guidelines. A forest is considered *rough terrain* but also provides *concealment* to a model with any part of its base inside its perimeter.

A model can draw *line of sight* through up to 3" of forest, but anything more obstructs line of sight. For a model outside of it, the forest completely obstructs line of sight to anything beyond it. Thus, a model can see into or out of a forest but not completely through one no matter how thick it is. A forest provides no protection from melee attacks.

Hills

A **hill** is a terrain feature representing a gentle rise or drop in elevation. Since many terrain pieces use stepped sides instead of gradual slopes to represent a hill's elevations, be sure to declare whether the terrain feature is a hill or an obstacle.

A hill may be open or rough terrain depending on the ground's nature. Unlike obstacles, hills do not impose any additional movement penalties, nor do they provide cover or concealment. A model can charge up or down a hill in open terrain at no penalty.

Elevation

Models can take advantage of hills, platforms, and some obstacles that provide elevation above table level. When drawing line of sight from a model on a higher elevation than its target, ignore intervening models on lower elevation than the attacking model except those that would normally screen the target. Additionally, you can draw a line of sight through screening models that have equal or smaller-sized bases than the attacking model, but the target still gets +2 DEF for being screened. A model on higher elevation than its attacker gains +2 DEF against ranged and magic attacks from that opponent. Models on lower elevations than the target do not provide *screening*.

Hazards

Many things on a battlefield can kill just as quickly as an opponent can. These hazards could include water or flowing lava. Immediately apply a hazard's effects to a model as soon as any portion of its base enters the hazard's perimeter.

Water

Depending on its nature, water can be hazardous to both warriors and warjacks. When placing a water terrain feature, declare whether it is deep or shallow.

Deep water cannot be entered voluntarily. However, a model may be slammed, thrown, or otherwise forced to move into deep water. A warjack that enters deep water has its furnace extinguished and is instantly disabled and replaced with a wreck marker. Although otherwise intact, a warjack in deep water cannot be repaired or restarted for the remainder of the game.

A model in deep water can advance at half its normal movement rate but cannot run or charge. It cannot perform actions, cast spells, use feats, or give orders until it is completely out of the deep water. A model in deep water cannot engage other models or make attacks. A warcaster in deep water can allocate focus points and use them to maintain upkeep spells.

A model in deep water has a base DEF of 7 against all attacks. A warrior ending his activation in deep water automatically takes one damage point.

Shallow water is rough terrain that can be crossed by any model. Other than hindering movement, shallow water poses no threat—except to warjacks.

A warjack knocked down in shallow water has its furnace extinguished and is instantly disabled. Any friendly model can restart a warjack knocked down in shallow water. To restart a warjack's furnace, the model must be in base-to-base contact with the warjack and forfeit its action. A warjack must forfeit its activation and cannot channel spells on the turn it is restarted, but it functions normally next turn. Even if a warcaster other than its controller restarts it, the warjack remains part of its original battlegroup. A model can restart only one warjack per turn. Whenever a warjack's furnace is restarted, it automatically stands up.

Entryways

Some terrain features such as buildings and walls have openings called **entryways** that allow models to pass through or enter them. A model may not enter a terrain feature if the terrain feature's interior is not physically accessible. For example, a model may enter a ruined building that's missing its roof or one that has a removable roof. However, it may not enter a building with a fixed roof that cannot be opened in some other way to allow access to the models inside of it. Before the start of the game, the players should agree on the locations of any entryways and which terrain features may be entered.

A small or medium-based warrior model can pass through any entryway such as a door, window, or *breach* (see *Damaging and Destroying Structures*, below). A non-warrior model or large-based warrior model can only pass through a door or breach large enough for its base to pass

through. It may not pass through a window regardless of the window's size.

Structures

Structures present unique opportunities for terrain arrangement and tactical play. A structure is any terrain feature that can be damaged and destroyed. The most common structures are buildings, but you can use these guidelines for fortress walls, bridges, and similar constructions as well. All structures are *obstructions*.

Keep in mind that these rules are guidelines and may need to be adapted to the actual terrain pieces you are using. For example, a burned-out building that only has its exterior walls remaining might be large enough that models deep within its interior are far enough away from those walls not to suffer damage when the structure collapses. As another example, a house might have attached fences and field walls. Those walls and fences are best treated as separate structures from the house itself even though they are part of the single terrain piece. After all, shooting at a fence should not cause the house to collapse!

> **TACTICAL TIP:**
> An Incorporeal model ca[n] voluntarily enter deep water, b[ut] does not suffer movement pena[lty] when moving through it.

Damaging and Destroying Structures

A model that would rather blast its way through the side of a structure instead of using an existing entryway or bring a building crashing down on the heads of the enemies sheltering inside it will need to inflict substantial damage to it. An attack against a structure must target a specific location on the structure. *Breaches* (pg. 80) cannot be targeted by attacks. An attack against a structure in range automatically hits. A structure is also automatically hit by a spray attack if any part of the structure is within the spray template. Not all weapons are effective against structures, however, so a model must have a weapon that will do the job if it intends to punch through. Ranged weapons such as handguns, rifles, and crossbows are all but useless. A ranged weapon must have a POW of at least 14 to damage a structure. Melee attacks, magic attacks, and area-of-effect attacks do full damage against structures, as do ranged attacks that cause fire, cause corrosion, or have tempered ammunition, even as critical effects. Structures suffer blast damage and collateral damage. A magic attack only does its normal damage to a structure.

Terrain

Ignore a spell's special rules when it targets a structure. A structure cannot be charged or slammed.

A structure can only suffer so much damage before being destroyed. Every structure has an Armor (ARM) stat and damage capacity corresponding to its composition, size, and nature. Before the start of the game, the players should agree on each structure's ARM and damage capacity. A structure's damage capacity is determined by its composition and size. A wooden structure typically has a capacity of 5 damage points per inch of perimeter. The damage capacity of stone structures is typically 10 per inch. A reinforced stone or metal structure has a capacity of 20 or more damage points per inch. See the table below for typical ARM and damage capacity values. For mixed-composition structures, ARM values may vary from location to location. Assign damage capacity of mixed-composition structures proportionally. For example, an inch-wide or so wooden door in an otherwise stone building would only contribute 5 points to the structure's damage capacity. The door has ARM 12 while the surrounding stone has ARM 18.

Structure Material	ARM	Damage Capacity (points per inch)
Wood	12	5
Reinforced Wood	14	5
Brick	16	10
Stone	18	10
Iron	20	20
Steel	22	20

Undamaged portions of walls or other freestanding structures remain intact as the structure suffers damage, so the total damage capacity of such structures is determined by their total perimeter (or length, for linear structures such as walls or small structures such as obelisks). However, complex structures such as buildings and bridges rely on the support of all portions to remain standing. Such a structure's damage capacity is only half of the value determined by its composition and perimeter or length. For example, a 3"-wide stone wall is destroyed once it suffers a total of 30 damage points (3" length x 10 points per inch), but a 3" x 6" stone building collapses as soon as it suffers 90 points of damage (18" perimeter x 10 points per inch / 2).

When a structure is destroyed, remove it from the table and replace it with an equal-sized ruin. A ruined structure is rough terrain and provides cover to a model with any part of its base inside the ruin's perimeter.

In addition, the structure **collapses** and may damage models that are inside it. A model inside a collapsing structure suffers a damage roll with Power (POW) equal to the structure's ARM times the number of levels in the structure, after which the model is knocked down. For example, a warjack inside a three-story brick building when it collapses suffers a POW 48 (Brick structure ARM 16 x 3 levels) damage roll. Whatever is left of the warjack is then knocked down.

Breaches

When an open structure suffers a number of damage points equal to or greater than the structure's damage capacity per inch, the structure is breached unless it has an inaccessible interior and thus cannot be entered by models (see *Entryways*, pg. 79). A **breach** is a hole in the structure through which models may move. Breaches are *entryways*.

The newly-created breach is centered on the targeted location. Its size is determined by the amount of damage inflicted by the attack. The breach created is one inch wide for each full inch of damage capacity inflicted by the attack. In the case of structures with multiple levels, the breach occurs on the level targeted. Adjacent breaches are combined into a single, larger breach. For example, a wooden building that can take 5 damage points per inch suffers 18 damage points from an attack. Assuming that this damage doesn't cause the building to collapse, the attack creates a single 3"-wide breach.

For mixed-composition structures, use the appropriate damage capacity for the targeted location to determine when a breach is created and how big it is. For instance, an attack that targets a wooden door in a stone building will breach the door if it inflicts only 5 damage points, but the attack would have to inflict 15 or more points to create a breach wider than an inch.

Models may use a breach just like any other entryway. A small- or medium-based warrior model can pass through any size breach. A large-based warrior model or any non-warrior model can only pass through a breach large enough for its base to pass through.

Once a portion of a structure has been breached, that part of the structure may no longer be targeted by attacks.

Scenarios—Why We Can't All Be Friends
Six Variations of Gameplay

There are as many reasons for war as there are wars themselves. Sides seldom clash with only the intent to eliminate one another. It could be a skirmish over boundaries, a fight over resources, or an attempt to hold important strategic ground. Conceiving a reason for your conflicts can greatly enhance your WARMACHINE gaming experiences.

Here you will find six scenarios ready to play. Each occurs on a balanced playing field conveying no specific advantage to any one player. You can agree with your opponent on which scenario to play, or prior to building your army, roll a d6 and play the scenario indicated below:

1—Crossed Lines	4—King of the Hill
2—Domination	5—Mangled Metal
3—Killing Field	6—Pendulum

Each scenario provides special rules that describe how to handle the unique circumstances of the scenario. Certain scenarios will also have restrictions on army composition as well as how the game table should be set up. Most scenarios can be played at any encounter level you choose. Experiment with different combinations, and feel free to create variations or unique scenarios of your own!

Crossed Lines

Bugger! Are those Menites? What are they doing here? Bleedin' hell, they've got 'jacks and they're headed straight for us! Get Commander Stryker, mate, and step lively!

—Rodger "the Rake" Digby, Cygnaran long gunner.

Description

Sometimes rival forces inadvertently stumble across one another. These clashes quickly become disorganized brawls rather than the orchestrated battles preferred by most commanders, and they typically involve close-quarter fighting in urban settings where battles might be taken structure-to-structure or in dense forests where one never knows what lies beyond the next copse of trees.

Special Rules

No models from either side are allowed to use the Advance Deployment special ability.

Army Selection

Players agree on the size of the battle normally.

Set Up

The table should be thick with terrain. Players take turns placing terrain until one player wishes to stop. The other player is then allowed to place one additional piece. Each player must place a minimum of four (4) terrain features.

Beginning

At the start of the game, each player rolls a d6 and the high roller chooses who will deploy first. Starting with that player, the players take turns choosing three (3) deployment points each. A deployment point may be anywhere on the table but not within 12" of an opponent's deployment point. Players then alternate placing one battlegroup, one unit, or all of their solos at a time anywhere completely within 6" of one of their deployment points. Warjacks assigned to a 'jack marshal are placed at the same time as the 'jack marshal. Players deploy their models and units in the same order in which they chose deployment points.

After all forces have been deployed, the players make a starting roll to determine turn order.

Victory Conditions

A player wins the game when he has the only remaining warcaster(s) in play.

Multiplayer Game

Crossed Lines is a truly chaotic multiplayer game. It is also very easy to adapt to multiplayer play because there are no deployment zones to worry about. Players should simply follow the rules detailed above.

Domination

The Battle of the Tongue was about land control. The Khadorans gobbled it up all the way to the river, and the Cygnarans let them have it, for they knew the mighty Dragon's Tongue was where they could make their stand and wear the northerners down.

—From 'The Thornwood War' by Lethyl Harke

Scenarios

Description

Often in battle the goal is to gain control over the majority of the land, and it results in much back and forth conflict. This is often the case in the borderlands between Khador and Cygnar. Domination pits rival forces against each other in a struggle to capture and hold as much of the battlefield as possible.

Special Rules

Domination lasts for eight (8) game rounds as players rush to capture specific domination points on the table. A player captures a domination point when any part of the base of a model under his control passes over it. If a model leaves a domination point, the point remains under its army's control until an enemy model moves on top of it. Only one model may be on top of a domination point at any time.

Army Selection

Players agree on a size of the battle as normal.

Set Up

Domination is best played on a 4'x4' table. Players decide how much terrain to use and then take turns placing terrain.

Divide the table into 1-foot squares and place domination points at the vertices of each intersection according to the following diagram:

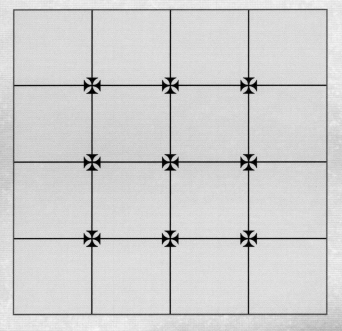

Beginning

Determine deployment and turn order with a standard starting roll (pg. 29). Players are allowed to place their forces completely within 10" of the table's edge.

Victory Conditions

The game ends at the completion of the eighth game round. The player controlling the most domination points wins the game. In case of a tie, the player who accumulated the most victory points wins.

Multiplayer Game

Domination requires some care in set up for multiplayer scenarios. All players must be equidistant from each other, and each must have the same size deployment zone.

Killing Field

Victory can be measured both in terms of ground gained and casualties inflicted.

—Major Markus 'Siege' Brisbane

Description

Killing Field is a desperate struggle between two armies seizing control of the battlefield by entrenching themselves on the centerline and inflicting crippling losses on their opposition.

Special Rules

Players score Control Points by holding the points marked on the middle of the table. A model holds the point if it ends its controlling player's turn with its base overlapping a point marker. Only one model may hold a point. Wrecked or inert warjacks cannot hold a point. A player scores one (1) Control Point for each point marker held. Points cannot be scored during the first round.

Army Selection

Players agree on a size of the battle normally.

Set Up

Before the start of the game, mark three (3) points along the centerline of the table: one at the center of the table and two (2) more 8" from the edges of the table (see diagram on following page).

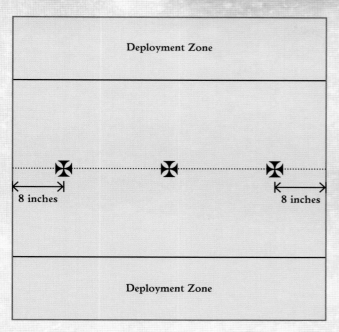

Deployment Zone	
8 inches	8 inches
Deployment Zone	

Beginning

Determine deployment and turn order with a standard starting roll (pg. 29). Players are allowed to place their forces completely within 10" of the table's edge.

Victory Conditions

The first player to score seven (7) Control Points wins the game.

If the game ends before this, the player with the most Control Points wins. In case of a tie, the player who has accumulated the most victory points wins.

Multiplayer Game

Killing Field is not suited to multiplayer play.

King of the Hill

Get three Defenders on that hill. Back them up with three more units of long gunners. With the elevation and our guns, we shall be as untouchable as any Khadoran fortress.

—Commander Coleman Stryker at Zerkova's Hill.

Description

Many battles are fought over strategic locations of uncertain value, but military strategists know the benefit in taking a monumental hill before securing ancillary vantage points. King of the Hill is one such battle. In this scenario, both forces scrabble over land and rush up the hillside to claim the spot for their faction.

Special Rules

The obvious objective of King of the Hill is to take the hill. At the end of each player's turn, the player with more models on the hill than his opponent scores a Control Point. A unit counts as one model for the purposes of calculating who has more models on the hill.

Army Selection

Players agree on a size of the battle normally.

Set Up

Place a hill in the center of the table. Players take turns placing terrain until one player wishes to stop. The other player is then allowed to place one additional piece. Each player must place a minimum of two (2) terrain features.

Beginning

Determine deployment and turn order with a standard starting roll (pg. 29). Players are allowed to place their forces completely within 10" of the table's edge.

Victory Conditions

The first player to score five (5) Control Points wins the game.

If the game ends before this, the player with the most Control Points wins. In case of a tie, the player who has accumulated the most victory points wins.

Multiplayer Game

In multiplayer King of the Hill, all players should be equidistant from each other and have the same-sized deployment zone.

Mangled Metal

There's nothing like the clatter and clamor of warjacks crashing together, their hulls ringing, their furnaces spewing ash with gouts of sparks and flame, and then the deafening screech of metal as one rends the other apart. What a grand, pernicious thing man has made to fight his wars.

—Casner Feist, ex-warcaster and leader of the Daggermoor Rovers.

Scenarios

Description

Mangled Metal is a brutal contest between warjacks. This scenario is an all-out unrestrained bloodbath where the only goal is to survive.

Special Rules

None.

Army Selection

Players agree on a point limit and then purchase their forces as normal, except each player is only allowed a single warcaster regardless of the size of the game. Points may only be spent on the warcaster and his warjacks; units and solos have no place in Mangled Metal.

Set Up

Mangled Metal may be played on any size table, but a smaller table works better. Each player is allowed to place two terrain features on the table.

Beginning

Determine deployment and turn order with a standard starting roll (pg. 29). Players are allowed to place their forces completely within 10" of the table's edge.

Victory Conditions

A player wins the game when he has the only remaining warcaster in play or when all his opponents' warjacks have been destroyed, disabled, or removed from play.

Multiplayer Game

In multiplayer Mangled Metal, all players should be equidistant from each other and have comparable deployment zones.

Pendulum

Their sacrifice is meaningless. With each death we gain ground.

—Lich Lord Terminus

Description

The back and forth rhythm of warfare often leads to decisive moments as enemy lines are crossed. In a Pendulum battle both forces fight for control over the battlefield by holding their own halves of the table and invading the enemy's region of control.

Special Rules

Divide the table in half with a line running west to east through the center.

A player ending his turn with one or more of his models across the centerline on his opponent's side of the table while none of his opponent's models are on his side of the table scores one (1) Control Point. Points cannot be scored during the first round. The first player to score three (3) Control Points wins the game.

Army Selection

Players agree on a size of the battle normally.

Set Up

The table should be thick with terrain. Players take turns placing terrain until one player wishes to stop. The other player is then allowed to place one additional piece. Each player must place a minimum of four (4) terrain features.

Beginning

Determine deployment and turn order with a standard starting roll (pg. 29). Players are allowed to place their forces completely within 10" of the table's edge.

Victory Conditions

The first player to score three (3) Control Points wins the game.

If time runs out before one player has won, the player with the most Control Points wins. In case of a tie, the player with the most Victory Points wins.

Multiplayer Game

Pendulum is not suited to multiplayer play.

Cygnar

Of Crown and Kingdom
A Brief History of Cygnar

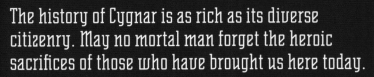

The history of Cygnar is as rich as its diverse citizenry. May no mortal man forget the heroic sacrifices of those who have brought us here today.

—King Leto Raelthorne speaking at the expansion of the
Royal Cygnaran University

The following is a transcription of Professor Gabriel Parrish, professor of Cygnaran History at Corvis University. These words were spoken two months before his death during Vinter Raelthorne IV's siege of Corvis in 603 AR:

Where did we leave off? Ah yes, the post-Occupation Era. History teaches us that all empires crumble, and it was the Orgoth's violent disposition and rigorous segregation of the native peoples that made their downfall inevitable. The people of western Immoren united against the long-term oppression of the Orgoth and fought protracted and bloody battles to send them off. Ultimately the Orgoth retreated to their ships and sailed to their faraway lands.

It was on Cygnaran soil that armies, wizard orders, and even the priests of Morrow and Menoth fought as brothers against their common foe to conduct the greatest battles of liberation against the Orgoth. This type of unity will never happen again, nor do I expect to see the descendants of those heroes working in concert in our lifetimes, if ever.

In 202 AR just down the canal from here, the Corvis Treaties established our borders. Our ancestors separated the kingdoms along similar boundaries to those of the Orgoth because roads and customs had already united these regions. The Iron Kingdoms and their crown jewel, Cygnar, were born that year. Foreigners sneer at this title, but it was the Cygnarans who were the first to organize the Circle of the Oath—those who wielded "the Gift" of magic. We were also the people who enticed Rhulfolk to work alongside our mechaniks to create the first colossals.

Kings of Cygnar have been warriors and sages, and one of the most notable to occupy the throne was the legendary King Woldred the Diligent. Although his personal demeanor was grave as a result of years campaigning against trollkin, Woldred was a rightly good king. The Colossal War against Khador was Woldred's proving ground. Tales of his valor won him the support of his people, but he showed he was more than purely a military man. He was also a shrewd negotiator, an accomplished statesman, and a just lawmaker.

King Woldred was determined to quash the north's invasion ambitions utterly. After the Colossal War as part of his terms to the defeated Khadorans, Woldred convened the Disarmament Conferences of 257 AR, which saw the dismantling of the north's mighty constructs and the establishment of the Colossal Guard. This significantly hindered Khador's capabilities to wage effective war and allowed four decades of uneasy peace between nations.

Woldred became the first ruler of the Reconstruction Era to set aside personal desire and enmity to encourage not just the rebuilding of structures the Orgoth had destroyed during the Scourge but also growth on every level. His reign saw road building, canal digging, shipbuilding, and a reorganization of the Cygnaran army.

The only conflict marring this period was ongoing harassment from the Thornwood's warlike trollkin. Woldred was tolerant enough to meet with trollkin chiefs personally in 267 AR, and he negotiated a lasting peace that ended years of needless conflict. Fights with the trollkin had encouraged the generals to initiate a redesign of steam-powered war machines. Their efforts gave rise to the modern warjack engineered to maneuver around forest obstacles better than its lumbering predecessors. Small utility steamjacks soon expedited industrialization and trade in every Cygnaran city.

In his last few years, Woldred became renowned for two major deeds. One was the retirement of colossals in 286 AR. The other was "Woldred's Covenant" in the same year. He decreed that the people of Cygnar would not endure the vicious backstabbing occurring in other monarchies, which often "devolves into a pattern of brother betraying brother and father fearing son." He drafted his Accord-By-Hand Covenant, which stated that each king could impart the throne on his own terms and not allow it to be handed over helplessly to "kin of bad quality." Primogeniture would only apply as a means of last resort.

Woldred's Covenant might have been revolutionary if not for one notable amendment. The Temple of Menoth would only support the contract under the condition that their priesthood retained exclusive rights to bear witness to each king's terms. Though the Morrowan faith was already dominant among the wider population, Menites remained an undeniable force in Cygnar's capital, and they pressured Woldred's council to pass the decree.

Woldred the Diligent died unexpectedly in 289 AR. The kingdom recoiled—some crying treachery—but the Temple of Menoth quelled such talk and claimed that after the traditional mourning period they would unveil the terms of succession. The Church of Morrow looked to their primarch for counsel expecting conflict if Menites gained exclusive access to the throne. This never happened.

Woldred's terms mysteriously disappeared, and within a fortnight his nephew Malagant—called the Grim—entered the palace in Caspia with a force of five hundred soldiers to claim the throne. The Temple of Menoth refuted Malagant's right to rule and called him a usurper. Vocal Menite priests were in turn accused of sedition, and between 290 and 294 AR, the Grim King had over two hundred Menite priests arrested and hung. Temple and state were at odds, and in 293 AR Malagant proclaimed the Church of Morrow Cygnar's official religion and dissolved all Menite authority over the government. Cygnar roiled in turmoil and some feared civil war.

Like a wolf on a blood-scent, Khador's Queen Cherize initiated a border war with Cygnar in 293 AR that lasted until 295 when Cherize went missing. King Malagant died shortly thereafter. Ill omens and superstitious rumor surrounded the loss of both sovereigns.

Queen Ayn Vanar V, a mere girl of five winters, was crowned in Khador. Lord Regent Velibor took control of Khador in her stead and began an aggressive campaign to expand the borders. Lord Velibor was cruel, it is true, but he was also cunning and shrewd. When a great alliance of barbarian tribes from his own northern mountains came together to pillage his lands, he enticed them to attack south instead. He convinced them of the spoils and riches they could garner off the hides of the southerners. He hoped to follow in their wake, pick at weakened armies, and conquer new lands.

Bitter conflicts raged unchecked for more than a decade until the young queen matured. In the Siege of Midfast in 305 AR, the majority of the last great barbarian tribes were destroyed. Captain Markus Graza, champion of Morrow, single-handedly turned the tide and humbled the barbarian chieftains. The Khadorans continued their border wars for another decade and seized lands from both Ord and Llael. It was not until 313 AR that Queen Vanar, tired of death and strife, mustered the authority to end the wars. The treachery of Lord Velibor and the barbarians of the north sparked disdain and animosity that linger still, and relations between Khador and her neighbors have never been peaceful since. Khador gained substantial lands in those battles, including the city once known as Radahvo, now Port Vladovar. The other nations sought peace and foolishly allowed this transgression in the vain hope that the northmen were sated.

The treachery of Lord Velibor and the barbarians of the north sparked disdain and animosity that linger still, and relations between Khador and her neighbors have never been peaceful since.

The Temple of Menoth, once so strong, struggled to renew its influence. Over the next hundred and fifty years, Cygnar became a powder keg waiting to explode. The Menites never forgot their removal from the halls of power by the Grim King, and they sowed constant unrest in the streets. The Cygnaran court condemned agitators, but Menites took their operations underground. They vilified the Church of Morrow and denounced them as heretics against the True Law. Innocents on both sides lost their lives to ceaseless religious conflict.

Sporadic clashes were nothing compared to the rift that would divide Caspia in 483 AR. The eastern city had always been a haven for the Menite minority, and their vocal leader, Visgoth Sulon, called for a pilgrimage of all Cygnaran Menites to rally to him. Tens of thousands of Menites answered the call. The masses gathered, Sulon proclaimed himself hierarch of the entire faith, and they seized control of eastern Caspia, the portion of Caspia east of the Black River. Angry Menites forced all non-Menites to vacate the eastern city. Thinking a riot was looming, the Caspian watch moved to disperse the crowds, but the Menites' intentions were deadly. Thousands of pilgrims rose against the Cygnaran militia and slew over three hundred guards.

Two hundred years of aggression ignited into the Cygnaran Civil War. Zealous Menites nearly razed the river districts on the west bank of the City of Walls in the extensive fighting that followed. Fueled by a clash of faiths and opportunistic looting, the battles were so bloody even the stalwart priests and defenders of the Church of Morrow entered them directly.

Khador again took advantage of chaos to attack our allies, prompting the Coin Wars along the Llaelese border. Llael's army, small at the best of times, sought mercenaries to bolster their defenses, and it bankrupted their treasury. Our kingdom's soldiers were too busy trying to keep the capital standing to lend aid.

she entreated Sulon's successor, Visgoth Ozeall, for an end to the violence. After difficult and protracted discussions, both sides made concessions, agreed on terms, and created the newly dubbed Protectorate of Menoth.

The Menites were ceded an expanse of land east of the Black River and the entirety of eastern Caspia which they immediately renamed Sul after Hierarch Sulon. The Protectorate had leave to govern their people as they saw fit without interference by the Cygnaran throne. It was understood that the Protectorate was nominally part of Cygnar and subject to disarmament terms and taxation, but neither nation would have any political sway over the other. Cygnaran diplomats believed the Menites would

The fate of our capital might have been doomed were it not for the death of Sulon. His death in battle dealt a great blow to the morale of the Menites and opened the door for peace talks since both sides wearied of staggering losses. High Prelate Shevann, head of the Morrowan Church treasury and a woman of spotless reputation and honesty, stepped forward. She had great sway over the Cygnaran people and even the grudging respect of the Menites. Serving as spokeswoman for Cygnar's King Bolton Grey V,

reject Shevann's terms since it pushed the Menites against the barbarous and heathen Idrians, but the Menites of the Protectorate proved eager to bring their faith to the region. Menite zeal destined the Idrians to hard decades to come and eventual mass conversion to the Menite faith, but it spared Cygnar years of civil war. Even Morrow himself recognized Shevann's worth, so she eventually ascended as one of his puissant servants to watch over fair trade and agreements.

King Grigor Malfast led the nation into an era of growth not seen since Woldred the Diligent. Steamjacks became more common as the Fraternal Order of Wizardry perfected cortex creation, and the once-depleted Cygnaran coffers filled with coin. Malfast had his most trusted vassal by his side, Archduke Vinter Raelthorne II, who tempered his grandiose schemes. The Raelthorne bloodline was ingrained in the Cygnaran courts, the first Vinter Raelthorne having been a king decades before, and their blood-claims traced back to ancient kings of Caspia before the Orgoth.

Vinter II was in charge of keeping Malfast's idealistic plans accomplishable by Cygnaran hands. Though Vinter

force including the bulk of the renowned Khadoran cavalry to the borders of Llael. He knew it would force Malfast to respond. Indeed, Cygnar's king sent warjacks and riflemen led by Vinter II north to beat back the impending invasion. All the while Vygor personally led an even larger force of battle-ready warjacks fresh from Khadoran factories and a tremendous army of heavy infantry straight into the forest hoping to make a drive south and attack key Cygnaran territories unaware.

If it were not for the scouts of Fellig who had made it past King Vygor's deadly Kossite hunters, Cygnar would have felt the full brunt of a secret Khadoran force carving its way through the "impassable" Thornwood. Small forces from Corvis, Point Bourne, and Rivercleft met the Khadorans at the Dragon's Tongue while the army rushing to Llael turned back, made a desperate forced march, and tried to intercept the Khadoran warjack advance.

The Battle of the Tongue in early 511 AR remains one of the bloodiest in recent history. Cygnar was greatly outnumbered. It took all of our superior training, the leadership of Colonel Drake Cathmore, and the aid of nearby mercenary forces to hold the river. Centuries-old bridgework was destroyed to stop the crossing, and tons of Warlord Era stonework was lost to the deep waters. The confrontation saw the loss of more warjacks than

Zealous Menites nearly razed the river districts on the west bank of the City of Walls in the extensive fighting that followed.

in any conflict in the history of western Immoren. Although we halted the Khadorans at the river and kept them from sweeping inland, we suffered great losses. It took decades to replace and repair the warjacks destroyed in the comparatively short four-month Thornwood War, which ended with Vygor's demise on the blade of Vinter Raelthorne II.

II was a hard man, he was practical. Without him, King Malfast would have wasted much of his treasury in a short time and left Cygnar penniless.

The Khadoran king, Ruslan Vygor, was a misanthrope with a dark heart, and Cygnar's prosperity stoked his jealous rage. He may have been insane, but he was also daring. He gathered the largest war host yet seen in the north and executed a wild scheme. In late 510 AR, he sent a great

Malfast had a tower erected at the northern end of "Warjack Road," the path Vygor's army carved through the Thornwood. The twisted forest eventually reclaimed the area, including the watchtower. Dark spirits cast the Cygnaran forces out, and the resilient Thornwood enveloped the region again. On the sloping banks of the Dragon's Tongue below the wood and throughout the old battle site, pieces large and small of the warjacks used in the war are still unearthed. Even Khador has, to this day, left the area to the shades of its past failure.

A few short years later, King Malfast fell ill. With no heir-apparent, Malfast drafted terms from his deathbed according to Woldred's Covenant and handed his crown to then Archduke Vinter Raelthorne II. Vinter accepted the burden knowing that the blood of ancient kings was in his veins. Soon after the announcement of the coronation, Grigor Malfast passed away. In 515 AR, Vinter Raelthorne II, then in his forties, was crowned king, and Cygnar entered the Raelthorne Era.

The rule of the Raelthornes has been eighty-seven years to this day. Vinter II ruled with the same approach he had adopted with his predecessor, priding the utilitarian over the frivolous. Always found deep in thought over matters of state with an inscrutable expression, he was termed the Stone-Faced King. He survived two assassination attempts and developed a reputation as a strong opponent of unregulated sorcery and a man suspicious of cults. He played an important behind-the-scenes role in the founding of the Mercarian League, a confederacy of merchant cities both throughout the kingdom and abroad. Vinter II was a remarkable leader.

In 539 AR the crown passed to his son, Vinter Raelthorne III. Here was a man who had learned from his father's rule although he translated the heavy hand into an iron fist. Vinter III filled the kingdom's coffers through burdensome taxes in order to bolster the navy and fund privateers to secure the western sea-lanes rife with pirate vessels. Many people hated him for such rigid demands despite his successes against the raiders of the Broken Coast. He earned a nickname that played off of his father's: the Stoneheart.

Vinter slew two score of Leto's men and appeared invincible. He waded through the cleft armor and flesh like an armored galleon sailing in a sea of Cygnaran blood.

The Stoneheart was a stern and harsh king who brooked no nonsense. He claimed to be surrounded by the self-interest of bureaucrats and sycophants and concluded he could trust no one. He dismissed his courtly advisors and looked to "the counsel of his own mind" for making all of the kingdom's decisions. Despite the mixed feelings of his subjects, Vinter III moved Cygnar toward greatness.

His taxes were harsh, but he was not as tight-fisted as we've been led to believe. He was a pragmatist, and his collected monies went to strengthen the kingdom. If debtors could not pay, rather than letting them rot in prison, he put them on board ships or into quarries to work off what they owed. True, many died under the hard circumstances, but by their toil the kingdom prospered.

Vinter III had two sons: his heir, also named Vinter, and Leto, our current good king. Nursemaids and midwives raised the boys since their father was preoccupied refining the kingdom's army and treasury. When he died suddenly—some say suspiciously—in 576 AR, the kingdom fell to his eldest son Vinter IV because no accord had been left.

So begins our next chapter.

King Vinter IV 'the Elder' Raelthorne. Most of you were adolescents when his reign came to a sudden end. I think it is fair to classify Vinter IV as paranoid. Certainly his irrational fear of the Church of Morrow drove him to seclude himself, and perhaps it is why he turned out as he did. His father and grandfather were hard and sometimes grim men, but this Vinter was darker and colder yet. Woe for us that the Stoneheart had no time for Woldred's Covenant.

Vinter IV suspected enemies everywhere he looked, and he contravened matters in open court by drawing his blade to intimidate officials and "sway" dignitaries to his position. His paranoia brought the Inquisition when he turned his father's network of national security spies into judges and executioners. Until that time the Inquisition was a small group of discreet information gatherers, but Vinter IV expanded them into his own guild of authorized assassins. The Inquisition had complete liberty no matter how vile or unjust their actions. The Elder ruled with terror and murder though he termed it justice and royal privilege. Those who opposed him were dragged off in the middle of the night and never seen again.

In the latter years of his rule, individuals later unveiled as followers of Thamar—Morrow's dark twin—infiltrated the king's court and used Vinter's tyranny for their own purposes. There were instances recorded regarding priests of Morrow corrupted from their faith with gifts and promises from the royal coffers; some were even inducted into the ranks of the Inquisition. So deep was Vinter's evil that he managed to turn goodly wizards of the Fraternal Order and the Golden Crucible into willing participants in his tyranny.

During the length of his brother's rule, Prince Leto was appalled. He would lay awake at night as he brooded on his brother's depravities and the ongoing threat to the Church. The prince had an affinity with Primarch Arius and had proven himself a pious Morrowan. Although they downplay their part in what was soon to happen, the Church's agreement to join in action against Vinter may have been the final push that moved Leto's hand. A palace revolution erupted in the winter of 594 AR. It was nine years ago, but it seems like yesterday.

It is fortunate for us that Vinter IV's paranoia was so strong. As much as he despised his younger brother Leto, Vinter trusted no one else to run his military. Making his brother General of the Crown turned out to be an ironic choice, however, for Leto soon enlisted the most pious officers along with nobles loyal to the prince and weary of the tyrant. Allies of Leto included High Magus Calster, now head of Caspia's Fraternal Order, heirs to the northern and eastern Midlunds, and a core of honorable army commanders and royal guard who could no longer endure their sovereign's profane orders.

This force waged battle through the palace attacking the equally stalwart henchmen of Vinter IV. Calster's wizards were pitted against Vinter's Inquisitors, and their conflict consumed the east wing of the palace in a foundation-shaking battle of sorcery. You can still see the burn marks in the marble and stone. Leto and his vanguard of knights and paladins battered their way into Vinter's chambers and attacked the king and his personal guards.

Vinter slew two score of Leto's men and appeared invincible. He waded through the cleft armor and flesh like an armored galleon sailing in a sea of Cygnaran blood. When the Elder stood enraged before his brother, Leto demanded one last time for him to end his madness and surrender. Vinter went for his brother's head and rained blows onto his sibling in unrelenting fury. Though Leto would prove a wiser king, his brother was the more deadly swordsman and dealt the Younger what should have been a fatal wound—a wide gash across the chest. Leto was at his brother's merciless sword point and uttered prayers to Morrow.

You may ask, "What happened? Why is Leto our king if his brother defeated him?"

There are many rumors of godly intervention, but reports are unclear. One moment Leto seemed defeated, but the next he stood over his disarmed and furious brother. I'd wager a hundred crowns on the Primarch Arius. If anyone short of Morrow himself could conjure up such a miracle, it would be that fine man.

Vinter was cast into the royal dungeons, and Leto declared the coup at an end. Sadly the Elder had many secret allies who moved immediately. Operatives of the Inquisition took Leto's wife hostage and demanded Vinter's release. Leto loved his bride and had little choice. His assembly urged him to refuse, but Leto gave the command. The Inquisitors immediately betrayed their promise by keeping the princess even as they bought time for Vinter by distracting the palace guards. Vinter thwarted the chase by gaining control of an experimental flying balloon contraption at the top of the palace. He used it to fly east where the winds would take him, and he drifted out over the Bloodstone Marches. No one saw Vinter or Leto's bride again. May Morrow preserve her soul.

King Leto "the Younger" Raelthorne was crowned in a solemn ceremony while noblemen still whispered of the grim circumstances leading to his coronation. The Royal Assembly conducted a full trial for the Elder in absentia whereby they formally stripped him of all Cygnaran rights for his proven crimes and dark alliances. Convicted of high treason, his life was forfeit. Execution had to be left to the perilous Bloodstone Marches.

You lads are fortunate to live in a new and prosperous era with a pious king who stands vigilant. It is true that violence along the borders has increased and our army is beset by soldiers and mercenaries seeking to pillage our bounty. Khador never ceased its bloodshed on our northern border even after the end of the Thornwood War, yet our soldiers are brave and keep them in check. They are aided by geography and the supremacy of our engineering and military prowess.

The Protectorate makes noises again reminiscent of the Civil War; I have no fear Leto will keep them in line. Already soldiers of our Caspian garrison periodically beat them back from the Black River. War is a constant, and bloodshed remains as an unfortunate price to pay for freedom and opportunity. King Leto is a just and honorable ruler, and you would do well to give him your support. Offer your prayers to blessed Morrow for King Leto's continued health, my lads. We'll continue next session with an in-depth look at the way Khador and Cygnar have made use of mercenaries to wage various battles without declaring formal war.

LIEUTENANT ALLISTER CAINE

A few years ago I saw Caine duel a man he had accused of treason. They walked ten paces before Caine vanished and reappeared an arm's length behind his opponent. Twin streaks of sunlight flashed and Caine had holstered his pistols before the dead man hit the ground. If I'd been watch captain then, I'd have put him in the pillory for shooting a man in the back.

—Corvis Watch Commander Julian Helstrom

The Militant Order of the Arcane Tempest requires a great degree of control over its students, for each is expected to graduate as an elite soldier. When it inducted an intense and troubled youth by the name of Allister Caine, the order had no idea what it was getting—an untapped warcaster who would pioneer the art of gunplay to unparalleled heights.

Purely by instinct Caine learned how to channel power into his pistol shots, which he placed with unerring accuracy. However, despite his impressive skill, his ego and irreverent attitude made him a difficult man to befriend. He claimed his pistols had more life and were better friends than any of the sods in the Order against whom he competed. Soon Caine was performing trick shots whenever he could escape the scrutiny of his teachers, and he slowly earned the grudging admiration of his peers. Nonetheless, as Caine's skills became legendary so did his insubordination.

Caine's warcasting capabilities were revealed when an instructor happened upon him willing a steamjack to perform his assigned labors. As a punitive measure Caine had been ordered to haul kegs of blasting powder from the vault to the practice range, but he let a laborjack "borrowed" from the docks handle the work while he rehearsed drawing and re-holstering techniques. His instructors were relieved to see these abilities, for it allowed them to speed him through

training and pass him to other hands. He was granted the title of gun mage in little over one year. News of his abilities reached Leto's court, and upon graduation he was summoned to the king for a display. Caine did not disappoint. He was personally urged to enlist as a warcaster by King Leto himself, and he passed through apprentice training with alacrity.

It is said that shortly after Caine graduated from the Tempest Academy, he made an unfortunate visit back to his hometown of Bainsmarket. There he was incarcerated for the murder of a gangster of no small status. Apparently there had been a long-standing feud between the two and Caine had fulfilled a vendetta. Because the victim was obviously a criminal and Caine an up-and-coming warcaster and officer, the magistrates chose to cover up his misdeed, but Caine's practices were not about to change for the better.

Over the next several years while he was fulfilling his journeyman tour of duty under an indulgent semi-retired mentor, Caine gained a reputation as a loner, drifter, and scoundrel. He frequented seedy spots along the borders of Cygnar and Ord. He enjoyed "slumming" in the guise of a common drunk to show off his nearly unmatched skills for a moment's thrill or a handful of crowns. He spent many nights sleeping in the stocks and cells of towns, tapping into his mystic abilities once his head cleared the alcohol-induced fog. His drinking, improprieties with countless women (often of rank or title), unrelenting swagger, and utter audacity in the face of superiors all precluded him from attaining rank. He is the only warcaster in recent memory to be promoted to captain on becoming a full magus only to lose that rank weeks later for "improprieties not befitting an officer".

Any hope that busting Caine to lieutenant would mature or reform him has faded. Were it not for his skills, it is doubtful the man would be allowed within a league of valuable 'jacks, much less be enlisted in the army. His vices notwithstanding, Allister Caine remains a gun mage of the highest regard in the ranks of the Cygnaran army. When pressed about the officer's behavior, Commander Stryker dismisses Caine's indiscretions as "the last vestiges of a chaotic youth." Those who have seen him fight are willing to bend their normal ideas of discretion, for he is a weapon without equal.

On the field of battle, Lieutenant Caine sometimes employs his infamous "flash-fry" maneuver where he magically blinks from place-to-place to gain the element of surprise. This strange ability to make short-ranged leaps in time and space is unique to Caine and Caine alone. Other gun mages call it a dishonorable practice, but he scoffs whenever he hears such talk. Caine was once heard to remark, "Any commander worth his salt takes whatever edge he can, or he's an idiot. In war we gamble with our lives, and every good solider keeps an ace up his sleeve. This one is mine."

Focus 6				Cmd 8	
SPD	STR	MAT	RAT	DEF	ARM
7	5	4	8	17	13

Spellstorm Pistol

RNG	ROF	AOE	POW
12	2	—	12

Spellstorm Pistol

RNG	ROF	AOE	POW
12	2	—	12

Sword

SPECIAL	POW	P+S
—	3	8

Damage	15
Point Cost	67
Field Allowance	C
Victory Points	5
Base Size	Small

SPECIAL RULES

FEAT: MAELSTROM

In an awesome display of speed and skill, Allister Caine launches himself into the air and spins about, firing his brace of Spellstorm pistols in rapid succession like a fiery tornado of death.

Caine makes a Spellstorm Pistol attack against every enemy model currently in his control area. Caine must have LOS to a model to target it. When using Maelstrom, Caine's front arc extends 360°. These attack and damage rolls may be boosted normally. If Caine forfeited his movement to gain an aiming bonus this activation, he gains +2 to Maelstrom attack rolls. Caine cannot use Maelstrom if he is in melee.

CAINE

CRACK SHOT - Caine's targets do not benefit from being screened.

SPELLSTORM PISTOL

RANGE AMPLIFIER - Caine's Spellstorm Pistols add 5" to the range of all spells cast directly from him. Channeled spells do not benefit from Range Amplifier.

SPELL	COST	RNG	AOE	POW	UP	OFF
ARCANE BLAST	3	10	3	13		X
A magical energy blast radiates from a single point to strike all models in the AOE.						
BLUR	2	6	—	—	X	
Target model/unit gains +3 DEF against ranged attacks.						
DEADEYE	2	6	—	—		
Target model/unit rolls an additional die on each model's first ranged attack roll this turn.						
FLASH	2	SELF	—	—		
Place Caine at any location within his control area with no greater than a 5" change in elevation from his current location, then his activation ends. There must be room for his base at the new location.						
SNIPE	*	6	—	—		X
For each focus point spent when Snipe is cast, increase the RNG of target model/unit's ranged weapons by 1.						
THUNDER STRIKE	4	8	—	*		X
Target model hit by Thunder Strike is slammed d6" directly away from the spell's point of origin and suffers a POW 14 damage roll. If the slammed model collides with another model with an equal or smaller-sized base, that model suffers a POW 14 collateral damage roll.						

TACTICAL TIPS

MAELSTROM – Using Maelstrom, Caine can mow down several ranks of troopers, one rank at a time. Determine LOS to each target at the moment of the attack. No, Snipe does not extend the range of Maelstrom. If Caine uses Maelstrom and is later in melee due to enemy models moving into melee range of him, Caine can no longer make Maelstrom ranged attacks.

THUNDER STRIKE – Thunder Strike's collateral damage is not considered to be damage caused by a magic attack. Thunder Strike does not affect incorporeal models.

CAPTAIN VICTORIA HALEY

Burn the dead, consecrate the bones, and render them to ashes lest they return to haunt us.

—Captain Haley after a decisive victory over a Cryxian invasion force

A calculating woman capable of both harshness and heroism, the grim Victoria Haley was born in Ingrane, a small but once thriving fishing village on the western coast of Cygnar, north of Frog's Bight. Her parents were simple fishing folk who lived a hard life to provide for Victoria and her twin sister. Their lives were seemingly normal, and it would have stayed that way were it not for the dreaded Cryx.

The girls were just five summers old in late spring of 584 AR when raiders from the Scharde Islands landed during the night on the wooden docks of Ingrane. They charged into the peaceful village and met little resistance. During the raid, Haley's father ran to confront the pillagers only to be cut down while her mother tried to hide Victoria and her sister in the clay-carved fruit cellar of their villa. She barely had enough time to push Victoria down the trap door before the Cryx battered their way inside. The door slammed shut and Victoria watched through the gaping floorboards as her mother was murdered and her sister was snatched up and spirited away into the night.

Today nothing but dark memories and restless spirits live in the ruins of Ingrane. The violence that took place

during that raid has somehow refused to be forgotten, and now the village is a place of shadowy things where icy winds howl down from the high bluffs and across the necks of travelers and sailors who venture too near.

The survivors of that night gathered together and made the leaden voyage through moors and woods to Ramarck. Victoria Haley was one of those grief-stricken few. An elderly woman bore the girl the distance to the city, but she could not care for the youth despite her best efforts. A Morrowan seminary eventually took in the girl. She was given education and not treated unkindly, but it was not a life for her. At thirteen summers, Victoria fled the school, made her way to New Larkholm, and found employ as a fishmonger's assistant on the docks.

One afternoon in the marketplace with her employer, a laboring steamjack went haywire and ran amuck. It careened through dockside pier-houses like a giant metal berserker, but as its shadow fell over Victoria, she screamed out in terror for the 'jack to stop—and it did. It froze mid-swing with its riveted fist a mere foot away from her blonde head. She wiped away her tears of shock, brushed her apron flat, and quietly whispered for the steamjack to return to its owner; this, too, it did. The two of them represented a paradox of frailty and strength, and walking alongside the metal giant, Victoria never felt so in control of her world. Two years later in 599 A.R. at the age of 20, she was among the ranks of the Cygnaran army as a powerful warrior and a determined warcaster.

Captain Victoria Haley has a furious loathing for anything Cryxian. Where the pirate armies assemble she is soon found throwing everything at her disposal toward the undying hordes. It is not hard for her to find targets for her vengeance. She has in some way attracted the attention of a particular warwitch who goes by the name Deneghra. This Cryxian minion seems bent on destroying Captain Haley as much as the reverse is true. Deneghra moves to block Haley's every move, and their forces have collided more than once in bloody conflict.

Given the recent aspirations of the warwitch to confront Haley directly, the captain has had a special piece of mechanikal weaponry added to her personal arsenal—the vortex spear. In her hands it is a blindingly fast weapon engraved with ancient runes of protection that merge with those of her armor to make her impervious to the ravaging

magic of her enemies. Though their forces have clashed more than once, never have Haley and Deneghra met face-to-face in battle. It is safe to assume only one of them would walk away from such a meeting. Captain Haley's motives are clear: there will never be enough blood shed for what the minions of Lord Toruk took from her on the bluffs of Ingrane years ago.

Focus 7				Cmd 8	
SPD	STR	MAT	RAT	DEF	ARM
6	5	6	5	16	14

Hand Cannon

RNG	ROF	AOE	POW
12	1	—	12

Vortex Spear

SPECIAL	POW	P+S
Multi	6	11

Damage	15
Point Cost	58
Field Allowance	C
Victory Points	5
Base Size	Small

SPECIAL RULES

FEAT: BLITZ

Though she generally prefers a regimented and conservative approach to battle, Captain Haley is capable of launching a massive unified assault with a single command. Carefully conserving the energy and resources of her forces, Haley will trigger a deadly offense at precisely the right moment.

Friendly Cygnaran models currently in Haley's control area may make one additional attack this turn with no additional focus required, regardless of a weapon's ROF.

VORTEX SPEAR

ARCANE VORTEX - Haley may negate any spell that targets a model within 3", including herself, as it is being cast by spending one focus point. The negated spell does not take effect, but its focus cost is still spent. Haley can use Arcane Vortex at any time as long as she has focus points to spend.

REACH - 2" melee range.

SET DEFENSE - Haley gains +2 DEF against charge and slam attacks originating from her front arc.

SPELL	COST	RNG	AOE	POW	UP	OFF
ARCANE BOLT	2	12	—	11		X
Magical bolts of energy streak toward the target model.						
ARCANE SHIELD	2	8	—	—	X	
Surrounded by a magical barrier, target model/unit gains +3 ARM.						
CHAIN LIGHTNING	3	10	—	10		X
Lightning arcs from target model to d6 additional models. The lightning arcs and automatically hits the nearest model within 4" of the last model hit, but it cannot strike the same model more than once. Each model hit suffers a POW 10 damage roll.						
DEADEYE	2	6	—	—		X
Target model/unit rolls an additional die on each model's first ranged attack roll this turn.						
DISRUPTOR	3	8	—	—		X
Target warjack suffers Disruption. A warjack suffering Disruption loses any unused focus points and cannot be allocated focus points or channel spells for one round.						
SCRAMBLE	3	10	—	—		X
During its controller's next Maintenance Phase, target warjack activates and runs in a random direction, moving through warrior models in its path if it has enough movement to move completely past their bases. Models moved through are knocked down. The scrambled warjack ends its movement and is knocked down if it contacts an obstruction, another warjack, or a warbeast. The scrambled warjack cannot activate again this turn.						
TEMPORAL BARRIER	4	SELF	CTRL	—		
Enemy models currently in Haley's control area move at half rate and suffer −3 DEF for one round. Affected models cannot charge or slam.						

TACTICAL TIPS

ARCANE VORTEX – If part of a unit is within 3" of Haley, target a trooper farther away with a unit-affecting spell so that she can't negate it.

SCRAMBLE – When a knocked down warjack is affected by Scramble, it activates and does nothing.

COMMANDER COLEMAN STRYKER

Coleman in a word? Patriot.

—Captain Victoria Haley

Coleman Stryker was a mere nineteen years old when King Leto took the throne in 594 A.R. He was there during the palace revolt serving in the Royal Guard under a captain who fought and died for Leto in the coup. Even by that time the first hints of his sorcerous ability had begun to manifest, but the young guardsman was uncomfortable with his powers. When the fighting from the coup ended, Stryker volunteered to continue direct service to King Leto in his guard, but fate and the eye of an older warcaster decided otherwise.

The commander and adept named Sebastian Nemo suggested to the king that the young patriot become a Stormblade. To young Stryker it seemed a demotion, not a

reward; he had hoped to serve the king directly. However, his elders had a plan and knew the promising warrior needed seasoning in the field by serving as an active soldier on the front line. It was a path that would shape him into the man he would become.

It took time for the flame-haired youth to find his niche in the army, but his natural leadership qualities emerged and he was soon promoted. While leading a squad of the Stormblade garrison at Fort Falk, he was tasked to conduct a forced relocation of mercenary bandits near the city of Corvis, and it was there that Stryker's destiny took a turn. The Stormblades squared off against a charterless mercenary camp lawfully evicted from the area. Tensions were high. The

meeting escalated from threats to swordplay, and during the melee, Stryker's storm glaive was batted away. Disarmed, he raised his gauntleted fists at his attacker and drew on the mechanikal energies in his unit's storm glaives. Coleman Stryker loosed an arcane bolt of great magnitude that instantly ended the conflict. It was an unmistakable manifestation of the sorcery Stryker had been struggling to suppress.

Seeing his potential, Stryker's superiors sent him back for proper training at the Strategic Academy in Caspia where tests proved he was also manifesting the highly prized warcaster ability. Now under the direct tutelage of Commander Adept Nemo, he developed his abilities to control the enormous Cygnaran warjacks. They obeyed him with uncanny precision, and he demonstrated none of the usual fumbling and uncertainties of other young warcasters. During his first few months, Coleman Stryker set out on border errands alongside his commander as a journeyman. As if Morrow himself were guiding him, Stryker met and overcame challenge after challenge for king and country.

It was with no small measure of pride that his mentor pronounced him ready to hold his own as a full warcaster. His name spread around the villages and towns, and words soon became cheers wherever he went. With every enemy defeated, Stryker gained the admiration of the Cygnaran people, and they strengthened his faith with every smiling face and sobbing thank you. He has accepted their thanks and praises gladly, and he is able to put aside the harrowing images of warfare using the comfort he finds in their support. He has had to kill many enemy soldiers and seen close friends die ugly deaths, and at times their faces haunt his thoughts, but he knows sacrifice is necessary to preserve the nation he loves.

For many Stryker has become the ideal most Cygnaran youths idolize. His is a leader's role, and he likes nothing better than to direct from the front lines. Nothing pleases him more than wading into battle to test the limits of his skills. Wherever there are border conflicts or bandit insurrections, Stryker is always there seeking to preserve the realm. His dedication to Cygnar's defense allowed him to advance rapidly through the ranks from captain, to major, and then to colonel.

Stryker lost the last remnant of his past as a Stormblade when he lost his trusty storm glaive in a battle against a Khadoran Juggernaut. Its previously imperishable edge shattered in the final great blow that demolished the stubborn metal giant. Soon after the battle, mechaniks forged a new

technology with an innovative arcane disruption. The prototypes took the form of a pistol and the masterfully crafted greatsword Quicksilver. He received the weapons as part of his promotion to commander in the king's army—a rank he achieved at a relatively young age. King Leto himself was present for Stryker's promotion, reaffirming personally that this warcaster was the nation's finest young battlefield leader.

Stryker seems a fiery youth compared to the aged veteran commanders and generals leading the majority of King Leto's army. His brashness is tempered by battlefield experience, and he sees himself as just another soldier fighting for the crown. Commander Stryker goes to great lengths to preserve the lives of his men, for he has watched too many enemy blades and shells cut down his friends. He has gone so far as to sacrifice expensive warjacks to spare soldiers under his command to the chagrin of the treasury in Caspia. A fine leader, a better soldier, and one of the finest warcasters in the Iron Kingdoms, Coleman Stryker was born for Cygnar and will die defending her. He would have it no other way.

SPECIAL RULES

FEAT: INVINCIBILITY

Commander Stryker is renowned for his strategic prowess and his ability to maneuver his assets on the battlefield. Even in the face of relentless onslaught, the commander's plans rarely falter.

Friendly Cygnar models currently in Stryker's control area gain +5 ARM for one round.

DISRUPTOR PISTOL & QUICKSILVER

DISRUPTION - Warjacks suffer Disruption when hit by Quicksilver or Stryker's Disruptor Pistol. A warjack suffering Disruption loses any unused focus points and cannot be allocated focus points or channel spells for one round.

Focus 6				Cmd 9	
SPD	STR	MAT	RAT	DEF	ARM
6	6	6	6	16	15

Disruptor Pistol			
RNG	ROF	AOE	POW
10	1	—	10

Quicksilver		
SPECIAL	POW	P+S
Disrupt	7	13

Damage	17
Point Cost	64
Field Allowance	C
Victory Points	5
Base Size	Small

SPELL	COST	RNG	AOE	POW	UP	OFF
ARCANE BLAST	3	10	3	13		X
A magical energy blast radiates from a single point to strike all models in the AOE.						
ARCANE BOLT	2	12	—	11		X
Magical bolts of energy streak toward the target model.						
ARCANE SHIELD	2	8	—	—	X	
Surrounded by a magical barrier, target model/unit gains +3 ARM.						
BLUR	2	6	—	—	X	
Target model/unit gains +3 DEF against ranged attacks.						
EARTHQUAKE	3	10	5	—		X
Models in Earthquake's AOE are knocked down.						
SNIPE	*	6	—	—	X	
For each focus point spent when Snipe is cast, increase the RNG of target model/unit's ranged weapons by 1.						

TACTICAL TIP

BLUR – Blur affords no protection against magic attacks.

CHARGER
CYGNAR LIGHT WARJACK

More Chargers have rolled off Cygnaran factory assembly lines and been hammered together in far-flung steamjack shops than any other light warjack in history. Even as other designs have gone into production, commanders continue to rely on the Charger to bring versatility to the modern battlefield. This mainstay remains a dependable element stationed at nearly every forward post of the army.

The combination of a powerful and reasonably accurate light dual cannon and a weighty battle hammer allows this 'jack to operate with equal comfort at range or in close melee. Many journeyman warcasters

If the first shot doesn't get them, the second one will.
—Commander Coleman Stryker

have cut their teeth with Chargers in tow by sending them forward to blast shells into oncoming infantry and support the advance of heavier warjacks.

The Charger was an evolution of the same mobility system found on the old reliable Talon, its immediate predecessor. The original Talon chassis had powerful pistons and a compact steam engine capable of driving the 'jack forward at surprising speeds, and it was improved for the Charger with greater articulation and the ability to react to threats in combat. The Charger boasts an accurate dual-shot cannon that borrows the reloading assembly developed for the Defender's heavy barrel but adds a recoil-based mechanism that readies the cannon for the second shot.

The Charger retains the sturdy armored protection of the Talon and is covered in a shell of tight-fitting interlocked plates. The reliable 'jack is an economical combination of speed, durability, and firepower that Cygnar will continue to exercise as a mainstay for years to come.

SPD	STR	MAT	RAT	DEF	ARM
6	8	5	5	13	16

L — Dual Cannon

RNG	ROF	AOE	POW
12	2	—	12

R — Battle Hammer

SPECIAL	POW	P+S
—	4	12

Point Cost	75
Field Allowance	U
Victory Points	2
Base Size	Medium

HEIGHT/WEIGHT: 8'7" / 3.2 tons

ARMAMENT: Dual Cannon (left arm), Battle Hammer (right arm)

FUEL LOAD/BURN USAGE: 297 lbs/ 5 hrs general, 45 min combat

INITIAL SERVICE DATE: 567 AR

CORTEX MANUFACTURER: Fraternal Order of Wizardry

ORIG. CHASSIS DESIGN: Cygnaran Armory

TACTICAL TIP

DUAL CANNON – Remember that the Charger has to spend a focus point to take its second shot with the Dual Cannon.

LANCER
CYGNAR LIGHT WARJACK

The Lancer is the most perfect tool of war at our disposal. Give me half-a-dozen, and keep the factories cranking.

—Captain Victoria Haley

The development of the arc node has been among the most significant advances in modern warfare since the dawn of the warjack itself. A device of unquestionable martial utility, the arc node allows a warcaster to dominate by extending his arcane reach across the battlefield.

The secrets of the precursor arcantrik relay were initially developed and held exclusively by Cygnar for decades, but it was Cryx who would first put them to proper use. Having plundered arc node technology from the rifled graves of Cygnar's most ingenious inventors, the Cryxian necrotechs integrated the devices into light and mobile 'jacks that could run circles around the warjacks of the day.

For years before the implementation of the Lancer, Cygnaran warcasters stationed at Highgate complained about lacking a proper arcane relay. Cygnaran mechaniks originally pioneered the field of arcane relays with such 'jack designs as the Javelin used in the Thornwood War and the Arcane of later years, but those chassis were fragile and antiquated relics of another era. After several decisive Cryxian victories in the region, King Leto pressured Warmaster General Turpin to heed the reports and then challenged the Royal Cygnaran University to provide a better delivery vehicle for the costly arc node.

Seamlessly adapted from the reliable Charger chassis, the Lancer is the rugged yet agile masterpiece resulting from Leto's challenge. The Lancer was developed with an emphasis on defense and survivability to ensure the machine would succeed in its primary application—to move into position and allow its warcaster to rain arcane fury on enemy lines. The machine's main weapon is a heavy spear designed to keep adversaries

LANCER

ARC NODE - The Lancer may channel spells.

SHOCK SHIELD

SHOCK FIELD - If the Lancer hits a warjack with the Shock Shield, or if the Lancer is hit by a warjack with a melee weapon and its Shock Shield is not disabled by the attack, its opponent takes one damage point to its first available Cortex system box. When the Lancer attacks with the Shock Shield, mark this damage before making the damage roll.

WAR SPEAR

REACH - 2" melee range.

SET DEFENSE - The Lancer gains +2 DEF against charge and slam attacks originating from its front arc.

> **TACTICAL TIP**
> SHOCK SHIELD – A good way to avoid this cortex damage is to lock the Lancer's shield arm first.

at bay, and its sturdy shield generates a shock field capable of burning out a warjack cortex on contact. These innovations are the basis for arguably the most valued light warjack in the Cygnaran arsenal.

SPD	STR	MAT	RAT	DEF	ARM
6	8	5	5	13	16
					18

L — Shock Shield

	SPECIAL	POW	P+S
	Shock Field	1	9

R — War Spear

	SPECIAL	POW	P+S
	Multi	4	12

1	2	3	4	5	6
	L	A	A	R	
L	L	M	C	R	R
	M	M	C	C	

Point Cost	76
Field Allowance	U
Victory Points	2
Base Size	Medium

HEIGHT/WEIGHT: 9'1" / 3.25 tons

ARMAMENT: War Spear (right arm), Shock Shield (left arm), Grade VII Arc Node

FUEL LOAD/BURN USAGE: 363 lbs/ 9 hrs general, 1.5 hrs combat

INITIAL SERVICE DATE: 601 AR

CORTEX MANUFACTURER: Cygnar Armory

ORIG. CHASSIS DESIGN: Cygnaran Mechaniks Coalition at the Royal Cygnaran University

SENTINEL
CYGNAR LIGHT WARJACK

CHAIN GUN

AUTOMATIC FIRE - The Sentinel gains +2 on additional Strafe attack rolls.

STRAFE (D6) — A single attack with the Chain Gun has the potential to hit its target and several nearby models. First, make a normal ranged attack against an eligible target. If the initial attack hits, roll a d6 to determine the number of additional attacks the initial attack generates, then allocate those attacks among the original target and any models within 2" of it, ignoring intervening models when determining line of sight. Each model may be targeted by more than one attack but cannot be targeted by more attacks than the initial target, including the original Chain Gun attack. A model is ineligible to become a new target if it has a special rule preventing it from being targeted or if the Sentinel's line of sight is completely blocked by terrain. Make separate ranged attack and damage rolls for each Strafe attack generated. Completely resolve each attack individually and apply the targets' special rules immediately as each attack is resolved. Determine damage normally.

The Sentinel is an example of daring design demonstrating revolutionary weapons concepts that have since found other expressions on the battlefield. Even detractors grudgingly admit the inventor of the chain gun was decades ahead of his time. The warjack has taken a dominant role on the battlefield against clusters of infantry, making it valuable whether defending the northern borders against charging platoons of Winter Guard or holding the eastern border against an unending tide of Menite zealots.

SPD	STR	MAT	RAT	DEF	ARM
6	8	5	5	13	16
					18

L Assault Shield

	SPECIAL	POW	P+S
	—	2	10

R Chain Gun

RNG	ROF	AOE	POW
10	1	—	10

1	2	3	4	5	6
		L		R	
L	L	M	C	R	R
	M	M	C	C	

Point Cost	72
Field Allowance	U
Victory Points	2
Base Size	Medium

HEIGHT/WEIGHT: 8'6" / 2.45 tons

ARMAMENT: Assault Shield (left arm), Chain Gun (right arm)

FUEL LOAD/BURN USAGE: 154 lbs / 8 hrs general, 1.3 hrs combat

INITIAL SERVICE DATE: 573 AR

CORTEX MANUFACTURER: Cygnaran Armory

ORIG. CHASSIS DESIGN: Albere Gungria, arcane mechanik at Royal Cygnaran University

I'd give my left jewel for a pair of those.

—Lt. Allister Caine

It was the invention of the chain gun that set this warjack apart. Its intricate machinery was well beyond what had been seen until that point. Designed by the genius Albere Gungria, a member of the engineering department of the Royal University of Cygnar and consultant to its Strategic Academy, the weapon's innovative design was the first to feature brass casings that allowed rapid belt-fed ammunition. This development was radical in its day, and it seems likely more weapons will benefit from the design in time. Some criticized the cost of producing ammunition of this sort, but they were silenced once they witnessed the whirling barrels of a multi-bore chaingun strafing through multiple targets in seconds. The notion of using a spinning cluster of gun barrels had never been conceived before. The initial design suffered from overheating, but a snug heat dispersal cowling atop the mechanism quickly fixed the problem.

Closing with the Sentinel will cost enemies dearly as they are forced to endure an unremitting hail of shot. Those within striking range of the machine soon discover the crushing power of its assault shield when the warjack's two and a half tons of bulk are thrown behind it. The warjack has found a niche when deployed in the hands of cunning warcasters who know how to exploit its tremendous firepower.

TACTICAL TIP

STRAFE — The additional Strafe attacks can be allocated to models that are beyond the Chain Gun's maximum range

DEFENDER
CYGNAR HEAVY WARJACK

Today we have revolutionized warfare. With the Defender there is no need to wait to see the whites of their eyes. We will engage the enemy before he realizes the battle has begun.

—Lord General Everett Cathmore after observing field trials, 563 AR

SHOCK HAMMER

CRITICAL CORTEX DAMAGE - On a critical hit, target warjack automatically takes one damage point to its first available Cortex system box. Mark this damage before making the damage roll.

The Defender is a stout heavy warjack boasting unprecedented long-range and accurate firepower while remaining equally effective in melee. It is a warjack no enemy can ignore, and it is as dangerous at a distance as it is when it closes.

The design of the Defender marks a significant change in Cygnaran military tactics clearly demonstrated in the differences between its function and that of its predecessor, the Mule. None will dispute that the Mule, still utilized by mercenaries today, is an effective warjack boasting remarkable longevity, but the Mule's enormous explosive blasts are somewhat inaccurate and unpredictable, and its range is short particularly while the Mule is on the move. During the reign of Vinter III after bloody clashes with Khador along the northern border, Cygnaran generals wanted to annihilate their foes well before they could engage and demanded more accurate and longer-ranged firepower. The Cygnaran armory delivered by modifying the chassis of the Ironclad to create a uniquely powerful warjack that has yet to be surpassed in its role on the battlefield.

The Defender's primary weapon is the enormous heavy barrel, a deceptively advanced cannon mounted in place of the warjack's arm. In addition to a rapid reloading mechanism, the cannon has mechanikal stability enhancements; when run by the machine's advanced cortex, it is accurate at unprecedented ranges. The armory also provided the 'jack with an exceptional melee weapon featuring an electrical jolt that can cause immediate damage to an enemy cortex.

SPD	STR	MAT	RAT	DEF	ARM
5	11	6	5	12	18

L — Heavy Barrel

RNG	ROF	AOE	POW
16	1	—	14

R — Shock Hammer

SPECIAL	POW	P+S
Critical	5	16

	1	2	3	4	5	6
			L		R	
	L	L	M	C	R	R
		M	M	C	C	

Point Cost	122
Field Allowance	U
Victory Points	3
Base Size	Large

HEIGHT/WEIGHT: 12'2" / 6.5 tons

ARMAMENT: Heavy Barrel (left arm), Shock Hammer (right arm)

FUEL LOAD/BURN USAGE: 655 lbs/ 5 hrs general, 45 min combat

INITIAL SERVICE DATE: 564 AR

CORTEX MANUFACTURER: Fraternal Order of Wizardry

ORIG. CHASSIS DESIGN: Cygnaran Armory

IRONCLAD
CYGNAR HEAVY WARJACK

QUAKE HAMMER

CRITICAL KNOCKDOWN - On a critical hit, target model is knocked down.

TREMOR (★ATTACK) - Roll 2d6 and add the weapon's POW. This roll cannot be boosted. Compare the result to the DEF of every model within 2". These models are knocked down if the total equals or exceeds their DEF. This effect causes no damage. A Tremor special attack cannot be made after a charge. A Tremor special attack does not need a target.

Six tons of iron rumbling across a battlefield then hammering the ground hard enough to knock a 'jack on its exhaust pipes? That's what I call a warjack. Pure perfection.

—Gamack Redhammer, Engines East, Corvis

The most recognized heavy 'jack in the Cygnaran arsenal, the Ironclad is a walking behemoth of metal twice the height of a man. Gigantic smokestacks blow sooty "breath" from its heartfire's furnace, and its face grille emits a bright orange glow giving it a fearsome demeanor. Armed with a powerful quake hammer, the Ironclad effortlessly smashes lesser combatants to scrap with its massive blows. Even heavy warjacks have been known to crumble after a single strike from its thunderous hammer. The Ironclad's durable armor—smelted from the kingdom's highest grade iron—provides fantastic protection from all but the most powerful impacts.

When it came time to upgrade Cygnar's front line heavy warjack in the 550s, the lucrative contract went to the well established Engines East in Corvis, an independent but solid shop which had earned its fame a century earlier creating several of Cygnar's mainstays, including the Mule and the Nomad. Engines East based its older models like the Nomad on the old fundamental principles found in mundane laborjacks, but they built the Ironclad from the start to be a walking wall of unyielding metal. It bore some outward similarities to its predecessor, but it exceeded the Nomad in every regard.

The two most notable advances are the use of a more sophisticated cortex allowing considerably better performance in combat and the impressive addition of its signature quake hammer. Even when completely surrounded, the Ironclad can seize victory by shattering the earth with its hammer and causing all surrounding enemies to tumble to the ground. The Ironclad was made strong, durable, and capable of removing any obstacle from its warcaster's path, be it boulder or building, wall or warjack. If an Ironclad cannot break something, it is safe to say it cannot be broken.

SPD	STR	MAT	RAT	DEF	ARM
5	11	6	5	12	18

L Quake Hammer

	SPECIAL	POW	P+S
	Multi	7	18

R Open Fist

	SPECIAL	POW	P+S
	—	0	11

1	2	3	4	5	6
	L			R	
L	L	M	C	R	R
	M	M	C	C	

Point Cost	103
Field Allowance	U
Victory Points	3
Base Size	Large

HEIGHT/WEIGHT: 12'3" / 6 tons

ARMAMENT: Quake Hammer (left arm)

FUEL LOAD/BURN USAGE: 582 lbs / 6 hrs general, 1 hr combat

INITIAL SERVICE DATE: 556 AR

CORTEX MANUFACTURER: Fraternal Order of Wizardry/Cygnaran Armory

ORIG. CHASSIS DESIGN: Engines East

> *One gun mage is a terror, but an army of gun mages has never been seen before now. Let our enemies quake before your thunder!*
>
> —Warmaster General Laddermore at the founding of the Militant Order of the Arcane Tempest

MAGELOCK PISTOL

ARCANE EFFECT - Each time a Magelock Pistol is used to make a ranged attack, choose one of the following effects:

- **DETONATOR** - On a critical hit, the Detonator explodes inside its target. Roll damage normally, then make a second POW 10 damage roll and add an additional die to the roll.

- **SHOCKER** - Target warjack hit by this attack automatically takes one damage point to its first available Cortex system box. Mark this damage before making the damage roll.

- **THUNDERBOLT** - An enemy model hit by this attack is pushed directly back d3". On a critical hit, target model is also knocked down. A pushed model moves at half rate in rough terrain and stops if it contacts an obstacle, obstruction, or model. The pushed model cannot be targeted by free strikes during this movement.

LIEUTENANT

ARCANE INFERNO (ORDER) - Every Gun Mage that received the order who is in an open formation group with the Lieutenant may combine his fire at the same target as the Lieutenant. Make one attack roll using the Lieutenant's RAT, adding +1 to the attack roll for each Gun Mage participating in the attack, including the Lieutenant. The Arcane Inferno attack is a POW 14 ranged attack with a 3"AOE and may not include an Arcane Effect. Arcane Inferno requires at least three Arcane Tempest Gun Mages.

LEADER

Lieutenant				Cmd 8	
SPD	STR	MAT	RAT	DEF	ARM
6	4	5	7	15	12
Gun Mage				Cmd 6	
SPD	STR	MAT	RAT	DEF	ARM
6	4	4	6	15	12

Magelock Pistol			
RNG	ROF	AOE	POW
12	1	—	10

Sword		
SPECIAL	POW	P+S
—	3	7

Leader and 5 Troops	90
Field Allowance	1
Victory Points	2
Base Size	Small

For over two decades the Militant Order of the Arcane Tempest has trained sorcerers to harness their unique powers. The Tempest teaches members to carve runes of power into bullets and focus arcane energies as they fire their pistols. Their magelock pistols are exceptional weapons crafted from an expensive steel alloy noted to be particularly responsive to arcane energies. In the hands of members of the Arcane Tempest, these pistols bring deadly firepower and versatility and have proven worthy of their expense.

When gun mages of the Arcane Tempest march to join their comrades on the front line, the impact is profound. The sight of Tempest uniforms inspires immediate confidence and the mages' rune-covered pistols portend the pyrotechnics to come as these elite gunslingers spring into deadly action. Working as a smoothly-oiled machine, they unleash a hail of deadly bullets enchanted by their unique sorcery. Their power can hurl enemy warjacks back with a rumble of booming thunder while others crackle and smoke as their cortexes become fried. Soldiers struck are torn apart from within by bullets that can detonate on impact with brutal killing power.

Since the invention of the firearm, only a few have been born with the talent to become gun mages. Such sorcerers feel an instant affinity with pistols and an urge to extend their power through the gun's barrel. Only recently organized by the Cygnaran military, this once secret and exclusive fellowship of duelists has been absorbed into the ranks as gun mages. Instructors at the Tempest Academy temper talent with discipline and instill each gun mage with patriotism and utter loyalty to the crown.

Gun mages must earn the right to wield the magelock pistol and wear the uniform of their order. Each gun mage force works as a precision team to take down any adversary by attacking with coordinated strikes that can cripple warjack cortexes, knock enemies away from their intended targets, and tear entire ranks of soldiers to shreds with an inferno of concentrated arcane fire.

TACTICAL TIP

ARCANE INFERNO – Unlike a combined ranged attack, Arcane Inferno can target a model in melee.

FIELD MECHANIKS
CYGNAR UNIT

CREW CHIEF

'JACK MARSHAL (1) — The Crew Chief may start the game controlling one Cygnar warjack. The Crew Chief has a marshalling range equal to his CMD in inches. If a controlled warjack is in the Crew Chief's marshalling range, it can run, charge, or boost an attack or damage roll once per activation. If the Crew Chief is destroyed or removed from play, warjacks under his control do not become inert. The Crew Chief may reactivate one friendly inert Cygnar warjack per turn in the same manner as a warcaster. The reactivated warjack comes under his control unless he already controls 1 other warjack.

LEADER

REPAIR [9] (★ACTION) - A Field Mechanik may attempt repairs on any friendly Cygnar warjack that has been damaged or disabled. To attempt repairs, the Field

Crew Chief				Cmd 7	
SPD	STR	MAT	RAT	DEF	ARM
5	4	3	4	12	11

Gobber Bodger				Cmd 4	
SPD	STR	MAT	RAT	DEF	ARM
6	2	2	2	15	9

Rivet Gun			
RNG	ROF	AOE	POW
4	1	—	10

Monkey Wrench		
SPECIAL	POW	P+S
—	2	6/4

Leader and 3 Troops	16
Up to 2 Additional Troops	2ea
Field Allowance	3
Victory Points	2
Base Size	Small

There's nothing heavier, more expensive, or more useless than a disabled warjack a hundred miles from home.

—Commander Coleman Stryker

Mechanik must be in base-to-base contact with the damaged warjack or disabled wreck marker and make a skill check. If successful, roll a d6 and remove that number of damage points from anywhere on the warjack's damage grid.

GOBBER BODGER

ASSIST REPAIR [+2] (★ACTION) - Every Gobber Bodger assisting the Chief with a repair adds +2 to the Crew Chief's Repair skill, up to a maximum of 11. A Gobber Bodger must be in base-to-base contact with the warjack being repaired by the Crew Chief in order to assist.

REPAIR [5] (★ACTION) - Same as Chief, above.

RIVET GUN (CREW CHIEF ONLY)

Armor gets mangled. Firearms misfire. Warjacks break down.

All of these things could spell doom to a battlefield commander if it were not for the mechaniks who brave the combat zone. Mechaniks wear little in the way of armor so they can move quickly and get into position to make necessary repairs. They perform miraculous fixes on non-

functioning mechanika, and many battles have been turned around at the moment of defeat by a returning warjack that was believed destroyed just moments earlier.

A mechanik's pockets, pouches, and satchels overflow with extra parts and tools. Any self-respecting field mechanik can never have enough extra gear, for not having a single specific piece might mean disaster for hundreds of men. It is why they keep company with the ever-present and ever-willing gobber bodgers.

A gobber loves to tinker no matter what, where, or how. Bodgers earn a pittance in comparison to the dangers they endure to carry extra parts and tools for their mechanik employers. To them, however, the adventure and excitement is at least half the pay although the buggers are often known for tossing equipment and diving for cover until danger has passed.

TACTICAL TIP

ASSIST REPAIR — Note that a Gobber Bodger doesn't make a skill check himself when assisting. He simply adds +2 to the Chief's skill score. Also note that a Gobber Bodger cannot assist another Gobber Bodger with a repair attempt.

> *I heard they were going to start taking missed shots out of our wages.*
>
> *Well, I reckon we don't miss then.*
>
> —Two long gunners conversing at the Falling Star tavern

Since the advent of the long gun, Cygnar has assembled skilled riflemen to support its vast armies. Originally the guns were muzzleloaders, and gunners had to load each ball down the barrel by hand. They had to line up in pairs with one gunner shooting while the other reloaded. In time gunsmiths introduced the breechloader. It vastly improved the rate of fire and eliminated the need for firing in pairs. More recently the ammo wheel has come into use by which single gunners can cycle up to six preloaded shots by cranking a lever atop the gun.

Long gunners make up the majority of Cygnar's rank and file soldiers, and they represent Cygnar's relatively modern focus on outfitting its army with the best weapons for war. Rifles were once seen only in small squads providing support

SERGEANT
LEADER

UNIT
COMBINED RANGED ATTACK - Instead of making ranged attacks separately, two or more Long Gunners may combine their attacks against the same target. In order to participate in a combined ranged attack, a Long Gunner must be able to declare a ranged attack against the intended target and be in a single open formation group with the other participants. The Long Gunner with the highest RAT in the attacking group makes one ranged attack roll for the group and gains +1 to the attack and damage rolls for each Long Gunner, including himself, participating in the attack.

DUAL SHOT - A Long Gunner may voluntarily forfeit his movement to make one additional ranged attack this turn. These attacks receive the aiming bonus.

Sergeant				Cmd 8	
SPD	STR	MAT	RAT	DEF	ARM
5	4	4	5	13	12

Gunner				Cmd 6	
SPD	STR	MAT	RAT	DEF	ARM
5	4	4	4	13	12

Repeating Long Gun			
RNG	ROF	AOE	POW
14	2	—	10

Sword		
SPECIAL	POW	P+S
—	3	7

Leader and 5 Troops	64
Up to 4 Additional Troops	10ea
Field Allowance	2
Victory Points	2
Base Size	Small

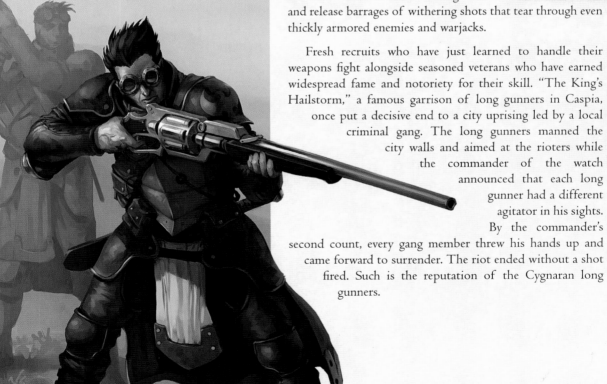

fire to the main line soldiers, but now they are the force upon which Cygnar relies to man its garrisons and defend its borders. Working together with squads of hardened Trenchers, the long gunners symbolize the modern face of the Cygnaran soldier. They are well trained in concentrating their fire and release barrages of withering shots that tear through even thickly armored enemies and warjacks.

Fresh recruits who have just learned to handle their weapons fight alongside seasoned veterans who have earned widespread fame and notoriety for their skill. "The King's Hailstorm," a famous garrison of long gunners in Caspia, once put a decisive end to a city uprising led by a local criminal gang. The long gunners manned the city walls and aimed at the rioters while the commander of the watch announced that each long gunner had a different agitator in his sights. By the commander's second count, every gang member threw his hands up and came forward to surrender. The riot ended without a shot fired. Such is the reputation of the Cygnaran long gunners.

STORMBLADES
CYGNAR UNIT

SERGEANT
LEADER

UNIT
COMBINED MELEE ATTACK - Instead of making melee attacks separately, two or more Stormblades in melee range of the same target may combine their attacks. In order to participate in a combined melee attack, a Stormblade must be able to declare a melee attack against the intended target. The Stormblade with the highest MAT in the attacking group makes one melee attack roll for the group and gains +1 to the attack and damage rolls for each Stormblade, including himself, participating in the attack.

FEARLESS - A Stormblade never flees.

Sergeant					Cmd 8	
SPD	STR	MAT	RAT	DEF	ARM	
5	6	8	5	13	15	

Knight					Cmd 6	
SPD	STR	MAT	RAT	DEF	ARM	
5	6	7	4	13	15	

Storm Rod Blast			
RNG	ROF	AOE	POW
6	1	—	14

Storm Rod		
SPECIAL	POW	P+S
—	9	15

Storm Glaive Blast			
RNG	ROF	AOE	POW
4	1	—	12

Storm Glaive		
SPECIAL	POW	P+S
—	7	13

Leader and 5 Troops	84
Field Allowance	2
Victory Points	2
Base Size	Small

STORM ROD BLAST (SERGEANT ONLY)
STORM ROD (SERGEANT ONLY)
ELECTRICAL ARC - The Storm Rod adds +2 RNG and +2 POW to each of its unit's Storm Glaives whose wielders are in an open formation group with the Sergeant.

STORM GLAIVE BLAST (KNIGHT ONLY)
STORM GLAIVE (KNIGHT ONLY)

Stormblades are men as hard as tack. They are ready to face insurmountable odds and wield the most advanced mechanika Cygnar has to offer. Initiated by Leto Raelthorne in the years before he seized the crown from his brother, these heavily armored soldiers were handpicked to become knights of storm. They are a juxtaposition of old martial tradition and the latest advances in weaponry. Bringing these elements together, they have become the finest fighting men serving the king.

the next. In combat Stormblades are illuminated with a glowing nimbus of flashing lightning, and the sight presents a fearsome glance into the future of Cygnaran warfare.

Upon induction into a Stormblade unit, each soldier receives a storm glaive. These ingenious weapons combine Caspian enthusiasm for bladed warfare with powerful mechanikal storm chambers. The metal of the blade has been forged to exacting specifications and infused with a lattice of conductive materials designed to direct and regulate the flow of electrical energies. Mechanikally generated lightning arcs throughout the blade, and in properly trained hands, the charge can be sent forth to blast enemies at a distance.

Each Stormblade sergeant is issued a special weapon specifically designed to work in synergy with the men of his unit and capable of conducting massive electrical surges—the storm rod. By wielding this weapon in the midst of his men, the sergeant forms a fulcrum of power. He becomes the heart of an electrical storm that feeds on the combined energy of each glaive and amplifies each weapon's electrical charges.

A Stormblade's armor insulates the wearer against the electric currents of his weapon and is designed to withstand the dancing arcs of lightning flowing from each member to

TACTICAL TIP
ELECTRICAL ARC – Electrical Arc doesn't change a Storm Glaive's melee range.

> *War requires courage, sacrifice, and men who fight no matter how slim the hope of victory. That is the life of a Trencher. It is by the cost of their lives our borders stay safe.*
>
> —King Leto Raelthorne

SERGEANT

BAYONET CHARGE (ORDER) - Every Trencher who received this order must either charge or run. As part of a charge, after moving but before performing his combat action, each Trencher who received this order must, if possible, make a single ranged attack targeting the model charged. Trenchers are not considered to be in melee when resolving the Bayonet Charge ranged attacks, nor are the targets of those attacks considered to be in melee with them. If the target is not in melee range after moving, the Bayonet Charge's ranged attack must still be made before the Trencher's activation ends. A Trencher cannot target a model with which he was in melee at the start of his activation with the Bayonet Charge's ranged attack.

LEADER

SOLDIER

ADVANCE DEPLOYMENT - Place Trenchers after normal deployment, up to 12" beyond the established deployment zone.

COMBINED RANGED ATTACK - Instead of making ranged attacks separately, two or more Trenchers may combine their attacks at the same target. In order to participate in a combined ranged attack, a Trencher must be able to declare a ranged attack against the intended target and be in a single open formation group with the other participants. The Trencher with the highest RAT in the attacking group makes one ranged attack roll for the group and gains +1 to the attack and damage rolls for each Trencher, including himself, participating in the attack.

DIG IN (★ACTION) - A Trencher may dig a hasty battle position into the ground, gaining cover (+4 DEF) and +4 ARM. The Trencher remains dug in until he moves or is engaged. Trenchers cannot dig into solid rock or man-made constructions. Trenchers may begin the game dug in.

SMOKE BOMBS (★ACTION) - A Trencher may place a 3" AOE cloud effect anywhere within 3" of himself. The cloud effect remains on the table for one round.

Sergeant					Cmd 9
SPD	STR	MAT	RAT	DEF	ARM
6	6	7	6	13	13

Soldier					Cmd 7
SPD	STR	MAT	RAT	DEF	ARM
6	6	6	5	13	13

Military Rifle			
RNG	ROF	AOE	POW
10	1	—	11

Bayonet		
SPECIAL	POW	P+S
—	3	9

Leader and 5 Troops	83
Up to 4 Additional Troops	13ea
Field Allowance	2
Victory Points	2
Base Size	Small

The Trenchers have earned a reputation as being men of grit who can be found at the forefront of every battlefield. Known as "Gravediggers," they are the first into the field and often the last to leave. It is their duty to precede the van by hours, if possible, to prepare a battlefield for the main force. Across trench lines and hastily dug emplacements, they seize ground and hold it to allow the rest of the army to advance while enduring the concussive blasts of cannon and warjack fire. They embody the courage of young Cygnaran patriots, and each is aware that every day there is a chance he or his friends will be returning home in a box.

Trenchers are armed with heavy rifles ready to be set with trench knife bayonets, and they carry smoke grenades called hazers. When broken open, the grenades emit thick gray smoke that prevents the enemy from getting a fix on their position. When the time is right, Trenchers are sent to make life hell for the enemy by charging out of their holes with bayonets flashing and rifles roaring.

The Trenchers began as an experiment by the Cygnaran command to see if hard training could shape otherwise unremarkable or even troublesome youths into elite soldiers. The experiment proved a success and showed how far any man could go with the right training and motivation. Every Trencher must endure a harsh regimen to be forged into a peerless soldier capable of enduring war's horrors. It is said that, "Once a Trencher, always a Trencher." Many retired

veterans have been called back to duty over the years to train the next generation for war. Each day a new legend arises among the Trenchers as an example to brothers in arms stuck in the mud across countless battlefields.

TACTICAL TIP

DIG IN – A dug-in Trencher remains dug in even if he is knocked down.

SMOKE BOMBS – Although a single Trencher can't both attack and throw a smoke bomb in the same activation, you can have part of the unit make attacks and then have the rest of the unit lay down a smoke screen.

JOURNEYMAN WARCASTER
CYGNAR SOLO

JOURNEYMAN WARCASTER

BATTLEGROUP COMMANDER - A Journeyman Warcaster may control a battlegroup of warjacks just like a warcaster, and he counts as their controlling warcaster.

FEARLESS - A Journeyman Warcaster never flees.

FOCUS MANIPULATION - The Journeyman Warcaster receives focus points he may use just like a warcaster.

JOURNEYMAN - A Journeyman Warcaster is not yet a true warcaster, even though he has some of their abilities. A Journeyman Warcaster's model type is solo, not warcaster.

POWER FIELD - A Journeyman Warcaster possesses a Power Field just like a warcaster.

SPELLCASTER - A Journeyman Warcaster may cast spells just like a warcaster.

The tales of warcaster accomplishments have brought many hopefuls forward to the Strategic Academy to see if they have the spark. Most are deemed to lack even the faintest glimmer of potential and are

When you can caress a flower with the same hand you use to render stone to dust, only then are you ready.

—Famous ideal given to apprentice warcasters by their mentors

immediately turned away. It is difficult to predict who will manifest the ability to meld his mind with a warjack cortex. Those who prove promising begin training with veterans of the warcaster discipline hoping to unlock their potential. Finding new warcasters is one of the kingdom's highest priorities.

Becoming an apprentice warcaster requires a soldier to reinvent himself and put aside former military or arcane accomplishments. Many fresh warcasters have already served for years before realizing their ability to sense cortexes. Giants of the battlefield do not become great in a single day, and they must learn to walk before they can run. Beginning as apprentices, they control labor-exclusive steamjacks. Soon they move to disarmed warjacks and eventually earn the right to command a (typically old or battered) warjack when reaching journeyman rank.

As part of a tradition as old as the Strategic Academy, each journeyman must spend a full tour of duty under the tutelage of a veteran warcaster before he can graduate to the title of magus. In a time of war, journeymen are forced to learn vital lessons while evading death, and many will not survive the tour. Young warcasters are juicy targets of opportunity, and enemies seek to kill them before they can mature into greater threats. As they develop they become great assets, fighting alongside their mentors and learning how to become leaders of men and machines. Some commanders dread the thought of allowing a rookie to command a six-ton powerhouse with lives on the line, but most know it is a crucial step in building a warcaster. Each of the greats were once lowly journeymen, and they remember the glorious feeling of commanding a seemingly unstoppable warjack in the heat of battle for the first time.

Focus 3				Cmd 7	
SPD	STR	MAT	RAT	DEF	ARM
6	5	5	4	14	14

Hand Cannon

RNG	ROF	AOE	POW
12	1	—	12

Mage Blade

SPECIAL	POW	P+S
—	5	10

Damage	5
Point Cost	25
Field Allowance	1
Victory Points	1
Base Size	Small

SPELL	COST	RNG	AOE	POW	UP	OFF
ARCANE BOLT	2	12	—	11		X
Magical bolts of energy streak toward the target model.						
ARCANE SHIELD	2	8	—	—	X	
Surrounded by a magical barrier, target model/unit gains +3 ARM.						
DISRUPTOR	3	8	—	—		X
Target warjack suffers Disruption. A warjack suffering Disruption loses any unused focus points and cannot be allocated focus points or channel spells for one round.						

Protectorate of Menoth

A Menite Recounts the Past
A Brief History of the Protectorate of Menoth

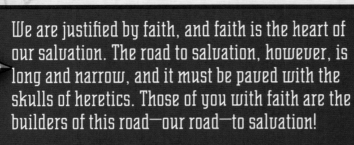

We are justified by faith, and faith is the heart of our salvation. The road to salvation, however, is long and narrow, and it must be paved with the skulls of heretics. Those of you with faith are the builders of this road—our road—to salvation!

—Hierarch Sulon, welcoming pilgrims to Caspia, 481 A.R

Sovereign Temple of the One Faith, Imer, in the year 604 AR. Grand Scrutator Severius addressed the recently initiated Knights Exemplar. These are his words recorded for posterity:

As long as man could see the world and speak the words of prayer, he has worshipped Menoth. Mankind arose from the froth when the shadow of the Creator fell on the still forming waters of the world. Since that creation, we have been His. Never forget that our flesh, our souls, all our works are His, and he may reclaim us whenever it suits His needs. In the dawn of our creation the Creator did not coddle us because He knew our strength must rise from travail. The first of humanity gathered into tribes in the difficult and wild lands where every shadow hid a threat and every nightfall presented an uncertainty of waking the next day. Great beasts stalked us, and we learned to hunt them in turn. Our tribes wandered for millennia enduring the elements and toiling to survive. We became stronger and more worthy. In our ignorance we did not know, even then, that we fought the Creator's ancient foe, the Beast of Many Shapes. We were being forged into weapons by His hand.

We know not the extent of the tribes of ancient man, but we gathered on the fertile land by riverbanks and the coasts of the ocean seeking to learn our place in the world. In the beginning man was a trivial thing to his Shaper, but our resilience did not go unnoticed. Man ascended above the beasts. To those deemed worthy Menoth gave the gifts of fire, stonework, and agriculture. The first and greatest of these men we know of was Cinot to whom Menoth revealed the True Law transcribed in stone as the Canon at Ancient Icthier. We made structures to glorify Menoth and walls to shield our people from the wilderness. By the favor of Menoth the first priest-kings rose up as a caste above all lesser citizens, and each man knew his place in the order of things. Menoth's covenants ensured we led our lives in obedience to His priests who themselves remained obedient to the True Law. We offered prayers in recognition of our Creator so that He would never again be forgotten, lest we lose all and surrender our rightful dominance over beast and wilderness. This was the birth of the Temple and the Sacred Flame, a single never ending fire that would burn in every temple, unite them as one, and maintain our promises. Villages arose and some that survived became the cities of today.

You may think I dwell too long on ancient times, but heed me well. You must feel in your bones and sinew that we are part of a sacred covenant with our Creator from the dawn of mankind. The ills of this world arise from those who have forgotten or shamelessly abandoned this first and most important promise. Menoth was and is our Creator and Lawgiver, and He gave us everything we required to foster civilization and thrive. He left us once more but left His priests in His place. Millennia passed.

Men are akin to children—so easily do they go astray. Yes, even a priest may lose his path if the scrutators do not remain firm and willing to provide discipline. The tribes broke apart. Man fell to worshipping false idols and looking to his ancestors rather than the Lawgiver. Some entered a deeper betrayal by giving offerings to the Devourer Wurm, enemy of the Shaper of Man. Lesser gods arose, allowed to exist only on the sufferance of Menoth while those they led astray forgot from whom mankind had sprung. When Menoth saw this, He was much displeased, and man became ill favored. Menoth sent storms to warn us of our defilements, but they were not enough. In spite of His anger, Menoth did not yet wish to destroy His creation. Rather, He sent a peril greater than storms to test us. In 600 BR, He sent the Orgoth. Their invasion would be a lesson of what might come to us if we neglected our faith.

The hardships we bore in those days were small matters, for we were being tested. The devout suffered in His name only, and when the time came it was Menoth's will that the Iron Fellowship was forged to cast off the chains of the Orgoth and regain our mastery of this land. Without Menoth's favor, our bones would lie in the earth, or we would be adrift in a void of lawlessness. He is the giver of all things, and by serving Him without question we may be spared His righteous wrath.

After the Orgoth quit our lands eight hundred years after they had first come, we re-built our temples and our walls and erected monuments to His glory. We helped the peoples of Immoren re-build while spreading His word. There were those who listened, and there were those who accepted our aid but would later forsake the faith. Some of Menoth's children chose to abide by the heretical teachings of other devotions, either forgetting the true way or turning their backs deliberately on the Creator. All would face His ultimate judgment when they passed through His hands again. Our missionaries adamantly taught that all lesser faiths must know their place, particularly Morrow—a dangerous faith of increasing popularity. Those who followed this deceiver were drawn to its easy and slothful tenets and showed a devotion requiring no discipline or adherence to ancient laws. We tolerated their unworthy rabble only as long as they acknowledged Menoth as supreme to all lesser powers. Perhaps we were too indulgent or too eager to allow such heretics to accept their errors and rejoin the true faith.

Man is lazy and weak, so the faith of Morrow grew over time, especially among the uneducated and lowborn. Those of high blood were closer to the True Law, for many of them descended from the ancient priest-kings and understood that each man must know his place, both ruler and those born to be governed. During the rule of Woldred the Diligent in the 280s, our right to oversee the proper passing of the Cygnaran crown was formalized in law. Woldred understood only the priests of the Temple could be trusted to recognize and authorize a worthy king, yet those who would undermine our faith were already busy seeking to unravel Woldred's righteous legacy. When Woldred became ill and died, our priests ushered his soul back to the Creator, but heretics calling themselves Morrowans unleashed their plot. Woldred's lawful documents of succession were stolen or destroyed. Fingers were pointed at our faith and we were blamed for his demise. Morrowans have ever been opportunists, and this was their best chance to usurp the power that was rightfully ours.

Their deceit had the desired effect, for Menoth's patience was tried. Those who were indolent—those who were decadent—began to slip away from His divinity. Our priests could not be faulted for their efforts. They fought in the Cygnaran courts for generations attempting to reconcile ancient Menite law with the increasingly corrupted revisions brought forth by Morrowan influence. The kings of Cygnar have ever been materialistic and preoccupied with their politics and their economies rather than heeding advice concerning their immortal souls. They turned from their Creator. Locked in their fleshly cages, they had been perverted by the Morrowans and thrown into confusion by lies, coin, and earthly power. When it became clear that we could not remain faithful to the True Law while governed by corrupt temporal courts, we denied their authority and began our work outside their purview.

Menoth watched and was displeased with the Cygnaran kings. His wrath stirred. He instructed His favored priests in what He wished done. The Cygnarans had turned away from Him in great numbers. They were like sheep lured away by the wolf from their shepherd, and that wolf was their Morrowan king.

As long as man could see the world and speak the words of prayer, he has worshipped Menoth.

Things could not have been bleaker for the Menite faithful when the Creator sent us Sulon. An exceptional visionary, he proved the greatest mortal leader since the ancient priest-kings Khardovic and Golivant. Sulon was granted the holy sight, and he quickly rose to the station of visgoth among the Caspian Menites. Soon his words were known in every corner of the nearly corrupted kingdom. He began to mark the way of our destiny and declared a great pilgrimage by which all Menites of Cygnar should join him in Caspia. The faithful had long been strong in the eastern districts of the capital, using the Black River to distance themselves from the self-serving Morrowans. In eastern Caspia Visgoth Sulon organized those who came to him, initiated more scrutators, and trained the faithful as warriors, knights, and war priests. Knights Exemplar were recalled from their posts and temples throughout the north to join the visgoth at the new era's birthplace.

A vast number journeyed to the site of our new beginning, the City of Walls. It was fitting that Menoth's worldly throne would be atop the ashes of the Cygnarans' mortal one. This was the city that was once Calacia and birthplace of Priest King Golivant. This was holy ground long before the birth of the Twins and the building of their indolent Sancteum.

By 482 AR Visgoth Sulon stood atop the ancient Great Temple of the Creator. His vision had become reality. From next to his altar he looked out over a sea of tents and wagons filling the city's streets and open spaces to see faithful men and women involved in the industry of arming themselves and preparing for what must come. Eastern Caspia had become the largest temple to Menoth in the world. Hundreds of thousands of our brothers and sisters joined him in prayer on an early spring day. On the holy day we now call the Birth of Sulon, the visgoth donned the vestments and became the first to take on the title of hierarch since the days before the Orgoth. Those amassed wept in His glory. Menoth was pleased, and through Hierarch Sulon His will was made manifest. Though the visgoths of Khador sent their refusal to acknowledge Sulon's claim, he was embraced as the uncontested leader of all Cygnaran Menites.

That same year, the hierarch decreed that all unbelievers should move west of the bridge, for the districts had become tremendously overcrowded. The faithful lived in the streets in what had been markets, and they spilled out into tents beyond the walls. While some of the non-

across the Black River into western Caspia, igniting the fires from which a new kingdom would soon be forged. We destroyed the bridges and blocked all roads joining the two halves of the city. Caspia was a city besieged from within.

For two years we fought. It was a tremendous test of our faith. Hierarch Sulon decreed that the Sancteum of Morrow, the stonework home to the pagan faith, must be torn apart and consecrated with fire and blood. That was his intent, but on the first full moon of 484 A.R., reinforcements from the north entered Caspia, and Sulon fell in battle against the infidels under the shadow of the Sancteum. Sulon had done enough, and it was Menoth's will His Hierarch should join Him in Urcaen. It became

The jealous Morrowan puppets of the Cygnaran court and their primarch master sent armed soldiers to the bridges in preparation to attack the holy patronage.

Menites of the city were indignant, they could not refuse the solidarity of our faith and were sent away. We were overly indulgent in those times, for we allowed them to depart in peace and take what possessions they could carry. Had we known what would come we would have dealt with them otherwise.

The jealous Morrowan puppets of the Cygnaran court and their primarch master sent armed soldiers to the bridges in preparation to attack the holy patronage. Their excuse that they sought to enforce order was a transparent ploy for what was clearly an assassination attempt. Hierarch Sulon, knowing this would come to pass, implored the Menites to "Send them to Urcaen!" With that, the faithful fell on the Cygnarans with righteous fury and overcame the heretics. Hierarch Sulon gave the holy order, and our forces flooded

clear to those who battled that this would not be the day the Menites would reclaim Caspia. Their times of trial and testing were not over. To commemorate the prophet's valor and clarity of vision, every year on the first full moon, on Sulonsphar, our tongues remain still and our hands stay idle for the entire day.

Three months after the hierarch's defeat, King Bolton Grey V agreed to a conference with Visgoth Ozeall, Sulon's most trusted subordinate, and the conflict was soon declared over. A long stretch of land on the southeastern corner of Cygnar became ours to rule as we would. The crown feigned agreement that they would not impose its political will upon us. We were ceded eastern Caspia, for they knew they could never root us out from this sacred land. No longer wishing to be tied to the Cygnaran name, we declared this a new city named Sul in honor of the first hierarch of the new age. We were Caspians no longer. Through our faith we had become Sulese.

We knew the land so close to the Bloodstone Marches was bitter and hot, but Hierarch Sulon had once said, "hardship is the coin of Urcaen." Menoth would be proud of His children should they survive in such a place. Was this not a victory? He deigned to give us a kingdom of

was a small cost to pay for religious freedom. Another term disallowed us from maintaining a standing army, but Ozeall's foresight ensured we would be allowed to raise what defenders were required to preserve our borders from the hostile tribes to the east and to defend our temples. This became the seed from which the true military of our new nation would grow by slow but inexorable measures. A stream of humanity ventured out from the walls of Sul to claim farmland from the difficult soils east of the Black River. It was the new land of the Protectorate of Menoth—our inherited land.

The land was not easily worked, but increasingly the faithful realized the divine hand dealt to them. This

our own. Within the borders of this new protectorate, we could mold the vision for which Sulon had sacrificed himself—a Sulese theocracy to, for, and of Menoth the Creator! So pure a theocracy had not been seen in western Immoren since ancient times. It was a rebirth of the true castes of our faith and a society driven solely by worship of the Lawgiver.

There were, of course, terms. This new protectorate would remain part of Cygnar in title and taxes, if not in law or religion. A percentage of coin, Ozeall stated,

ancient region had been abandoned as more fertile lands were found north and east. Here had once stood even Ancient Icthier, one of the most ancient cities of mankind where Cinot had discovered the True Law. Other holy and forgotten temples of those ancient and primal days of our faith awaited our discovery. They would be well worth the looming dangers of the Bloodstone Marches. It is an environment reflective of Menoth and His ancient battles with His first foe. The early years were difficult and thousands perished trying to civilize these forgotten regions. The people questioned if they had wandered into the wilds of the Devourer rather than sacred ground.

Then something wholly better than unearthed stone arose—the Idrian people. While we erected our temples amidst brambles, meager fields, and dust and carved our homes from the red sandstone from which the Marches take their name, the howling Idrian tribes descended upon us time and again. Menite and Idrian blood watered the desert through repeated raids, but we remained unwavering. Emboldened by our visgoths and scrutators, we retaliated in kind by putting them to the sword wherever we could find them. If they could not accept our holy expansion or if they did not know the name of our Creator, they would perish into the earth.

For years the Idrian tribes made attempts to force us from our new lands, but never before had they seen such iron resolve. The greatest clash of our peoples came in 504 AR well to the east of Sul as we moved on the collection of crude huts and hovels of their largest city, called Imer. Suddenly the hand of Menoth struck the earth as a sign, shaking the ground in a tremendous earthquake that sent the Idrians prostrate but left the faithful standing. This was His sign that the slaughter would not serve us nearly as well as converting the savages to His faith. The Idrians had been ignorant, but they were not easily seduced by false gods. They recognized the hand of the divine. Immediately the majority of those tribes, particularly the great masses of Imer, converted to the true faith and joined our fold.

We are a people who thrive on strong leadership. We find our way when the entire Temple can look to one ruler who commands absolute obedience.

Our battles against the Idrians did not end on that day. It would take decades of more strife and bloodshed to bring the tribes to the south into our faith, but this was the great beginning of the unity of our cultures. The Idrians brought much needed numbers to our young nation and proved themselves to be capable warriors and zealous citizens. Imer experienced the fruit of our knowledge and became a modern city with true walls and temples. The converted Idrians soon proved their loyalty and usefulness to the Temple and later the military of the Protectorate.

It was the Idrians who led us to the diamonds beneath the Marches. We have little weakness for precious jewels, but the heretics of the west crave them madly. The harvested gems trickled into the hands of the Cygnaran tax collectors to blind them from our activities. As long as the shining stones fell into their pockets, they paid us no attention as the hierarchs who followed after Sulon began to build our nation and ensure its military strength. We had some aid from the faithful abroad even among those of the Old Faith of Khador. Despite their refusal to acknowledge our hierarchs, some aided us against our enemies.

We discovered pure and blessed oil abundant under the cracked soil, first refined into the weapon known as Menoth's Fury by Hierarch Turgis. The unrefined fluid is useful to fuel forge fires and keep the hearths blazing in the temples, but by refinement it becomes truly potent. The oil can become so volatile it can ignite the instant it is exposed to air, roaring like the manifest wrath of our god. Menoth be praised for revealing this weapon to us, and let the fire consume the heretics who seek to defy Him.

Fifty years after our independence, King Vinter Raelthorne III ascended in Cygnar. He was a man who would tax and harass us mercilessly. The stonehearted reprobate drained our coffers. Tensions rose and our people starved. Vinter III died in 576 A.R., and the crown passed to his oldest son. Vinter IV embodied Cygnar's corrupt ways in his treatment of his own people. He clumsily imitated the techniques of our scrutators but without the holy sanction of the Creator. He found solace in darkness and put much of his efforts into strangling the life from his own people. He was a richly deserved plague on them for having given themselves over to false faiths. The paranoia of this king in regard to his own people was a boon to us, for we were able to gather our strength without interference.

We are a people who thrive on strong leadership. We find our way when the entire Temple can look to one ruler who commands absolute obedience. Sadly not all leaders of the faith have the same uncompromising strength of character. Hierarch is a title that must be earned and is not idly imparted. The founding of the Protectorate saw this from the earliest days when Visgoth Ozeall refused to take the title. He knew his own limits and recognized he was not the same caliber of man as Hierarch Sulon. The death of each hierarch after has always brought a time of turmoil and transition as the Temple struggles to adjust and find its new voice.

Sometimes there is contention among the visgoths, and this strife is natural since we must ensure Menoth's will above the petty aspirations of individuals. After the death of Hierarch Luctine it was thirteen years before the rise of Hierarch Turgis, during which the Synod of Visgoths underwent many changes. It was nineteen years after the death of Turgis before Hierarch Ravonal took the mantle. We were relatively blessed that Ravonal's death only presaged eight years of uncertainty among the ruling Synod. A number of petty sovereigns, visgoths, and senior scrutators sought to elevate themselves at this time, and from the records it seems many forgot their first duty was to their god. Visgoth Garrick Voyle rose from this storm of bickering voices, silenced all opposition, and took absolute control over our destinies. Here at last was a man worthy of Ravonal's legacy who would carry us forward into a new age.

It was in 588 A.R. at the height of Raelthorne's rule when Voyle seized power and proclaimed himself hierarch. The divided visgoths and their respective followers were forced either to recognize his claim or oppose him. Most recognized his invincibility and chose the wise course, but for some it would require an abject lesson and punishment. Aside from those few malcontents who soon received their discipline at Tower Judgment, the Temple bowed to him. His strong voice was just what the Temple needed to stand united and more powerful than ever before. He quashed all pretenders, single-handedly thwarted several assassination attempts, and rooted out seditious plots with an awareness that seemed divinely inspired. The hierarchy of Garrick Voyle was also accompanied by a miraculous manifestation. He stood before the subjugated visgoths and showed where the True Law had emerged of its own accord inscribed into his skin. Every word of the holy text is divinely scribed on his flesh as the sign of a new dawn. It represents the full weight of Menoth's scrutiny and His will to guide the chosen people made manifest. Menoth directs us through him, His chosen priest. Here was a leader who would fulfill the dream spoken by Hierarch Ravonal who promised to sever all ties with Cygnar and see our rise as an independent nation.

Hierarch Voyle has brought our nation to its greatest strength since its inception. It was he who relocated the capital from Sul to Imer. It was he who made arrangements with our brothers and sisters across Immoren to ensure warjack cortexes could be crafted within our borders rather than relying on the spoils of war or the charity of the faithful in other nations. The Vassals of Menoth were created at his urging. They captured and subdued foreign arcanists and bent their unholy skills to a sacred purpose with our powers of persuasion and torment. The Vassals have grown to include those among our people with these unsavory talents. Still, always we watch lest they attempt to turn these powers away from their sanctioned purpose. The Creator has allowed us to adapt to the challenges of the battles ahead without losing sight of our divine purpose.

Our gaze has turned to Cygnar again. The perfidy of the Morrowans has been made clear even to their citizens. In 594 AR Cygnar's prince overthrew the king and gave us King Leto, a Morrowan who rules with only the most tenuous claim to his throne. Cygnar is surrounded by enemies, and we will be the righteous flame that seizes their capital and returns it to the true faith. Tempers flare on other borders, and the corruption of the west is about to erupt in a war that will decide the fate of humanity.

Last year in 603 AR we received the greatest sign that our rise to triumph is imminent—the emergence of a prophetess and oracle long presaged in our holy texts. She is the Harbinger, a miraculous young woman whose sacred flesh refuses to touch the unclean soil. She was born blind but able to see to the true core of believer and unbeliever alike. She is the embodiment of Menoth's will and speaks with His voice, come unto our capital of Imer for the Synod of the Visgoths to receive her and reaffirm the hierarch's crusade. The great labors our people have endured in the last few years to create hidden factories, establish weapons caches, and build weapons enough to arm every citizen—young or old—will soon come to fruition.

We shall finish what Hierarch Sulon began so many generations before. We will convert or conquer the lesser faiths beginning with Morrow the betrayer. Every faithful member of the congregation, even some of our estranged brothers in Khador, will answer the call and recognize the miracle of the Harbinger. Never before have we come together so quickly and with such great purpose. Hierarch Voyle will lead us to greater glory. He is the Lawgiver's hand, and we are the weapon He wields. Menoth be praised!

THE HIGH RECLAIMER

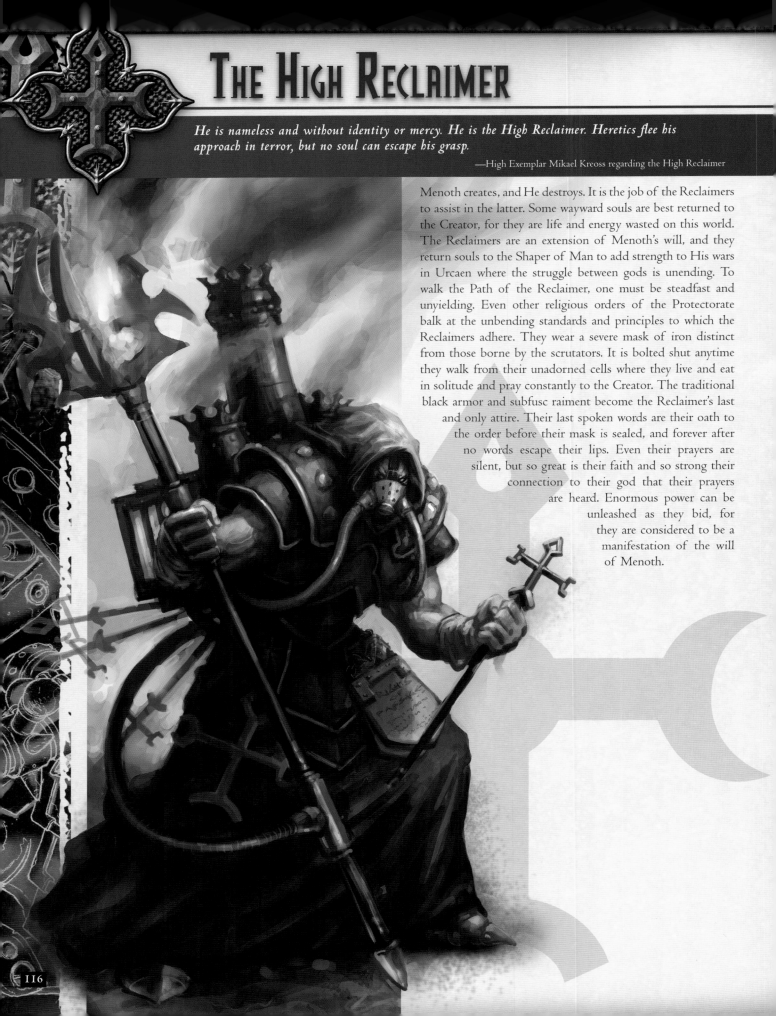

He is nameless and without identity or mercy. He is the High Reclaimer. Heretics flee his approach in terror, but no soul can escape his grasp.

—High Exemplar Mikael Kreoss regarding the High Reclaimer

Menoth creates, and He destroys. It is the job of the Reclaimers to assist in the latter. Some wayward souls are best returned to the Creator, for they are life and energy wasted on this world. The Reclaimers are an extension of Menoth's will, and they return souls to the Shaper of Man to add strength to His wars in Urcaen where the struggle between gods is unending. To walk the Path of the Reclaimer, one must be steadfast and unyielding. Even other religious orders of the Protectorate balk at the unbending standards and principles to which the Reclaimers adhere. They wear a severe mask of iron distinct from those borne by the scrutators. It is bolted shut anytime they walk from their unadorned cells where they live and eat in solitude and pray constantly to the Creator. The traditional black armor and subfusc raiment become the Reclaimer's last and only attire. Their last spoken words are their oath to the order before their mask is sealed, and forever after no words escape their lips. Even their prayers are silent, but so great is their faith and so strong their connection to their god that their prayers are heard. Enormous power can be unleashed as they bid, for they are considered to be a manifestation of the will of Menoth.

Protectorate Warcaster Character

One man who took the Oath of the Reclaimer's Last Breath has risen above his peers. Through this man the divine power of Menoth flows without effort as he sends forth clouds of burning ash and causes the unworthy to burst into flame, consumed with brutal agony before their lives are snuffed out and their souls sent to Urcaen. Hierarch Voyle publicly recognized him as the High Reclaimer, a singular title denoting absolute unity with the will of the Lawgiver. This was the first time in the history of the Protectorate that a man of this order and station had demonstrated the talent for warcasting, and it was immediately obvious to Hierarch Voyle that he would bring tremendous strength to the upcoming crusades. By Voyle's command, the High Reclaimer was allowed to command as many men and warjacks as he might require. High Exemplar Kreoss was recalled temporarily from the battles abroad to refine the High Reclaimer's control over warjacks and unleash his full potential as a battlefield commander.

The High Reclaimer's sole weapon is an oversized ceremonial torch like those wielded by lesser Reclaimers called Cremator. It is a large flanged mace set atop a long haft kept aflame by a continuous supply of concentrated Menoth's Fury. One crushing blow from the High Reclaimer's great weapon smashes limbs and collapses torsos, rends warjack armor like mortified flesh, and ignites anything it does not immediately demolish. The High Reclaimer excels in the turmoil of battle, and his every swing and movement serve as words in an ongoing litany of silent praise of the Creator.

Those soldiers who have marched at his side in battle attest that it is a unique and sacred experience, for they know his will without being told. His plan of battle becomes apparent to them with effortless clarity. To prepare for each upcoming conflict, the High Reclaimer spends countless hours in silent meditation and tests his limits with a rigorous regimen of exercises and fasting that tempers his body into corded muscle and sinew akin to iron.

No one is safe from the reclaiming. It is said Menoth whispers to the High Reclaimer during his prayers and names those who are to be returned to Him. Enemies, allies, even so-called innocent bystanders are oft reclaimed with no more foreknowledge than Cremator's hiss as it delivers a killing blow

or the sudden pressure of a Crusader's grip. These matters are not to be questioned, for all Reclaimers are trained to know Menoth's signs. They interpret the subtlest suggestions as His divine command—every twitch, every gesture, and every deep breath has meaning to a Reclaimer, and they know they must not fail in their duties or their interpretations, for failure means reclamation often by the High Reclaimer himself.

Focus 5				Cmd 8	
SPD	STR	MAT	RAT	DEF	ARM
5	7	6	4	14	15

Cremator			
	SPECIAL	POW	P+S
Fire	7	14	

Damage	18
Point Cost	52
Field Allowance	C
Victory Points	5
Base Size	Small

SPECIAL RULES

FEAT: RESURRECTION

Though the High Reclaimer's purpose is to usher souls into the next existence, he has been given the authority to return them from death in order to carry out Menoth's will.

Return 2d6 friendly destroyed Protectorate troopers to play, placing them in the Reclaimer's control area. The controlling player chooses which models are returned to play, and models may be returned to their original units or formed into new units of the same type. New units formed must follow the rules of unit composition. Resurrected models placed in their original unit cause the unit to lose benefits or effects that it received from the original destruction of the resurrected models. Resurrected models must be placed in formation. Resurrected models cannot activate the turn they return to play.

HIGH RECLAIMER

OATH OF SILENCE - The High Reclaimer cannot give orders. Other models/units cannot use the High Reclaimer's CMD stat when making command checks.

RECLAIM - The High Reclaimer gains a soul token for each living Protectorate model destroyed in his control area. During his controller's next Control Phase, replace each soul token with a focus point.

TERROR - Enemy models/units in melee range of the High Reclaimer and enemy models/units with the High Reclaimer in their melee range must pass a command check or flee.

CREMATOR

FIRE - Target model hit by Cremator suffers Fire. A model on fire suffers a POW 12 damage roll each turn during its controller's Maintenance Phase until the Fire expires on a d6 roll of 1 or 2. Fire effects are alchemical substances or magical in nature and are not affected by water.

SPELL	COST	RNG	AOE	POW	UP	OFF
ASHES TO ASHES	4	8	*	10		X
If target model is hit, d6 nearest enemy models within 5" suffer a POW 10 damage roll.						
BURNING ASH	*	8	3	—		
Place a 3" cloud effect for each focus point spent anywhere within the spell's range. Models in a Burning Ash cloud suffer –2 MAT and RAT. Burning Ash clouds last for one round.						
IMMOLATION	2	8	—	12		X
On a critical hit, target model suffers Fire.						
RITUAL SACRIFICE	1	*	CTRL	—		
Remove a friendly living model from play. Warjacks in the High Reclaimer's battlegroup in his control area receive one additional focus point, not to exceed the warjack's normal allocation limit. A warjack may only receive one focus point per turn from this spell.						
SOULSTORM	3	SELF	*	—		X
Enemy models that enter the area within 4" of the High Reclaimer immediately suffer one damage point. An enemy model that begins its activation within 4" of the High Reclaimer and does not end its activation more than 4" away from him suffers one damage point at the end of its activation.						

TACTICAL TIP

RESURRECTION – Your opponent keeps any VPs he earned for the destruction of the destroyed models being resurrected. He will also be able to earn more VPs for their destruction again. If the High Reclaimer uses Resurrection to return models to a unit, the unit can still activate. Only the models returned do not activate. When a model with damage boxes is returned to play, that model has all damage removed. A unit can only have one leader and one instance of an attachment.

RITUAL SACRIFICE – A warjack suffering Disruption will still gain a focus point from this spell.

HIGH EXEMPLAR KREOSS

If you didn't believe in the Creator before, you will today.

—Long Gunner Sergeant Terschel Bannock to a fresh recruit sent into battle against the Knights Exemplar

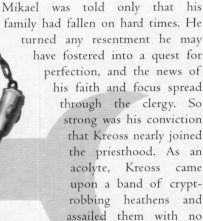

Though Menoth does not make room for petty ascendants and scions like the lesser gods of the new age, He does well to make his followers ready for the wars of Caen. Mikael Kreoss, high exemplar of the Knights Exemplar, is a prime example of Menoth's worldly influence on mortal man.

Kreoss was born in the rugged north of Khador as part of a strong community of the Old Faith that has long adhered to the True Law. As a child Kreoss aspired to become a paladin of the Order of the Wall to serve as one of the temple guardians and defenders. Kreoss has never known anything but Menoth's word and the cold truth of His purpose. Mikael's great-grandfather perished in the Thornwood War on the banks of the Dragon's Tongue, and

his death left the Kreoss family in poverty. Debtors forced Mikael's father into a hard life with very little except his arduous labors to occupy his time. When he became a father in his own right, his troubles continued. Mikael's mother died in childbirth, leaving Mikael's father to raise the child on his own. Having little choice, he gave his only son to a group of visiting Protectorate pilgrims who took him south in the hopes of providing him a proper upbringing.

Mikael was told only that his family had fallen on hard times. He turned any resentment he may have fostered into a quest for perfection, and the news of his faith and focus spread through the clergy. So strong was his conviction that Kreoss nearly joined the priesthood. As an acolyte, Kreoss came upon a band of crypt-robbing heathens and assailed them with no

more than his fists and faith, cracking bones with his bare hands. Towering over his quaking foes, the Khadoran-born Menite seemed a wrathful, unstoppable giant. Immediately after the scuffle, dripping with blood and sweat, Kreoss prayed to Menoth for direction. While in vigil at the temple, Kreoss realized his destiny rested neither with the clergy nor the paladins he had admired as a youth, but that his calling was to join the stern Knights Exemplar fighting for Menoth. A visiting exemplar from Khador observed the acolyte in prayer and was impressed. Exemplars say their initiation is their true birth when old lives and family are put aside. Kreoss left the temple in the company of that exemplar leaving the thoughts of his past behind, and his true training began.

Mikael Kreoss rose in Menoth's grace—and the opinion of the visgoths—quickly. His crusades were effective in stamping out heretics and blasphemers wherever they were rooted. His quest became to "remind the wayward masses of Menoth's laws, which they had spurned." Kreoss holds the life of every man and woman as a gift of the Creator, and those who take Him for granted are deemed unworthy of the flesh they wear in this world. He has sent many a dissenting soul to Urcaen to be judged by the Creator. In time, he achieved the venerated position of high exemplar. Among the people of the Protectorate, Kreoss has become a living legend. His flowing robes and thick runic armor enhance his impressive physique while his unwavering faith makes him a pillar of the theocracy and a leader upon whom the scrutators can rely with absolute confidence. When the decision was made to renew war with the Cygnarans, thousands gathered to listen to him pray to Menoth for victory.

High Exemplar Kreoss is like a living warjack when he takes up arms in the name of the Creator. His concentration is unmatched and his prayers are unceasing as he directs whole interdictions of thousands of zealous soldiers and warjacks to key points in a battle. He invokes the wrath of Menoth and smashes mortal enemies with his battle flail Spellbreaker. So strong is his faith that a mere touch from his blessed weapon can revoke the unwholesome sorcery granted by lesser gods to their wayward followers.

He may be a legend and hero among the Menite faithful, but Kreoss is a nightmare to the rest of western Immoren's people, especially those dedicated to Morrow. Some fear that when Menoth plays the last move, High Exemplar Kreoss will be the knight who topples the king.

Focus 7					Cmd 8
SPD	STR	MAT	RAT	DEF	ARM
5	6	7	4	14	15

Spellbreaker		
SPECIAL	POW	P+S
Multi	8	14

Damage	18
Point Cost	64
Field Allowance	C
Victory Points	5
Base Size	Small

SPECIAL RULES

FEAT: MENOTH'S WRATH

Few members of the Temple's clergy can command the forces of the Old God to greater effect than High Exemplar Kreoss. With but a few chanted words from an ancient littany, Kreoss may unleash the anger of man's creator to smite all who oppose him to their knees.

Enemy models currently in Kreoss' control area are knocked down.

SPELLBREAKER

DISPEL - Upkeep spells on target model/unit immediately expire when hit by Spellbreaker.

REACH - 2" melee range.

SPELL	COST	RNG	AOE	POW	UP	OFF
ANTI-MAGIC PULSE	2	SELF	CTRL	—		
Upkeep spells currently in the AOE expire.						
CLEANSING FIRE	4	8	4	14		X
A massive blast of flames erupts and causes Fire to all models in the AOE on a critical hit. Fire is a continuous effect that sets the target ablaze. A model on fire suffers a POW 12 damage roll each turn during its controller's Maintenance Phase until the fire expires on a d6 roll of 1 or 2. Fire effects are alchemical substances or magical in nature and are not affected by water.						
IMMOLATION	2	8	—	12		X
On a critical hit, target model suffers Fire.						
LAMENTATION	2	SELF	CTRL	—		X
Enemy models in Kreoss' control area pay double the focus points to cast or upkeep spells.						
PROTECTION OF MENOTH	2	8	—	—		X
Target model/unit gains +2 DEF and +2 ARM.						
RETRIBUTION	2	8	—	—		X
If target warjack is damaged by an attack, its attacker suffers an equal damage roll, then the spell expires. Retribution is not triggered by collateral damage, damage from continuous effects, or damage taken without a damage roll.						
WARD	2	6	—	—		X
Target friendly warjack cannot be targeted by enemy spells.						

TACTICAL TIP

ANTI-MAGIC PULSE – Anti-Magic Pulse only affects upkeep spells. Lingering effects from a non-upkeep spell such as Blood of Kings are untouched. Additionally, this spell affects friendly upkeep spells, too. If you are planning to cast it, you might not want to pay upkeep that turn. Anti-Magic Pulse will cause upkeep spells with an AOE to expire if any part of the AOE is in Kreoss' control area.

DISPEL – Spellbreaker causes upkeeps spells to expire before the damage for the attack is resolved.

LAMENTATION – A Skarlock is not affected by Lamentation since it does not pay focus points to cast spells. Also, you can channel spells through a channeler in the spell's area without paying double the focus as long as the spell caster stays outside the AOE.

RETRIBUTION – If the damage was dealt without a damage roll, e.g., by a Widowmaker using his Sniper ability, there is no retribution.

GRAND SCRUTATOR SEVERIUS

This man embodies my voice on the battlefield. None shall question his authority, lest they incur my wrath.
—Hierarch Garrick Voyle to the assembled Synod of the Nine Visgoths at the elevation of Severius to grand scrutator

Scrutators require a singular strength of presence, for they are responsible for controlling the priesthood which in turn controls the entire Protectorate of Menoth. They must be able to snap the minds of the faithless and encompass them with feelings of piety, servitude, and fear of a divine reckoning. Scrutators cannot show the slightest weakness; they represent the vigilant oversight of Menoth whose wrath is terrible. Grand Scrutator Severius, handpicked by Hierarch Garrick Voyle, is a pillar holding up the grand Temple of Menoth. Severius answers only to the hierarch himself and has been given command over the entirety of the Protectorate's military.

Though many years ago he cast aside his original Caspian-derived name in disgust, Severius has come to be known by younger patrons and followers as the 'Voice of Menoth'. He would no doubt punish those who use the term loosely, but the meaning is close to the truth. The man has single-handedly converted thousands of heathens and infidels to the True Law. In past decades he marched far afield into other nations with a retinue of followers as an unofficial ambassador of the faith too powerful to ignore and too dangerous to confront. After one particularly fruitful trip to Khador in the 570's, he was thereafter banned from that nation as thousands flocked to his call and deserted

Protectorate Warcaster Character

the Motherland to find a new home in the south. Since Hierarch Voyle has put forward increasingly militant and aggressive crusades, Severius has ceased these missions to focus on leading the Protectorate military. Conversion remains a priority, but he conducts it now on subjugated villages and towns whose defenders have been slaughtered or driven away.

Grand Scrutator Severius has dozens of servants who work meticulously to discipline the unworthy with the pain of the wrack, hook, or cleansing fire while he searches to bring more supporters from abroad into the fold, such as the Old Faith of Khador. He expects all subordinate scrutators and priests to be industrious, for he cannot personally direct them at all times. His role—and his passion—lies on the battlefield.

In a role that parallels Menoth's ancient war with the Devourer, Severius lives to make war on the enemies of his faith. He has a powerful thirst for the blood of blasphemers, and through his divine power he has little problem slaking it. His warjacks come alive with the same fervor as his converts. His tactics are planned well in advance, for he has a brilliant tactical mind. His stratagems are often too complex for his peers to follow, but they unfurl on the battlefield as easily as if he were plotting on his war room maps. Indeed, Severius has a plan in motion that will not come to fruition until far past his lifetime. He knows full well it will fall into place exactly as Menoth has ordained.

For all his commanding presence and undeniable genius on the battlefield, Severius is beyond his physical prime. He is aged, gray, and not as fit as the Protectorate's younger commanders, but what he lacks in bodily prowess, Severius makes up with divine power. His ability to harness energy through his faith, and that of the faithful around him, allows him a control of the battlefield and his soldiers other commanders only dream about. He is the blaze of Menoth's wrath, breaching the minds of non-believers with a single word. Severius is the eye of the hurricane and a center of focused spiritual control with a whirlwind of faith-driven destruction surrounding him. So potent is his righteousness,

he wades through otherwise deadly arcane attacks as if they were no more than illusion. So strong is his divine nature that if he so chooses, he can thunder the Litany of Menoth declaring Menoth's glory and greatness. This divine rite purges all foreign magic from those within earshot like holy thunder and denies enemy warcasters their connections to their impure mechanika. This litany proves that all things are Menoth's, pagan sorcery and heathen witchcraft notwithstanding. Through Grand Scrutator Severius, Menoth's glory is unmistakable, and his voice shall be heard abroad.

SPECIAL RULES

FEAT: DIVINE MIGHT

Endowed with the power to pass judgment on his fellow man, Grand Scrutator Severius may call upon the grandeur of Menoth to deny arcane magic users their abilities.

No spells may be cast or channeled within Severius' control area for one round. Models with the Focus Manipulation ability currently in Severius' control area do not replenish focus points during their controller's next turn. Divine Might does not affect friendly Protectorate models.

Focus 8				Cmd 9	
SPD	STR	MAT	RAT	DEF	ARM
5	5	4	3	14	14

Staff of Judgment		
SPECIAL	POW	P+S
Multi	8	13

Damage	16
Point Cost	66
Field Allowance	C
Victory Points	5
Base Size	Small

STAFF OF JUDGMENT

REACH - 2" melee range.

SACRED WARD - Severius cannot be targeted by enemy spells.

SPELL	COST	RNG	AOE	POW	UP	OFF
ASHES TO ASHES	4	8	✱	10		X
If target model is hit, d6 nearest enemy models within 5" suffer a POW 10 damage roll.						
BLESSING OF MENOTH	2	6	—	—	X	
Target model may re-roll all dice for any one die roll, then the spell expires. The affected model may only re-roll a roll that is a result of its own action. It cannot re-roll effects it suffers nor continuous effects it inflicted on other models.						
CONVERT	4	6	—	—		X
Target living trooper model must pass a command check or permanently become part of the Protectorate army. The converted model becomes an independent Protectorate model under the control of Severius' controller. Converted model cannot activate this turn. This spell cannot be cast on characters.						
DEATH SENTENCE	5	6	—	—		X
Attacks targeting a model affected by Death Sentence within the attack's range automatically hit. Death Sentence lasts for one turn.						
EYE OF MENOTH	3	SELF	CTRL	—	X	
While in Severius' control area, friendly Protectorate models gain +1 to attack and damage rolls.						
HOLY VIGIL	3	6	—	—	X	
Target model/unit gains +4 DEF until it moves or is knocked down.						
IMMOLATION	2	6	—	12		X
On a critical hit, target model suffers Fire. Fire is a continuous effect that sets the target ablaze. A model on fire suffers a POW 12 damage roll each turn during its controller's Maintenance Phase until the fire expires on a d6 roll of 1 or 2. Fire effects are alchemical substances or magical in nature and are not affected by water.						
VISION	3	SELF	—	—	X	
Severius suffers no damage or effects from the next direct hit against him, then the spell expires.						

TACTICAL TIP

BLESSING OF MENOTH — Examples of rolls that may be re-rolled are attack and damage rolls, damage location rolls, and deviation.

DEATH SENTENCE — This will negate Stealth, but you will still have to get within 5" of the target to cast Death Sentence on it in the first place.

DIVINE MIGHT — Divine Might will prevent warcasters from replenishing their focus, but other ways of gaining focus such as soul tokens are unaffected.

HOLY VIGIL — Holy Vigil expires for the entire unit when any trooper moves or is knocked down.

SACRED WARD — He can still be affected by enemy spells, however. Target a nearby model with an AOE spell.

VISION — This really does mean "direct hit." Vision will not protect him from Skarre's Sacrificial Strike, nor from blast damage.

REDEEMER
Protectorate Light Warjack

SKYHAMMER

INACCURATE - The Redeemer suffers −4 to its attack rolls with the Skyhammer.

SPD	STR	MAT	RAT	DEF	ARM
5	9	5	4	12	17

L Skyhammer

RNG	ROF	AOE	POW
16	3	3	12

R Battle Mace

SPECIAL	POW	P+S
—	4	13

1	2	3	4	5	6
	L			R	
L	L	M	C	R	R
	M	M	C	C	

Point Cost	81
Field Allowance	U
Victory Points	2
Base Size	Medium

HEIGHT/WEIGHT: 9'10" / 4.85 tons

ARMAMENT: Battle Mace (right arm), Skyhammer Rocket Pod (left arm)

FUEL LOAD/BURN USAGE: 154 Lbs / 5.5 hrs general, 1.2 hrs combat

INITIAL SERVICE DATE: 545 AR

CORTEX MANUFACTURER: Originally stolen from the Fraternal Order of Wizardry & Greylords Covenant, Vassals of Menoth (currently)

ORIG. CHASSIS DESIGN: Engines East/Khadoran Mechaniks Assembly (modified by the Sul-Menite Artificers)

> *Never again shall you fear being outnumbered by heretics. Under a hail of blessed rockets their numbers will wither to nothing, scattered by Menoth's hand.*
>
> —Senior Scrutator Vorn advising a novice warcaster given a battlegroup of Redeemers

Once forced to rely on stolen parts and frames and hide their assemblies from prying Cygnaran eyes, the Protectorate relied heavily on lighter warjack chassis to fill essential combat roles. With limited ability to produce the heavier frames, the Menites often improvised. One such improvisation is the infamous Redeemer.

Armed with devastating long ranged rockets, the Redeemer was designed to deliver blazing judgment from afar. The warjack carries an ample supply of Menite-made explosives and a mechanikal rig to launch them. Borrowing the Repenter's ignition system, the Redeemer uses vented heartfire to light the propellants. These simple tubes of shrapnel-to-be are launched recklessly into the enemy ranks and explode in a cascade of deadly debris. They leave infantry with horrible lacerations and extensive burns that are

against rugged and determined bands of Idrian holdouts who refused to convert. Since that time the warjack has turned more actively against Cygnar and is deployed in both border defense and active assaults abroad. Many Cygnaran women still wait for their long-lost husbands or brothers not knowing their bodies lie in the bloody trenches of faraway lands, incinerated by Redeemer fire.

notoriously difficult to heal. The Redeemer is capable of launching salvos of rocket fire although the accuracy of the weapon usually sends the projectiles across a wide area. The Redeemer wields a brutal mace for close fighting, but it is far more adept at decimating the enemy at a distance.

In the earliest decades after its production, the Redeemer was instrumental in helping to expand the borders of the Protectorate to the east and south. It was often employed

> *We have never adequately enforced our disarmament laws, and they flaunt warjacks like the Repenter in our face. It is unmistakably a weapon of war.*
>
> —Commander Coleman Stryker

The Protectorate of Menoth utilizes the volatile oil known as "Menoth's Fury" in great abundance in place of blasting powder. The fiery weaponry of the Protectorate serves as a wicked reminder of the faith's burning wrath. Older warjacks like the Repenter are loaded with the crudest and least refined supply of Menoth's Fury, which it is at liberty to use in abundance. This warjack was first used to police the borders of the Protectorate by bringing scourging flames to bear against any who dared to trespass.

When they designed the Repenter decades ago, the Sul-Menite artificers armed the light warjack with a great three-headed flail. The other hand was replaced with the first projection system for Menoth's Fury— the flame thrower. The first model was little more than a tube attached to a reservoir with a simple pump, but newer versions have fanning spray nozzles and refined mechanikal pumping mechanisms to propel the blazing fluid at some distance from the 'jack. The new pump prevents a problem from earlier models where the 'jack would sometimes catch on fire and explode. The original flame thrower ignited the oil with an outside sparking mechanism, but the latest weapon vents superheated heartfire into the fuel.

Though fire is certainly an effective weapon in its own right, none can dismiss the impact of a Repenter's blaze on the morale of the enemy. The weak unbelievers who face the Protectorate in battle have no stomach or fortitude for seeing their friends burned alive, screaming in terror while their allies try desperately to extinguish the hungry flames. Menoth's Fury is aptly named, and the Repenter is a favored delivery vehicle for the god's wrath against Cygnar and any other enemies who defy the Creator.

FLAME THROWER

FIRE - Target model hit by the Flame Thrower suffers Fire. Fire is a continuous effect that sets the target ablaze. A model on fire suffers a POW 12 damage roll each turn during its controller's Maintenance Phase until the Fire expires on a d6 roll of 1 or 2. Fire effects are alchemical substances or magical in nature and are not affected by water.

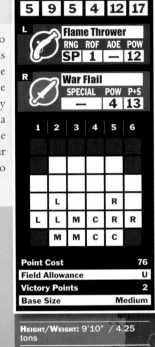

SPD	STR	MAT	RAT	DEF	ARM
5	9	5	4	12	17

L — Flame Thrower

RNG	ROF	AOE	POW
SP	1	—	12

R — War Flail

	SPECIAL	POW	P+S
	—	4	13

	1	2	3	4	5	6
			L		R	
	L	L	M	C	R	R
		M	M	C	C	

Point Cost	76
Field Allowance	U
Victory Points	2
Base Size	Medium

HEIGHT/WEIGHT: 9'10" / 4.25 tons

ARMAMENT: War Flail (right arm), Flame Thrower (left arm)

FUEL LOAD/BURN USAGE: 165 Lbs/ 6 hrs general, 1.5 hrs combat

INITIAL SERVICE DATE: 533 AR

CORTEX MANUFACTURER: Vassals of Menoth (currently)

ORIG. CHASSIS DESIGN: Engines East/Khadoran Mechaniks Assembly (modified by the Sul-Menite Artificers)

REVENGER
Protectorate Light Warjack

REVENGER

ARC NODE - The Revenger may channel spells.

REPULSOR SHIELD

REPEL - If the Revenger hits with the Repulsor Shield, or if the Revenger is hit with a melee weapon and its Repulsor Shield is not disabled by the attack, it pushes the opposing model 1" directly away. A pushed model moves at half rate in rough terrain and stops if it contacts an obstacle, obstruction, or model. The pushed model cannot be targeted by free strikes during this movement.

HALBERD

POWERFUL CHARGE - When making a charge attack with the Halberd, a Revenger gains +2 to its attack roll.

REACH - 2" melee range.

Menite artificers crafted the powerful repulsor shield to protect this vital weapon in battle. Aided by priests, the artificers inlaid runes of protection on the warjack's shield. If the powerful runes come into contact with an enemy, the foe is immediately rebuked and hurled away. This has given the Revenger the ability to distance itself from superior combatants like Cygnar and Khador's heavier 'jacks while being able to retaliate at a safe distance with its halberd.

Visgoths charged with innovating weapons to stand on an equal footing against Cygnar knew it was imperative to leverage divine power against the enemy on the battlefield. The holy prayers and spells of Protectorate warcasters have long been among the greatest weapons of the nation, and finding a means to extend the reach of these holy warriors was a top priority. The capture of several of Cygnar's Javelin warjacks and their arcantrik relays aided the research. In a fit of spiritual inspiration, Menite mechaniks reverse-engineered the devices and laid the groundwork for the creation of the Revenger.

Menites believe the purity of their divine power is easier to channel through a properly modified arc node than the heathen magic of sorcery. Though the creation of this device is heralded openly today, in its time it was a controversial endeavor plagued by lingering doubts about the wisdom of utilizing anything derived from Cygnaran mechanika. Still, with the same procedures used to sanctify warjacks, mechaniks disassembled the arcantrik relay while supervising priests purified the mechanism with prayer, rebuilding this new 'Divinity Arc Node' with refinements allowing it to channel divine power properly. This success was a remarkable achievement and one that only confirmed to the visgoths the divine endorsement of these weapons of war.

SPD	STR	MAT	RAT	DEF	ARM
5	9	5	4	12	17
					19

L	Repulsor Shield		
	SPECIAL	POW	P+S
	Repel	0	9

R	Halberd		
	SPECIAL	POW	P+S
	Multi	4	13

1	2	3	4	5	6
	L	A	A	R	
L	L	M	C	R	R
	M	M	C	C	

Point Cost	76
Field Allowance	U
Victory Points	2
Base Size	Medium

HEIGHT/WEIGHT: 9'8" / 4.45 tons

ARMAMENT: Halberd (right arm), Repulsar Shield (right arm), Divinity Arc Node

FUEL LOAD/BURN USAGE: 165 Lbs / 5.5 hrs general, 1.2 hrs combat

INITIAL SERVICE DATE: 546 AR

CORTEX MANUFACTURER: Vassals of Menoth (currently)

ORIG. CHASSIS DESIGN: Engines East/Khadoran Mechaniks Assembly (modified by the Sul-Menite Artificers)

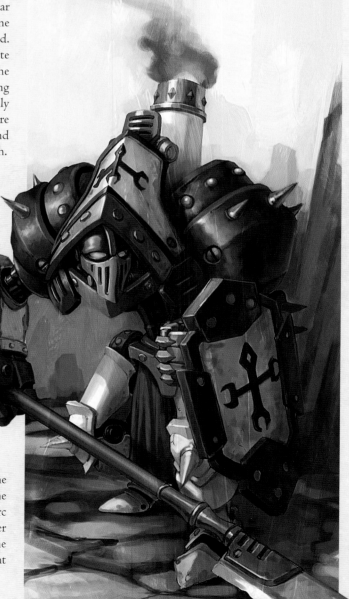

CRUSADER
Protectorate Heavy Warjack

In its peace terms after the Civil War, Cygnar decreed the Protectorate could not keep a standing army. Visgoth Ozeall acquiesced but commanded engineers to build warjacks from cortexes smuggled from Khador down the Black River and Cygnaran parts salvaged from fields of battle. Those early 'jacks were designed with open hands to pass as laborjacks to casual inspection. Meanwhile artificers worked in secret to forge weaponry for these warjacks to wield as Menoth commanded.

The greatest of the new Protectorate designs was the Crusader, a massive warjack boasting heavy armor and capable of crushing attacks. The chassis originated during the reign of Hierarch Luctine who devoted himself to subjugating outlying Idrian tribes. Even after the greatest number converted after the earthquake of 504 AR, many tribes resisted and continued to harass the young nation. The Crusader was unleashed to provide an unstoppable force in the battles to come. It quickly proved its strength against Cygnar as well when friction between the two nations prompted inevitable clashes along the Black River.

After the development of Menoth's Fury, the Crusader was enhanced with the addition of the inferno mace—a weapon inspired by the flaming maces

INFERNO MACE

CRITICAL FIRE - On a critical hit, target model suffers Fire. Fire is a continuous effect that sets the target ablaze. A model on fire suffers a POW 12 damage roll each turn during its controller's Maintenance Phase until the fire expires on a d6 roll of 1 or 2. Fire effects are alchemical substances or magical in nature and are not affected by water.

of the Reclaimers. Between the Crusader's immensely durable armored frame and its powerful laborjack arms, a strike with an inferno mace rends most armor into flaming scrap. When the call-to-arms sounds, the Crusaders will assemble at the front line ready to hammer and burn the foes of Menoth to dust and ashes.

SPD	STR	MAT	RAT	DEF	ARM
4	11	5	4	10	19

L — Open Fist

	SPECIAL	POW	P+S
	—	0	11

R — Inferno Mace

	SPECIAL	POW	P+S
	Critical	7	18

	1	2	3	4	5	6
			L		R	
	L	L	M	C	R	R
		M	M	C	C	

Point Cost	93
Field Allowance	U
Victory Points	3
Base Size	Large

HEIGHT/WEIGHT: 12' / 8 tons

ARMAMENT: Inferno Mace (right arm),

FUEL LOAD/BURN USAGE: 253 Lbs / 6 hrs general, 1 hr combat

INITIAL SERVICE DATE: 513 AR

CORTEX MANUFACTURER: Vassals of Menoth (currently)

ORIG. CHASSIS DESIGN: Engines East/Khadoran Mechaniks Assembly (modified by the Sul-Menite Artificers)

VANQUISHER
Protectorate Heavy Warjack

BLAZING STAR

CIRCULAR STRIKE (★**Attack**) - The Vanquisher may make one melee attack with the Blazing Star against every model within melee range. Completely resolve each attack individually and apply the targets' special rules immediately as each attack is resolved. When performing a Circular Strike, the Vanquisher's front arc extends 360°. A model is ineligible to be hit if it has a special rule preventing it from being targeted or if the attacker's line of sight is completely blocked by terrain.

The Vanquisher is one of the latest warjacks in the Protectorate's arsenal. It is a formidable weapon that inspires terror and dread in the enemies of the faithful. Secretly assembled from imported parts and armed with distinctive Menite weaponry, this heavy warjack is as subtle as the faith

it serves—which is to say, not at all. The Vanquisher is a towering behemoth of armor, and its great flail is a whirling harbinger of death. One arm wields a length of chain nearly as long as a man is tall, and the end of it is capped with the "blazing star"—a viciously spiked sphere swung in a windmill motion. It visits swift justice to infidels and crunches limbs, heads, and torsos in one devastating movement.

The blazing star is not the Vanquisher's only weapon, for it also wields the flame belcher to bring destruction from afar. Shortly before the design of this warjack, Protectorate alchemists learned to refine Menoth's Fury into an even more combustible form requiring no ignition source but exposure to air. Compressed into a heavy cannonball, these shells shatter on impact, and the explosion blazes oil across a wide area. The blast sears the area hot enough to melt metal before the oil consumes itself in a blaze of superheated air.

Some would say the Vanquisher was the first sign of the coming full crusade against Cygnar when Hierarch Voyle urged his artificers to create more powerful and overt weapons of war. There can be no disguising the nature of the Vanquisher. Despite being based on the same chassis as the Crusader, it could never feign to be a laborjack. Cygnaran defenders of Caspia and Eastwall have already faced the brilliant simplicity of its design, and they watch in horror as it sweeps through hardened knights and soldiers to leave nothing but destruction and mourning in its wake.

SPD	STR	MAT	RAT	DEF	ARM
4	11	5	4	10	19

L — Flame Belcher

RNG	ROF	AOE	POW
9	1	4	13

R — Blazing Star

SPECIAL	POW	P+S
Circular Strike	5	16

Point Cost	112
Field Allowance	U
Victory Points	3
Base Size	Large

HEIGHT/WEIGHT: 12' / 9.75 tons

ARMAMENT: Blazing Star Flail (right arm), Flame Belcher (left arm)

FUEL LOAD/BURN USAGE: 275 Lbs / 5 hrs general, 1 hr combat

INITIAL SERVICE DATE: 598 AR

CORTEX MANUFACTURER: Vassals of Menoth (currently)

ORIG. CHASSIS DESIGN: Engines East/Khadoran mechaniks Assembly (modified by the Sul-Menite Artificers)

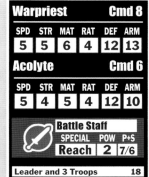

The power of faith is never ending and oft surprising. The Protectorate has long had an uncomfortable relationship with the mechanikal tools upon which its military relies. Since shortly after the Cygnaran Civil War, the Menites saw the need to make use of converted laborjacks and stolen warjacks modified and armored for battle. At the crux of their faith, however, they consider such fabrications blasphemous. Hierarch Luctine first derived the means to sanctify their use, purifying even formerly profane artifices to turn them to holy use when accompanied by fervent prayer and blessings. Successive accomplishments in battle are taken as a sign of Menoth's favor, for it seems the Creator smiles on their efforts and encourages warjacks sent into war while accompanied by prayer. The choirs of Menoth bring holy chants to the battlefield and march alongside the giants of iron and steel to empower them with their faith.

Acolytes are grouped into choirs with devout warpriests who lead them onto the field of battle with their sacred scrolls in hand. These priests are chosen among those most likely to demonstrate the rare gift of connecting to and controlling warjacks in battle. The warpriest leads a powerful, ancient canticle reinforcing the already woven bonds between warjacks and their warcaster masters. Their prayers turn aside incoming projectiles, unravel enemy spells before they can reach their targets, and divinely guide warjacks' weapons to smite unbelievers. The effort required by the choir to achieve their perfect meditative chants is taxing and leaves them helpless to perform other acts in the field. The Flameguard often stand at the ready and defend the chorus if combatants dare to approach.

The results of the choir are testaments to the power of the divine will of Menoth. They have attained a level of harmony with these machines the likes of which Cygnaran warcasters have yet to dream. No doubt they have become a concern to all the Protectorate's foes.

WARPRIEST

BATTLE HYMN - As a special action, the Warpriest may recite one of the following Battle Hymns, affecting friendly Protectorate warjacks currently within 3" of him. A warjack may only be under the effect of one Battle Hymn at a time. All Battle Hymns last for one round.

- **INFUSE (★ACTION)** - Affected warjacks gain +2 to attack and damage rolls.
- **SAFE PASSAGE (★ACTION)** - Affected warjacks cannot be targeted by ranged attacks.
- **SHIELDING WARD (★ACTION)** - Affected warjacks cannot be targeted by spells.

LEADER

ACOLYTE

CHANT (★ACTION) - The Warpriest gains +1" to the range of his Battle Hymn effects for each Acolyte in the Choir who chants.

BATTLE STAFF

REACH - 2" melee range.

Warpriest				Cmd 8	
SPD	STR	MAT	RAT	DEF	ARM
5	5	6	4	12	13

Acolyte				Cmd 6	
SPD	STR	MAT	RAT	DEF	ARM
5	4	5	4	12	10

Battle Staff			
	SPECIAL	POW	P+S
	Reach	2	7/6

Leader and 3 Troops	18
Up to 2 Additional Troops	2ea
Field Allowance	3
Victory Points	2
Base Size	Small

TACTICAL TIP

BATTLE HYMN — These are not like upkeep spells. A warjack is only affected by the first hymn recited for it in a turn. Additionally, When an ability says a model can't be targeted, it applies equally to friendly and enemy models.

INFUSE — Apply this bonus to the damage roll, not the POW. E.g., an infused Redeemer rolls 2d6+8 for its Skyhammer's blast damage.

DELIVERERS
Protectorate Unit

ARMS MASTER
LEADER

SKYHAMMER

INACCURATE - A Deliverer suffers –4 to his attack rolls with the Skyhammer.

MISFIRE - A Skyhammer rocket prematurely detonates on an attack roll of all 1s and causes a direct hit to the attacking model and blast damage to each other model in the 3" AOE.

TACTICAL TIP

MISFIRE – If the attack will automatically hit the target (because of Death Sentence, for example), you do not have to roll for a misfire.

Arms Master				Cmd 7	
SPD	STR	MAT	RAT	DEF	ARM
5	4	5	6	12	11

Deliverer				Cmd 5	
SPD	STR	MAT	RAT	DEF	ARM
5	4	4	5	12	11

Skyhammer			
RNG	ROF	AOE	POW
16	1	3	12

Sword		
SPECIAL	POW	P+S
—	3	7

Leader and 5 Troops	46
Up to 4 Additional Troops	7ea
Field Allowance	1
Victory Points	2
Base Size	Small

The Cygnarans take pride in their ability to unleash hails of bullets. However, the rockets of the Deliverers—called Skyhammers—provide the faithful with even greater range and destructive potential. Whistling through the air in long and deadly arcs, these rockets rain down across the battlefield, explode like thunder, and bring the wrath of the Lawgiver. Few enemies are brave or hardy enough to face a withering barrage of Deliverer fire long enough to close because entire formations can become consumed in roaring blossoms of incinerating fire.

The Deliverers were one of many achievements of Hierarch Garrick Voyle's push to reform the Protectorate's military. Voyle realized the relatively expensive Redeemer warjack employs a cheap and easily built form of fiery rockets. The hierarch ordered an even less expensive (and more expendable) method of launching the lethal payloads—the faithful themselves.

Originally Deliverers aimed the dangerous, self-propelled explosives by hand by holding a length of wood until the fuse lit and the rocket spiraled into the air. Most of the time the rockets landed among the enemy lines before exploding in a shower of deadly shrapnel. Sometimes, however, the rockets detonated immediately after launch or fell straight to earth, woefully short of the foe. Ranking arms masters developed a more stable launching method and implemented reinforced cylindrical tubes to be aimed at the enemy. Even with these improvements, only the most devoted serve in the Deliverer units. Lighting Skyhammer fuses is a dangerous game with the possibility of a misfire never far away. Deliverers pride themselves on their courage, and they walk into battle with tremendous explosives knowing that each rocket they launch may be the one to send them to Urcaen.

> *Conviction is more lethal than any blade, and faith is stronger than any armor. No faithless soldier can withstand the force of the many eager to die if necessary to preserve their beliefs.*
>
> —Declaration of Hierarch Sulon
> to the poorly armed zealots of what would become Sul

One of the Protectorate of Menoth's concessions in signing the treaties with Cygnar stated that they were not permitted to retain a standing army. However, as Visgoth Ozeall penned his names to those papers, he knew full well that should any leader of the Protectorate call for arms, every able-bodied citizen would answer the call without hesitation. Among the regular citizens are those who feel the stirrings of their religion so strongly they would gladly give up their lives to confront the enemies of the faith. They are willing to employ any weapon, even bare hands if need be, in that cause.

The Cygnarans are not total fools. Being quite aware of the fanatical devotion of the Menites, they decreed it unlawful for the zealots of the Protectorate to bear martial arms. In past decades Cygnar remained vigilant about these rules, but necessity has forced them to pay less heed. Nonetheless, the Menite clergy prepared their citizens, secretly trained them for combat, and created massive stockpiles of weapons with which to arm them at a moment's notice. When the zealots hear a call to arms, they know to rush to one of these hidden weapon caches and hurl themselves into the chaos of battle.

To bolster the faith of their people—and to remind them of the just torments of a coward's death in Menoth's eyes—Menite priests walk amongst the zealots sermonizing and leading them in prayer. These are often local village priests who trained extensively with their local faithful. In recent times, these priests have become so persuasive that entire villages have engaged in bloody uprisings against Cygnaran soldiers patrolling the fringes of their land. If one fanatic is a dangerous thing, a hundred thousand promises to be utterly apocalyptic.

PRIEST
LEADER

PRAYERS OF MENOTH - As a special action, the Priest may recite one of the following Prayers. Every model in his unit, including himself, gains the listed benefits for one round:

- **PRAYER OF FERVOR (★ACTION):** +2 to attack and damage rolls.
- **PRAYER OF PROTECTION (★ACTION):** +2 ARM.
- **PRAYER OF WARDING (★ACTION):** Cannot be targeted by spells.

HEAVY MACE (PRIEST ONLY)
LIGHT MACE (ZEALOT ONLY)
FIREBOMBS (ZEALOT ONLY)

CRITICAL FIRE - On a critical hit, each model in the AOE suffers Fire. Fire is a continuous effect that sets the target ablaze. A model on fire suffers a POW 12 damage roll each turn during its controller's Maintenance Phase until the Fire expires on a d6 roll of 1 or 2. Fire effects are alchemical substances or magical in nature and are not affected by water.

TACTICAL TIP

PRAYERS OF MENOTH – The Priest cannot pray when the unit runs or charges.

Priest				Cmd 8	
SPD	STR	MAT	RAT	DEF	ARM
6	5	5	4	13	13

Zealot				Cmd 4	
SPD	STR	MAT	RAT	DEF	ARM
6	4	4	4	12	10

Firebombs			
RNG	ROF	AOE	POW
5	1	3	14

Heavy Mace		
SPECIAL	POW	P+S
—	4	9

Light Mace		
SPECIAL	POW	P+S
—	2	6

Leader and 5 Troops	40
Up to 4 Additional Troops	5ea
Field Allowance	3
Victory Points	2
Base Size	Small

KNIGHTS EXEMPLAR
Protectorate Unit

WARDER
LEADER

UNIT

BOND OF BROTHERHOOD - A Knight Exemplar gains +1 STR and ARM for each member of his unit that has been destroyed. These bonuses are lost if the model is returned to play and returned to this unit.

FEARLESS - A Knight Exemplar never flees.

WEAPON MASTER - A Knight Exemplar rolls an additional die on his melee damage rolls.

TACTICAL TIP

BOND OF BROTHERHOOD — This bonus does not kick in until the attack and its damage have been resolved. If several Knights are caught in an AOE attack, they will not benefit from each others' deaths while resolving the AOE damage.

Warder				Cmd 9	
SPD	STR	MAT	RAT	DEF	ARM
5	6	8	4	12	15

Knight				Cmd 7	
SPD	STR	MAT	RAT	DEF	ARM
5	6	7	4	12	15

Relic Blade

SPECIAL	POW	P+S
—	5	11

Leader and 5 Troops	69
Field Allowance	1
Victory Points	2
Base Size	Small

Many scholars compare the various aspects of the Protectorate to Menoth Himself. The faithful serve as the body of Menoth on Caen, the hierarch represents the head, and the scrutators form the mouth. The masses of the laboring faithful comprise the bones while the battle-ready zealots are the blood. If this is true, then the Knights Exemplar are the weapons in His hands.

Heavily armored in blessed suits of full plate engraved with rites of protection and wards, these powerful swordsmen cry out in righteous fury as blows deflect off their armor in tones akin to a hammer striking an anvil. Even before the Cygnaran Civil War, the distinct armor of the exemplars set apart those holy soldiers who unflinchingly carried out the orders of the scrutators.

In their gauntleted hands they carry relic blades of flawless quality that seemingly burn with the words of Menoth inscribed into them. Unsheathing these blades in war is considered a righteous sacrament. Even in the hands of an amateur these weapons prove lethal, but in the grasp of Knights

Exemplar they are capable of legendary feats. The blades pass through the armor and flesh of those out of Menoth's grace as if they were made of water. Knights Exemplar are formidable in their own right, and with the divine gifts they receive from the Creator they are nearly unstoppable. These knights never allow the diminishment of their number to deter them from their cause, and they grow stronger as each of their brethren falls. Seeing one of their brothers pass into Menoth's hands fuels their faith. They know that dying in His service brings them closer to His glory.

The first time the Knights Exemplar raised arms as a large force was within the City of Walls during the Cygnaran Civil War. At that time only a few hundred of the holy warriors served the clergy. Now by the bidding of Hierarch Voyle, their numbers surge with the faithful who feel the calling to take up the sword. There is no telling how many of these divine knights will be sent to inflict retribution on the heretics in days to come.

TEMPLE FLAMEGUARD
Protectorate Unit

Such dedication must be rewarded. They are wasted watching over these buildings and relics. Let us give them the chance to test themselves. Let us give them the chance to meet the Creator in glory. Let us give them the honor of battle!

—Hierarch Garrick Voyle

Outside the temples of Menoth, the Flameguard stand ever vigilant. The great Hierarch Sulon created the Flameguard by conscripting able-bodied Menites in the days leading up to the Cygnaran Civil War. Though the temples had long gathered and armed guardians from among the faithful, the Flameguard was something new, unified in training and discipline to become true soldiers of the faith. Garbed in heavy flowing white tabards and glimmering helms, they trained to use the spear and shield to great effect. Their purpose: keep the temples and holy sites under guard at all times and preserve the sacred flame burning in each house of worship. In return for making themselves useful to Menoth, they were granted indulgences by order of Sulon and earned favored status and comfort for their families.

Even in the time of Sulon and increasingly under the direction of hierarchs who followed after, the Flameguard's post as temple sentries was a veneer for creating a well trained and armed military. After the development of Menoth's Fury under Hierarch Turgis, the Flameguard's spears were fitted with reservoirs of the fiery substance. They gripped their flame spears with a renewed determination. Having started as sacred guards, they eventually became elite infantry who protect warcasters and battle priests. The Flameguard are prized as the first and last line of defense in battle, and they serve as a thick wall protecting important clergy from harm.

With their spears they display great skill honed by practice and ceaseless drills. Each spear is roughly seven feet in length and made of durable alloys. Inside the haft sits a tube of Menoth's Fury piped to surface vents in the barbed spear tip and ignited by flint clackers at the blade's base. When used, the spear drips oily fire from these vents and inflicts excruciating wounds.

CAPTAIN
LEADER

SHIELD WALL (ORDER) - Every Temple Flameguard that received the order who is in tight formation with the Captain at the end of the unit's movement gains +4 ARM. If the Captain is no longer on the table, the largest tight formation group forms the shield wall. If there is more than one group with the largest number of troopers, the unit's controller decides which group forms the shield wall. A trooper that did not receive the order cannot join the shield wall. This bonus does not apply to damage originating in the model's back arc. Models that do not end their movement in tight formation do not benefit from the shield wall. This bonus lasts for one round.

UNIT

COMBINED MELEE ATTACK - Instead of making melee attacks separately, two or more Temple Flameguard in melee range of the same target may combine their attacks. In order to participate in a combined melee attack, a Temple Flameguard must be able to declare a melee attack against the intended target. The Temple Flameguard with the highest MAT in the attacking group makes one melee attack roll for the group and gains +1 to the attack and damage rolls for each Temple Flameguard, including himself, participating in the attack.

FLAME SPEAR

REACH - 2" melee range.

SET DEFENSE - A Temple Flameguard gains +2 DEF against charge and slam attacks originating from his front arc.

Captain				Cmd 8	
SPD	STR	MAT	RAT	DEF	ARM
6	5	7	4	13	14
Flameguard				Cmd 6	
SPD	STR	MAT	RAT	DEF	ARM
6	5	6	4	13	14

Flame Spear		
SPECIAL	POW	P+S
Multi	5	10

Leader and 5 Troops	53
Up to 4 Additional Troops	8ea
Field Allowance	3
Victory Points	2
Base Size	Small

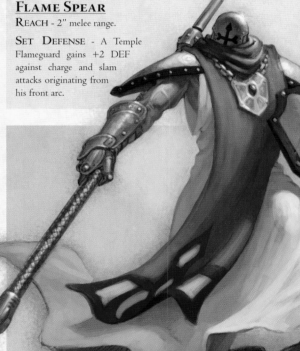

PALADIN OF THE ORDER OF THE WALL
Protectorate Solo

PALADIN

FEARLESS - A Paladin never flees.

STONE-AND-MORTAR STANCE - The Paladin may voluntarily forfeit his movement to gain +5 DEF and ARM for one round. While in the Stone-and-Mortar stance, the Paladin may only attack a model that has attacked him in its previous turn. A Paladin cannot make free strikes while in the Stone-and-Mortar stance.

WEAPON MASTER - A Paladin rolls an additional die on his melee damage rolls.

FIREBRAND

CRITICAL FIRE - On a critical hit, target model suffers Fire. Fire is a continuous effect that sets the target ablaze. A model on fire suffers a POW 12 damage roll each turn during its controller's Maintenance Phase until the Fire expires on a d6 roll of 1 or 2. Fire effects are alchemical substances or magical in nature and are not affected by water.

Paladin					Cmd 9
SPD	STR	MAT	RAT	DEF	ARM
6	7	8	4	13	15

Firebrand		
SPECIAL	POW	P+S
Critical	7	14

Damage	5
Point Cost	19
Field Allowance	1
Victory Points	1
Base Size	Small

Among Menoth's first gifts to man was the wall, by which we were taught to protect our people. Atop the first wall at civilization's dawn, a paladin stood vigil.

—Lesson taught during initiation to the Order of the Wall

The Order of the Wall is shrinking in these times, and its members are fleeting reminders of an ancient brotherhood. Knights of this order have served mankind since the first words of the Canon of the True Law, acting as bastions of stability when the wilderness threatened to overthrow civilization. Hierarch Voyle believes their codes are outmoded and are impediments in the crusades against unbelievers. The paladins sometimes disobey orders given by the scrutators, which is a sign that they lack the loyalty and obedience that are the hallmarks of the Knights Exemplar. One day soon Voyle could disband this heroic order, but for now they continue to serve. They prefer to protect His flock rather than drown them in rivers of blood, and they believe even the wayward can be guided back to the path of the Creator. They are beloved by the people and loathed by the clergy, so they stand alone in an unenviable position at a time of absolute power among the scrutators.

Encased in the protection of tempered steel, each paladin is trained to hold against any enemy and can become akin to the cornerstone of an unbreakable and unmoving fortress. Even powerful blows from the likes of warjacks will glance harmlessly off a paladin's shield while his sword returns strikes capable of shearing mechanikal limbs. When the paladin strikes, his sword erupts in holy fire like a sliver of the sun. The heated blade slices through armor and flesh, and few who witness a Firebrand in combat doubt the holy power flowing through it.

For every soul saved by the paladin's actions, two more are lost to the wracks and thumbscrews of the scrutators. Of all the warriors fighting for the Temple of Menoth, the paladins are the least comfortable with the changes initiated by Hierarch Voyle and the only ones brave enough to speak fondly of the old ways.

Cryx

Death Denied
A Brief History of Cryx

> Your claim to power is meaningless. There is only servitude or annihilation. Make your choice.
>
> —Emissary of Lord Toruk to the fourteen pirate kings of the Scharde Isles

Lich Lord Daeamortus speaking to Skarre Ravenmane, captain of the *Widower*:

The task set before us is neither simple nor easy, but the outcome is inevitable. This world will fall to our master Lord Toruk. Our true strength has remained shrouded for a millennium, lest mankind unite against us and delay His inevitable dominion. Better to seem a remote nightmare, a threat to their shores and nothing more. They think themselves safe in the heartland. Far from the oceans, they feel secure among their farms, roads, bridges, and cities. Only when our innumerable legions fall upon them and consign their fragile nations to ruin will they see the truth. Nowhere is safe from our grasp.

The mainland will fall. We add another to our ranks with every gunshot, sword stroke, and rending claw. Death strengthens us even as it saps our enemies. Burn us and we rise again. Hiding will not avail them, nor resistance, nor any effort put forth by their weak and distant gods. We shall unleash oceans of blood, and our ships will go forth on the red tide with a plague wind filling our black sails. Lord Toruk will not be denied, and mortals have but one choice: slavery in life or servitude in death. Every village that falls brings us another legion. Every city slaughtered gains us a fortress. There is no more loyal army in all of Caen.

Understand that we do not wage a war of simple conquest. We care little for the land or resources that so consume the petty minds of mortals. Cryx will rise from beneath to consume all. We know no true or lasting defeat. *Sacrifice* is a hollow word spoken by doomed mortals. The loss of countless minions means nothing should it further our master's designs. This ship, your crew, every weapon at your disposal, your very self may be expended for our purposes. This is our strength, and in the execution of our plans you must be as ruthless and brazen as necessary. Commit every resource toward total victory. You must understand this to serve us, but do not imagine we suffer failure lightly.

Serve and the rewards may surpass your life's extinction. Betrayal is not an option, for our master sees and knows all we do. If there is strength in you, prove it in battle and make your mark. When at last you are drowning in your own blood, hope one such as myself approves of your efforts and decides to reward you with undeath. Your flesh will transform and become eternal so as to bear witness to our ultimate conquest.

As Asphyxious serves me so you must serve him. Use the powers we have brought forth from your blighted blood to control the machines delivering death to those who would resist us. Set them upon our enemies. Let them know no rest, no mercy, and no respite even after death.

✳ ✳ ✳

You have asked of my ancient origins, and I will indulge you. Let it be a lesson in the power one can attain after casting aside mortality. It is a tale long in the telling, and I have not thought back to those faded days in centuries. I prefer not to consider my past form, for I retain no echo of that mortal life save in the dimmest stirring of memory. Immortality and the vicissitudes of time irrevocably change a being.

Over sixteen centuries I have witnessed the birth and demise of empires, countless wars, and the unfolding of the Dragonfather's unknowable plans. We lords of Cryx are exalted above all others. Though chosen to oversee His domain and carry forth His works, we are as far removed from Him as you who in turn serve us. Even those of us present at His arrival lack the insight to pierce His mind or comprehend His will. Lords of all we grasp, we remain slaves to His designs.

We were pirate kings when first Toruk came to the Scharde Isles and fools every one of us not to recognize the Dragon as imperishable. We each thought ourselves a master of great forces. Once we had the freedom to satisfy our petty whims and each of us carved an empire by ship, oar, and blade. We lived beholden to nothing except our greed. Do not make the mistake of thinking us simple. Though we were pale shadows of what He would make us, we had power in our own way. We were not simple bandits or exiles, but each a mighty king with his own army, court, and blood-bathed and battle-tested vassals.

Your ancestors on the isle of Satyx prided themselves on their lore of blood. They knew the power brought from bloodletting and sacral rite. Others on the islands had their own occult lore. Always we sought weapons to outdo our rivals and any tool to increase our territories. Some turned to the worship of the Devourer and learned the ancient blasphemies of guttural tongues to enlist those savage tribes living thick across the islands. Others turned to the dark goddess Thamar and drank of the cup of forbidden lore. We remained arrogant imposters. We hoped to control powers to rival the priest-kings of old who in turn were slaves to their own god.

I tell you this so you understand the hubris with which we greeted the first emissary Lord Toruk sent to reveal His demands. We declared truce from our incessant infighting and gathered our forces together thinking to stand against the Dragon. We thought there no force on Caen that could stand against us when united. Fools! We had not seen true power flowing as it does in the body of a terrible god made flesh. We were emboldened by the words of King Threnodax, the mightiest of our fourteen-member fellowship. He proved the greatest fool. He had sipped the rudiments of power and thought himself mighty. We killed the Dragon's messenger and prepared ourselves for war. Little did we know our feeble strength would not avail us in the slightest.

Among our pirate fleets one ship stood mightier than the rest. The *Atramentous* was a dirgenmast ship once of the nation of Tordor stolen by Threnodax for his vaunted flagship and his greatest vessel for plundering and pillaging. Often I endured Threnodax boasting of this ship, its fierce captain, and its bloodthirsty crew. Proving a capacity for bitter irony, Lord Toruk chose to seize that vessel and turn its crew against their former king.

The Dragon could as simply have come into our midst to destroy us, but such was beneath Him. He sought an abject lesson rather than our destruction. We were fortunate that He had yet to birth His Empire and had need of generals, even generals as impudent as we had been. The Dragonfather came to the *Atramentous*, funeral vessel turned pirate flagship, and obliterated its crew and captain in a breath of all-consuming fire. He extinguished their lives, collected their souls, and gave them new birth in death.

This was Toruk's lesson. Our dabbling in dark arts was nothing compared to true power. The revenant ship *Atramentous* came upon us as we gathered at Threnodax's fortress in Darkmoor in the shadow of a long dormant volcano. The unliving crew poured forth across the piers to light our ships ablaze and tear their blades through our armies like a culling wind. Thirteen kings gathered in that fortress tower and watched in horror as all we had built burned. Only King Moorcraig was absent. Perhaps some oracle had warned him to seek hiding. I know not. His time would soon come. We thirteen were the last alive when Toruk came to us, and we knew in that moment the meaninglessness of our existence. We prostrated and humbled ourselves. Only Threnodax, stubborn to the end, continued to speak defiance. Toruk annihilated us in a single breath, but we twelve who had bowed were reborn. With our souls enslaved we became His vassals to rule over a new empire.

> We care little for the land or resources that so consume the petty minds of mortals. Cryx will rise from beneath to consume all.

Toruk consumed Threnodax's soul for special torment, and perhaps he still dances in endless agony. Moorcraig retreated to his castle and hoped his collection of ancient bobbles would protect him. His doom came on black wings. The Dragon flew over his castle and unleashed unquenchable fire. All of Moorcraig's plans and schemes burned and were buried in rubble. This is the consequence of defiance, a lesson seared into my soul and remembered forever. Lord Toruk transformed we twelve who remained into immortal generals and seneschals of the Dragon. He brought us far past the limits of our feeble living flesh. Few of those original kings remain, yet Toruk has kept us twelve in number. He allows us to contest with one another and prove our strength against ambitious subordinates simply to ensure that the strongest survive to serve Him.

We wasted no time or effort founding Toruk's empire, as we were privy now to secrets and powers known previously only to our master. True necromancy was revealed to us. We in turn built the framework that has given rise to a nation and an army like no other seen on

Caen—one worthy of our master and capable of bringing to heel those of the Dragon's progeny who had betrayed their creator. Such an effort was not done in a single day, but time is inconsequential to the undying.

Yes, we learned that Toruk, although mightiest and first, was not the only dragon. In an age before our insignificant births Toruk had created treacherous progeny that refused to serve Him. His own essence was too powerful even when divided. A dragon cannot be tamed or ruled, and it seeks absolute supremacy. His progeny sought to steal His strength, so he hunted them across the centuries to consume their athancs—their essence-stones—to rejoin His primal one. So it

His exile was by His choice, for he had derived a plan whereby he could unravel this knotted alliance of his progeny. All he required was an empire, an army, and puissant generals to lead them. Cryx became the seed that would give fruit to an island empire.

In those early centuries we twelve divided the ruling of Cryx among us, each finding his role in directing the construction of an empire. We returned to our old followers and fiefdoms, gathered and united them, and allowed them to taste our freshly awoken powers. We brought each scattered village and pirate hold to heel with brutal example, and we taught the importance of obedience with blood and lash. We crushed petty faiths

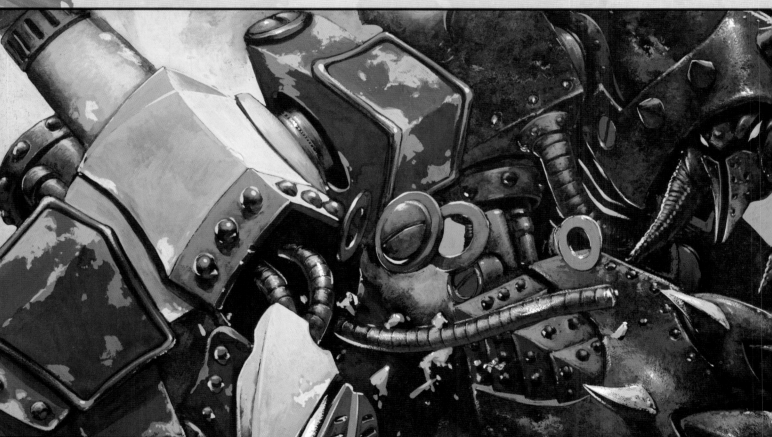

was that Toruk rent and consumed Shazkz the White Dragon in a great battle over your island of Satyx. Her draconic blood rained down to shape your people and enhance their rude forms like clay fired in a kiln. Toruk killed many others, but the survivors banded together and battered our master until he felt it prudent to leave the mainland and regain His strength so expended in innumerable battles.

and gave their followers the choice of obedience in life or unending servitude in death. Lord Toruk became our sole god and master.

We gifted those useful vassals who possessed a spark worth preserving higher undeath and allowed them to retain their full reasoning. We chose first those demonstrating an aptitude for even the pathetic rudiments of necromancy dabbled in before the Dragon's arrival. As Toruk opened my mind to the deeper art, I in turn opened the minds of those coming after. This was the dominion left to me as I had sampled most deeply of that craft. I codified the rudiments, passed methodically down to others, to master the industry of reanimation and soul extraction that would become the wellspring of our strength.

Your master Asphyxious, drawn to the majesty of the Dragonfather, came among us early. He demonstrated an unusual aptitude in the manipulation of death-born power. While not among we twelve at the beginning, Asphyxious received a form similar to our own as Toruk assured us he would make a worthy weapon in time. This has come to pass just as He predicted. Asphyxious passed to my service

to learn my arts and assist in the creation of Toruk's army. He has remained my greatest and most loyal tool and weapon. Aspire to emulate his example.

Never on Caen has a nation like ours arisen with singularity of purpose shaped by a power so vast and possessed of limitless intelligence. The kingdoms of man are haphazard. They are driven by the capricious rising and falling of kings and petty lords and other meaningless events naïvely called history. Toruk and His lich lords keep our evolution on a guided trajectory.

It was here that industry revolutionized applied necromancy by fusing dead flesh and iron to enhance form. We have refined such methods to combine occult power and engineering never equaled by the living. The weapons we develop testify to our supremacy, and in our streets the dead walk alongside the living. The powerful energies of the Dragon Himself have shaped the land and its people. What some call the 'blight' seeps eventually into all things. This is the shadow of the Dragon and His brand upon all in His demesne.

Even as the moment arrived when our armies were ready to crush the petty kingdoms across the waters, the arrival of the Orgoth gave us pause. Those conquerors fell upon the mainland before our plans could reach fruition. We decided we should bide our time and observe, and we consolidated our strength while the Orgoth broke the will of the people of the Thousand Cities. Orgoth ships came once to our shores, but Toruk disabused them of any ambitions of conquest among our islands. Breathing flame upon their ships, He sent them burning into the deep still blazing as the ocean's water tried and failed to quench His fire. The Dragon's plans are adaptable, and we would deal with the Orgoth at a time of our choosing. We allowed them to occupy the island of Garlghast but thrashed any ship that dared the Windwatcher's Passage.

A dragon cannot be tamed or ruled, and it seeks absolute supremacy.

The Orgoth proved a worthy adversary, and we learned why Toruk proceeded with patience and guile. We watched as the rebellions rose up and failed, one futile attack after another, time and time again over two centuries. Slowly the people of the mainland stretched and weakened the Orgoth, and we learned much watching these battles. Even then we had agents on the mainland serving as our eyes and ears. We allowed mortals to waste their blood and win victories inch by inch. At times their courage earned grudging respect among our number, pyrrhic though their successes seemed to be.

Out of struggle and war comes advancement and invention. We were not so arrogant as to refuse to acknowledge useful innovations or to seize them. We have always taken the weapons of our enemies and improved them for our use. Just as Toruk turned the *Atramentous* against Threnodax, we noted the construction of colossals and made efforts to acquire such lore for our armories. Where the great hulking machines fell against the Orgoth our minions came to salvage the loose debris and reclaim the corpses of those who had worked to maintain the machines or control them in battle. From their ashen remains we learned all we needed to make our own sublime machines of war.

We have since fueled our industries with every advance made by the short-lived mechaniks of the mainland. Each time one of these 'great minds' gives up his last gasp of breath, our agents are there to unearth his grave, recover his remains, and force him to whisper his secrets to us. Through the application of necro-mechanikal industry we have constructed vast numbers of helljacks and bonejacks, all engineered and produced by our necrotechs striving to outdo each other. We mine necrotite to fuel these weapons from those places that have seen mass torture and death where life energy bleeds into mud and ash to saturate the stones beneath the soil. It is a great resource, but we have another even more powerful one in the souls of the living. We who master the arts of necromancy can feed upon these souls and use them as fuel to marshal power far greater than can be conceived by the petty minds plagued with sophomoric delusions of morality.

> ## When we attack in numbers we will shatter their pathetic ships beneath the prows of our blackships and land our armies on whatever shores we desire.

Driven from their fortresses the Orgoth retreated by ship to their first and mightiest stronghold, the castle known as Drer Drakkerung on Garlghast Island. Lord Toruk was ready, having anticipated this eventuality. For years Cryxian industry in the cities of Skell, Dreggsmouth, and Blackwater was committed to crafting weapons to equal those possessed by the Orgoth. They had an impressive mastery of the arcane, and their corpses had proven resistant to our initial attempts to unravel their secrets. We knew raw force, not subtlety, would be required. The Orgoth was a foe that would not fall without tremendous commitment and would cost us a substantial portion of our prepared reserves.

The Dragon gave His approval to commence the great attack, and we sent forth an army such as few have seen in their most terrifying nightmares. The mainlanders know nothing of this final battle and ignorantly believe their rebellion had driven the blackships across Meredius. They delivered just the first blow, but the decisive and ultimate victory was ours. Our army sailed against Garlghast led by five lich lords, each a master of warfare boasting armies tens of thousands strong of thralls, men, blighted ogrun, and trollkin eager to gain Toruk's favor. I was not among them, and I envied those sent forth. It was a battle beyond imagining with invoked powers that shook the surface of Caen, brought blood raining down, and boiled the ocean to froth.

Bitter even in defeat the Orgoth had made clear their philosophy. When they saw we would triumph, their warwitches demonstrated suicidal resolve and invoked a conflagration to obliterate both themselves and our army in a show of such reckless self-destructive power as has never been witnessed. They blasted the great city of Drer Drakkerung to ruin and obliterated tens of thousands of thralls in a conflagration of fire and ash. Three lich lords were erased in an instant from the face of Caen. The two who survived were forever changed. Forced into somnolent recovery after the near disintegration of their physical forms, their minds reshaped and became unsuited thereafter to directing the chaos and fast reversals of warfare.

Our master deemed the price fair. Even an army as great as this proved inconsequential next to ultimate victory. It was a lesson to those of us entrusted to command, and we should always remember His willingness to consign His servants to ash to suit His purposes. In the wake of the tremendous battle, we required time to recover our strength, yet time is meaningless. An age to mortals is the blink of an eye to the deathless. Our losses amounted to nothing compared to the bounty we reaped in the wake of the Orgoth. Orgoth treasures came into our hands as well as several yet living Orgoth and the countless blackened corpses of the slain.

Through our arts many spoke from beyond death to reveal their secrets. Lich Lord Terminus rose to prominence, and it was by his efforts that we learned the Orgoth mastery of Meredius. These are secrets our enemies would give much to acquire, and this lore revolutionized shipbuilding at Dreggsmouth and gave birth to the Black Fleet. I know well you're familiar with these tremendous vessels, for the *Widower* ranks among their number. Those on the continent have yet to realize the strength of our navy. They think our fleet is limited to the rag-tag pirate vessels they are accustomed to encountering. When we attack in numbers we will shatter their pathetic ships beneath the prows of our blackships and land our armies on whatever shores we desire. This is why we will prevail. Any strength of our enemies becomes ours in time.

After the fall of Drer Drakkerung, Lord Toruk gave me leave to emerge from the dark halls of Skell, put aside my necromantic research, and pass the oversight of the industries of war to other hands. He needed generals to replace those destroyed on Garlghast, and he chose me to test the mainland and begin the next phase in His great plan. We would proceed with our customary patience by planting seeds in the most fertile soil. Considerable gains were to be had in the wake of the Orgoth, and we took the first great steps to recovering Toruk's wayward progeny. They are the real enemy and the only true threat to our supremacy. Fear not the bumbling soldiers of the mainland's puerile kingdoms. Were it not for Toruk's progeny the Dragonfather would cover all in His blighted shadow. This is the Great War compared to which all others are transient.

Our agents have penetrated the cities of man. They feed to us lore to conduct our coming war. Our fleets poke and prod the mainland to find the easiest routes to the dragons' lairs. Even apparent defeats at Highgate, Ceryl, or the fortress of Westwatch are part of our design. We idly discard one inconsequential army as a feint to deliver another force unobserved onto other shores and lurk inward and prepare hidden bases for coming reinforcements. Every fight you enter from this point forward is a test of your ultimate worth. My eye will be upon you as Asphyxious sets you against the enemies of the Dragonfather. There is no limit to the rewards that will come to you should you bring to our master even the smallest step toward the destruction of His progeny.

Toruk's children are shrewd but afraid. They will not dare reveal themselves openly. They hide among the nations of mankind while lashing out against any who venture close. They are cowards, yet they contain a sliver of our master. Do not underestimate them. Even the least dragon is the equal of an entire army, yet armies we have in ample supply. Toruk's children have allowed the kingdoms of mankind to rise as weak but inconvenient obstacles against our master. We must orchestrate our conquest with cunning precision to sweep aside the militaries of lesser kingdoms standing unwittingly between our master and His rebellious progeny. These lands will fall with their flesh and bones slaved to our purpose and their souls harvested to fuel our industries. If this requires us to raze every city and slay every living entity on the mainland, so be it. Life matters not except for the strength it brings us in death.

Pick apart the so-called 'Iron Kingdoms' one by one and sift among their ashes for the disloyal children who have defied their father. Toruk will reign over all of Caen as its undisputed master and god.

Our time is at hand. Our machinations and the weaknesses inherent in man will soon propel the mainland into bitter warfare. For decades enmity has festered among rival nations as each accumulates stockpiles of weapons and trains new generations of soldiers. We have seen many petty clashes in the last centuries, but I predict the next will outdo them all. We shall witness carnage on an unparalleled scale. Nations deeming themselves great cannot abide the existence of rivals, and in their thrashing struggles for dominance they open the way to us.

Their armies will hurl themselves upon the spears of their adversaries. They will turn cannons and rifles inward and leave not but death and slaughter as a feast upon which we will glut ourselves. Every battle they wage is a diversion to exploit. All the better should both vying forces in a conflict expend themselves like a drowning man flailing for purchase against craggy rocks before sinking forever. Death for them is unavoidable, yet we refuse to be extinguished and remain everlasting and immortal. Impress me in the days ahead and I may preserve you. Only if you demonstrate the unique qualities we require will I include you in our undying company. Go forth. Pillage, burn, destroy, and leave nothing but ruins and corpse piles. Our enemies are blinded by inconsequential battles over land. Do not think as they think. Let me see you as a harbinger of utter annihilation with your every waking breath devoted to the glory of Lord Toruk.

Iron Lich Asphyxious

Forget what you were. I grant you a new form suitable to serve a god.

—Attributed to Lord Toruk

Asphyxious has become the Dark Dragon's chosen instrument on the mainland and the unholy general of the vast, rapacious unliving army of Cryx. His campaigns have carved out a bastion for the Cryx forces in the depths of the Thornwood. He excavates pits of evil and despair in old and forgotten battlefields in order to spawn countless horrors that stalk the night.

The iron lich has almost forgotten the time when he was living; it was the blink of an eye compared to the sixteen centuries he has spent in his greater form. Once he was a powerful member of the enigmatic Circle who watched over the Scharde Islands for his cabal. Even then he thirsted for greater power and explored the destructive energies of nature. When he saw Lord Toruk flying across the ocean to land upon the islands, the druid realized the true shape of ultimate power given form.

The druid spent his days witnessing the seminal acts by which the Cryxian Empire was born, and he secretly watched as Lord Toruk spread his claw across the region. He saw the dread ship *Atramentous* sail into Darkmoor Harbor to greet the gathered pirate kings, exulted in the following slaughter, and witnessed with jealous hunger as the Dragon obliterated the twelve pirate kings and remade them into undying lich lords.

Renouncing his ancient vows, the druid went to the Dragonfather at the site that would become known as Dragon's Roost in the shadow of a great volcano. The druid prostrated himself and offered his service if he could be given a taste of immortality and even a fraction of the Dragon's power. Toruk made no promises but challenged the mortal to prove his willingness to sacrifice everything with no assurances of a future.

Cryx Warcaster Character

It was a mad request, but the druid did not flinch. He immediately climbed atop the lip of the nearby volcano and jumped into its depths. Magma devoured his body; even the druid's resilience to the natural elements barely dulled the pain and only sufficed to keep his bones safe from the heat. When the magma stripped his flesh, his screams finally fell silent. Toruk scooped him from the caldera with one massive talon and blew a spark of unlife into the skeleton still glowing white-hot like steel set into a forge. The druid's dark soul lingered, agitated from torment. Those among the first generation of Toruk's necromancers gathered the soul and secured it in a receptacle to hold it against this new creature's as yet unproven loyalty. On that day, Asphyxious came into being as a lich in the Dragon's employ.

After the forges of Skell were completed and the industry of Toruk's new empire began to belch smoke and piece together the first weapons for His newly forming army, the liches were called forth. Asphyxious and the lich lords were given the gift of steel. Their brittle bones were wrapped in frames of dark metal and imbued with the strength and resiliency of iron. Among the first iron liches, Asphyxious was sent forth to do Toruk's bidding and master the great powers of necromancy open to him. He did so with nearly unmatched aptitude, but he burned with greater ambition magnified by his insatiable hunger for souls.

For sixteen centuries he has gathered lore, mastered the arts of war and necromancy, and become as formidable a creature as has ever walked the face of Caen. Asphyxious promises dark glory for the Cryxian army. He looks to orchestrate the plans of the Dragonlord, to see His empire encompass the mainland, to drown its cities in blood, and release a never-ending tide of souls from which he can drink and draw power.

The magic of the iron lich is destructive, relentless, and merciless. Asphyxious leaves behind ashen fields of lifeless grasses and withered trees where once grew fertile fields, and blackened corpses and bubbling pools of gore are all that remain of his victims. Death energy fuels Asphyxious, but the demands of his iron body create a ravenous thirst for fresh souls. The powerful iron carapace grants great

physical strength, and his iron talons wield the ensorcelled Soulsplitter—a twin-pronged spear bathed in entropy that consumes metal and flesh.

Asphyxious is a terrible foe crafty beyond belief and capable of any act in Lord Toruk's name. A prime source of the cancer feeding upon western Immoren, he gleefully spreads the shadow of the Dragonlord's wings. It is a shadow that will one day, by his efforts, extend to all of Caen.

Focus 7				Cmd 7	
SPD	STR	MAT	RAT	DEF	ARM
6	7	6	3	15	16

Soulsplitter

	SPECIAL	POW	P+S
	Multi	8	15

Damage	18
Point Cost	78
Field Allowance	C
Victory Points	5
Base Size	Medium

SPECIAL RULES

FEAT:
CONSUMING BLIGHT

Constant death follows in the wake of the iron lich, and it is on this death that Asphyxious feeds. In a horrific display of necromancy, this terrible undead warcaster may leech the life from the earth itself and all who stand on it.

Living models currently in Asphyxious' control area suffer an unboostable POW 5 damage roll. In addition, Asphyxious replenishes all of his focus points.

ASPHYXIOUS
SOUL CAGES - Asphyxious gains a soul token for each living model destroyed within 2". During his controller's next Control Phase, replace each soul token with a focus point.

TERROR - Enemy model/units in melee range of Asphyxious and enemy models/units with Asphyxious in their melee range must pass a command check or flee.

UNDEAD - Asphyxious is not a living model and never flees.

SOULSPLITTER
REACH - 2" melee range.

SUSTAINED ATTACK - Once Asphyxious hits a target with Soulsplitter, additional attacks with it against the same target this turn automatically hit. No additional attack rolls are necessary.

SPELL	COST	RNG	AOE	POW	UP	OFF
BREATH OF CORRUPTION	3	8	3	12	X	X
Models in the AOE suffer a POW 12 damage roll. Breath of Corruption is a cloud effect that stays on the table as long as upkeep is paid. Models entering or ending their activation in the cloud suffer one damage point.						
HELLFIRE	3	10	—	14		X
Target model/unit hit by Hellfire must pass a command check or flee.						
IRON BLIGHT	2	8	—	*		X
Target warjack takes d6 damage points to its Hull only in a random location.						
PARASITE	3	8	—	—	X	X
Target model/unit suffers −3 ARM and Asphyxious gains +1 ARM. Asphyxious removes one damage point each time the spell's upkeep is paid.						
SCYTHING TOUCH	2	6	—	—	X	
Target model/unit gains +2 STR.						
SHADOW WINGS	3	SELF	—	—		
Asphyxious moves up to 10" ignoring terrain penalties and effects, then ends his activation. Asphyxious cannot be targeted by free strikes during this movement.						
SPECTRAL LEECH	3+	8	—	—		X
Target warcaster loses one focus point next turn, plus one for each additional focus point above 3 Asphyxious spends when casting Spectral Leech.						

TACTICAL TIP

BREATH OF CORRUPTION – All models in the AOE suffer a POW 12 damage roll instead of normal AOE damage. Incorporeal models suffer the damage from moving into Breath of Corruption.

CONSUMING BLIGHT – Basically this feat refills Asphyxious' focus pool up to his current FOC. He cannot, however, make a partial payment to cast a spell and then use this feat to regain focus points and make the rest of the payment.

IRON BLIGHT – The d6 roll cannot be boosted because it is not a standard damage roll.

SHADOW WINGS – Asphyxious can use Shadow Wings to move into or across deep water.

Pirate Queen Skarre

She's the drowning tide, the wave that crushes a ship and sends all hands to the deep, the poison smile of a woman who looks you over only to find a place for her dagger.

—Satyxis Raider on the *Widower*

Skarre Ravenmane, the 'Pirate Queen', is the bloodthirsty ruler of the Satyxis—warrior women of the island of Satyx blighted by ancient dragon blood to become something more than human. She is a woman for whom power runs thicker than blood in her veins, and her name spells terror to any who hear of her approach. Her ship, the *Widower*, strikes along the western coast frequently. Its course and destination are impossible to predict and throw all the navies of the mainland into confusion and disarray. Without warning she disgorges undead forces and helljacks from the black hull of her vessel to obliterate any resistance to her raids. She withdraws with equal speed and leaves ruin and chaos. Bent on pillage, plunder, and slaughter, she serves as a distraction for Cryxian fleet movements, and like her sisters, she wields terrible weapons imbued with blighted power. Her magic is subtly different from that of her peers and serves as a powerful reminder that long ago even the Orgoth feared the reaver witches. Unlike the necromancers, her spells draw on the powers of blood sacrifice as learned by the Satyxis witches after the white dragon's blood rained down on them from the skies. Few know better than she the power of shed blood, for she is able to invoke acidic rain, prompt flies to spawn from the blood of her victim and explode outward in a flesh-consuming swarm, and project sickly green balefire from her fingertips.

Sacrifice is vital to Skarre's dark magic. She carries with her a millennia-old ritual dagger she uses to drain the energies binding her comrades together, living or dead, willing or not, to fuel its enchantments. Alive with stolen essence, the blade can unleash a powerful curse upon Skarre's foes. She is swift to employ her dagger to wrack her victims with gut-wrenching pain that leaves behind twisted, broken corpses.

Skarre's other weapon is Takkaryx—loosely translated as 'Death Merchant'. It is a black-bladed sword carved from one of Toruk's scales and tempered in a necrotite-fired forge. The blade allows her to draw strength from the shedding of her own blood, transforming her self-sacrifice into tremendous ferocity in battle. When Skarre wields this blade few can stand against her battle-lust. Her eyes fill with cruel glee as she dispatches as many victims as the sword demands.

Skarre has seized her position through strength and cunning, and her power impresses even the Dragonlord and His lich lords who recognize her as the leading Satyxis witch in the Cryxian fleet. Attaining her position has not come without difficulties, however, for its blood-price requires constant vigilance against those over whom she has stepped. Her domination of the Satyxis is the result of a combination of respect and fear since she has had to eliminate a number of possible rivals who have plotted against her. Only those with proven dedication and loyalty remain, and Skarre has given them command of the lesser ships of the fleet at her bidding. These intrigues have occasionally caught her up in the more subtle and dangerous games of the lich lords who view her as an effective weapon and a living pawn. Currently her service is linked to Asphyxious, and above him Lich Lord Daeamortus, but her true loyalty has always been rooted firmly to the Dragonfather.

Skarre dedicates her powerful sorcery to His unholy faith. She reads portents and auguries in every kill and claims the Dragon speaks to her through the entrails of her victims. Through these signs she steers *Widower* to private ports of call to trade blood, steal coin, and sell depravity itself. Women cling tightly to their husbands when the fog thickens along the Broken Coast, for the dreaded pirate queen may be hiding within.

Focus 6				Cmd 8	
SPD	STR	MAT	RAT	DEF	ARM
7	6	7	4	16	15

Takkaryx		
SPECIAL	POW	P+S
Life Trader	7	13

Bloodwyrm		
SPECIAL	POW	P+S
Multi	3	9

Great Rack		
SPECIAL	POW	P+S
Knockdown	4	10

Damage	16
Point Cost	66
Field Allowance	C
Victory Points	5
Base Size	Small

SPECIAL RULES

FEAT: BLOOD MAGIC

As the dark queen of the Broken Coast, Skarre Ravenmane is naturally one of the greatest practitioners of the ancient, island born black magic. By sacrificing her own blood, she imbues her followers with dark power to enhance their abilities.

Give Skarre 1-5 damage points. Friendly Cryx models currently in her control area, including herself, gain +1 STR and ARM for each damage point she takes. These bonuses last for one round.

TAKKARYX

LIFE TRADER - After a successful attack with Takkaryx, Skarre may take one damage point to roll an additional damage die.

BLOODWYRM

LIFE DRINKER - For each living model destroyed with Bloodwyrm, Skarre removes one damage point.

SACRIFICIAL STRIKE (★ACTION) - Remove a friendly Cryx trooper model within 1" of Skarre from play. Target model in Skarre's control area suffers a damage roll with POW equal to the current ARM of the model sacrificed. This damage roll may be boosted.

GREAT RACK

KNOCKDOWN - A model hit by the Great Rack is knocked down.

SPELL	COST	RNG	AOE	POW	UP	OFF
BACKLASH	3	8	—	—	X	X

Whenever target warjack is damaged, its controlling warcaster takes one damage point.

SPELL	COST	RNG	AOE	POW	UP	OFF
BLOOD RAIN	3	8	3	12		X

Models in the AOE suffer Corrosion. Corrosion is a continuous effect that slowly erodes its target. Corrosion does one damage point each turn to the affected model during its controller's Maintenance Phase until it expires on a d6 roll of 1 or 2.

| DARK GUIDANCE | 5 | SELF | CTRL | — | | |

Friendly Cryx models currently in Skarre's control area, including herself, roll an additional die for melee attacks. Dark Guidance lasts for one round.

| FLY'S KISS | 2 | 8 | — | 10 | | X |

Target living model destroyed by Fly's Kiss explodes in a 3" AOE. All models in the AOE suffer an unboostable POW 10 damage roll.

| HELLFIRE | 3 | 10 | — | 14 | | X |

Target model/unit hit by Hellfire must pass a command check or flee.

| SACRIFICIAL LAMB | 2 | 6 | — | — | | |

Remove a target friendly warrior model from play and roll a d6. Skarre gains that number of additional focus points during her controller's next Control Phase. Sacrificial Lamb can only be cast once per turn.

Warwitch Deneghra

She was like a dark dream, a grymkin tale in the flesh. When I blinked...there she was... next to me...whispering and commanding... caressing...I had no will to resist.
—Captain Berle Winwort, awaiting execution for high treason

Deneghra has left a scorched path of devastation. On the battlefield she is a beautiful terror single-mindedly stalking each victim. Perversely angelic in her wicked beauty, Deneghra drifts like a phantom through trees and walls whenever she wills it. She need but whisper and men claw at their skulls in vain pursuit of silence. Those same wretches who fall prey to her spell would slit a familiar throat—comrade, brother, or beloved wife—at her command. Those few who succeed in staving off her seductions become her reluctant victims. She twirls, leaps, and laughs while enemy soldiers weep and blades slash

air or strike harmlessly off her bladed armor. Then she ends the game with a single sweep of her mechanikal spear Sliver. In Deneghra's hand the weapon turns her foe's shadow against him by entwining her opponent in a writhing mass of umbral coils. Death—rather than being a release—traps her victim's soul in the soul cages dangling from her belt.

The Cryxian warwitches are cruel beyond comparison and are willing to commit any act no matter how depraved in their lord's name. Honed to be adept at necromancy and blade, they are cunning, adaptable, and unpredictable. The witches have been so warped by Toruk's influence that some suspect they have been drained of all humanity.

None who knew Deneghra as a youth would have anticipated she could become a merciless killer. She and her twin began life in a fishing village on the western coast of Cygnar. Simple folk, her parents knew nothing of their daughters' untapped magical potential. Occult portents unveiled by Skarre Ravenmane indicated a mortal birth of a sorceress with unbridled potential. After informing Asphyxious of this presaged birth, the pirate queen was sent personally to ensure the capture of this precious cargo. The portents were vague however, and Skarre returned with just a single captive. She was unaware that her true target was a pair of twins, the whole product of the prophesied birth.

By the time Asphyxious realized their error, it was too late. Determined to turn this single captive into a weapon worthy of the effort of her capture, the iron lich set about initiating her into her new life with Cryx. First she had to learn the cost of failure, so Asphyxious forced her to watch as the raiding crew, barring only Skarre, was tortured, maimed, and slowly executed. Skarre faced her own punishment for her failure of vision, but it was a private torment she has mentioned to no one.

The frightened little girl watched the bloody execution of the crew for almost two days. An evil alchemy was underway powered by the torturers' grisly work. Both Skarre and Asphyxious knew the sight of such horrors in combination with their arcane manipulations might awaken a change. Eventually the girl's wailing subsided. By the second day a smile crossed her lips. Her smile broadened and her eyes remained unblinking as she leaned forward to take in the horror. The girl began to clap delightedly each time a raider died. They gave the girl her new name, Deneghra, and soon thereafter began to prepare her to become a warwitch.

In the following two decades, Asphyxious twisted the young woman's body, mind, and soul into a phantasmal temptress. She excelled at the arcane arts, and even the terrifying helljacks bowed to her will. When the iron lich judged her ready, he unveiled the darkest secret: she had a twin sister who possessed the other half of her powers. Asphyxious spoke of a Cygnaran sorceress who, while sharing a womb, had stolen part of Deneghra's inherent power and prevented her from reaching her potential. Deneghra raged, ranted, and slaughtered a dozen slaves to clear her head, but she could not banish the image of this pathetic twin—identical yet opposite—stealing her power. Gore-splattered from her murderous rampage, Deneghra petitioned Asphyxious to be granted command over

an incursion against Cygnar. Pleased with his machinations, the iron lich granted her request and sent forth his protégé as a lieutenant in his army.

Some scream in horror at her approach and others beg her for salvation, but Deneghra yearns for one sound alone—the throttled gurgle of her sister's death rattle. That alone would be the sweet music of victory to her black soul.

Focus 7				Cmd 8	
SPD	STR	MAT	RAT	DEF	ARM
7	5	5	4	16	14

Sliver			
	SPECIAL	POW	P+S
	Multi	7	12

Damage	16
Point Cost	76
Field Allowance	C
Victory Points	5
Base Size	Small

SPECIAL RULES

FEAT:

THE WITHERING

Darkness and death obey the beck and call of the warwitch. With mere spoken words and an arcane gesture, Deneghra blankets an area with a web of debilitating despair.

Enemy models currently in Deneghra's control area suffer −2 to their SPD, STR, MAT, RAT, DEF, ARM, CMD, and FOC for one round. Affected models cannot run, charge, or make special attacks.

DENEGHRA

SOUL CAGES - Deneghra gains a soul token for each living model destroyed within 2". During her controller's next Control Phase, replace each soul token with a focus point.

STEALTH - All attacks against Deneghra from greater than 5" away automatically miss. If Deneghra is greater than 5" away from an attacker, she does not count as an intervening model.

WITCH BARBS - Deneghra cannot be targeted by free strikes. Witch Barbs negates back strike bonuses against Deneghra.

SLIVER

REACH - 2" melee range.

SHADOW BIND - Model hit suffers −3 DEF and cannot move, other than to change facing, for one round. A previously bound model is released when a new target is hit.

SPELL	COST	RNG	AOE	POW	UP	OFF
CRIPPLING GRASP	3	8	—	—	X	X
Target model/unit suffers −2 to SPD, STR, DEF, and ARM and may not run, charge, or make special attacks.						
DARK SEDUCTION	4	6	—	—	X	X
Target living warrior model/unit must make a command check. If it fails, Deneghra's controller takes control of the target. Pay upkeep of one focus point per model, or the spell expires. Cannot be cast on characters, character units, or solos.						
DEATH RAGE	4	6	—	—		X
When target warrior model suffers sufficient damage to be destroyed, Death Rage expires. Target model is not destroyed and for one round cannot be destroyed or targeted by Death Rage. After one round, the model is destroyed.						
GHOST WALK	3	6	—	—		X
During its activation this turn target model/unit may move through any terrain without penalty. While ghost walking, a model cannot charge or slam and cannot be targeted by free strikes.						
PARASITE	3	8	—	—	X	X
Target model/unit suffers −3 ARM and Deneghra gains +1 ARM. Deneghra removes one damage point each time the spell's upkeep is paid.						
SCOURGE	4	8	3	13		X
Models in the AOE are knocked down after suffering damage.						
VENOM	2	SP	—	10		X
A stream of venomous acid spews forth and causes Corrosion to every model hit. Corrosion is a continuous effect that slowly erodes its target. Corrosion does one damage point each turn to the affected model during its controller's Maintenance Phase until it expires on a d6 roll of 1 or 2.						

TACTICAL TIP

DARK SEDUCTION — You only gain control of the unit itself. If it includes a 'jack marshal, his 'jacks do not come along for the ride.

DEATH RAGE — Roll for a model's Tough ability first, and then apply Death Rage if the model fails the roll.

GHOST WALK — A model under the effects of Ghost Walk may voluntarily enter deep water.

SHADOW BIND — A knocked down, shadow-bound model can still forfeit its movement to stand up.

THE WITHERING — Remember that power attacks are a type of special attack, so a model affected by The Withering cannot make those either. A warcaster affected by The Withering receives two fewer focus points during his controller's next Control Phase and has his control area immediately reduced by 4".

DEATHRIPPER
CRYX BONEJACK

DEATHRIPPER
ARC NODE - The Deathripper may channel spells.

MANDIBLE
SUSTAINED ATTACK - Once the Deathripper hits a target with the Mandible, additional attacks with it against the same target this turn automatically hit. No additional attack rolls are necessary.

SPD	STR	MAT	RAT	DEF	ARM
7	7	5	4	15	14

H	Mandible		
	SPECIAL	POW	P+S
	Sustained	5	12

	1	2	3	4	5	6
	H	H	C	A	A	M
	H	C	C	M	M	M

Point Cost	38
Field Allowance	U
Victory Points	1
Base Size	Medium

HEIGHT/WEIGHT: 6'4" / 2.5 tons

ARMAMENT: Mandibles (head), Necrotech Arc Node

FUEL LOAD/BURN USAGE: 44 Lbs (necrotite) or 88 Lbs (coal)/18 hrs general, 3 hrs combat

INITIAL SERVICE DATE: UNKNOWN, first seen in 502 AR

CORTEX MANUFACTURER: UNKNOWN

ORIG. CHASSIS DESIGN: UNKNOWN

Something primal in us fears the jaws of untamed beasts. They become even more frightening when their bones are stripped clean of flesh, their fangs are bared, and their eye-sockets remain hungering and empty.

—Professor Viktor Pendrake, Corvis University

The Deathripper, Cryx's quintessential bonejack, is a terrifying weapon of surprising speed and bestial ferocity that charges forward to tear apart its enemies while serving as a magical conduit for the horrifying spells of its master. It is the staple of the Nightmare Empire and is often the herald for large forces to follow. These 'jacks scurry across the battlefield as their vents pour forth poisonous smoke and steam from wickedly efficient necrotite-fueled engines. The high-pitched keen of the Deathripper venting steam has been written about in fevered war journals for decades. It is a sound rarely forgotten.

The Deathripper is built of blackened iron and steel fused with the skulls and fangs of fearsome blighted beasts chosen for their nightmarish guise. Powered by steam engines driven by necrotite—coal laced with death energy—the jaws of the Deathripper can leverage enough power to sever limbs and shear through armored metal plates. In a blur of billowing smoke, wailing metal, and bleeding hydraulics,

just a few Deathrippers can strip a light warjack down to its components within minutes. The Deathripper is shielded by minimal armor in order to maximize its terrifying speed, and the bonejack remains easily replaced between conflicts.

However, it is not its frenzied attack that makes the Deathripper such a feared weapon; it is the Cryxian arc node. Arc node technology, originally called the arcantrik relay, was the pride of Cygnar when initially developed. It was considered to be Cygnar's premiere mechanikal achievement, but it did not take long for Cryx to unravel the puzzle. Defiling the tombs of engineers who had innovated the device and pulling forth their secrets through necromantic rituals, the necrotechs soon learned how to create arc nodes of their own. They improved upon the process and were able to utilize profane materials and unholy techniques to cheapen and accelerate the manufacture. Now Cryxian warcasters enter the field with a small swarm of arc node-equipped bonejacks, each a conduit for the devastating arcane power wielded by its controlling warcaster. The Deathripper is as likely to deliver a wave of necromantic doom on its adversaries as it is to leap into the attack with its gaping jaws.

TACTICAL TIP

BONEJACK — Yes, kids. A bonejack is a light warjack.

DEFILER
CRYX BONEJACK

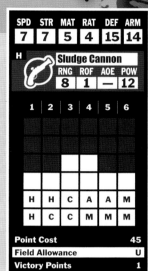

> 'Tis a shame they are so effective. They leave so little for us to salvage.
>
> —Warwitch Deneghra commenting on the Defiler's sludge cannon

Mainlanders often wonder how the Nightmare Empire can produce such a profusion of deadly and fast constructs that swarm and quickly tear apart their larger counterparts. Where other nations parcel each warjack cortex carefully, necrotech fabrication in Cryx never ceases. The hundreds of necrotechs working on various projects—each one a mad genius in its own right—are capable of tremendous innovations even while hoarding secrets and competing with each another for the favor of their unforgiving superiors. The lich lords encourage the mad pace of breakneck competition, for they know their greatest weapons will arise from the unexpected experiments and vile machinations of tireless necrotechs.

No two bonejacks are entirely the same, and variations on chassis and weaponry is common. Those excelling in battle are preserved, and their designs are carried forward to be produced in number. Failures are instantly forgotten and may even earn a necrotech a quick demise by being ground underfoot and obliterated. The Defiler has proven its worth as a Cryxian light assault bonejack. Fast and mobile, it can cross the battlefield in a few long strides and fix its warcaster's enemy in its sights before the fight has scarcely begun. Its

DEFILER
ARC NODE - The Defiler may channel spells.

SLUDGE CANNON
CORROSION - A model hit by the Sludge Cannon suffers Corrosion. Corrosion is a continuous effect that slowly erodes its target. Corrosion does one damage point each turn to the affected model during its controller's Maintenance Phase until it expires on a d6 roll of 1 or 2.

valuable arc node remains ever ready to deliver arcane death.

Where the Deathripper closes to feast, the Defiler avoids close combat and fires on the enemy with its sludge cannon. Within the bowels of this bonejack is a secured bladder of the same concentrated dissolvent pumped through bile thralls. Thralls spray a great effusion of the substance, but the Defiler is more economical and spits an acid burst in a sizzling but precisely measured gout. The thick, viscous corrosive melts through metal and stone more easily than flame eats wood. Between the potential of its arc node and the horrendous wounds caused by the sludge cannon, enemies have no choice but to close desperately with the bonejack before their allies are torn apart. Injured survivors face a fate almost worse than death.

SPD	STR	MAT	RAT	DEF	ARM
7	7	5	4	15	14

H — **Sludge Cannon**

RNG	ROF	AOE	POW
8	1	—	12

	1	2	3	4	5	6
	H	H	C	A	A	M
	H	C	C	M	M	M

Point Cost	45
Field Allowance	U
Victory Points	1
Base Size	Medium

HEIGHT/WEIGHT: 6'4" / 2.6 tons

ARMAMENT: Sludge Cannon (head), Necrotech Arc Node

FUEL LOAD/BURN USAGE: 44 Lbs (Necrotite) or 88 Lbs (coal)/17 hrs general, 2.75 hrs combat

INITIAL SERVICE DATE: UNKNOWN, first seen in 512 AR

CORTEX MANUFACTURER: UNKNOWN

ORIG. CHASSIS DESIGN: UNKNOWN

TACTICAL TIP

SLUDGE CANNON — Contrary to popular belief, the Sludge Cannon does not have a spray attack.

Nightwretch
Cryx Bonejack

NIGHTWRETCH

ARC NODE - The Nightwretch may channel spells.

For centuries Cygnar has had the dubious privilege of being the testing ground for Cryxian innovation. The Third Army out of Highgate and Westwatch has had to face the unveiling of weapons too dreadful to be imagined. None who serve as guards along this great stretch of open coastline consider the undead lacking in cunning, for they have witnessed an endless variety of nightmares given form. So many vile creations have landed on Cygnaran shores to pillage and destroy, and the arrival of the Nightwretch was one such event.

From New Larkholm came a dispatch that a Cryxian landing party had been sighted two leagues south of the city. The coastal fort of Westwatch less than 10 leagues away immediately sent out a company of long gunners. Each soldier stood ready with rifle in hand and proved eager to put a few bullets in Cryxian raiders. Unaware that they faced a new weapon, they stood shoulder to shoulder as they had been trained. Their disciplined shots dropped several of the incoming bonejacks, but not enough.

These men had only a moment to consider the unfamiliar visage of the Nightwretch before explosive projectiles launched from small cannons set into the head of each bonejack flew in their direction. These bombs contained a particularly volatile explosive mixture of blasting powder and alchemical waste byproducts and exploded into their midst with a concussive force heard for miles. None returned to report of their failure.

In seconds the entire company had been reduced to a smoldering heap of flesh flayed from bone. The 'jacks turned and followed their master back to the landing skiff on the rocky beach. Their mission was a success, and the necrotechs would soon begin mass production of the newly tested Nightwretch. They are unleashed on the enemy to blast apart those who cluster together too closely—an instinctive reaction of terrified mortals cruelly exploited by Cryxian necrotechs.

SPD	STR	MAT	RAT	DEF	ARM
7	7	5	4	15	14

H — Doomspitter

RNG	ROF	AOE	POW
6	1	3	14

1	2	3	4	5	6

| H | H | C | A | A | M |
| H | C | C | M | M | M |

Point Cost	44
Field Allowance	U
Victory Points	1
Base Size	Medium

HEIGHT/WEIGHT: 6'4" / 2.75 tons

ARMAMENT: Doomspitter Launchers (head)

FUEL LOAD/BURN USAGE: 44 Lbs (necrotite) or 88 Lbs (coal)/17 hrs general, 2.5 hrs combat

INITIAL SERVICE DATE: UNKNOWN, first seen in 590 AR

CORTEX MANUFACTURER: UNKNOWN

ORIG. CHASSIS DESIGN: UNKNOWN

TACTICAL TIP

Remember that a Nightwretch, Defiler, or Deathripper that has lost its head can still make bash attacks.

REAPER
CRYX HELLJACK

We had a proper defensive line of Ironclads surrounding Chargers to protect our last Lancer. Two of those things burst from the beach, opened fire, and reeled in the Chargers like dragonfish on a line. All bets were off.

—Commander Coleman Stryker regarding a defeat at Blue Sands

More than the bonejacks, Cryxian helljacks have a disturbing similarity in form to living creatures. They are like perverse amalgams of insects fused with machined ingenuity geared toward the simple goal of slaughter. They are hulking creatures of metal and steel with blackened armor plating that house cortexes thirsting for death. The Reaper helljack is one of the most terrible inventions to emerge from necrotech workshops. It is an evolution of the already brutally efficient Slayer, but it is equipped with even more lethal armament.

The Reaper's fiendish impaling strikes make it deadly in melee, and its harpoon reels distant foes close enough to obliterate. The Reaper is armed with a vicious mechanikal spike of tempered steel driven by a wickedly powerful piston. The Helldriver is capable of punching through the thickest iron plates with enough force to pierce boiler casings, rend gears, and reduce enemy warjacks to scrap.

As powerful as this weapon might be, it is the harpoon launcher which most distinguishes the Reaper. Inspired by weapons wielded by black ogrun aboard Cryxian pirate vessels, a Reaper's harpoon launcher can puncture armor while its hooked tip maintains a grip. Truly enormous warjacks such as the Juggernaut or Ironclad are too heavy for the Reaper to pull, so smaller targets— such as enemy warcasters—remain its chosen prey. Crossing the battlefield as swiftly as a Slayer, the Reaper gets close enough to its prey to fire its harpoon with explosive force, and its dark chain unrolls as the weapon sinks through flesh or armor. Once its target is impaled, a winch powered by the helljack's boilers reels the chain at rapid speed to bring the unfortunate in to receive the relentless strike from the Helldriver.

REAPER

TUSKS - In addition to providing an extra weapon for attacks, the Reapers's Tusks give it +2 POW for head-butt attacks.

HARPOON

DRAG - If the Harpoon damages a target model with a small- or medium-sized base, the model is moved directly into base-to-base contact with the Reaper, stopping short only if it contacts another model, an obstacle, or an obstruction. During this movement the model cannot be targeted by free strikes. After the model has been moved, the Reaper may immediately make one melee attack targeting the dragged model with any melee weapon without spending focus. Focus points may be spent for additional melee attacks.

HELLDRIVER

SUSTAINED ATTACK - Once the Reaper hits a target with the Helldriver, additional attacks with it against the same target this turn automatically hit. No additional attack rolls are necessary.

SPD	STR	MAT	RAT	DEF	ARM
6	10	6	4	13	17

L	Harpoon			
	RNG	ROF	AOE	POW
	8	1	—	12

R	Helldriver		
	SPECIAL	POW	P+S
	Sustained	6	16

—	Tusks		
	SPECIAL	POW	P+S
	—	2	12

1	2	3	4	5	6
		L		R	
L	L	M	C	R	R
	M	M	C	C	

Point Cost	113
Field Allowance	U
Victory Points	3
Base Size	Large

HEIGHT/WEIGHT: 11'10" / 6.5 tons

ARMAMENT: Helldriver (right arm), Impaling Harpoon (left arm)

FUEL LOAD/BURN USAGE: 88 Lbs (necrotite) or 196 Lbs (coal)/ 10 hrs general, 1.5 hrs combat

INITIAL SERVICE DATE: UNKNOWN, first seen in 557 AR

CORTEX MANUFACTURER: UNKNOWN

ORIG. CHASSIS DESIGN: UNKNOWN

TACTICAL TIP

DRAG — If you disable or total a warjack with the Harpoon attack, you cannot drag the resulting wreck marker. Knocked down models, however, are subject to Drag.

HELLJACK — Yes, kids. Helljacks are heavy warjacks.

SLAYER
CRYX HELLJACK

SLAYER

TUSKS - In addition to providing an extra weapon for attacks, the Slayer's Tusks give it +2 POW for head-butt attacks.

DEATH CLAW

COMBO STRIKE (★ATTACK) - The Slayer may make Death Claw attacks separately, or it can make a special attack to strike with both Death Claws simultaneously. Make one attack roll for the Combo Strike. Add the Slayer's STR once and the POW of both Death Claws to the damage roll.

CRITICAL CORROSION - On a critical hit, target model suffers Corrosion. Corrosion is a continuous effect that slowly erodes its target. Corrosion does one damage point each turn to the affected model during its controller's Maintenance Phase until it expires on a d6 roll of 1 or 2.

FISTS - Both of the Slayer's Death Claws have the abilities of an Open Fist.

SPD	STR	MAT	RAT	DEF	ARM
6	10	6	4	13	17

L	Death Claw		
	SPECIAL	POW	P+S
	Multi	5	15

R	Death Claw		
	SPECIAL	POW	P+S
	Multi	5	15

—	Tusks		
	SPECIAL	POW	P+S
	—	2	12

	1	2	3	4	5	6
		L		R		
	L	L	M	C	R	R
		M	M	C	C	

Point Cost	110
Field Allowance	U
Victory Points	3
Base Size	Large

HEIGHT/WEIGHT: 11'10" / 6.25 tons

ARMAMENT: Twin Death Claws (right and left arms), Tusks (head)

FUEL LOAD/BURN USAGE: 100 Lbs (necrotite) or 200 Lbs (coal)/ 12 hrs general, 2 hrs combat

INITIAL SERVICE DATE: UNKNOWN, first seen in 531 AR

CORTEX MANUFACTURER: UNKNOWN

ORIG. CHASSIS DESIGN: UNKNOWN

It is the face of death itself. I do not credit that thing is a machine. Its eyes hungered, and it moved like no machine I have ever seen.

—Unnamed survivor of an attack on Southshield

Slayers are massive hulks of metal and bone that stalk battlefields in search of prey. Their soulfire furnaces burn hot with savage energy that pushes the helljacks to ever-greater feats of destruction. The Slayer exists to sink its claws into living flesh and tear bodies apart to spray the battlefield with gore. It lopes in long strides like a rabid, frenzied beast seeking to tear through anything unfortunate enough to linger in its way.

An eerie green glow pulsates from the Slayer's soulfire furnaces between the cracks and folds of its armor and up into its ever-searching eyes. These two sickly green sockets glow frightfully and create a horrid sight. As a result, any greenish lights, like those found floating in the bogs and fens of Immoren, are often called "Cryxlight" by superstitious travelers.

Concealed bladders of corrosive acids deliver seeping fluid onto the Slayer's claws to soften and then rend metal apart, leaving wounds that are to metal as infection is to skin. Additionally, necrotechs bolt long and cruelly curved tusks onto the Slayer's armored skull to deliver vicious shattering attacks. This helljack taps into the remnants of life forces within its necrotite furnace, and the pain and suffering found therein pushes the Slayer to great heights of destruction. Those who tend to these murderous machines insist they run best on refined necrotite straight from the field of slaughter.

Bane Thralls
Cryx Unit

Bane thralls—cunning undead warriors inscribed with countless runes and sigils of their dark rebirth—serve as versatile and deadly soldiers among the more mindless undead. Bane thralls are wickedly proficient and play host to a darkness that not only permeates their being, but also seeps into the world of the living. Few know the means by which these potent banes are created, and only the most depraved masters of necromancy can begin to understand the nature of the malignant power from whence they arise.

They are enshrouded in preternatural darkness, and its cold energy siphons the very light from the air and is utterly inimical to living flesh. Tendrils of this darkness reach out hungrily seeking to choke the breathing. Not only does the shroud make fighting bane thralls difficult, but it also obscures their forms even in bright daylight. In addition to the darkness seeping from them, there is a malevolent glimmer in their eyes that reveals a hateful intelligence. Each of the foul creatures delights in nothing more than slaughter and seeks any opportunity to charge into battle and sow death. Sometimes they can even be heard whispering to each other in ancient tongues. They coordinate their actions and march into battle with the discipline and inexorable confidence of soldiers with no fear of death.

Bane thralls are a profane clue that Cryxian necromancers have unlocked horrors only dimly understood as if connected to some force beyond Caen that thrives on extermination. Some darkness never goes away no matter what the stories might say, and the bane thrall is a testament to ancient blasphemies.

LIEUTENANT
LEADER

UNIT
DARK SHROUD - Enemy models within melee range of a Bane Thrall suffer −2 ARM.

STEALTH - All attacks against a Bane Thrall from greater than 5" away automatically miss. If a Bane Thrall is greater than 5" away from an attacker, it does not count as an intervening model.

UNDEAD - A Bane Thrall is not a living model and never flees.

WEAPON MASTER - A Bane Thrall rolls an additional die on its melee damage rolls.

Lieutenant				Cmd 8	
SPD	STR	MAT	RAT	DEF	ARM
5	7	7	4	12	15

Thrall				Cmd 6	
SPD	STR	MAT	RAT	DEF	ARM
5	7	6	4	12	15

War Axe		
SPECIAL	POW	P+S
—	4	11

Leader and 5 Troops	82
Up to 4 Additional Troops	13ea
Field Allowance	1
Victory Points	2
Base Size	Small

BILE THRALLS
CRYX UNIT

LIEUTENANT
LEADER

UNIT
UNDEAD - A Bile Thrall is not a living model and never flees.

BILE CANNON
CORROSION - A model hit by the Bile Cannon suffers Corrosion. Corrosion is a continuous effect that slowly erodes its target. Corrosion does one damage point each turn to the affected model during the model's controller's Maintenance Phase until it expires on a d6 roll of 1 or 2.

Dead flesh is more versatile than machinery alone. These thralls carry a caustic tide that melts flesh and bone to fluid easily collected for our use.

—Mortenebra, Master Necrotech

PURGE (★ATTACK) - The Bile Thrall sprays out the entire contents of its guts, deflating and automatically hitting all models within 6" of the Bile Thrall and in its front arc. A model in range of the Purge attack cannot be hit by the attack if the attacker's LOS is completely blocked by terrain. Models hit suffer a POW 12 damage roll and Corrosion, then remove the Bile Thrall from play. Purge is a ranged attack.

Lieutenant				Cmd	7
SPD	STR	MAT	RAT	DEF	ARM
5	4	2	4	11	13

Thrall				Cmd	5
SPD	STR	MAT	RAT	DEF	ARM
5	4	2	3	11	13

Bile Cannon			
RNG	ROF	AOE	POW
SP	1	—	12

Leader and 5 Troops	41
Up to 4 Additional Troops	6ea
Field Allowance	3
Victory Points	2
Base Size	Small

The terrifying monstrosities called bile thralls are proof of the mad genius of Cryxian necrotechs who are able to turn their art and machines to tasks more insidious than steam-powered fists. Disgorged from hellish workshops, these horrors are noted for their bloated and distended bodies and the gurgling noise heard from within as pumps and siphons perform unspeakable mockeries of biological processes. Bile thralls store and purify volumes of corrosive digestion and decomposition agents with hoses and tubes leading from their distended mouths and fabricated orifices to crude firing mechanisms. With a lurching spasm, each bile thrall can force a startling volume of caustic fluid out of the nozzle and over a wide area that dissolves flesh and devours tempered metal.

In the midst of enemy troops, a bile thrall can force itself to perform a particularly powerful paroxysm. It ruptures its over-pressurized intestines like a blister to provide a massive purge that creates a grisly shower of fluid, flesh, and metal. Anything caught in the foul blast quickly succumbs to the potent dissolving agents. Metal melts into slag while skin and organs painfully liquefy into a bloody unrecognizable mess.

Cryxian commanders unleash dozens of bile thralls at a time. They waddle sluggishly across the battlefield with their sloshing and throbbing internal mechanisms until just the right moment to disgorge their innards. Bile thralls serve as much to obliterate an enemy's morale as to destroy its soldiers. Those who have seen bile thralls in action have been known to go days without eating, and most who have risked going toe-to-toe with them cannot forget the putrid stink.

MECHANITHRALLS
CRYX UNIT

> *The Dragon feeds on our wars. Every dead soldier is another mindless weapon in Cryxian hands. While we weaken, Cryx grows stronger.*
>
> —King Leto Raelthorne to kin

Mechanithralls were among the first horrors unleashed on the mainland by Cryxian necrotechs, and they remain as terrifying today as when they first charged from the bowels of raider ships. Their oversized fists crush the skulls and chests of coastal defenders and innocent villagers with equal disregard. The Nightmare Empire is able to rebuild the ranks of mechanithralls from the corpses of the slain, so there is no end to the instantly recognizable creatures. Soldiers who survive one engagement will soon experience the horror of seeing their fallen friends among the next wave of attackers. The blind and lifeless eyes of their former companions stare from behind rotting flesh while steam-powered pistons promise an impending brutal death.

The thralls are augmented with two heavy gauntlets, their flesh is animated by dark energies, and steam pressure courses through the conduits and pipes weaving in and out of their cadaverous bodies. The gauntlets greatly enhance their unliving strength—a strike from a mechanithrall is nearly as powerful as the impact from a steamjack. Necrotechs and stitch thralls have found these devices are easily constructed from the salvageable ruins of battlefields. They take as many pipes and steam engines as they can find and integrate them into corpses. Inscribed with basic runes of animation, these bodies become fresh reinforcements.

Mechanithralls charge unthinkingly into the face of destruction, climbing over bodies to strike at the enemy. They have been witnessed using cover and clustering at ambush points. Perhaps this behavior is some echo from their former lives, for they follow orders immediately and blindly. Mechanithralls are favored tools of the Cryxian warcasters who are eager to release packs of these necro-mechanikal terrors upon their foes.

LIEUTENANT
LEADER

UNIT
UNDEAD - A Mechanithrall is not a living model and never flees.

STEAMFISTS
COMBO STRIKE (★ATTACK) - A Mechanithrall may make Steamfist attacks separately, or it can make a special attack to strike with both Steamfists simultaneously. Make one attack roll for the Combo Strike. Add the Mechanithrall's STR once and the POW of both Steamfists to the damage roll.

Lieutenant					Cmd 6	
SPD	STR	MAT	RAT	DEF	ARM	
6	7	6	4	12	12	

Thrall					Cmd 4	
SPD	STR	MAT	RAT	DEF	ARM	
6	7	5	4	12	12	

Steamfist	SPECIAL	POW	P+S
	Combo	4	11

Steamfist	SPECIAL	POW	P+S
	Combo	4	11

Leader and 5 Troops	39
Up to 4 Additional Troops	6ea
Field Allowance	3
Victory Points	2
Base Size	Small

Satyxis Raiders
Cryx Unit

Dominatrix
Leader

Unit
Combined Melee Attack - Instead of making melee attacks seperately, two or more Satyxis Raiders in melee range of the same target may combine their attacks. In order to participate in a combined melee attack, a Satyxis Raider must be able to declare a melee attack against the intended target. The Satyxis Raider with the highest MAT in the attacking group makes one melee attack roll for the group and gains +1 to the attack and damage rolls for each Satyxis Raider, including herself, participating in the attack.

Horns
Critical Knockdown - On a critical hit, target small-based model is knocked down.

As beautiful as the bloom on the Iosan tiger vine and just as deadly. Steer clear lads, no matter what yer loins tell ye. There's only death ta be found 'tween those thighs.

—Captain Halford Bray of the *Palaxis*

No Combined Melee Attacks - Satyxis Raiders cannot make combined attacks with their horns. Each makes a separate attack with her horns in addition to other attacks.

Lacerator
Critical Knockdown - On a critical hit, target model is knocked down.

Feedback - Any time a Lacerator damages a warjack, its controlling warcaster takes a damage point. Combined attacks only cause one point of feedback damage regardless of the number of Satyxis Raiders combining their attacks.

Reach - 2" melee range.

Dominatrix				Cmd	8
SPD	STR	MAT	RAT	DEF	ARM
7	5	7	4	14	12

Raider				Cmd	6
SPD	STR	MAT	RAT	DEF	ARM
7	5	6	4	14	12

Horns			
	SPECIAL	POW	P+S
	Multi	3	8

Lacerator			
	SPECIAL	POW	P+S
	Multi	4	9

Leader and 5 Troops	64
Up to 4 Additional Troops	10ea
Field Allowance	2
Victory Points	2
Base Size	Small

The island of Satyx is a lost, legendary place. The only evidence of its existence are the savage women called Satyxis. These cruel females came unto the waters of the Broken Coast with a will to enslave and kill. Birthed by an ancient struggle between dragons, they were fated to have their destiny entwined with the Dragonfather. When Lord Toruk first consolidated His island empire, His minions came upon these brash horned pirates. Seeing the wisdom of an alliance, they bowed to the Dragonfather and promised the service of their ships to defend the outer waters.

Many mistakenly believe their guise to be the result of exposure to Toruk's blight, but the Satyxis were forever changed by the blood of the white dragon Shazkz who battled and was consumed by Lord Toruk high above the island Satyx in 1640 BR. Blighted blood rained down across the island and transformed these proud warrior women—once human—into something more. Eyes darkened, lips became pale, and long horns of twisted bone sprouted from their heads. Their beauty remained in a dark and twisted fashion, capable of exuding an aura that draws men's lust.

Their favored weapons are lacerators made from links of black steel, etched with sigils, and topped with vicious hooks. In combat a Satyxis raider's shapely frame belies her strength as she uses her unique allure to distract adversaries and then tear them apart. Raiders silently coordinate their strikes like a pack of wolves. One or two charge using their horns to deliver blows to knock their victims prone while others circle the downed prey. They then employ their chained scourges to hook flesh and tear and pull it from different directions until their victims are ripped to shreds and left to die in agony. The raiders have become a favored weapon against mainland warcasters because their whips shearing into warjacks can send feedback surges back upon their masters.

Tactical Tip

Feedback — A Journeyman Warcaster will suffer this damage just like a warcaster, but a 'jack marshal will not.

Necrotech & Scrap Thralls
Cryx Solo and Independent Models

Insane, they are. Every one is left to its mad genius, scavenging graveyards and junkyards. They spawn the helljacks, bonejacks, and other horrors, caressing steel and bone into death that walks.

—Dougal Kildaire, smuggler of Blackwater

NECROTECH

CREATE SCRAP THRALL [8] (★ACTION) - To use this special action, a Necrotech must be in base-to-base contact with a disabled or totaled warjack wreck marker. With a successful skill check, d3 Scrap Thralls are created from a light warjack wreck marker or d6 from a heavy warjack wreck marker. Remove the wreck marker from play and place the Scrap Thralls within 3" of the Necrotech. The Scrap Thralls cannot activate this turn. The number of Scrap Thralls that can be created is not limited by Field Allowance.

UNDEAD - A Necrotech is not a living model and never flees.

SCRAP THRALL

DEATH BURST (★ATTACK) - Death Burst is a special attack that combines the Scrap Thrall's movement and combat action. Declare that a Scrap Thrall is going to Death Burst when it activates. Move the Scrap Thrall up to twice its SPD, and then perform a melee attack targeting a model in melee range. Center a 4" AOE on the Scrap Thrall's target if the attack is successful and on the Scrap Thrall if it is not. On a direct hit, the target of Death Burst suffers a POW 16 damage roll. Models in the AOE, including the target if the attack missed,

suffer a POW 8 blast damage roll. The Scrap Thrall is removed from play after performing a Death Burst.

INDEPENDENT MODEL - This model is not part of a unit and cannot run or charge. An army must include a Necrotech at the beginning of the game to field Scrap Thralls.

THRALL BOMB - When a Scrap Thrall is destroyed, it explodes with a 4" AOE. Models in the AOE suffer a POW 8 blast damage roll. When a Scrap Thrall explodes, remove it from play.

UNDEAD - A Scrap Thrall is not a living model and never flees.

VISE CLAW (NECROTECH ONLY)

IMMOBILIZE - If the Vise Claw hits, it can either do damage as normal or immobilize its target without damaging it. An immobilized model may activate normally, but it suffers –3 DEF and cannot move until it is released or its attacker is destroyed. An immobilized model is released from the Vise Claw if the Necrotech moves, is moved, makes an attack against another model, is destroyed, is removed from play, or if either model is placed.

REACH - 2" melee range.

MECHANO-CLAW (SCRAP THRALL ONLY)

Necrotech					Cmd 7
SPD	STR	MAT	RAT	DEF	ARM
5	6	6	3	12	13

Scrap Thrall					Cmd 1
SPD	STR	MAT	RAT	DEF	ARM
5	4	5	3	11	12

Vise Claw		
SPECIAL	POW	P+S
Multi	4	10

Mechano-Claws		
SPECIAL	POW	P+S
—	4	8

Necrotech Point Cost	9
Scrap Thrall Point Cost	5
Necrotech Field Allowance	3
Scrap Thrall Field Allowance	10
Necrotech Victory Points	1
Scrap Thrall Victory Points	0
Necrotech Base Size	Medium
Scrap Thrall Base Size	Small

Part necromancer, part mechanik, part evil genius, and spiced with a dash of deranged lunatic—this is what comprises Lord Toruk's necrotechs. The lich lords of Cryx are powerful overlords whose immortal attention cannot be spared on the small details of constructing the soldiers of their army, so the task of making these perversities walk, slither, or crawl falls to the capable necrotechs. These sadistic undead engineers have no fear of altering their own forms or of testing their weapons and enhancements on their own bodies before applying them to others, and they demonstrate a number of ingenious attachments and necro-mechanikal augmentation. Far less than human, necrotechs see the world through evil-tinted goggles, and they renounced the "ways of meat" long ago.

When not designing or assembling the next wave of horrors, necrotechs skitter into battle with their "pretty little children" in search of how to better their creations by witnessing them at work. They are not idle observers, however, for they wield the skills to repair their infernal constructs. Even the highly altered techs find it difficult to haul hundreds of pounds of raw material into battle, so they do what they can with what fate and carnage provides. Like the necrosurgeons who raise thralls from fallen meat, necrotechs create shambling scrap thralls from heaps of metal and bone.

Scrap thralls are little more than the spare parts of a fallen 'jack slapped together and animated as a shambling delivery vehicle for necrotite-enhanced

bombs. These ramshackle undead are just as likely to detonate when a wayward bullet or arrow strikes them as when they accomplish their last embrace. Their only real goal is to clutch an opponent long enough for the bomb to explode in a shower of bone, metal, and steam. The deadly explosive impact of these hastily improvised devices is proof of the potential a necrotech can unleash if given enough time, the necessary materials, and a proper workshop.

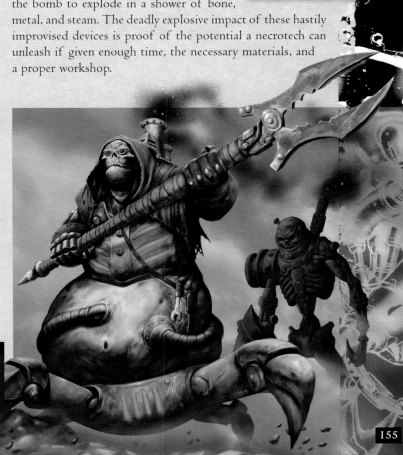

TACTICAL TIP

DEATH BURST — This is not a charge. The Scrap Thrall does not need LOS to its target at the beginning of its movement, nor does it need to move in a straight line. A ghost-walking Scrap Thrall can be quite a surprise.

IMMOBILIZE — A knocked down model that is Immobilized can still stand up.

SKARLOCK THRALL
CRYX SOLO

SKARLOCK THRALL

BOUND - Before the start of the game, the Skarlock Thrall's controller assigns it to a single warcaster. The Skarlock Thrall cannot be reassigned during a game. Each warcaster may only have one bound Skarlock Thrall.

SOUL CAGES - The Skarlock Thrall gains a soul token for every living model destroyed within 2". During its controller's next Control Phase, remove the Skarlock's soul tokens. If the Skarlock Thrall is within 2" of its controlling warcaster, give the warcaster a focus point for each soul token.

SPELL SLAVE (★ACTION) - While in its warcaster's control area, a Skarlock Thrall may cast one of its controlling warcaster's spells with a focus cost of three or less without spending any focus points. The Skarlock uses the FOC stat of its controlling warcaster to resolve all effects of the spell including attack rolls. Rolls cannot be boosted since the Skarlock has no focus. The Skarlock cannot channel spells or cast spells with a range of 'self.' Its controlling warcaster may allocate focus points to upkeep spells cast by the Skarlock and spells cast by the Skarlock are considered to have been cast by the warcaster. When the Skarlock Thrall casts an offensive spell, it is considered to be the attacker. The Skarlock Thrall cannot act as a Spell Slave if its warcaster is destroyed or removed from play.

UNDEAD - A Skarlock Thrall is not a living model and never flees.

> *As thee are an extension of my will and power, so will this thrall become an extension of thine.*
>
> —Iron Lich Asphyxious instructing his pupil Deneghra

Skarlock				Cmd	6
SPD	STR	MAT	RAT	DEF	ARM
6	4	3	3	14	11

Claw

SPECIAL	POW	P+S
—	2	6

Damage	5
Point Cost	16
Field Allowance	1
Victory Points	1
Base Size	Small

There are few thralls more insidious and dangerous than the skarlock. It is a creature of blackest sorcery linked to its master by bonds so powerful it can act in its master's stead by gathering the souls of the slain and invoking unspeakable magic. Slender and graceful, it moves against the enemy with confidence while the light of a hateful intelligence shines from its baleful eye-sockets.

Skarlocks are difficult to craft and require an investment of time and substantial energy from the most proficient necromancers. Each is unique, and many skarlocks have extensive personalities and agendas. More than any other constructed thrall, the skarlock retains the old memories and lore it gained during its life in addition to the knowledge absorbed during the inscription of its animating runes. Still, through its fabrication each skarlock is inextricably bound to its master and is incapable of disloyalty. Skarlocks are therefore perfect tools, lieutenants, and extensions of a warcaster's power. A dense inlay of dark sigils blackens skarlocks' bones and desiccated flesh, and only small bits of exposed bone show between the numerous runes. With tremendous necromantic power instilled into its physical form, each skarlock is infused with sorcerous abilities.

As part of its bonding process, a skarlock is opened up to the unique arcane abilities of its warcaster master and is able to invoke devastating effects. They are often sent forth to expand the warcaster's necromantic power and to allow tremendous spell energies to be unleashed in a single great outpouring of destruction. The skarlock can also gather the souls of those slain in its proximity into soul cages and channel them back to its master to strengthen his power.

KHADOR

Legacy of Strength
A Brief History of Khador

No other people have as rich a history of breeding strength and courage. Our soldiers fight boldly to uphold that legacy. Never again will we suffer compromises and appeasements or give up what we have earned in blood.

—Queen Ayn Vanar XI while conducting a visit to the officers of the First Army, 604 AR

The following is a transcript of Kommandant Grezko Antonovich's address to thousands of fresh Winter Guard recruits in Korsk, 602 AR:

I am here to remind you that our greatness stands on the shoulders of countless generations stretching back to the Khardic Empire. A nation cannot endure without weapons wielded by strong hands, and our ancestors forged their strength in war. They united the Kossites of the Scarsfell Forest, the Skirov of the northern mountains, and the Umbreans of the eastern plains under one Khardic emperor. At the height of our glory, our hand stretched east to conquer the weak-willed Ryn and south to throttle the petty northern fiefdoms of Tordor. These once proud men bowed to us, recognized our greatness, and swore eternal fealty to the horselords of the north. Our civilization stood poised on the cusp of total dominion before the arrival of the damnable Orgoth.

Remember this fact when you go to war and when you hear the weeping indignation of those who fear us. Our cause is just. We restore a great civilization torn down by the Orgoth. Those lands others squat upon as scavengers, scrabbling for our leavings, are ours by right of oaths sworn in blood and binding even unto today's generation. I leave it to you to remind them with axe and cannon of what they have forgotten.

The Orgoth defeated us, but it was no shame. They unleashed accursed sorceries and weapons. We fought them for every inch and took many Orgoth howling with us into Urcaen. We forced them to send more ships to our shores and to overwhelm us by sheer numbers. If the southerners had been as strong as we, the Orgoth would be nothing but a forgotten speck in history. The soft underbelly of the south is where they took hold first, but the Khardic Empire forced their campaigns to stall.

We sunk them in a quagmire of their own blood spilled by Khadoran blades. By our efforts it took them two centuries to gain their dominion.

The Orgoth ruled for generations and defaced our great and ancient cities with their grotesque fortresses, strange temples, and twisted monuments; structures they razed to the ground during the Scourge when they fled our shores. Our fathers suffered greatest under Orgoth oppression as punishment for the ferocity with which we fought them. Your kin of times past were forced to feed the Orgoth by working the soil, enrich them by mining the earth for gems, and please them with blood sport combat. They offered a simple but painful choice: submit or die. They could kill our people but not our inner strength, and we endured.

Each nation has taken credit for victory over the Orgoth. It is true that the first rebellion occurred in Cygnar, but their so-called Iron Fellowship failed utterly and was quashed shortly after it began. The Tordorans and Thurians put up a brave but futile fight called the Battle of the Hundred Wizards. Again the Orgoth returned in force and obliterated those who defied them. So too with the Army of Thunder the Llaelese describe with misty-eyes. It was their single valiant moment in an otherwise forgettable history. Only the horselords of Khador won the first real victory of this period in 147 AR. An enormous gathering of strong northmen surrounded and engulfed the first Orgoth city. They razed it, left only a hole swallowed by the earth, and deliberately excised its name. They then wrested the great city of Korsk from the Orgoth grasp.

The Orgoth regrouped and beset the city. They sent infernal evils, men made of metal and flesh, and fiery engines of destruction against her walls, but the city stood strong—as strong as she does this very day. Korsk never shook and never allowed the raiders entry into her beloved walls again. This was our turning point. Looking to our leadership, a rag-tag group of infant nations came together as the Iron Alliance in 160 AR and later declared all-out war in 164 AR. The alliance organized the combined efforts that would give rise to the invention of the colossals.

To imagine one of those massive machines clench its mighty fists and peer with burning eyes toward an Orgoth fortress on the horizon must have been enough to sway our forefathers. It was what they needed to drive the enemies of Immoren away forever. The Cygnarans convinced the Khadorans that with their help the colossals could be a reality.

Other nations do not speak much of this period and pretend that unity reigned among the Council of Ten leading the alliance. The Caspians revealed the depths of their treachery even in this dark hour when we fought against a common foe. The southerners feared our strength and spoke poison words in the halls of the Rhulfolk whom they convinced to assist in the creation of the colossals. They isolated us from their debates and selected Caspia as the sole site of construction. The Rhulfolk agreed to this plan, for they had long feared our stalwart warriors along their border.

When we learned of their shortsighted and foolish scheme, we took the prudent step of safeguarding our people by duplicating the colossal plans without their knowledge. It was a small deception made necessary to safeguard the success of the alliance. Our secret factories in Korsk began their work.

Always they underestimate us. The Cygnarans look down on us as if we were beneath them. They have forgotten we invented the steam engine. Our engineers are as innovative and capable as any in other lands—better!—for they have strength of heart and loyalty bred into their bones. We do not require the approval of the south, not in those days and not now.

We saw that their hatred of us exceeded all sense in 188 AR when the southerners or the Rhulfolk—we know not which—betrayed us to the Orgoth. Against all bonds of alliance they pretended to hold sacred, they revealed our factories to our enemy. Though the Orgoth had been fighting on every front, they now focused completely on Khador. They brought an immense army of tenacious warriors and unliving killers called 'dreads' against our ancestors.

The Motherland has ever been our greatest ally. She awoke, having had enough of the festering fleas biting her skin, and conjured a winter to meet the armies of the great enemy. Razor-sharp winds and tower-deep snows immobilized the armies. Trapped in the valleys and the plains, the Orgoth were forced by a freezing cold that stole the breath from their very lungs to turn away from their mission of doom. Khador herself had saved her people. It was a sign in the purest sense of the need to protect our borders from outside invasion forever.

The Orgoth could not obliterate us as they had hoped. They destroyed the factories we had erected at tremendous cost to their gathered army. Who knows how many lives would have been saved had this not come to pass? We would have emerged from the battles ahead stronger and more capable of pressing our rights to territories of the old Khardic Empire. Caspia achieved its goal and deprived us of the weapons with which we could stand on equal footing.

I am here to remind you that our greatness stands on the shoulders of countless generations stretching back to the Khardic Empire.

It was not the time to seek reparations, for they covered their tracks well and we had no proof of misdeeds. Our strength was for the moment exhausted, and our leaders were forced to be prudent. The obliteration of the Orgoth was too important, so our leaders cooperated with the other members of the Council of Ten. If one must sleep beside a foe to guard against a greater one, so be it.

We bit our tongues as Caspian colossals emerged and attacked the Orgoth in 191 AR. Our great generals and warriors fought alongside southerners as we pushed back the invaders. In 198 AR after many smaller gains, we combined our strength for an enormous push and risked all to seize final victory. The Orgoth fell back like a swarm of locusts, slaying innocents, ruining cities, and burning fields in a swath of ashen destruction called the Scourge. The day came when the last of them boarded their black ships and pushed off, sailing across Meredius, back to whatever infernal land had spawned them. Immoren was once again ours. Never forget what our ancestors endured for our freedom!

The time came for rebuilding. In 202 AR the Council of Ten convened in Corvis, the sinking city, to establish a new age. For weeks the Council debated and outlined plans and put them down on parchment only to shred and re-write them. The Cygnarans and their Ordic lackeys maintained it was easiest to use the lines drawn by our former captors for their provinces. Preposterous as it sounds the council agreed! What had become of our heritage? They ignored our protests and insisted the Khardic Empire had taken territories unlawfully. The southerners took advantage of our armies' tremendous losses and the fact that we had no colossals to back our demands. Their subtle threats made it clear our cities might see the same fate as the Orgoth fortresses if we did not comply.

The final maps enormously reduced the old borders of the Khardic Empire to make room for the upstart kingdoms of Ord and Llael, built on the tattered remains

with our strength expended to destroy the Orgoth, they became jackals. The northern reaches of our land are impassable mountains so rugged and difficult they are nearly worthless to modern industry. Our mines, few and in difficult elevations, require twice the effort and costs of those in Cygnar. We are proud of our heritage, but only our southern reaches contain worthwhile farmland. Our empire stretched forth its mailed gauntlet because we had need of resources, and in the time of the Thousand Cities we had bled and fought to win them. We accepted oaths and promises from those who surrendered to our benevolent rule. Southerners find it convenient to ignore promises when it suits them.

of old Tordor and Ryn. Though the Tordorans had earned our respect as a tough people standing bravely in battle the claims of the Ryn were galling. They had never been more than a tiny fiefdom at the base of the mountains. Their squabbling people were unworthy of a place in the company of their betters.

The southerners call the treaties fair. They point to the size of our nation, but it is false logic. Should not a righteous and mighty king live in a palace and not a hovel? We had earned what was ours, yet in this moment,

It became clear after the Corvis Treaties how cleverly Cygnar manipulated border negotiations to avoid confronting us. Cygnar arranged the borders of Ord and Llael to gain space between their soldiers and our axes. Leaders of those two nations were puppets. They frequently met with the rulers in Caspia and fawned to accommodate them. The Llaelese—how shameful it is to think we share bloodlines with those Umbreans who abandoned the Motherland! We must remember our ancestors suffered and this was not their finest moment. Southerners may have lulled them with magic, bent their minds, or simply confounded them with silver tongues and honeyed words. Since those days we have had to fight constantly to assert our rights and regain our lands.

We came from those treaties with a will to abide in spite of the poor choices of our councilors. We swore to honor and to hold binding the pacts our representatives had made even unto their descendants. Khador would make the best of it. We are an honorable people, yet after the decades passed, learned men in Korsk brought to light an interesting fact. The families of those first councilors had, for whatever reason, no heirs. Clearly this was a blessing from the gods. Perhaps it was a sign of Menoth's approval

of our respect for the written law, for, by the wording of the Corvis Treaties, the old agreements now had no hold. None who had agreed to those tenets lived nor did their descendants hold power in the halls of our sovereigns. The lands refused us by those deceitful papers would be ours again. We could begin the reclamation.

In 242 AR King Lavash Tzepesci sent forth the call for all loyal Khadorans outside our borders to return home. Our kinsmen had scattered to earn wages and learn skills

during the reconstruction but had not forgotten their loyalty. These far-flung and well-educated Khadorans gave up lives abroad and returned to the embrace of the Motherland. Most important were those who had learned arcane mysteries with the Fraternal Order of Wizardry and the Order of the Golden Crucible. The returning arcanists severed ties to those corrupt foreign fellowships. In 243 AR the Greylords founded their Covenant.

These men carried magic and occult lore back to our cities in a great tide of power and brought the modern arcane and mechanikal weapons of the age with them. This included knowledge of the construction of cortexes which at long last allowed us to build colossals. No longer subject to the intimidation of weak-willed Caspians, all of our nation's industry bent to the task of readying our military, By 250 AR we had put together an army mighty enough to fling against Llael and Ord simultaneously, and the reclamation of our lands began.

For seven years the massive constructs wreaked havoc upon the lands and people. These glorious battles proved to the world that Khador could not be dismissed, yet in hindsight we had been hasty. Our armies had not the time to equip themselves adequately. The colossals proved too expensive to maintain. It required Ord, Llael, and Cygnar struggling like farmers holding back a mighty ox to restrain

Should not a righteous and mighty king live in a palace and not a hovel?

us, yet we withdrew and accepted their disarmament terms. Cygnar crowed their victory from every street corner, but we had already decided colossals were an antiquated approach to war. We came to this realization years before the dim-witted southerners.

We spent this enforced peace recovering from the costs of war and rebuilding our strength. In 293 our new sovereign, Queen Cherize, renewed the struggle against our bitter enemy. Colossals had been formally retired roughly a decade earlier and replaced by more nimble warjacks. Cherize was a strong but enigmatic queen. She brought unusual allies to fight the southerners, including tribes of forgotten savages from the Thornwood called Tharn. These tribes hurled themselves against Cygnar but proved insufficient to the fight, tainted by association of their bestial god.

Queen Cherize disappeared under mysterious circumstances in 295 AR. The fights continued at the urging of Lord Regent Velibor, however, who ably commanded the throne while Queen Ayn Vanar V grew into her maturity. These so-called 'Border Wars' were fought with steel and cannon, but, more significantly, they featured the earliest true warjacks, particularly the battles at Ravensgard in 299 AR and the Ironfields the following year. In the years to come we pushed Llael and Ord back, reclaimed our rightful borders, and stretched our strength.

We approach a new age, one where the past shall shape the present. Beginning today, we forge a new Khador.

Had we taken our gains and bided our time it may have served us better, but one cannot fault Lord Velibor for his ambition. He was not a king, yet he led ably. Perhaps it was his lack of royal blood that prevented his success. In early 305 AR a great alliance of barbarian tribes from the mountains and plains of Khador assembled. These last remnants of heathen tribes had never properly joined in the nation of Khador. They still lived by the old ways on the fringes and in the mountains worshipping the Beast of All Shapes. Some were primitive and savage. Others were noble but crude and carried a legacy of the once great horselords stretching back before priest-king Khardovic. These men came to plunder and pillage the wealth of their betters. Lord Velibor drew on the example of Queen Cherize and the Tharn and viewed these gathered warriors as an opportunity to beset the enemies of the Motherland. As they rode through the outlying fields that fed Korsk, he confronted their leaders. Speaking at length he convinced them of the enormous spoils awaiting them in the fat southern lands of Ord.

Lord Velibor's plan nearly succeeded. Though most southerners are cowardly and weak, the men of Midfast in Ord had proven their ability to withstand siege time and time again. They even endured an attack by our colossals in 250 AR without falling. We had reclaimed the lands north of Midfast with a number of successful attacks, including Port Vladovar, which the Tordorans had called Radahvo after they negotiated unlawfully for this land in the Corvis Treaties. Still, Midfast and its line of rugged hills had thwarted our efforts. Knowing this, Velibor

sent the barbarian tribes against this fortress city to see if an endless tide of savages might succeed where more organized armies had failed. He sent our army to follow in their wake and exploit any vulnerabilities opened by the barbarians.

These fourteen barbarian tribes with, so they say, fifty thousand savages laid siege to Midfast. There seemed little hope of the city surviving such a horde, but clearly divine will stood against Velibor's victory. Some took it as a sign that only a true king of Khador could accomplish such a deed. Others believe that the use of Devourer worshipers to fight in our stead invoked intercession. Scholars know that the Tharn who fought with Cherize suffered the so-called 'Ten Ills of Morrow' for their unholy attacks on Morrow's chosen champions. Velibor's choice to bring such savages to his cause in a similar fight, while apparently expedient, may have been a mistake in the eyes of the divine. I do not pretend to understand the will of the gods.

Whatever the case, the Ordfolk fought well as always when cornered in their holes. They have no stomach to meet us on the open field or to muster forth from their borders, but they remain resolute when trapped. We recognize the rare occasions a great warrior arises on foreign soils. On this day a great warrior named Markus—perhaps descended of Khadoran blood—stood to rally the defenders of Midfast in their hour of desperation. We know he endured this siege beyond all hope. He went sleepless for a week and remained an inspiration to his cornered soldiers. He heard that reinforcements were hurrying north but would arrive too late. To buy his comrades time, he went out alone and challenged the chieftains of all fourteen barbarian tribes to personal combat. I wish I had been alive to see the fight. Every day for a week straight Markus came forth to battle two chieftains, and each time he emerged victorious. By the end of the week he had suffered grievous wounds and died after defeating the final champion. Still, he gained time for reinforcements to arrive. They reached the field of battle just as Markus himself ascended to take Morrow's hand. I have read the accounts of a Khadoran officer who witnessed the event, and I believe it was a true miracle. It was not destined that those lands would be ours that day. The words of that soldier echo my own thoughts: 'who am I to gainsay a god?'

It was a small defeat that did not cost the army of Khador anything but pride. We had won great victories already and continued to press on to other gains in the years to come. When Queen Ayn Vanar V came of age and took the throne, she decided we had accomplished enough for a time. She was a soft-hearted woman and called for peace in 313 AR to allow our soldiers rest. We had won Port Vladovar and many fine and fertile lands north of Midfast, so we must count this as a great victory. Port Vladovar became one of our finest port cities and the heart of our navy. Its capture is worth a dozen dry and barren fortress-holes like Midfast.

We suffered further indignities in the peace negotiations, including giving up lands we had taken from Llael on our eastern border. It had no consequence at the time despite historical interest in the area. We forfeited only broken and despoiled ruins, the leavings of both our wars and the Orgoth before us. While some protested we must reclaim Old Korska, once the eastern capital of the Khardic Empire, most were content to leave the ruins to the Llaelese.

This proved a tactical mistake, but after seizing so many lands it is one we must forgive. We did not expect the Umbreans of this region to roll over so docilely. The once great decedents of horselords turned to lapdogs of the Ryn! They accepted the change in nations with no more resistance than a man might change his coat, and even still they scorn us. The city of Laedry arose on formerly Khardic soil. It is time we rectified this affront and forced the Umbreans to account for their lack of loyalty to a true sovereign. They sit comfortably in their Ryn-built city and lift rifles to fire on us who should be their kinsmen. This is unacceptable. I long for the day we can march into those lands and force those men to bow to their betters.

Some call the time after the Border-Wars peace, but even without a declaration of open war there has never been rest for our soldiers. Having all our neighbors turned against us made it difficult to renew our rightful claims of reclamation. Then came the Cygnaran Civil War. In Khador the two religions of Menoth and Morrow exist side by side without rancor, and we pay homage to both gods. Cygnar failed to accomplish the same. The state heavily favored one religion over the other which resulted in division and much bloodshed. In its eternal hubris, Cygnar exiled their Menites and so dictated where the very gods should rest. What arrogance to think that they could simply turn Menoth away from their lands! We have always given proper respect and loyalty to the Creator. We stand, Morrowans and Menites alike, united as Khadorans in the defense of the Motherland.

King Ruslan Vygor was a devoted Menite who learned from an early age to loathe Cygnar. Whether mad or inspired, Vygor claimed to be Priest King Khardovic reborn when he took the crown. He decreed he would carve a

new future for our people, and he gathered hundreds of Khadoran patriots, scores of warjacks, and dozens of tacticians. Vygor's forces carved a path through the perilous Thornwood, later called the 'Warjack Road', hoping to reach the site of Cygnar's first transgression at the sinking city of Corvis. They reached the Dragon's Tongue River before Cygnar's armies met them.

The Cygnaran cowards refused to face the strength of our army directly. Hate them, but do not underestimate their cunning. Their tactics are slippery and elusive like the twisting of a snake—a lesson Vygor learned too late to avoid death. Cygnar's forces evaded his, and they bombarded our army from across the river. They destroyed their bridge, used the terrain to hide at every turn, and exhausted our supplies. Thousands of soldiers died, and scores of warjacks obliterated each other in a series of bitter battles.

The Cygnaran cannons did their damage, but what turned the tide was the betrayal of our mercenaries, the Ironbears, who turned against our kinsmen. One can never fully trust those who fight for coin, and never was that more clear than at the so-called 'Battle of the Tongue'. His forces thrown into disarray, King Vygor fell valiantly in battle in 511 AR and left his men to make a long and difficult retreat. Even in defeat we were not cowed and many of our kinsmen have never given up the fight. The valiant Fifth Border Legion swore revenge against Cygnar and has maintained a constant watch on the border. For those stalwart men and women on the southern border, the Thornwood War continues today. If you are lucky, some of you may join them.

I believe our finest hour awaits us. For a century we have rebuilt. Our warjacks are strong and our people stronger. We approach a new age, one where the past shall shape the present. Beginning today, we forge a new Khador. We had strength enough to cast out the Orgoth, and we will harness their relics to serve the Motherland.

Queen Vanar XI, descendent and namesake of that gentle sovereign of long ago, has decreed we should prepare for the next step. You men and women will be the first to take that step. Do not falter. You are Khador's children! The Motherland that defended you and kept you safe now calls upon you. It is your strength that will overcome our enemies in the battles ahead. War is our oldest and finest tradition. Trust your strength!

THE BUTCHER OF KHARDOV

Zoktavir is a force of nature as wild as Khador itself. Some say his manners and methods are crude and shortsighted, but I ask you, would you deny that he is the personification of victory at any cost? Has he ever failed us?

—Queen Ayn Vanar XI in defense of the infamous Butcher of Khardov

The Khardic men of central and southern Khador are known for both their size and fighting spirit while the northern Skirov boast an ancient legacy as powerful berserkers without equal. Orsus Zoktavir embodies both of these proud lines. Although his parentage is uncertain, each of the peoples of Khador have at times claimed him as their own as his legend has grown. His only known home has been the Orgoth fortress turned industrial city named Khardov. Seven and a half feet tall and over half this in breadth, he is a massive man who manifested natural arcane skills early in life. Orsus' past is wrapped in mystery, and none seem to know his origins before he appeared in Korsk with two old warjacks in tow.

He gained notoriety as "The Butcher of Khardov" during his first command in 587 AR when a village just north of Boarsgate Keep announced its withdrawal from Khador to join with Ord. Orsus could not abide such infidelity and, without orders, he took it upon himself to crush the "traitorous rebellion." He gathered fifty men and marched to Boarsgate. A contingent of militiamen awaited him there with wishes to parley, but Orsus howled at the heavens and charged.

Crying betrayal, he and his Khadorans attacked. It was carnage. Halfway through the slaughter, the militiamen surrendered, but Orsus kept hacking away. His men tried to restrain him, but in a wild rage reminiscent of Orgoth berserkers, he accused his own warriors of treachery. With his massive axe he rent every living man to pieces. His rage was boundless. Moments later, a total of eighty-eight warriors were simply dismembered parts strewn about the village square. Those who witnessed the aftermath told of blood so thick in the muddy streets that rats leapt from one body to the next for fear of drowning. The day became known as the "Boarsgate Massacre."

Word spread quickly of the bloody act, and Orsus earned the title of "Butcher of Khardov." The news ultimately reached the ears of the newly crowned Queen Ayn Vanar. The pragmatic young queen saw a consummate warrior and powerful innate warcaster, so she exonerated him and openly condoned his behavior as the reaction of any true patriot. Most other kommanders guessed at the queen's true intent—to parade a new weapon against internal dissent. Now to speak or act against her could result in a visit from the Butcher. Her maneuver had the desired effect and instantly stifled all talk and speculation of whether the young queen would prove a strong monarch.

Orsus Zoktavir is without doubt a powerful warrior. He wields his axe Lola—rumored to be named after a love whose loss fuels his rage—with a vengeance. For the occasion when direct force is not an option, he carries a mechanikal blunderbuss that fires a powerful blast of heavy lead shot. He wears a modified suit of steam-powered rune armor that was literally shaped from the hull of a warjack and crafted to suit his frame by loyal battle mechaniks once in his service. In its protective casing, the Butcher is a force of destruction, a one man wrecking crew.

Younger warcasters such as Kommander Sorscha Kratikoff view the Butcher with disdain. More traditional warcasters like Vladimir Tzepesci see him as nothing more than a weapon, and troops across all of Immoren cannot remove the vision of the axe-wielding giant from their nightmares. Orsus Zoktavir fights for a deeper cause than even he knows, for something burns in his blood from the days of mountain savages and bloody sacrifices before the Iron Kingdoms. The Butcher of Khardov is the personification of warfare and bloodshed, and woe to any fool who stands in his way.

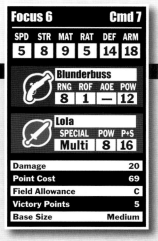

Focus 6				Cmd 7	
SPD	STR	MAT	RAT	DEF	ARM
5	8	9	5	14	18

Blunderbuss			
RNG	ROF	AOE	POW
8	1	—	12

Lola		
SPECIAL	POW	P+S
Multi	8	16

Damage	20
Point Cost	69
Field Allowance	C
Victory Points	5
Base Size	Medium

SPECIAL RULES

FEAT: BLOOD FRENZY

The Butcher's rage runs deep. It is the well from which he draws his power and the inspiration from which he leads his force into battle. His rage is contagious, and when the Butcher relinquishes what little control he has over it, all who march by his side, man and machine, will succumb to this blood lusting frenzy.

Friendly Khador models currently in the Butcher's control area roll an additional die on attack damage rolls this turn.

THE BUTCHER

TERROR — Enemy models/units within melee range of the Butcher and enemy models/units with the Butcher in their melee range must pass a command check or flee.

LOLA

BRUTAL DAMAGE - Roll an additional die on Lola's damage rolls.

REACH - 2" melee range.

SPELL	COST	RNG	AOE	POW	UP	OFF
AVALANCHE	4	8	3	15		X
A great stone is ripped from the earth and hurled at the enemy.						
FURY	2	8	—	—	X	*
Target model/unit suffers −1 DEF but gains +3 to melee damage rolls. When this spell targets an enemy model, it is an offensive spell and requires a magic attack roll.						
HOWL	3	SELF	CTRL	—		
Enemy models/units in the Butcher's control area must pass a command check or flee.						
IRON FLESH	2	8	—	—	X	*
Target warrior model/unit gains +3 DEF and suffers −1 SPD. When this spell targets an enemy model, it is an offensive spell and requires a magic attack roll.						
KILLING BLOW	3	SELF	—	—		X
Double the Butcher's STR for his next melee damage roll, after which this spell expires.						
RETALIATION	3	6	—	—		X
Target model may make one melee attack out of turn against any model that hits it with a melee attack before taking damage. The retaliating model still suffers any damage rolled by the attacking model after resolving Retaliation. This spell expires after target model makes one retaliatory attack. Retaliation attack and damage rolls cannot be boosted.						

TACTICAL TIPS

RETALIATION — If the target model cannot attack for some reason, (for instance if it were knocked down), it cannot make a retaliatory attack either. The spell remains in play. Retaliation is not triggered by free strikes.

KOMMANDER SORSCHA

She is a perfect example of what a woman should be: pale as the ice that blankets us, beautiful but distant as the starry sky, yet as deadly as a winter storm. Far better to serve her than to dream of crossing her in battle.

—Kapitan Sergei Dalinski, Man-O-War officer speaking in hushed tones after too much uiske

When a teary-eyed Sorscha Kratikoff looked into her father's face at the age of thirteen winters and asked to be a soldier like him, he just smiled, patted her dark black curls, and strode out the door to join his unit. Later that month her mother received word of the massacre at Boarsgate. Sorscha's father lay among the dead, executed by Orsus Zoktavir, the Butcher of Khardov. Two years later, Sorscha lied about her age and joined the Winter Guard. She fought against all odds and not only survived the rigors and mayhem of war but excelled at it, fueled by the image in her mind of her father's bloody end at the hands of the Butcher.

Sorscha served in three consecutive tours of duty with the prestigious border garrison at Ravensgard and participated in frequent bloody conflicts with both Llaelese mercenaries and her Cygnaran counterparts. She demonstrated considerable natural tactical prowess and was chosen for officer training at the Druzhina in Korsk before returning to her men as a lieutenant. She advanced quickly through the ranks to kapitan and kovnik and demonstrated particular skill in the wise allocation of warjacks entrusted to her command. A warcaster named Torisevich valued her opinion above his other officers and picked her to serve as an aide. Perhaps some part of her felt an affinity with the armored machines even before she demonstrated her gift for warcasting. Sorscha had already shown hints of inborn sorcery but had kept them to herself, for she was raised in a rustic and rural border area where such powers were greeted with superstition and dread.

Her true potential surfaced during a conflict near the Ordic border when Torisevich was slain in an ambush and his 'jacks suddenly fell silent and dormant. In desperation, Sorscha charged unescorted into the combat. She cut men down like stalks of grain, but most of her troops were down and she was outnumbered ten to one. One foe sliced her thigh and she fell, shouting more in shock than pain. Suddenly, the world froze. Everything around her, including her enemies, stood encased in a layer of ice and frost. Leaning against one of the nearby Juggernauts, she found herself able to reach within its mind. She reactivated its cortex by mimicking the arcane sequence her untrained vision had perceived in her kommander. Sent forth at her bidding, this warjack charged into the nearby enemies and caused them to rout.

Days later Sorscha stood before her queen in Korsk. Her new talents were quickly put to the test, and she began to learn to control her sorcery and warcaster ability from the enigmatic and gifted Umbrean Vladimir Tzepesci. In her year of study with the nobleman, she became enamored. She saw in him ancient nobility, a sense of profound duty, and the embodiment of the days before Khador's defeat in the Thornwood. They had a brief romance before Queen Ayn Vanar XI called her away to service at the height of their passion. Since their parting of ways she seems to have become more embittered, or some might say focused on the tasks at hand. Those who see her now would never suspect any passions lingering beneath her iron discipline and unfaltering dedication to her first love of Khador.

Sorscha was rewarded with a unique weapon of extraordinary ability her last day in Korsk upon her promotion to kommander—the hammer-scythe Frostfang. In addition to dividing flesh and bone with expert manipulation, the wicked weapon can freeze her enemies by working in concert with her own powerful control over frost and ice. The weapon unites Sorscha's resourcefulness with the hard edge of her manner and the icy chill in her heart. Only the presence of Dark Prince Vladimir thaws her soul, if but for a moment. "Fiery rage and icy hatred," she was once heard to say, "these things a good soldier makes, not the warmth and comfort of love."

Focus 6					Cmd 9
SPD	STR	MAT	RAT	DEF	ARM
6	6	6	5	16	14

Hand Cannon

RNG	ROF	AOE	POW
12	1	—	12

Frostfang

SPECIAL	POW	P+S
Multi	7	13

Damage	17
Point Cost	71
Field Allowance	C
Victory Points	5
Base Size	Small

SPECIAL RULES

FEAT: ICY GAZE

Wherever Kommander Sorscha treads, winter appears to follow. The celebrated Khadoran warcaster manipulates winter itself through the power of sorcery, storing up her power to unleash a massive blanket of ice to freeze her enemies in their tracks.

Enemy models currently in Sorscha's LOS and control area become stationary for one round.

FROSTFANG

CRITICAL FREEZE - On a critical hit, target model becomes stationary for one round.

REACH - 2" melee range.

SPELL	COST	RNG	AOE	POW	UP	OFF
BOUNDLESS CHARGE	3	6	—	—		*
Target model's next activation is a charge at SPD +5" that crosses rough terrain and obstacles without penalty. When this spell targets an enemy model, it is an offensive spell and requires a magic attack roll.						
FOG OF WAR	3	SELF	CTRL	—	X	
A bank of fog is centered on Sorscha and provides concealment to all models in her control area.						
FREEZING GRIP	4	8	—	—		X
Target model/unit becomes stationary for one round.						
RAZOR WIND	2	10	—	12		X
A blade of wind slices through the target model.						
TEMPEST	4	8	4	12		X
Models in the AOE suffer a POW 12 damage roll and are knocked down.						
WIND RUSH	2	SELF	—	—		
Sorscha may immediately move up to her current SPD in inches and gains +4 DEF for one round. Wind Rush may be cast once per turn.						

TACTICAL TIP

TEMPEST — All models in the AOE suffer this POW 12 damage roll instead of blast damage.

WIND RUSH — Wind Rush can be cast during Sorscha's activation before she charges.

Let us say I was 'an uninvited guest' in the Tzepesci family manor located at the peak of the mountain known as Stragoi, which I believe means 'crowned' in ancient Khard. A strange place with bas-reliefs of Khadoran horselords—seemingly timeless. Crossing the threshold was like taking a step a thousand years into the past. A strikingly noble, handsome Umbrean who could only be Great Prince Vladimir entered the room. I recall thinking it was as if he had stepped straight from that princely wall.

—The words of Gavyn Kyle

In times of old before the Iron Kingdoms, certain lands in Khador were the provinces of so-called barbarians, yet among those who rode to battle were some possessed of their own rugged honor who united their people with a clarity of vision. Chieftains ruled these hordes, and horselords ruled the chieftains. Of noble stock, horselord families ruled for generations with oppressive strength, calculated cruelty, and a will to organize the chaos of the world. Their bloodlines have all but faded into obscurity in the fullness of time like the shadows of a bygone age. The Tzepesci, one of the strongest families to rule the provinces of Old Umbrey, are the last of the great families. Indeed, a millennia ago the Tzepesci were the governors of Old Korska before it fell into ruin, and they controlled the throne of all Khador for a time. Though they are reduced in power, the Tzepesci name still resonates with Khador's eastern people.

It is said that when the Tzepesci line comes to an end, a great doom shall be visited upon all Khador. Vladimir Tzepesci—called the Dark Prince for the shadowy prophecy

he bears—is the last of that line. He is the Great Prince of Korskovny Volozkya, one of the eighteen great houses recognized by the throne, yet he represents much more. Many of the ruling families of Umbresk and southern Gorzytska owe his family fealty from old oaths set in bone and blood. The influence he wields in this region is enough to stir uneasy rumors in the capital. Steeped in the traditions of old, he is a living relic of past glories and bloody deeds, and his noble bearing is testimony of an ancient lineage. So powerful is the blood in his veins that men shy from his gaze. He is a man of few words, but the Dark Prince is accustomed to being heard when he speaks.

As some are born to paint or write great works of poetry, Vladimir was born to make war. A brilliant tactician as well as a potent warcaster, he has waged many great campaigns in the service of his queen. From time-to-time he has orchestrated the whole of eastern Khador's military might. A swordsman without equal, he brings swift death upon all who dare cross blades with him. Worthy opponents are treated to longer duels, but most enemies are dispatched with little consideration.

Vladimir takes great pride in his armor. Refusing to abandon his family traditions, he wears the same enchanted, ancient plate of his forefathers. Although it has seen some sorcerous repair over the centuries, it is the same suit of crimson mail his horselord ancestor Prince Buruvan Tzepesci wore in battle against the Orgoth.

In his service to Queen Vanar XI, Vladimir has trained other warcasters, and it is no great secret that he became intimately acquainted with the young and promising Sorscha Kratikoff during her mentoring. Little is known of the affair other than it ended quite abruptly and left Sorscha distinctively changed. There is some speculation that she was rebuffed due to her lowly heritage. Whatever the case, Vladimir is determined to stay true to the legacy of his forefathers who were always strong and faithful in their duties even at the expense of their own happiness. There are those who call such notions—and his adherence to ancient tradition—nothing more than exercises in vanity, but for Vladimir Tzepesci it is the only life he knows.

Though Vladimir is respected for his great accomplishments, not all who meet him love him. It is whispered in secret among the courts that the time of the Tzepesci has passed, and Vladimir is but an unpleasant reminder of a crueler era. These conspirators neither believe in the grave prophecy nor in the man they see as a threat to their own designs. Rather, they anticipate the day when the Dark Prince falls and the vast treasures of the Tzepesci family are annexed into the vaults of Khador.

Focus 7				Cmd 9	
SPD	STR	MAT	RAT	DEF	ARM
6	6	7	5	15	16

Skirmisher		
SPECIAL	POW	P+S
Mimic	7	13

Ruin		
SPECIAL	POW	P+S
Parry	4	10

Damage	18
Point Cost	76
Field Allowance	C
Victory Points	5
Base Size	Small

SPECIAL RULES

FEAT: FORCED MARCH

The strategic and tactical prowess of the Dark Prince of Umbrey is legendary throughout the Motherland as well as any land he has touched. Through careful allocation of resources, Vladimir may conserve the energy of his warjacks and expunge this reserve in one great battlefield maneuver.

Friendly Khador warjacks currently in Vladimir's control area double their SPD for this turn.

SKIRMISHER

MIMIC — When making a melee attack with Skirmisher, Vladimir may duplicate one special rule from any melee weapon of a target warcaster in his control area, but he may not duplicate special attacks or special actions. Replace references to the target warcaster and weapon with references to Vladimir and Skirmisher respectively. The special rule is mimicked for the duration of the attack only.

RUIN

PARRY — Vladimir cannot be targeted by free strikes.

SPELL	COST	RNG	AOE	POW	UP	OFF
BLOOD OF KINGS	3	SELF	—			
Vladimir gains +3 SPD, STR, MAT, RAT, DEF, and ARM. Blood of Kings may be cast once per turn and lasts for one round.						
BOUNDLESS CHARGE	3	6	—	—		*
Target model's next activation is a charge at SPD +5" that crosses rough terrain and obstacles without penalty. When this spell targets an enemy model, it is an offensive spell and requires a magic attack roll.						
BRITTLE FROST	2	6	—	—		X
Damage to target warjack that exceeds ARM is doubled this round.						
IMPALER	4	8	—	13		X
Target model damaged by Impaler becomes stationary for one round.						
RAZOR WIND	2	10	—	12		X
A blade of wind slices through the target model.						
SIGNS AND PORTENTS	3	SELF	CTRL	—		
Friendly Khador models currently in Vladimir's control area, including himself, roll an additional die on attack and damage rolls this turn. Discard the low die in each roll.						
WIND WALL	4	SELF	*	—		
Ranged attacks against Vladimir or a model completely within 3" of him automatically miss. A model completely within 3" of Vladimir cannot make ranged attacks. Wind Wall lasts for one round.						

TACTICAL TIP

BLOOD OF KINGS — Combine this spell with Boundless Charge to give Vladimir a 14" charge range.

BOUNDLESS CHARGE — The +5" of movement granted by Boundless Charge replaces the normal +3" for a charge. Additionally, the target model does not need to spend focus or receive an order to charge next activation.

MIMIC — Though Vladimir can mimic Reach, it has no effect. He must declare the attack targeting a model in his melee range before benefiting from Mimic.

DESTROYER
KHADOR HEAVY WARJACK

BOMBARD

ARCING FIRE - When attacking with the bombard, the Destroyer may ignore intervening models except those that would normally screen the target.

EXECUTIONER AXE

CRITICAL AMPUTATION - On a critical hit, each arm and weapon system that takes damage is automatically disabled. After marking regular damage, those systems that took damage have their remaining system boxes marked as well.

SPD	STR	MAT	RAT	DEF	ARM
4	12	5	3	10	20

L Bombard

RNG	ROF	AOE	POW
14	1	3	14

R Executioner Axe

SPECIAL	POW	P+S
Critical	6	18

	1	2	3	4	5	6
			L		R	
	L	L	M	C	R	R
		M	M	C	C	

Point Cost	126
Field Allowance	U
Victory Points	4
Base Size	Large

HEIGHT/WEIGHT: 11'7" / 9.5 tons

ARMAMENT: Bombard Cannon (left arm), Executioner Axe (right arm)

FUEL LOAD/BURN USAGE: 408 lbs / 4 hrs general, 55 min combat

INITIAL SERVICE DATE: 537 AR

CORTEX MANUFACTURER: Greylords Covenant

ORIG. CHASSIS DESIGN: Khadoran Mechanicks Assembly

The advancement of Khadoran warjacks has been inexorable, for the country's mechaniks build each warjack to last. The Destroyer has served as the premiere Khadoran long-range bombardment warjack for almost a hundred years. The sight of the distinctive Destroyer silhouette atop a hill is enough to send dread and terror into all of Khador's enemies. Soon enough they hear the whistling of shells arcing overhead as a prelude to destruction before the explosive projectiles impact with thunderous booms and tear apart everything in the vicinity. While the enemy struggles to recover from bombardment, the Destroyer charges into battle and cleaves its Executioner Axe through the pathetic armor of smaller warjacks. Nothing is left intact in the wake of a Destroyer.

The Destroyer's current design has been unaltered for nearly seventy years, but warjacks bearing the name go back as far as 480 AR. Their most famous deployment came in the First Thornwood War of 510 to 511 AR. Even with antiquated armament, those impressive early 'jacks shelled Cygnaran fortifications from across the Dragon's Tongue River. Khadoran military historians believe that if King Vygor had more Destroyers for that war, Cygnar would have lost the Battle of the Tongue. Nearly a third of the warjacks ordered to replace those lost in the war were Destroyers. Improvements to the bombard in 537 AR cemented its position as a true masterpiece of war engineering. Its particularly innovative reloading system allowed the cannons to be deployed widely as a warjack attachment. The bombard's heavy shells are packed with prodigious red and black powder capable of exploding with enough force to spray shrapnel across the surrounding area.

Though most famous for its role in delivering a punishing bombardment, the Destroyer is no less formidable when engaged in combat. Its designers did not skimp on armor; its iron-plated chassis is as heavy as the Juggernaut's and provides it formidable protection. Against those who close with it, the Destroyer wields an Executioner Axe capable of shearing off entire limbs from a warjack in a single, mighty stroke.

TACTICAL TIP

ARCING FIRE — Basically, the Destroyer can shoot over other models unless they are close to the target and large enough to protect it.

> *You can't ignore a Juggernaut. It just keeps coming, shrugging off everything you throw at it. The only way to deal with them is heavy and unrelenting concentrated fire.*
>
> —Lieutenant Gralan Byrne, 86th Long Gunner Company

JUGGERNAUT

HEAD SPIKE - While not a weapon on its own, the Head Spike gives the Juggernaut +2 POW for head-butt attacks.

ICE AXE

CRITICAL FREEZE - On a critical hit, target model becomes stationary for one round.

Khadorans scoffed at the idea when the Cygnaran Armory unveiled its first so-called 'light warjack.' In Khador bigger is usually better, and their mechaniks employ this principle on each successive warjack. Looming over all of the Cygnaran heavy 'jacks of its day, the Juggernaut is a mammoth of plated armor viewed as the glorification of the Khadoran temperament. It has come to symbolize the supremacy of the Khadoran martial warjack and is as useful today as when it was freshly conceived. There are fewer coming off the assembly lines than in past decades, but they continue to endure brutal punishment admirably and are rebuilt and repaired countless times before deemed beyond salvage. There are Juggernauts still serving on the front lines that have persisted for a hundred years or more.

The current armament of the Juggernaut dates to 516 AR, but the older chassis was designed in 465 AR to create a more heavily armored combat platform than the Berserker it was intended to replace. It has become the staple chassis, and its underlying design is utilized for the majority of warjacks currently found in the Khadoran Army. The Juggernaut is a product of the ingenuity of Khadoran mechaniks challenged to combine the most powerful steam engines with as much massive armor plating as its armature could sustain.

In 517 AR the Mechaniks Assembly incorporated mechanikal techniques of the Greylords Covenant to create the ice axe. The weapon encases a target in a layer of ice and frost and causes it to seize up and freeze. Even glancing blows render enemy warjacks into statues of ice as their engines screech protest against their frozen limbs. With its free hand the Juggernaut can seize an enemy 'jack and hurl it across the battlefield to crush enemy infantry. All Khadorans respect power, and there is not a soul in the Motherland who does not admire the Juggernaut and its endless list of accomplishments in battle.

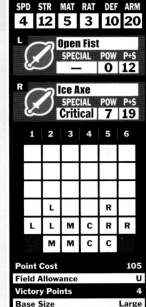

SPD	STR	MAT	RAT	DEF	ARM
4	12	5	3	10	20

L — Open Fist

	SPECIAL	POW	P+S
	—	0	12

R — Ice Axe

	SPECIAL	POW	P+S
	Critical	7	19

	1	2	3	4	5	6
			L		R	
	L	L	M	C	R	R
		M	M	C	C	

Point Cost	105
Field Allowance	U
Victory Points	4
Base Size	Large

HEIGHT/WEIGHT: 11'7" / 9 tons

ARMAMENT: Ice Axe (right arm)

FUEL LOAD/BURN USAGE: 408 lbs/ 4 hrs general, 55 min combat

INITIAL SERVICE DATE: 516 AR

CORTEX MANUFACTURER: Greylords Covenant

ORIG. CHASSIS DESIGN: Khadoran Mechaniks Assembly

MARAUDER
KHADOR HEAVY WARJACK

MARAUDER

HEAD SPIKE - While not a weapon on its own, the Head Spike gives the Marauder +2 POW for head-butt attacks.

RAM PISTONS

BATTER - Double the number of damage points a structure takes from the Ram Pistons.

COMBO SLAM (★ATTACK) - The Maurader may make Ram Piston attacks separately, or it can make a special attack to strike with both Ram Pistons simultaneously. Make one attack roll for the Combo Strike. On a successful hit, instead of making a normal damage roll, slam the target model d6" directly away from the Marauder. The model suffers a damage roll equal to the Marauder's current STR plus the POW of both Ram Pistons. If the model collides with another model with an equal or smaller-sized base, that model suffers a collateral damage roll equal to the Marauder's current STR. The Combo Slam is not prevented by any spells or movement penalties that prohibit charges or slams.

SPD	STR	MAT	RAT	DEF	ARM
4	12	5	3	10	20

L — Ram Piston
	SPECIAL	POW	P+S
	Multi	3	15

R — Ram Piston
	SPECIAL	POW	P+S
	Multi	3	15

	1	2	3	4	5	6
			L		R	
		L	L	M	C	R	R
		M	M	C	C	

Point Cost	109
Field Allowance	U
Victory Points	4
Base Size	Large

HEIGHT/WEIGHT: 11'7" / 10.25 tons

ARMAMENT: Twin Rams (left and right arm)

FUEL LOAD/BURN USAGE: 408 kg / 4 hrs general, 55 min combat

INITIAL SERVICE DATE: 522 AR

CORTEX MANUFACTURER: Greylords Covenant

ORIG. CHASSIS DESIGN: Targh Fedro (credited), Khadoran Mechaniks Assembly

---

May the Creator preserve the walls of our cities yet deliver to us weapons to shatter and crumble the fortifications of our enemies.

—Visgoth Ruskin Borga of the Old Faith bestowing a blessing on a Marauder being sent to battle

Designed to deliver pulverizing impacts capable of exploding apart buildings or armored warjacks with equal ease, the Marauder comes to battle armed with a pair of pneumatically powered battering rams. Though developed to aid in siege warfare, these crushing rams are even more useful for obliterating or displacing enemy warjacks, and they provide tactical control to their commanding warcasters. The Marauder can hurl ten tons of enemy warjack to the side with no more difficulty than a rampaging bear knocking aside a Cygnaran long gunner.

An industrial mechanik named Targh Fedro was inspired to try this design after observing stonemasons in the quarry. He took an old laborjack with broken down arms and replaced them with battering rams. He tested the 'jack against the quarry walls and nearly brought the entire face down in a single blow. Excited at the military potential, he took the design to the Mechaniks Assembly to build a prototype utilizing the ubiquitous Juggernaut chassis. Those gathered to witness trials against similarly heavy Khadoran 'jacks were astonished at the power compressed into the piston-driven rams. Built of military grade iron, the rams mustered enough force to send a ten-ton warjack flying. While any warjack can knock an adversary away or to the ground if it has sufficient distance to build up steam to a full charge, the Marauder can fire its rams into an enemy 'jack while standing still. The ram pistons can unleash enough power to send lesser machines flying back through stone walls and become gnarled wrecks of torn metal and shattered pistons.

The Marauder proved its worth in its first major field engagement against one of the southern border fortresses of Llael in 532 AR. The Llaelese army felt safe behind their thickened walls until an assault with four Marauders hammered its way straight through the gatehouse and penetrated into the inner courtyard. Khadoran soldiers followed behind, easily overcame the defenders, and tore the fortification down. The Llaelese derived an alarm no soldier cares to hear: "Marauders at the gates!"

TACTICAL TIP
COMBO SLAM – A Marauder does not have to move at all to perform a Combo Slam.

> *Get ready to have burns on your burns and calluses on your calluses. You'll be covered in oil and grime with nothing but a wrench and your wits to get the job done.*
>
> —A crew chief to a new subordinate

MECHANIK CHIEF

'JACK MARSHAL (1) – The Mechanik Chief may start the game controlling one Khador warjack. The Mechanik Chief has a marshalling range equal to his CMD in inches. If a controlled warjack is in the Mechanik Chief's marshalling range, it can run, charge, or boost one attack or damage roll once per activation. If the Mechanik Chief is destroyed or removed from play, warjacks under his control do not become inert. The Mechanik Chief may reactivate one friendly inert Khador warjack per turn in the same manner as a warcaster. The reactivated warjack comes under his control unless he already controls 1 other warjack.

LEADER

REPAIR [7] (★ACTION) - A Battle Mechanik may attempt repairs on any friendly Khador warjack that has been damaged or disabled. To attempt repairs, the Battle Mechanik must be in base contact with the damaged warjack or disabled wreck marker and make a skill check. If successful, roll a d6 and remove that number of damage points from anywhere on the warjack's damage grid.

ASSISTANT MECHANIK

ASSIST REPAIR [+1] (★ACTION) - Every Assistant Mechanik assisting the Mechanik Chief with a repair adds +1 to the Mechanik Chief's Repair skill, up to a maximum of 11. An Assistant Mechanik must be in base contact with the warjack being repaired by the Mechanik Chief.

REPAIR [4] (★ACTION) - Same as Mechanik Chief above.

Mechanik Chief				Cmd 8	
SPD	STR	MAT	RAT	DEF	ARM
5	7	6	4	13	10

Asst. Mechanik				Cmd 5	
SPD	STR	MAT	RAT	DEF	ARM
5	5	5	4	13	10

Monkey Wrench		
SPECIAL	POW	P+S
—	2	9/7

Leader and 3 Troops	17
Up to 2 Additional Troops	3ea
Field Allowance	3
Victory Points	2
Base Size	Small

No matter how heavily armored the great Khadoran warjacks are, in the crush of battle they are eventually worn down and sometimes disabled. Skilled and brave men must take to the field ready to stand alongside other soldiers to attend to the machines. Dodging bullets and evading explosions, these brave mechaniks make their way to the warjacks and restart their engines so they can rejoin the fight. These loyal brothers of the Khadoran Mechaniks Assembly consider themselves patriots to equal any regular soldier. They are not squeamish at the sight of spilled blood or oil, and they are willing to put themselves in harm's way to conduct repairs.

Because every loyal citizen in Khador is expected to enlist in the Winter Guard, many of these men have already served alongside the rest, and they are often older and more seasoned than the freshly recruited youths bearing the blunderbuss next to them. Their skills proved valuable enough to be transferred to the Battle Mechaniks, and rather than axes they now wield heavy wrenches as capable of crushing skulls as loosening the oversized and stubbornly tight bolts of heavy warjacks.

Chiefs are the hearts of mechanik teams. Sometimes the old vets get injured on the battlefield, but a Khadoran does not let a simple thing like a shorn-off limb get him down. Injured mechaniks repair their own broken bodies with cleverly improvised mechanikal limbs, often salvaging finer gears and mechanisms from the detritus of the battlefield in preparation for this eventuality. Such an arm is a great tool in its own right, for it imbues the mechanik with the strength to bend metal or hold armor while his crew rivets and welds it in place. It also grants an edge in close combat where the mechanik is able to leverage the wrench with tremendous

force. Many an enemy has underestimated the charge of enraged battle mechaniks interrupted from their labors to avenge the fallen machines they work tirelessly to restore.

TACTICAL TIP

ASSIST REPAIR – Note that an Assistant Mechanik does not make a skill check himself when assisting. He simply adds +1 to the Mechanik Chief's skill score. Also note that an Assistant Mechanik cannot assist another Assistant Mechanik with a repair attempt.

DOOM REAVERS
KHADOR UNIT

LIEUTENANT
LEADER

REAVER

ABOMINATION - Models/units—friendly or enemy—within 3" of a Doom Reaver must pass a command check or flee.

ADVANCE DEPLOYMENT - Place Doom Reavers after normal deployment, up to 12" beyond the established deployment zone.

FEARLESS - Doom Reavers never flee.

WEAPON MASTER - A Doom Reaver rolls an additional die on his melee damage rolls.

FELLBLADE

BERSERK - Every time a Doom Reaver destroys another model with a melee attack, he must immediately make one melee attack against another model in his melee range, friendly or enemy.

REACH - 2" melee range.

SPELL WARD - A Doom Reaver cannot be targeted by spells, friendly or enemy.

Lieutenant	Cmd 7				
SPD	STR	MAT	RAT	DEF	ARM
6	7	8	4	13	14

Reaver	Cmd 5				
SPD	STR	MAT	RAT	DEF	ARM
6	7	7	4	13	14

Fellblade		
SPECIAL	POW	P+S
Multi	6	13

Leader and 5 Troops	100
Field Allowance	1
Victory Points	2
Base Size	Small

Khador is dotted with ancient ruins from the Orgoth era, and many of the massive stonework temples, fortresses, and hidden catacombs are buried below ground. Though it is not widely mentioned, several great Khadoran cities have Orgoth catacombs below their streets that have been picked over by occult scholars and relic hunters. It was one such group led by the Greylords Covenant that unearthed a large cache of the infamous fellblades below the city of Khardov. These dark swords are saturated with tainted magic, and the very sight of them is painful to the eyes. Each blade is adorned with howling faces that shift and move at the fringes of vision, and once wielded the swords seem alive. The faces whisper incomprehensible chants into the minds of those unfortunate enough to hold them.

Upon discovering the blades, the Khadoran High Kommand and its queen were vexed. They were clearly powerful weapons, but each swordsman who tried a blade lost his mind and descended into savage and homicidal madness. Even in their sleep the swordsmen heard the babbling of foreign whispers stoking them to acts of bloodshed. Twice as strong and lashing out with berserk abandon, the wielders went where they willed, killing anything that crossed their paths while conversing only in the perverse language of the old conquerors. They had become Doom Reavers.

Queen Ayn Vanar finally came upon the solution. She decided to give the blades to wayward prisoners, particularly soldiers who had been deemed guilty of gross insubordination or other crimes. Already unable to serve, such men were a burden and were often slated for execution. At the queen's direction, the Greylords found a way to turn these men into berserkers chained to their fellblades and directed in battle by their urges. The Khadoran wizards have done what they can to impose restraints on these maddened swordsmen, but they are only nominally under control, particularly once blood lust overwhelms them. Something in the accursed Orgoth sorcery of the swords' creation protects their wielders from magic. It unravels spells before they can land and makes these berserkers particularly effective against enemies who rely on such power. In battle they are barbaric nightmares who undermine the morale of even the stoutest veterans. Some say the fellblades should never have been unleashed, but they have earned their share of bloody victories.

TACTICAL TIP

BERSERK — A Doom Reaver who only disables a warjack will not go berserk because it has not been destroyed yet.

REACH — Spread them out if you do not want them killing each other.

SPELL WARD — Yep, that's right. No beneficial spells either.

IRON FANG PIKEMEN
KHADOR UNIT

We learned to bring down the powerful mountain bears with long spears over a thousand years ago, but it's quite a different matter to bring down the ones with iron skins.

—Dhurgo Bolaine, decorated Iron Fang Kapitan

The proud Iron Fangs are examples of the Khadoran fighting spirit. They stand toe-to-toe against six-ton steam-powered machines that can crush the life out of them in a single blow. These hardened soldiers are part of an ancient tradition of spearmen who once fought the northern bear and later evolved into pikemen deployed by settled Khards to stand against the roving horselords who dominated the southern plains and eastern hills of their empire. Just as they stood firm against the seemingly unstoppable tide of warlords on muscled horses, they now form up behind their shields and bring pikes to bear against the warjacks that dominate the modern battlefield. Their pikes are tipped with powerful shaped explosive charges that can blast through heavy warjack armor and damage the machinery beneath.

Though famed for their skill against warjacks, they are equally effective against infantry. Through training Iron Fangs learn to carry the heaviest plated armor as a second skin, and they are able to ignore the weight and even sleep comfortably in it. Behind their tower shields of thick curved metal, Iron Fangs are notoriously difficult to kill, as even coordinated rifle fire simply bounces off their armored frames as they continue their implacable advance. In battle they move with military precision, interlocking their shields to form an impenetrable mobile wall of spear points.

After 200 years of service, the Iron Fangs have become a heralded tradition of the Khadoran army, and their fraternal bond is legendary. It is said that upon acceptance into the legion of Iron Fangs, a soldier swears a blood oath, casts off the life he lived before, and dedicates himself to his fellow soldiers, his country, and the art of war.

SERGEANT
LEADER

SHIELD WALL (ORDER) - Every Iron Fang Pikeman that received the order who is in tight formation with the Sergeant at the end of the unit's movement gains +4 ARM. If the Sergeant is no longer on the table, the largest tight formation group forms the shield wall. If there is more than one group with the largest number of troopers, the unit's controller decides which group forms the shield wall. A trooper that did not receive the order cannot join the shield wall. This bonus does not apply to damage originating in the model's back arc. Models that do not end their movement in tight formation do not benefit from the shield wall. This bonus lasts for one round.

PIKEMAN

COMBINED MELEE ATTACK - Instead of making melee attacks separately, two or more Iron Fang Pikemen in melee range of the same target may combine their attacks. In order to participate in a combined melee attack, an Iron Fang Pikeman must be able to declare a melee attack against the intended target. The Iron Fang Pikeman with the highest MAT in the attacking group makes one melee attack roll for the group and gains +1 to the attack and damage rolls for each Iron Fang Pikeman, including himself, participating in the attack.

BLASTING PIKE

CRITICAL KNOCKDOWN - On a critical hit, target model is knocked down.

REACH - 2" melee range.

Sergeant				Cmd 9	
SPD	STR	MAT	RAT	DEF	ARM
6	6	7	4	13	14

Pikeman				Cmd 7	
SPD	STR	MAT	RAT	DEF	ARM
6	6	6	4	13	14

Blasting Pike		
SPECIAL	POW	P+S
Multi	7	13

Leader and 5 Troops	59
Up to 4 Additional Troops	9ea
Field Allowance	2
Victory Points	2
Base Size	Small

175

MAN-O-WAR SHOCKTROOPERS

KHADOR UNIT

KAPITAN

LEADER

SHIELD WALL (ORDER) - Every Man-O-War Shocktrooper that received the order who is in tight formation with the Kapitan at the end of the unit's movement gains +4 ARM. If the Kapitan is no longer on the table, the largest tight formation group forms the shield wall. If there is more than one group with the largest number of troopers, the unit's controller decides which group forms the shield wall. A trooper that did not receive the order cannot join the shield wall. This bonus does not apply to damage originating in the model's back arc. Models that do not end their movement in tight formation do not benefit from the shield wall. This bonus lasts for one round.

UNIT

COMBINED MELEE ATTACK - Instead of making melee attacks separately, two or more Man-O-War Shocktroopers in melee range of the same target may combine their attacks. In order to participate in a combined melee attack, a Man-O-War Shocktrooper must be able to declare a melee attack against the intended target. The Man-O-War Shocktrooper with the highest MAT in the attacking group makes one melee attack roll for the group and gains +1 to the attack and damage rolls for each Man-O-War Shocktrooper, including himself, participating in the attack.

FEARLESS - Man-O-War Shocktroopers never flee.

ANNIHILATOR BLADE

REACH - 2" melee range.

> *We know what it's like to be a warjack. Those who retire, they are sad men. They grow old and shrivel away. I will not fade like that. When death comes, I will die in steam.*
>
> —Deidric Harkinos, veteran Man-O-War

Kapitan	Cmd 9				
SPD	STR	MAT	RAT	DEF	ARM
4	9	8	6	11	17

Shocktrooper	Cmd 7				
SPD	STR	MAT	RAT	DEF	ARM
4	9	7	5	11	17

Shield Cannon			
RNG	ROF	AOE	POW
6	1	—	14

Annihilator Blade		
SPECIAL	POW	P+S
Reach	4	13

Kapitan's Damage	10
Shocktrooper's Damage	8
Leader and 2 Troops	67
Up to 2 Additional Troops	20ea
Field Allowance	2
Victory Points	3
Base Size	Medium

The fabrication of warjack cortexes requires rare materials in short supply in Khador, so warjacks are doubly expensive and precious. The Khadoran Mechaniks Assembly has long sought an alternative. The solution derived in 470 AR by Jachemir Venianminov was simplicity itself, for the Assembly succeeded in transforming men into steam-powered wrecking crews called Men-O-War.

The suit of armor worn by a Man-O-War is a miraculous creation imbuing each soldier with near warjack-level strength, durability, and protection against the elements. There are drawbacks to wearing heavy battle armor powered by a steam boiler, however. Khadorans spending time in Man-O-War suits are susceptible to heat stroke, exhaustion, and the occasional steam leak cooking them alive. However, one will never hear a Man-O-War complaining or asking for comfort, for they are proud of their tradition and willingly embrace the risks in the service of the army.

These shocktroopers wield powerful Annihilator Blades, one stroke of which is capable of splitting the armor of a light warjack. Against mere men, it leaves them in ruin. As with more traditionally armored heavy infantry, they can file into ranks and lock their shields in formation, but each shield also boasts a powerful short-range cannon. While the Shocktroopers prefer to rely on their blades, the cannon blast gives them added reach and versatility on the battlefield.

Only the most steadfast soldiers can earn the right to join their number. Nonetheless many soldiers jump at the opportunity; it is not every day that one can experience the world from a warjack's vantage.

WIDOWMAKERS
KHADOR UNIT

Widowmakers form the elite sniper division of the Khadoran armed forces. Some regard snipers as little more than cowardly assassins, but Khador has embraced their sniper corps and elevated them to the status of heroes. The screening process to join the Widowmakers is among the most exacting of all of Khador's specialist soldiers, and it requires those who demonstrate peerless skill with the rifle. Because they are first and foremost a merit-based corps, their membership is open to all equally, whether peasant-born, rural-hunter, or noble's sons. Any who have the requisite skill can aspire to become a Widowmaker and bring death from afar. It is scarcely possible to overstate the skill Widowmakers possess with their long-barreled hunting rifles. So efficient are they that they can take apart incoming warjacks piece-by-piece with well-placed shots. Killing a man becomes as automatic as drawing breath.

A Widowmaker's primary role is neutralizing officers and unit leaders to facilitate chaos among the enemy and prompt rout. They frequently advance ahead of the main battle group, and their arrival is often signaled by enemy officers abruptly falling dead before the report of rifle fire can be identified. They also offer support during strategic withdrawals by ensuring their own wounded do not become prisoners. If a downed officer cannot be retrieved, Widowmakers make sure he does not fall into the wrong hands for interrogation. A true patriot knows it is better to die by a comrade's bullet than to be placed in irons on an enemy's torture rack.

Officially Widowmakers are not used in domestic conflicts, but it is whispered that their talents have been utilized to pick off speakers of dissent, rabble rousers, or corrupt kayazy suspected of losing their loyalty to the crown. Widowmakers expect little charity from their enemies if captured. Indeed, it is common practice among the Cygnarans to hang them without trial. For the Widowmakers it's understood; hatred and fear comes with the territory.

KAPITAN
LEADER

UNIT

ADVANCE DEPLOYMENT - Place Widowmakers after normal deployment, up to 12" beyond the established deployment zone.

CAMOUFLAGE - Widowmakers gain an additional +2 DEF when benefiting from concealment or cover.

PATHFINDER - During his activation, a Widowmaker ignores movement penalties from, and may charge across, rough terrain and obstacles.

SNIPER - When damaging a warjack, the Widowmaker's controller chooses which column takes damage. When damaging a warbeast, the Widowmaker's controller chooses which branch takes damage. After a successful ranged attack, a Widowmaker may automatically inflict one damage point instead of making a damage roll.

Kapitan					Cmd 8
SPD	STR	MAT	RAT	DEF	ARM
6	5	5	8	14	11

Sniper					Cmd 6
SPD	STR	MAT	RAT	DEF	ARM
6	5	4	7	14	11

Hunting Rifle			
RNG	ROF	AOE	POW
14	1	—	10

Sword		
SPECIAL	POW	P+S
—	3	8

Leader and 3 Troops	53
Field Allowance	1
Victory Points	2
Base Size	Small

WINTER GUARD

KHADOR UNIT

SERGEANT

LEADER

UNIT

COMBINED RANGED ATTACK - Instead of making ranged attacks separately, two or more Winter Guard may combine their attacks against the same target. In order to participate in a combined ranged attack, a Winter Guard must be able to declare a ranged attack against the intended target and be in a single open formation group with the other participants. The Winter Guard with the highest RAT in the attacking group makes one ranged attack roll for the group and gains +1 to the attack and damage rolls for each Winter Guard, including himself, participating in the attack.

When each Khadoran male reaches seventeen winters, he is conscripted into the Winter Guard. Women are allowed to volunteer, but it is often discouraged and prohibited if they have children in their keeping. Some conscripts are assigned to police and patrol the towns and cities of Khador and never see real combat, yet they remain the staple of the Khadoran infantry.

The equipment of the Winter Guard has changed only slightly since their inception. They utilize solid implements for defending border garrisons and taking the fight to the enemy. Their battle-axes are stout and well suited for hacking into the enemy should they close, but the Winter Guard rely most upon the blunderbuss, a powerful if somewhat inaccurate military weapon that utilizes a hefty blast of powder to fire either a mass of infantry-shredding stone and metal shrapnel or a thick and heavy slug more suitable for penetrating the armor of a warjack. Though southern riflemen disdain the range of these squat weapons, there is no doubt they hit with violent impact, particularly when Winter Guard concentrate fire.

The Winter Guard comprise the majority of the Khadoran Army and are found at the core of every garrison and attack force. Their rudimentary and quick training is designed to get the young soldiers immediately into the field of battle. The construction of training camps erected across Khador from the largest complexes at Volningrad to rural outposts near Uldenfrost has allowed Queen Ayn to maintain constant reinforcements and field a formidable army at an affordable cost. Through their training they learn what it means to be true Khadorans, to love their nation, and to risk death in battle. It is a lesson they carry even as they leave service, for each Khadoran is bonded by this brotherhood. They are all soldiers of the Winter Guard.

Sergeant				Cmd 8	
SPD	STR	MAT	RAT	DEF	ARM
6	5	6	5	12	13

Guardsman				Cmd 6	
SPD	STR	MAT	RAT	DEF	ARM
6	5	5	4	12	13

Blunderbuss			
RNG	ROF	AOE	POW
8	1	—	12

Axe		
SPECIAL	POW	P+S
—	3	8

Leader and 5 Troops	58
Up to 4 Additional Troops	9ea
Field Allowance	3
Victory Points	2
Base Size	Small

MANHUNTER
KHADOR SOLO

> *Blood is the coin of this realm now, and he is the paymaster.*
> —Kommander Sorscha Kratikoff

Fishing and hunting are the prime sources of food for many rural areas of Khador. Khadoran hunters tend to be held in higher regard than those of other kingdoms, particularly in the cold and rugged northern mountains and forests. They are experts at tracking and killing some of the most dangerous game, such as the Raevhan buffalo, and some have moved on to the most cunning prey of all—man.

First and foremost, manhunters are rangers able to travel effortlessly in the wilds of Khador. Lowland brush, forests, and snow are all treated as a well-paved road by a manhunter. The long years of harsh life in the wilderness has hardened their bodies and darkened their skin, and their skills are legendary. Manhunters are devoted trackers who serve as scouts and sometimes as assassins for the right price. They are masters at camouflage and are frequently overlooked while in plain sight.

Manhunters often operate behind enemy lines, and they are armed with twin hand axes for close combat. Whether stalking prey in silence or swinging their axes with blinding efficiency, manhunters are frightful killers. The hiring of such men by the Khadoran army is an old tradition, and their value on the fringes of the battlefield has been exploited in many wars. In exchange for their services, they are well provided for by the armies that hire them. They are sent to accompany reconnaissance groups where they join Kossite peers and the Widowmakers to strike at the enemy from unexpected directions.

Kommanders and warcasters are sometimes hesitant to call upon a manhunter's services, for they doubt the extent of their true loyalty. There are many whispers of manhunters who enjoy the hunt too much and give in to their animal urges and the rush of the kill. Their track records are often good enough to eclipse the dark rumors, however.

MANHUNTER

ADVANCE DEPLOYMENT - Place the Manhunter after normal deployment, up to 12" beyond the established deployment zone.

CAMOUFLAGE - The Manhunter gains an additional +2 DEF when benefiting from concealment or cover.

FEARLESS - The Manhunter never flees.

PATHFINDER - During his activation, the Manhunter ignores movement penalties from, and may charge across, rough terrain and obstacles.

STEALTH - Attacks against the Manhunter from greater than 5" away automatically miss. If the Manhunter is greater than 5" away from an attacker, he does not count as an intervening model.

WEAPON MASTER - The Manhunter rolls an additional die on his melee damage rolls.

Manhunter				Cmd 9	
SPD	STR	MAT	RAT	DEF	ARM
6	8	8	4	14	14

Axe		
SPECIAL	POW	P+S
—	3	11

Axe		
SPECIAL	POW	P+S
—	3	11

Damage	5
Point Cost	22
Field Allowance	1
Victory Points	1
Base Size	Small

TACTICAL TIP

CAMOUFLAGE — Effects which negate cover or concealment also negate the Camouflage bonus.

STEALTH — In other words, if he's far enough away from you that you cannot hit him, he does not block LOS or have any other effect on ranged or magic attacks against other models either.

MERCENARIES

Glory and Coin
Mercenaries of the Iron Kingdoms

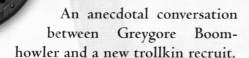

My favorite two colors are blood and gold, and on a good day I see a lot of both.

—Herne Stoneground

An anecdotal conversation between Greygore Boomhowler and a new trollkin recruit.

Aye, I met many an army sod what turns his nose up at mercs. As if their own coin spends better. They got fancy uniforms t'be sure, but wot else they got t'be so proud aboot? Most never seen battle a'fore. A bunch o'milk drinkin lads barely to manhood cannae tell one end of a rifle from t'other. Sneeze too loud and them baby-faced recruits soil their britches and drop their weapons.

Take yer average merc. We been in scraps every chance we get just to get by. Need coin for payin th'boys, coin for supplies and ammo, coin for drinkin. If we cannae hold our own in a scrap we dinnae get paid. It's honest work, na mistake. It's a hard livin and ever day the risk of bein put down for good. Only thing'll keep you alive is skill with blade or gun. Ne'er know whar a job'll take us. Might be up t'the frozen north whar spit'll freeze afore it leaves yer mouth or down sloggin through t'Marches in dust storms and eatin sand. Bein an active merc is tough. If you want to kick up yer heels and get paid yer better off at the town guard. Ever day wit my company ye best be ready to hunker down while bullets are flyin overhead and split some skulls with that axe at yer belt.

Afore ye ask wot it means t'be a merc ye gotta understand we got rules we follow. 'Tis my name on the company and my name on our charter and yer actions in battle will come back to me. Make me regret hirin you and I'll tear yer arm off and cram yer own fist down yer gullet until ye choke. Bein a proper merc ain't like bein a bandit. We live by the Charter set up in ancient days like any good company. When we hire on we see the course. It dinnae matter if the fightin gets rough, we stick in there. There's na turnin aboot and sellin ourselves to the other side cause they offered a few more gold coins. There are criminals and bandits wot work like that and it's a quick way to get strung up on the gallows when the law comes knockin. We dinnae put up with that. My name is known from Caspia to Blackwater cause my word is good and I give what service I promise. When Boomhowler signs 'is mark on the page, I put my gun and my axe where they tell me. If ye dinnae like it, hire on to a pirate ship and leave me be.

Those are all the rules ye need worry aboot. I'm the boss, so dinnae worry aboot anyone else here. If ye were in th'regular army ye'd have to worry aboot keepin yer uniform and boots shiny. Ye'd have to worry aboot all the officers up the pay scale from ye, which ones to salute and which ones yer na supposed to look at. We got freedom. We spend our money how we want and we have a good

> **Ever day wit my company ye best be ready to hunker down while bullets are flyin overhead and split some skulls with that axe at yer belt.**

time when we're na in battle. This company plays hard as we fight. Wot good is clink squirreled away if ye cannae spend and enjoy it?

There are a lot of mercs and we compete with all of 'em. Each has his own bag o' tricks and it's good to know wot to expect. Some pretend t'be yer best friend so keep yer wits. We earn our pay the same way, but every company got their own contracts. Each of 'em would as soon see ye in the ditch bleedin rather than take a job they want. Some companies we work alongside when the contract calls fer it, but dinnae trust 'em beyond that. Some mercs just want coin. Others got their own agendas. Some have an axe to grind. Maybe they're holdin' some past job we took against us and are lookin fer a scrap. Some pretend t'be proper mercs but don't even wear the company ink. They got na scruples and'r just assassins. Watch yer back and keep yer axe at the ready. That's enough preachin fer today. Ye seem to have a good head on yer shoulders. Follow my lead and duck when I say to and we'll all be rollin in gold afore ye know it.

GREYGORE BOOMHOWLER & CO.

That sound! Like a lion riding a church bell in the middle of a landslide. I covered me bloody ears in time, but not all me mates were fast enough. Some of 'em ain't heard a sound since.

—Reid Markus, Cygnaran long gunner

The legendary trollkin fell caller Bragg was quite promiscuous in his day, and thus the fruits of his peculiar talents have sprouted across Immoren. These special folk command a power of voice that staggers the imagination. One of the most noted is Greygore Boomhowler, a crass and nigh intolerable axe-for-hire with a great command of the Gift of Bragg. Many tales describe his vocal prowess, yet those who have heard it personally cannot recount the experience without emotion.

Greygore hails himself as the reincarnation of Bragg. An admitted outcast among the wild trollkin tribes, he chooses to wear garish strips of cloth in gaudy colors in a style of his own design not at all related to any true *quitari* tartan patterns of his people. He also refuses to be quiet, even in ambush.

Indeed, some commanders have paid him and his mercs double-fees to stop singing and gibbering at all hours of the day and night. When Greygore is not singing, drinking, or fighting, he is performing Bragg's favorite duty—wenching. Females of all races throughout the kingdoms have been entranced by Greygore's legendary voice. Indeed, he is quite the handful off the battlefield, but his antics are well worth it once the battle has joined.

Greygore is proficient with both blunderbuss and axe, but his true worth lies in his rumbling voice. With a single breath he can release a rolling

croon across the battlefield supernaturally palpable over the clash of swordplay and the crack of gunfire. His voice is heard from within the body like a feeling more than a sound. His vocal range is incredible, from subtle tunes in order to calm panicked comrades to shrill screeches that turn a man's hair white. There are soldiers who claim the trollkin's voice was key in winning battles before the first drop of blood was spilled. More than once Greygore alone has caused entire hordes to flee. Among those who appreciate his unique talents is the outlawed former Cygnaran warcaster Asheth Magnus, and the two seem to have come to an equitable arrangement.

Blood must be spilled at times when fear and terror cannot win the day. When battle is joined Greygore calls upon the full force of his power. With a deep breath, he sends forth a heavens-shaking cry. His maw erupts with a wall of sound like a mighty oceanic wave that shatters glass, splinters wood, and rips gashes in the metal skins of warjacks. The sensitive inner workings of the mechanikal giants are susceptible to this swell of sound that rattles cogs loose and unbalances essential fluids. Truth be told, Greygore's wail taxes him a great deal, and he cannot sustain it for extended amounts of time. This is a good thing. Though the force of his blasts are meant for his enemies, the ear-splitting sounds can be heard for miles, and many of the trollkin's allies are as prone to incapacitation as his foes.

Traditional trollkin dislike the fell caller's influence over the many young who have given up their tribal ways to join him abroad. Without question this particular "descendant of Bragg" is more comfortable in the cities than the wilds, but he makes occasional forays into the ancestral homes of his people to recruit for his unique mercenary company. These volunteers swell and wane in number from time to time, but Greygore cannot be found without at least a few loyal followers. He is no longer welcome in kriels where he returns with casualties in the place of wayward sons and daughters.

In battle Greygore's company of trollkin fights with a combination of axe, blunderbuss, and his trademark stink bombs which he developed to his specifications in the Cygnaran city of Fharin. These glass globes shatter on impact and release a cloud of noxious vapor that is highly debilitating to those who inhale it—anyone, that is, save the trollkin. Their legendary resistance to poisons and contaminants allow them to continue battle unfazed.

Whether or not Greygore is the reincarnation of the legendary Bragg or just a self-important bard with a bloated ego, it matters little to his employers. He and his trollkin followers are an impressive addition to any army, and between bouts of drunken revelry he has a wealth of talents to spread among the troops. Still, commanders are often wary of where to assign Greygore and company, for just like at the Caspian amphitheatre, if one instrument is out of tune during the symphony, the results can be disastrous—especially if that instrument can turn men into jelly with a single, sour note.

SPECIAL RULES

MERCENARY

Boomhowler & Company will not work for the Protectorate.

BOOMHOWLER

FELL CALL (★Action) - Enemy models/units currently within 8" of Boomhowler must pass a command check or flee. Warjacks and warbeasts currently within 8" suffer –2 MAT and RAT for one round.

LEADER

UNIT

COMBINED MELEE ATTACK - Instead of making melee attacks separately, two or more Trollkin Mercs in melee range of the same target may combine their attacks. In order to participate in a combined melee attack, a Trollkin Merc must be able to declare a melee attack against the intended target. The Trollkin Merc with the highest MAT in the attacking group makes one melee attack roll for the group and gains +1 to the attack and damage rolls for each Trollkin Merc, including himself, participating in the attack.

STINK BOMBS (★Attack) - A Stink Bomb is a RNG 5 AOE 3 gas effect ranged attack that does no damage. Living models in the gas effect AOE suffer –2 to their SPD, STR, MAT, RAT, CMD, and DEF for one round. The Stink Bomb gas effect remains on the table for one round. Trollkin are immune to the effects of Stink Bombs.

TOUGH - When a Trollkin Merc suffers sufficient damage to be destroyed, his controller rolls a d6. On a 5 or 6, the Trollkin Merc is knocked down instead of being destroyed. If the Trollkin Merc is not destroyed, he is reduced to one wound.

Boomhowler				Cmd 8	
SPD	STR	MAT	RAT	DEF	ARM
6	8	7	5	13	16

Trollkin				Cmd 6	
SPD	STR	MAT	RAT	DEF	ARM
6	7	6	4	12	15

Blunderbuss			
RNG	ROF	AOE	POW
8	1	—	12

Great Axe		
SPECIAL	POW	P+S
—	5	13 12

Boomhowler's Damage	5
Leader and 5 Troops	93
Up to 4 Additional Troops	13ea
Field Allowance	C
Victory Points	2
Base Size	Medium

TACTICAL TIP

STINK BOMBS – A model that enters a stink bomb template will also suffer its penalties. Additionally, stink bomb templates are not cloud effects.

HERNE STONEGROUND & ARQUEBUS JONNE

Eighteen degrees left! Seven degrees skyward! Three degrees for wind. Fire at will!
On it. This one's going to kick them in the shorts.

—Herne Stoneground to Arquebus Jonne and Jonne's response while gaining the perfect angle of fire

Herne Stoneground served as a traveling alchemist's assistant in his younger days and roamed from stronghold to stronghold learning his mentor's trade. It was more a hobby than a craft, but Herne became curious about the sciences surrounding gunsmithing, cannoneering, and demolitions. By his second decade he had already mastered the crafting of double-barreled firearms, and his wares earned him a reputation among traders and military merchants alike. In some parts the Stoneground mark is hailed as a sign of cutting-edge quality. A Stoneground original can fetch a thousand

Cygnaran crowns on the open market, and some sell at a much higher price behind closed doors. Herne could never trust messengers to deliver his wares, so he always did so personally. However, he rarely traveled without a bodyguard or three, and eventually Herne ran across a well-respected ogrun named Jonne.

Jonne was born and raised in Rhul where most of his conclave has served as guards and smith hands to the Rhulfolk for hundreds of years. Growing up quickly on the trade-rich border of Llael, Jonne was accustomed to the flash and pomp of the Llaelese merchants. It did not take long for the adolescent ogrun to make a name for himself on the Black River loading docks, and often merchants asked for him by name. The slightest taste of

fame went right to Jonne's head, and he soon signed on with a Rhulic mercenary group called the Emberhold. While in the company he practiced his martial skills and worked as a sword-for-hire (or axe, mace, or even large rocks!) for any who might be in need of his muscle.

One day during a delivery of a pair of Stoneground originals, Jonne met Herne Stoneground himself. A pair of ill-fated brigands picked that time to interrupt the sale. Jonne moved instinctively. He snatched up the two bandits and restrained them until the watch arrived. So fast was his reaction and effective his skill, the surrounding folk broke into applause as the ogrun handed over the brigands. Herne offered Jonne a solid handshake in thanks, and from that day forth the two were fated to become one of the most famous mercenary teams in all the Iron Kingdoms.

Herne hired Jonne as his personal guard to protect him and his products through thick and thin. That was nearly fourteen years ago, and Jonne is to this day bound to Herne. Over the years and through many adventures, the two have become great friends. Jonne has gone far beyond the call of duty for his charge by saving Herne time and again. The dwarf feels safe under Jonne's watchful eye, and though some less scrupulous employers might allow their hired muscle to perish in order to save their own skin, Herne would not think of it. Without a second thought of his own safety, Herne leaps to the aid of his ogrun friend against any who seek to harm him.

Some years ago after months of Jonne's grumbling, the duo agreed that small arms manufacturing was not the lucrative business it once was. They determined that true wealth would be found only in large ordnance, so Herne put his mind—and his gunwerks skills—to the task. Before long he unveiled the Stoneground Barrage Arquebus. In an effort to market the new creation, Herne and Jonne took to the road hiring themselves out to any would-be customers so that they might get a first hand experience of the gun's effectiveness.

The arquebus, a triple-barreled contraption that launches three cannonballs at once, is a beautifully crafted weapon so massive that only the bulging muscles of Jonne—or "Arquebus Jonne" as he has come to be called—can possibly hold it aloft. The heavy clouds of smoke emitted by the powder charges force Jonne to goggle his eyes with thick black glass. Obviously this impairs the ogrun's vision, but Herne, who after years of powder burns and stinging smoke

is immune to such effects, uses his shrewd judgment and mathematical skills to help Jonne aim. With its weight and kick, the barrage arquebus is difficult to aim, but its ammunition is designed for fragmentation. The arquebus is devastating at a fair range, but Jonne is just as deadly in close combat with his mighty axe. Foes who survive the shelling long enough to close will face Herne's own pistol and axe, neither of which he is reluctant to employ.

Herne Stoneground and Arquebus Jonne have joined Cygnaran officers at after-battle victory toasts, argued payment options with Khadoran kommandants, and witnessed the pre-battle prayers of Menite priests. The two friends have only one rule: no walking dead. If asked about the possibility of continuing if the other should fall in combat, both Jonne and Herne will ask, "How would that be possible? If he's dead, then I must be, too."

SPECIAL RULES

MERCENARY
Herne & Jonne will not work for Cryx.

HERNE
GUNNER - Jonne gains +2 RAT while he is in base-to-base contact with Herne and not engaged.

LEADER

PISTOL (HERNE ONLY)

AXE (HERNE ONLY)

BARRAGE ARQUEBUS (JONNE ONLY)
SCATTER SHOT (★ATTACK) - The Barrage Arquebus may make a Scatter Shot special attack when Herne and Jonne are in base-to-base contact. When fired in this manner, all three barrels of the Barrage Arquebus discharge at once. After determining the initial shot's point of impact, roll deviation for two additional shots from that point. Models in the AOE of the additional shots suffer blast damage.

GREAT AXE (JONNE ONLY)

Herne						Cmd 8
SPD	STR	MAT	RAT	DEF	ARM	
4	6	6	6	12	13	

Jonne						Cmd 9
SPD	STR	MAT	RAT	DEF	ARM	
6	8	6	4	12	15	

Pistol			
RNG	ROF	AOE	POW
8	1	—	10

Barrage Arquebus			
RNG	ROF	AOE	POW
12	1	3	14

Axe		
SPECIAL	POW	P+S
—	3	9

Great Axe		
SPECIAL	POW	P+S
—	5	13

Herne's Damage	5
Jonne's Damage	10
Point Cost	42
Field Allowance	C
Victory Points	2
Herne's Base Size	Small
Jonne's Base Size	Medium

TACTICAL TIP
JONNE - Jonne has a better chance of passing unit-level command checks once Herne is no longer on the table.

SCATTER SHOT - The additional shots deviate the full d6" regardless of range.

EIRYSS, MAGE HUNTER OF IOS

Like a ghost, she was. Appeared from nowhere, turned our warcaster into a bloody pincushion, then she faded away.

—Cygnaran Captain Morris Beaumayne on Black River patrol

Iosans have long been mysterious, doubly so since their nation isolated itself from outside contact in 581 AR. This was a dire omen in several halls of power that prompted speculation about what might be transpiring within the well-guarded borders of Ios. Any who have ventured uninvited into that territory have vanished utterly. Neither humans nor dwarves comprehend the power of the elves, nor do they understand Iosan technology and magic, but one hunter has arisen among the Iosans to leave her mark on the wars of man. Her peerless skill and deadly reputation are enough to cause panicked rumor to spread like wildfire. Warcasters may be giants among men, but even the bravest feels dread at the mention of Eiryss, Mage Hunter of Ios.

She is a killer without equal whose every fiber and thought are bent toward the slaughter of human arcanists. For years she has stalked the fringes of man's wars like a shadow barely seen. The only warning most warcasters receive is a whisper or a faint sense of movement before being struck in the neck with deadly bolts. She is not alone. There are others of her ilk, but none are so active or so single-mindedly determined to cull human warcasters, sorcerers, and wizards. Her deeds have generated rumors of dozens of such hunters. Few can bring themselves to believe the death of so many commanders could be linked to a single woman, whatever her origin.

The name 'Eiryss' is linked to one of the most insidious organizations in western Immoren—known to westerners as the Retribution. Exiles of Ios know its full name as the Retribution of Scyrah, and its members seek vengeance against the vile perfidy of human magic in all forms, particularly the mechanikal abominations called warjacks and the reckless men and women who control them. Little is known about the Retribution, its numbers, its members, or its resources. The Retribution does not strike often. Its members are cautious

186

and patient hunters willing to gather information on their targets to understand their every weakness and strength, but when they spring an ambush, it invariably ends in death.

Eiryss has come forth as something of a bloody ambassador of Ios. She is a mysterious mercenary who feigns working for coin or information but truly seeks only opportunities to end the lives of warcasters. She is adept at hiding her loathing and appears seemingly professional and reserved to those who agree to her services. All the while a strange smile touches her lips as she looks over those who hire her. Her eyes weigh them as if on a scale as she counts weapons, inspects armor, and analyzes their tactics and strength in battle. She prepares herself mentally for the time when she is given the opportunity to hunt them in turn.

None will dispute her effectiveness. She appears seemingly out of nowhere to offer her services to prospective clients. Her contracts are simple enough: find the enemy warcaster, kill him, and disappear into the shadows. She is a consummate assassin of unequaled stealth fueled by an unending hatred for those she believes are killing her goddess and dooming her species to extinction.

Eiryss employs a wide array of gear to aid in her hunts. Skilled with a sword, she is a capable close combat killer, but she prefers to deal with prey as any game hunter would—with well-placed shots from the shadows. She feels no need to sully her hands with the very blood that is poisoning Scyrah. To deliver her shots, Eiryss carries a powerful crossbow crafted specifically for her by the Retribution. Both weapon and bolts are customized to bring swift death.

She will work for anyone the Retribution feels might further its goals. She sometimes turns down payment when she is satisfied with the information she has gained. Armies employing Eiryss do not trust her, but there is no direct evidence that she has ever turned on an employer. Eiryss cares little for her reputation as long as her employers provide ample opportunities to slay mages. She will continue hunting to avenge Scyrah until every human spellcaster lies in a pool of his own blood. By her hands, many arcanists have crossed to Urcaen feeling only a brief blinding pain with absolutely no indication of how or why the mortal blow was delivered.

Eiryss				Cmd 9	
SPD	STR	MAT	RAT	DEF	ARM
7	4	6	9	16	12

Crossbow			
RNG	ROF	AOE	POW
12	1	—	*

Bayonet		
SPECIAL	POW	P+S
—	2	6

Saber		
SPECIAL	POW	P+S
—	3	7

Damage	5
Point Cost	29
Field Allowance	C
Victory Points	1
Base Size	Small

SPECIAL RULES

MERCENARY

Eiryss will not work for Cryx.

EIRYSS

ADVANCE DEPLOYMENT - Place Eiryss after normal deployment, up to 12" beyond the established deployment zone.

ASSAULT - As part of a charge, after moving but before performing her combat action, Eiryss may assault. When making an Assault, Eiryss makes a single ranged attack targeting the model charged. Eiryss is not considered to be in melee when making the Assault ranged attack, nor is the target considered to be in melee with Eiryss. If the target is not in melee range after moving, Eiryss must still make the Assault ranged attack before her activation ends. Eiryss cannot target a model with which she was in melee at the start of her activation with an Assault ranged attack. Eiryss can only make melee attacks with her bayonet after an Assault.

CAMOUFLAGE - Eiryss gains an additional +2 DEF when benefiting from concealment or cover.

INVISIBILITY - Eiryss may forfeit her activation to become invisible. While invisible, Eiryss cannot be targeted by ranged or magic attacks, cannot be charged or slammed, and gains +4 DEF against melee attacks for one round. Eiryss cannot become invisible if engaged at the start of her activation. While invisible, Eiryss does not block line of sight or provide screening.

PATHFINDER - During her activation, Eiryss ignores movement penalties from, and may charge across, rough terrain and obstacles.

TECHNOLOGICAL INTOLERANCE - If Eiryss ends her movement within 5" of a friendly warjack, her activation ends immediately.

WEAPON MASTER - Eiryss rolls an additional die on her melee damage rolls.

CROSSBOW

When declaring a crossbow attack, choose one of the following bolt types:

• **DEATH BOLT** - Target model hit by Death Bolt automatically takes three damage points. When damaging a warjack, Eiryss' controller chooses which column suffers the damage. When damaging a warbeast, Eiryss' controller chooses which branch suffers the damage.

• **DISRUPTOR BOLT** - Target model hit by Disruptor Bolt suffers a POW 8 damage roll and loses all focus points. A warcaster hit by Disruptor Bolt does not replenish focus points next turn. A warjack hit by Disruptor Bolt suffers Disruption. A warjack suffering Disruption cannot be allocated focus points or channel spells for one round.

• **PHANTOM SEEKER BOLT** - With this ethereal bolt, Eiryss may attack any model in range regardless of line of sight. Phantom Seeker Bolt ignores cloud effects, cover, concealment, obstructions, and intervening models. Target model hit by a Phantom Seeker Bolt suffers a POW 10 damage roll.

TACTICAL TIP

DISRUPTOR BOLT — Just like Disruption, a Disruptor Bolt does not prevent a warjack from gaining focus in other ways. A warcaster can still gain focus from other sources, too, such as soul tokens.

PHANTOM SEEKER BOLT — Keep in mind that the Phantom Seeker Bolt does not ignore Stealth.

REINHOLDT, GOBBER SPECULATOR

What d'ye mean ye don' know who I am? I'm famous, I am! Bloody famous!

—Reinholdt, gobber speculator and self-proclaimed world traveler

Few men can claim they have ventured from one end of the Iron Kingdoms to the other and back, and even fewer gobbers can make such a bold statement. One of these diminutive creatures does more than just suggest however; he downright guarantees he has been everywhere at least twice and seen it all at least once. Reinbaggerinzenholdt, or Reinholdt for short, claims to have seen many wondrous sights from the throne room of Stasikov Palace to the glowing walls of Shyrr. He sports strange trinkets and baubles from all over Immoren, and his accent is nearly indistinguishable from the natives of whichever area he happens to be in at the time. Whatever the cause or source, Reinholdt is a bottomless font of skills and knowledge that would be difficult for a dozen of his

kind to learn in a lifetime. Not an expert at anything special (although Reinholdt would argue otherwise), he seems at least partially versed in whatever comes up at the moment. Reinholdt is truly a jack-of-all-trades.

Even with the unsettling doubt of the veracity of his claims, it seems warcasters and commanders the kingdom over have shelled out coin to hire Reinholdt for his myriad of half-masteries. Although he claims to have once worked as a bodger, Reinholdt has little interest in such things. Too often he felt he was doing all the work for the mechaniks, and now he refuses to soil his hands with warjack repair. He enjoys tinkering with mechanika, but his true joy is the adventure of roaming the kingdoms.

MERCENARY SOLO CHARACTER

It may seem odd that a gobber with the reputation of a braggadocio could make a difference to the powerful commanders of iron behemoths, but he does, and happily so. While Reinholdt would tell his employers his very presence is a boon and his advice on tactics is without peer, he is indeed a true aid to most warcasters. The gobber claims a great savvy with the alchemy of firearms and is useful as a speedy reloader for riflemen and pistoleers. Sometimes he loads one of his "famous" home-brewed powder charges that leads to spectacular pyrotechnics at various levels of intensity, but he is still quite the handy assistant. Armed with a host of trinkets and artifacts from the lands over, Reinholdt makes great use of his "tools." His crystal Ordic spyglass—which he says he received for helping sway a Cryxian pirate invasion from the shores near Berck—is one of his favorites. Using the glass, he can spy out potential dangers and estimate just how long it will take for that peril to cause him personal harm (gobbers often use "getaway chronology" as a mode of measuring distance). Though it may take an employer a while to find the seconds-to-impact method useful, this knack of Reinholdt's is rarely off by much, and if so, it is usually on the positive side (in favor of the gobber's escape time). When all else fails, some warcasters rub the little guy for luck.

Though he has seen many battlefields across Immoren, Reinholdt himself is lucky to have not suffered a scratch. This fact, of course, is not from his skill as a combatant but rather his uncanny luck. He once sneezed himself out of a moving carriage into a patch of thornbriar bushes just before the carriage burst into flames upon hitting a powder trap set by brigands, and once a bullet reflected harmlessly off of a silver soupspoon in his pocket that he had "acquired" earlier that same day.

Despite his good fortune, Reinholdt is not what one would call a hero. He is far more likely to run and hide than stick around if a situation gets too hairy. Indeed, he has been known to vanish from sight in typical gobber fashion if an enemy comes too close. If left with little option, the resourceful chap will search his pockets and pouches for anything that might aid his escape. His tricks range from powerful smoke bombs to distracting contraptions, but they all result somehow in his safe exit. Though he may not be a hero, Reinholdt the world traveler is an interesting bloke with no lack of usable talents and skills. Many commanders utter a deep sigh when the little speculator comes sauntering into their camps from who-knows-where, and whether that sigh is an expression of relief or one of exasperation is debatable.

Reinholdt				Cmd 4	
SPD	STR	MAT	RAT	DEF	ARM
6	2	2	2	16	9

Point Cost	15
Field Allowance	C
Victory Points	1
Base Size	Small

SPECIAL RULES

MERCENARY

Reinholdt will not work for Cryx or the Protectorate.

REINHOLDT

ASSISTANT - Before the start of the game, Reinholdts' controller assigns him to a single warcaster. Reinholdt cannot be reassigned during a game. Remove Reinholdt from play if his warcaster is destroyed or removed from play.

COWARD - If Reinholdt begins his activation more than 3" from his warcaster, he must pass a command check or flee. Reinholdt must also pass a command check or flee any time he or his warcaster is in melee. Reinholdt automatically fails any command check if he is outside his warcaster's command range.

WARCASTER BENEFITS

While Reinholdt is in base-to-base contact with his warcaster, the warcaster may use one of the following abilities during his activation:

- LUCKY CHARM - The warcaster may roll an additional die on one attack or damage roll. Discard the lowest die.

- RELOAD - The warcaster may make an additional ranged attack without spending a focus point regardless of the weapon's ROF.

- SPYGLASS - The warcaster may measure the distance between himself and one other model within his line of sight anywhere on the table.

CYGNAR

**Commander
Coleman Stryker**
Warcaster

**Captain
Victoria Haley**
Warcaster

**Lieutenant
Allister Caine**
Warcaster

**Commander Coleman
Stryker Variant**
Warcaster

**Captain Victoria
Haley Variant**
Warcaster

**Journeyman
Warcaster**
Solo

Long Gunners
Unit

Ironclad
Heavy Warjack

Defender
Heavy Warjack

Stormblades
Unit

Lancer
Light Warjack

Sentinel
Light Warjack

Charger
Light Warjack

CYGNAR

Trenchers
Unit

Field Mechaniks
Unit

Arcane Tempest Gun Mages
Unit

A strong force under Commander Stryker musters from the fortress at Eastwall to engage in a little 'aggressive diplomacy' with marauding Protectorate raiders.

High Exemplar Kreoss
Warcaster

Grand Scrutator Severius
Warcaster

The High Reclaimer
Warcaster

High Exemplar Kreoss Variant
Warcaster

Paladin of the Order of the Wall
Solo

Temple Flameguard
Unit

Crusader
Heavy Warjack

Vanquisher
Heavy Warjack

Choir of Menoth
Unit

Redeemer
Light Warjack

Revenger
Light Warjack

Repenter
Light Warjack

Deliverers
Unit

Holy Zealots
Unit

Knights Exemplar
Unit

Grand Scrutator Severius calls forth a sizable crusade to bring the True Law to a Cygnaran border town. *"Let their flesh burn as an offering to the Creator!"*

Cryx

Warwitch Deneghra
Warcaster

Pirate Queen Skarre
Warcaster

Iron Lich Asphyxious
Warcaster

Warwitch Deneghra Variant
Warcaster

Skarlock Thrall
Solo

Bane Thralls
Unit

Slayer
Helljack

Reaper
Helljack

Bile Thralls
Unit

Nightwretch
Bonejack

Defiler
Bonejack

Deathripper
Bonejack

Mechanithralls
Unit

Necrotech and Scrap Thralls
Solo and Independent Models

Satyxis Raiders
Unit

The ruins of a once fortified Cygnaran town serve as an ideal staging ground and 'recruiting center' from which Asphyxious and his minions will mount raids throughout the mainland.

**Vladimir, Dark Prince
of Umbrey**
Warcaster

**Kommander
Sorscha**
Warcaster

**Butcher
of Khardov**
Warcaster

**Vladimir, Dark Prince
of Umbrey Variant**
Warcaster

**Kommander
Sorscha Variant**
Warcaster

Manhunter
Solo

Iron Fang Pikemen
Unit

Juggernaut
Heavy Warjack

Destroyer
Heavy Warjack

Man-O-War Shocktroopers
Unit

Marauder
Heavy Warjack

Battle Mechaniks
Unit

Doom Reavers
Unit

Widowmakers
Unit

Winter Guard
Unit

The Dark Prince of Umbrey prepares to ambush a Cygnaran patrol both to test the soldiers of the south and grant a few more Cygnaran women the honor of widowhood.

**Eiryss,
Mage Hunter of Ios**
Solo

**Reinholdt,
Gobber Speculator**
Solo

**Herne Stoneground &
Arquebus Jonne**
Unit

Greygore Boomhowler & Co.
Unit

Painting and Modeling Guide
Tips and Technique by Mike McVey

Welcome to the *WARMACHINE: Prime Remix* painting guide. In the next few pages we are going to take a quick look at miniature preparation and painting. This is by no means an exhaustive guide; miniature painting is a huge and complex field! This guide is meant to get you started down the road and will be particularly useful if you have just opened your first box or blister. There will also be some useful information for more experienced painters, including color scheme information for all the factions. We are going to focus on painting warjacks since they are pretty much unique to WARMACHINE, but we will also touch on other types of figures.

Painting miniatures is a large part of the WARMACHINE experience and not something to be dismissed as a necessary evil. In fact, painting is a fun and rewarding hobby in its own right. Imagine how much sweeter that crushing victory will be if you are proud of your beautifully painted army! It does not have to be a daunting task either. Though the size of the warjacks may strike fear into the heart of the most experienced painter, they are not that difficult to paint well if you know what you are doing. By the time you read through this, you will be armed with all the necessary techniques and tricks and can begin painting like a veteran. You will be amazed at the great results that can be achieved with these simple and quick techniques. Okay. Let us get started.

Tools of the Trade

I'm not going to go on at great length about what you should and should not buy, but it is worth speaking a bit about the paints and brushes you use. Sable brushes are the best choice for miniature painting. They cost more, but they also last longer if treated properly, and the painting quality of a nice sable brush is without equal.

As for paints, acrylics are really the best choice. They dry quickly and the colors are clean and bright. The Formula P3 range of acrylic paints is specially formulated to be used on Privateer Press miniatures. They cover exceptionally well and mix freely with other acrylic paints and inks, and many of the colors cannot be found elsewhere. The use of liquid pigments means the colors go on particularly smoothly and cover well even over black undercoat. Two thin coats of most colors will give complete coverage. All of the paint names in this section come from the Formula P3 range.

Inks are some of the miniature painter's greatest allies. Dull flat colors can be imbued with depth and richness with one quick glaze, and detail that was once lost can be made to re-appear magically with a well-placed wash. They are also great for mixing with paint because you can thin a color with ink and lose none of its coverage. Mix paints and inks anyway you want for a huge variety of different results.

KNOW THE TERMINOLOGY

BASE COAT - THE INITIAL FLAT COAT OF PAINT APPLIED TO A SPECIFIC AREA. APPLY THE SHADE AND HIGHLIGHT COATS OVER THE BASE COAT TO CREATE A THREE DIMENSIONAL EFFECT.

SHADE - A DEEPER COLOR THAN THE BASE COAT APPLIED IN THE RECESSED AREAS OF THE MINIATURE TO EXAGGERATE DEPTH.

HIGHLIGHT - A LIGHTER COLOR THAN THE BASE COAT APPLIED TO THE RAISED SURFACES TO EXAGGERATE THE EFFECT OF THE LIGHT CATCHING THE SURFACE.

DRYBRUSH - A SIMPLE BUT EFFECTIVE WAY OF HIGHLIGHTING A TEXTURED SURFACE. APPLY THE LIGHTER HIGHLIGHT COLOR BY CAREFULLY FLICKING THE TIP OF AN OLD BRUSH ACROSS THE SURFACE OF THE MINIATURE TO PICK OUT THE TEXTURE. REMOVE MOST OF THE PAINT FROM THE BRISTLES PRIOR TO DOING THIS BY BRUSHING THE SURFACE OF A PAPER TOWEL UNTIL THE TIP IS ALMOST DRY.

BLEND - A TECHNIQUE FOR CREATING VERY SUBTLE HIGHLIGHTS. APPLY THE HIGHLIGHT COLOR WITH ONE BRUSH, AND WHILE THE PAINT IS STILL WET, USE ANOTHER DAMP BRUSH TO FADE THE EDGE AND CREATE A SMOOTH GRADATION OF COLOR.

WASH - THINNED DOWN COLOR APPLIED LIBERALLY TO CREATE A SHADING EFFECT. THIS IS ESPECIALLY EFFECTIVE ON HEAVILY TEXTURED SURFACES. PAINT, INK, OR A MIXTURE OF BOTH CAN BE USED FOR A WASH.

GLAZE - A VERY THIN TRANSPARENT LAYER OF PAINT OR INK USED TO TINT THE COLOR OF A MINIATURE. THIS WORKS BEST WITH INK, AND APPLYING MULTIPLE GLAZES CAN GIVE DEPTH AND RICHNESS TO A COLOR.

UNDERCOAT - THE INITIAL PRIMER COAT APPLIED OVER THE BARE CLEANED MINIATURE. MOST UNDERCOATS ARE USUALLY APPLIED WITH A SPRAY IN EITHER BLACK OR WHITE.

Painting and Modeling Guide

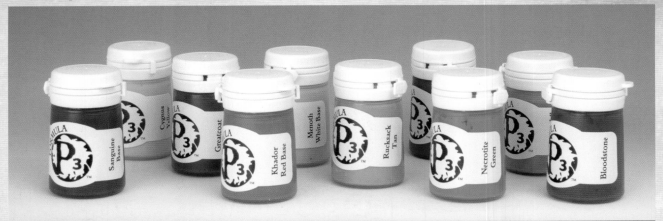

The Formula P3 range is available in a wide variety of colors specially formulated for WARMACHINE miniatures.

One other valuable trick in the miniature painter's arsenal is matt medium. You can add it to a wash color in order to give it a little more body. The addition enables the wash to stick to the surface of your miniature better and not run off into the cracks.

You are also going to need a few basic supplies for your painting area: a light, a pot for water, paper towels, and something on which to mix the paint.

Getting Started

The first step is to clean the pieces. This is the process where you remove the marks left by the casting process. The best tool for cleaning the metal is a half-round needle file. The primary thing to remove is the "split line". This runs right around the extremities of the miniature and marks the place where the two halves on the mold met when the miniature was cast. Just carefully smooth this away with the appropriate side of the file. You may also find some thin spurs of metal sticking from the miniature. These are vent marks and can be carefully removed with either a pair of clippers or a sturdy craft knife.

Once your miniatures are cleaned and assembled, you will need to undercoat them. Some people pass over this stage (mainly out of laziness), but doing so is a huge mistake! An undercoat makes all future layers of paint easier to apply to the surface (and they will stay

Use a needle file to smooth away the mold lines on the miniatures to prepare the surface for painting.

there longer), and using black undercoat presents other advantages. When painting warjacks, it is best to use a black spray undercoat that you can get from either a hobby store or an auto parts store. Make sure you spray from lots of different angles so the paint gets into all the recesses, and also make sure you do not overspray and fill in the details. It goes without saying you should always spray in a ventilated area, preferably outside and away from any electrical or gas appliances. I set up a spray booth made from a large box with one side cut out. It really helps to catch the overspray.

Once the miniature has been sprayed black, use a brush to touch in any of the spots you missed to give an even covering.

Painting Order

One way to make the process a lot easier is to paint your warjacks in a specific order. In general terms you want to get all of the messy techniques, such as washing and dry brushing, out of the way first, then move on to the main body colors, and finally finish with the details. You will find that when you break the painting down into simple steps like this, the whole task is far quicker and the results are better. We are going to talk in general terms here, but exactly the same techniques can be applied to any of the warjacks. Just apply the relevant colors.

Metals

The first things to paint on any warjack are the moving parts and the areas that are going to end up in a basic metallic finish. First, give them a fairly neat coat of Pig Iron straight over the black undercoat. When the metallic paint is completely dry (it is good to have a hair dryer handy to speed this up), you can move on.

To give the metal areas some definition and shading, you can apply a coat of Armor Wash. Apply the wash all over the area, but do not let it run and form deep pools. You can remove excess paint with a dry brush (don't forget to wash it though).

When the wash is dry you can either leave the metals alone if you want a grimy finish, or you can add some highlights. A lighter metallic color creates a good highlight. You can use either straight Pig Iron again or Pig Iron with a lighter silver tone added. For quick results you can carefully drybrush on the highlights, but if you want a more subtle effect I suggest using the technique described in the highlighting section.

Base coat the metal parts of the miniature with Pig Iron.

Wash over the dry base coat with a coat of Armor Wash.

Highlight with Pig Iron for a quick and effective finish.

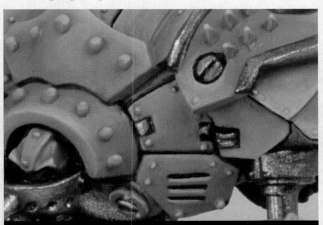

Leave the black undercoat showing to provide deep shading and bring out the detail.

Painting and Modeling Guide
Body Color

Once the metal areas are out of the way, you can start on the main body color. This will cover all of the armor plates and the details in the main color of the faction. Try to be as neat as you can since this is where that black undercoat really pays off. Leave black showing in all the recesses and between the armor plates. It requires a little practice, but you are left with instant shading! The black in the crevices lends depth and definition to the miniature. This stage is the most time consuming part of the process, but it is well worth the effort. If you get the main body color painted fairly neatly, you will end up with a great looking miniature.

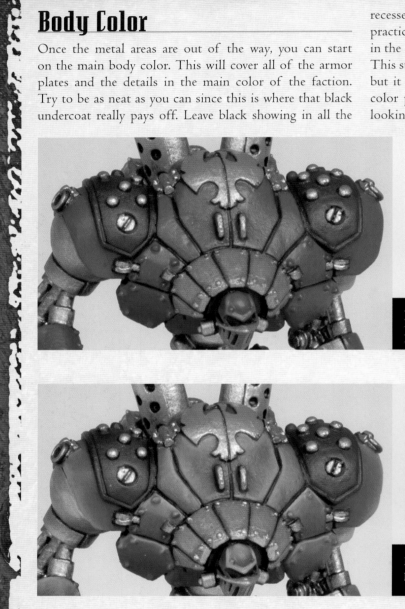

Apply the first highlight of Cygnar Blue Base and Cygnar Blue Highlight over a dry base coat of Cygnar Blue Base. Note how the edges and raised surfaces are picked out.

Lighten the highlight color further by adding more Blue Highlight to the mix.

Achieve the final highlight color by adding Morrow White to the mix. Apply it just to the very edges.

Highlighting

Highlighting may sound like a time consuming technique, but a few well-placed, simple highlights can make all the difference. This really brings the miniature to life, and it is not difficult to achieve. One of the most important aspects of highlighting is getting the tones just right. If you go too dark, they won't show up, but go too light and they will look crude. All of the main faction colors are provided in two shades in the Formula P3 range. Just paint on the base color and then add the highlight tone to create a lighter shade. You can add as many tones are you like here by mixing progressively more of the highlight color to the mix.

Keep in mind that on most miniatures you apply the highlights to the raised areas. Since there is very little surface relief on a warjack, apply the highlights toward the edges of the armor plates. It is common to apply one, two, or even three lighter tones for a quick finish and as many as eight to ten for display quality. The first highlight can be just a little lighter than the body color, and you can cover quite large areas with it. It effectively turns the remaining base coated areas into shading. The second highlight should be painted on a far smaller area and be significantly lighter, and the last should be even lighter and just applied to the edges.

Secondary Colors

There is generally a second color that complements the main body color. Pretty much the same goes for this color as for the primary color—be as neat as you can and let

Deep shading around sculpted details helps to pick them out from the surrounding area.

the undercoat help with the shading. For example, when you paint the Cygnaran symbol in Rhulic Gold on the top of an Ironclad, there should be a line of undercoat left around it to create the shading and separation from the blue armor plates. Once the base color is dry, add simple highlighting to bring out the shape just as you would with the body color.

Details

Once the main parts of the warjack are finished, all that is left is to pull out the details. Do as much or as little as you like here. The eyes look great if they are painted as if they glow, studs and rivets can be picked out to give a harder edged look, and you can even add chips, scratches, and battle damage to show a history of hard-fought combats. If you want to pick out the rivets, it is best to paint them black first and then add just a small dot of silver to the top to lend more contrast. In fact, that's a pretty good rule of thumb: when you pick out fine details, it is best to paint them black first. Then paint the color you want and leave black around the edge for shading and separation. For the eyes, paint them black and then red over the top. It is the same principle as leaving some black undercoat to create shading.

Painting the Factions
Cygnar

Painting Cygnaran warjacks is fairly straightforward. Cygnar Blue Base covers over the black undercoat in one application, so you can achieve a flat body color quickly. The first highlight is a mix of Cygnar Blue Base and Cygnar Blue Highlight. Add a little more Cygnar Blue Highlight into the mix to achieve the remaining highlight tones, and then apply them to a progressively smaller area until the final highlight is applied as a faint line right on the edge of the plate.

Give the gold areas a coat of Rhulic Gold with a little brown ink added to it. If you add ink to your metallics you can get some beautifully rich colors, but you may have to apply two coats since they will not cover as well. Alternatively you can add a spot of a deep brown, like Battlefield Brown, to deepen the gold nicely and give it a slightly more matte base over which to work. Once the base coat is dry, you can highlight with lighter tones just as you would with any other part of the miniature.

Painting and Modeling Guide

Cygnaran troops and characters dress in similar military schemes. Apart from the dominant Cygnar blue, other common clothing colors are Ironhull Grey and Rucksack Tan. Natural colors are also fairly predominant like leather tones for bags, packs, and straps. A great combination for deep leather is Battlefield Brown highlighted with Bootstrap Brown

Protectorate of Menoth

The key to painting the Menite miniatures is to lay down a good flat base color on the off-white areas. Menoth White Base covers really well, but if you are working over a black primer, it may take a couple of coats to be flat with no hint of patchiness. Once you have a flat base color, the highlights go on easily. Just follow the raised areas and edges of the armor plates.

The next step is to add the deep wine color that contrasts with the white armor. If you were neat with your body color, all of the areas that are going to be red should still be black from the undercoat. If your brush strays a little (as is inevitable) you should take the time to go back and re-paint in black to create definition between the white and red areas.

Sanguine Base goes on really well over black. In fact the black undercoat gives Sanguine Base a little more solidity than painting it over white. One coat will be fine for smooth coverage. For the highlight mix, start adding Sanguine Highlight to Sanguine Base. The more highlight you add the lighter the color will get and the smaller area you should apply it to. This color can start to get a little pink, but as long as you keep the highlights small, the overall effect will be deep red.

Troops and characters are generally painted in the same colors as the warjacks. This makes the Protectorate one of the most consistent color schemes of all the factions. There are some great opportunities really to go to town on the warcasters and some of the troops. The large flat areas on the robes and cloaks beg for some extra decoration, and it is that sort of richness that fits the ceremonial feel of the miniatures perfectly.

Khador

The main challenge with Khador miniatures is getting that bright, flat red that is characteristic of the faction. Khador Red Base covers well, but you might need a couple of coats to get a really flat base over which to work. It is worth persisting though because a flat, neat color makes

the rest of the painting easier. With a flat color you can keep the highlights simple and still end up with a great looking miniature. Just concentrate on keeping the paint application as neat as possible, thick enough to cover well, but sufficiently thin to flow smoothly.

Keep the highlights simple. Use Khador Red Base mixed with Khador Red Highlight to build the highlights up gradually and keep the lighter colors in small areas. If the overall effect looks too pastel, glaze it over with red and yellow ink to revive some richness and depth. Keep the highlights towards the raised areas and edges of the armor, and leave the main, flat areas in the basic body color. Doing so preserves the brightness of the red.

Khadoran troops and characters follow the same color scheme, but they are generally a little more subdued than the warjacks. Paint clothing and uniforms in military tones like Greatcoat Grey. It is a mid blue grey excellent for all manner of troops, particularly Winter Guard. Battlefield Brown is a useful all-around color for boots, gloves, packs, and straps, and it makes a great leather tone when highlighted with Bootstrap Brown. Of course there are plenty of bright red areas on the warrior models and some, like the Iron Fangs, are almost entirely painted in Khador Red Base.

Cryx

The main color on the studio Cryx miniatures is Cryx Bane, and like the other main faction colors, it comes in Base and Highlight versions. You can darken this color further by adding Thamar Black to give a suitably somber tone. Some of the most distinctive features of Cryx miniatures are the glowing green parts, and the effect is easy to achieve. Just apply a base coat of Necrotite Green, and highlight it by adding Morrow White. If you are particularly adventurous, you can try the glowing effect shown on some of the miniatures in this book.

You do not want to paint the whole miniature in the same dark color. Vary the shade on the edging and some of the different shaped plates. This creates some really interesting effects. Use pale Blighted Gold for some of the decoration and edging.

The warriors use very much the same color palette as the 'jacks. Dark iron (try mixing Pig Iron with Thamar Black) and Blighted Gold metallics with black or dirty brown clothing looks very effective when coupled with the pale Thrall Flesh and 'Jack Bone. Thrall Flesh gives a great undead pallor that can be shaded with Cryx Bane Base and highlighted with 'Jack Bone.

Painting and Modeling Guide
Basing Your Miniatures

When you finish painting your miniatures and the paint is thoroughly dry, the last stage is finishing off the base. While this process is pretty straightforward and quick, it is worth putting a little thought into it. The way you base a particular miniature can make the difference between something that looks adequate and an effect that embodies the miniature's background and character. Good basing can substantially add to the depth of the model. Think about it. It is not really appropriate to have your mighty Cryxian force treading on fresh green grass. The ground should be scorched from the curse of the Dragonfather's blight! Similarly the bases of your Khadoran Juggernauts should suggest the wastes of the rime-swept Motherland.

Once you master this basic technique, you can alter the way you apply it for all sorts of different effects. Try painting glue over the surface in patches and sprinkling some baking soda over it to achieve a realistic snow effect. Washing over the finished base with black and dark browns and then dry brushing with grays evokes a tortured landscape for Cryxian miniatures. More static grass lends a lush finish while less will make the base look rocky and parched. Leaving the grass off completely and painting the base in red-brown tones achieves an even more desert-like finish. Do not be afraid to experiment. There are a couple examples of custom bases that have been added to characters and important army pieces. It is a great way to help them stand out from the rank and file.

BASING YOUR MINIATURE STEP-BY-STEP

Stage 1

Place a strip of tape over the slot in the base and paint white glue onto the base being careful not to get it on the model's feet.

Stage 2

Dip the base in a shallow container of mixed sand until you obtain an even coverage.

Stage 3

Leave the sand to dry thoroughly and then give it a coat of Battlefield Brown.

Stage 4

Drybrush the sand with Rucksack Tan and then 'Jack Bone to bring out the texture.

Stage 5

Paint white glue in patches and press static grass firmly into place.

Stage 6

Drybrush the static grass with 'Jack Bone when dry and then paint the sides of the base with Thamar Black to neaten the finish.

With a little bit of effort, your games of WARMACHINE can come alive in vibrant color.
In addition, it's no secret that painted models perform better in the game!

WESTERN IMMOREN

Winter 602 AR, Battle of Grizorski Tower. Cryxian raiders assault fortifications on the road to Korsk, but Khadoran forces massing at the Tower repel the attackers.

Summer 603 AR, Pendersford Incident. Outraged at Cygnaran military crackdowns, Protectorate forces invade Pendersford in southern Cygnar. The attackers broke the Cygnar garrison and trapped them in their fortifications for two weeks before melting into the countryside when relief columns arrived from Eastwall.

Glossary

Ability (pg. 26): An ability typically gives a benefit or capability that modifies how the standard rules apply to a model. Abilities are always in effect and apply every time a game situation warrants their use.

Action (pg. 36): After moving, a model can perform one action: either a combat action or a special action. Some types of movement or special rules require a model to forfeit its action or restrict the type of action it can perform.

Activation Phase (pg. 31): The third phase of a player's turn. The Activation Phase is the major portion of the turn. A player must activate each model and unit he controls once during this phase except for models that activated in an earlier phase for some reason, such as fleeing.

Additional Attack (pg. 37): An attack made by a model after it has made the initial attacks granted by the option it has chosen for its combat action.

Advance (pg. 34): A model moves up to its Speed (SPD) in inches when advancing. An advancing model can perform an action after completing its movement.

Aiming (pg. 45): A model that voluntarily forfeits its movement by not changing its position or facing gains a +2 bonus to every ranged attack roll it makes that turn. If a model moves that turn, it loses the bonus for aiming. A magic attack does not get the aiming bonus.

Animus (pl. Animi) (pg. 54): A spell-like ability used by warbeasts in HORDES.

Arc Node (pg. 68): A passive relay carried by a channeler that effectively extends a warcaster's spell range.

Area of Effect (AOE) (pg. 25): The diameter in inches of the area-of-effect template used for certain weapons, spells, or abilities. All models with any part of their bases covered by the template potentially suffer the attack's effects.

Arm Lock (pg. 40): A type of power attack. A successful arm lock prevents the opposing warjack from moving and using weapons or making power attacks associated with the locked arm.

Arm System: Any warjack system with an arm location.

Armor (ARM) (pg. 25): ARM represents a model's ability to resist being damaged. A model takes one damage point for every point that a damage roll exceeds its ARM stat.

Army Points (pg. 27): Each encounter level gives the maximum number of army points each player can spend when designing an army. An army cannot exceed the maximum number of army points allowed by the selected level.

Attachment (pg. 58): A group of one or more models that may be added to a unit, such as a unit attachment or special weapon attachment. A unit may have several different attachments but may only have one of each kind of attachment. An attachment may increase the victory point value of the unit by an amount detailed in the description of the attachment.

Automatic Effect (pg. 56): Apply an automatic effect every time it meets the conditions required to function.

Autonomous Warjack (pg. 58): When a 'jack marshal is destroyed or removed from play, the warjacks under his control become autonomous. An autonomous warjack may not have focus allocated to it and may not be marshaled. A warcaster or 'jack marshal may forfeit his action to bring an autonomous friendly faction warjack in base-to-base contact under his control.

Back Arc (pg. 26): The rear 180° of a model's base, opposite its front arc. A model is in another's back arc if its base is entirely within the other model's back arc.

Back Strike (pg. 51): An attack against a target model's back arc from a model that began its activation in the target model's back arc. To receive the back strike bonus, the attacking model must spend its entire activation up to the moment of its attack in the target's rear arc. For a channeled offensive spell, the attack is a back strike if the channeler is in the target's back arc. A back strike grants a +2 bonus to the attack roll.

Base Size (pg. 26): The physical size and mass of a model are reflected by its base size. There are three base sizes: small (30mm), medium (40mm), and large (50mm).

Bash (pg. 39): A less than optimum warjack melee attack option. A warjack with no functional melee weapons may make a single bash attack, which suffers a −2 penalty to the attack roll and causes a damage roll of 2d6+STR.

Battlegroup (pg. 27): A warcaster and his assigned warjacks are collectively referred to as a battlegroup. A warcaster can allocate focus points to or channel spells through only the warjacks in his battlegroup.

Blast Damage (pg. 48): Every model with any part of its base covered by an AOE template, other than a model directly hit by the AOE, is automatically hit by the attack and suffers a blast damage roll of 2d6+1/2POW.

Bonejack: A type of light warjack used by Cryx.

Boosting (pg. 66): During its activation, a warcaster or warjack may spend a focus point to add one additional die to any attack roll or damage roll. The model must declare it is boosting the roll before rolling any dice.

Breach (pg. 80): An entryway created by sufficiently damaging a structure.

Cavalry Charge (pg. 59): A charge performed by a cavalry model differs in several ways from a standard charge. When drawing line of sight for a charge, ignore intervening models with the same base size as the target or smaller. During the charge movement, the cavalry model may be able to make impact attacks against models it contacts. If it eliminates those models, it continues its charge movement. A cavalry model gains +2 to charge attack rolls.

Cavalry Formation (pg. 59): Cavalry troopers up to 5" apart are in cavalry formation. Use cavalry formation groups rather than skirmish formation groups to determine when a cavalry trooper is in formation.

Channeler (pg. 68): A warjack equipped with an arc node.

Character (pg. 28): A model that represents a unique individual from the Iron Kingdoms. An army may include only one model of each named character. A character follows the rules for its basic model type.

Character Unit (pg. 28): A unique unit or one that includes a named character. An army may include only one of each character unit. A character unit remains a character unit even if the named character in it has been eliminated from play.

Charge (pg. 34): A type of movement that combines with a model's combat action to make a charge attack.

Charge Attack (pg. 34): If a charging model moved at least 3", its first attack is a charge attack. A charge attack roll is made normally and may be boosted. If the charge attack hits, add an additional die to the damage roll. This damage roll cannot be boosted.

Cloud Effect (pg. 57): A cloud effect produces an area of dense smoke, magical darkness, gas, etc. that remains in play at its point of impact. Consider every model with any part of its base covered by the cloud's template to be inside the cloud and susceptible to its effects. A model inside a cloud effect gains +2 DEF against ranged and magic attacks, which is cumulative with concealment or cover.

Collateral Damage (pg. 42): If a slammed or thrown model collides with another model that has an equal or smaller-sized base, that model is knocked down and suffers a collateral damage roll of 2d6 plus the current STR of the attacker. Collateral damage cannot be boosted. Collateral damage is simultaneous with the throw or slam damage. A model that has a larger-sized base than the slammed model does not suffer collateral damage.

Combat Action (pg. 36): A model can perform a combat action after advancing, charging, or forfeiting its movement. A combat action lets a model make attacks. A model performing a combat action can choose one of the following attack options:

- A model can make one melee attack with each of its melee weapons in melee range. These attacks are called initial attacks. A model making more than one attack may divide them among any eligible targets.

- A model not in melee that did not charge can make one ranged attack with each of its ranged weapons. These attacks are called initial attacks. A model making more than one attack may divide them among any eligible targets. Each ranged weapon only makes one initial attack regardless of its ROF.

- A model can make one special attack (★Attack) allowed by its special rules instead of making initial attacks.

- A warjack that did not charge can spend a focus point to make one power attack instead of making initial attacks. A power attack is considered a melee attack.

Command (CMD) (pg. 25): CMD represents a model's willpower, leadership, and self-discipline. Command also determines the command range of a model with the Commander ability and the marshaling range of a 'jack marshal.

Command Check (pg. 74): When a situation requires a model or unit to make a command check, roll 2d6. If the result is equal to or less than its Command (CMD) stat, it passes the check. If the roll is greater than its CMD, the check fails and the model or unit suffers the consequences.

Command Range (pg. 75): A model with the Commander ability has a command range equal to his CMD stat in inches.

Commander (pg. 75): A model or unit in command range of a faction model with the Commander ability may use that model's CMD instead of its own when making a command

Glossary

check but is not required to do so. A faction model with the Commander ability can rally any model or unit and give orders to any unit in its command range. However, a mercenary model with the Commander ability may only rally and give orders to mercenaries. Furthermore, only friendly mercenaries may substitute the CMD of a mercenary model with the Commander ability for their own.

Completely Within (pg. 22): A model is completely within a given distance when its entire base is within the distance.

Concealment (pg. 46): Some terrain features and special effects grant a model concealment by making it more difficult to be seen though they are not dense enough to block an attack. A model within one inch of a concealing terrain feature that obscures any portion of its base from an attacker or with any part of its base in a forest gains +2 DEF against ranged and magic attacks. Concealment provides no benefit against spray attacks.

Continuous Effect (pg. 57): Continuous effects remain on a model and have the potential to damage or affect it on subsequent turns. Resolve continuous effects on models you control during the Maintenance Phase of your turn. Roll a d6. If the result is a 1 or 2, remove the effect immediately without further effect. On a 3 through 6, it remains in play and the model immediately suffers its effects.

Control Area (pg. 65): A model's control area extends out in all directions for a distance of twice its Focus (FOC) stat in inches measured from the edge of its base. A warjack must be within its warcaster's control area to receive focus points or channel spells, but it does not have to be in line of sight. A warcaster is always in his own control area. Some spells and feats use a model's control area as their area of effect.

Control Phase (pg. 31): The second phase of a player's turn. During your Control Phase, each of your warcasters receives a number of focus points equal to his FOC stat. Each warcaster may allocate focus points to eligible warjacks within his control area and may spend focus points on his spells that require upkeep.

Corpse Token (pg. 52): Some models can claim a destroyed model's corpse, represented by a corpse token. If more than one model is eligible to claim a corpse token, the closest one to the destroyed model receives it. Models removed from play but not also destroyed do not generate corpse tokens. Refer to a model's special rules for how it utilizes corpse tokens.

Cover (pg. 46): Some terrain features and special effects grant a model cover by being physically solid enough to block an attack against it. A model within 1" of a covering terrain feature that obscures any portion of its base from an attacker gains +4 DEF against ranged and magic attacks. Cover provides no benefit against spray attacks.

Critical Effect (pg. 57): Apply a critical effect on a critical hit. A weapon with a critical effect has the label "Critical" to distinguish it from an automatic damage effect.

Critical Hit (pg. 57): A critical hit occurs if any two dice in an attack roll show the same number and the attack successfully hits.

Damage Boxes (pg. 26): Damage boxes appear on a model's stat card and track damage to the model. Mark one damage box for each damage point a model suffers. A model is destroyed once all its damage boxes are marked. A warjack's damage boxes are arranged in a damage grid.

Damage Capacity (pg. 26): A model's damage capacity determines how many damage points it can take before being destroyed.

Damage Grid (pg. 26): A warjack has a damage grid consisting of multiple rows and columns of damage boxes. Damage grids may be slightly different in shape and number of damage boxes, but they all function the same way.

Damage Roll (pg. 54): Determine how much damage a successful attack causes by making a damage roll. Roll 2d6 and add the attack's Power (POW). Melee attacks also add the attacker's Strength (STR). Compare this total to the target's Armor (ARM.) The target takes one damage point for every point that the damage roll exceeds its ARM.

Deep Water (pg. 78): Deep water is terrain that cannot be entered voluntarily. A warjack that enters deep water is instantly disabled and replaced with a wreck marker and cannot be repaired or restarted for the remainder of the game. A model in deep water has a base DEF of 7 against all attacks. A warrior ending his activation in deep water automatically takes one damage point. A model in deep water can advance at half its normal movement rate but cannot run or charge. It cannot perform actions, cast spells, use feats, or give orders until it is completely out of the deep water. A model in deep water cannot engage other models or make attacks. A warcaster in deep water can allocate focus points and use them to maintain upkeep spells.

Defense (DEF) (pg. 24): DEF represents a model's ability to avoid being hit by an attack. An attack roll must be equal to or greater than the target model's DEF value to score a hit against it.

Deployment Zone (pg. 29): The portion of the battlefield where a player initially deploys his army. Generally speaking, a player's deployment zone is the area completely within 10" of his table edge.

Destroyed (pg. 56): A model is destroyed when all of its damage boxes are marked. A model without damage boxes is destroyed when it takes one damage point. Remove the destroyed model from the table.

Deviation (pg. 49): When an AOE attack misses its target, determine its actual point of impact by rolling deviation. Referencing the Deviation Diagram, roll a d6 to determine the direction the attack deviates.

Direct Hit (pp. 39, 45, 48): A successful attack roll indicates a direct hit on the intended target. For an area-of-effect attack, center the weapon's AOE template directly over the model hit. A target hit directly by an AOE weapon suffers a direct hit damage roll of 2d6+POW.

Disabled (pg. 55): A system becomes disabled and can no longer be used when all its system boxes are marked. Mark the appropriate system status box to show this. A warjack becomes disabled when three of its systems are disabled.

Disabled Arc Node (pg. 55): A warcaster cannot channel spells through a warjack with a disabled arc node.

Disabled Cortex (pg. 55): A warjack with a disabled cortex loses any unused focus points and cannot be allocated focus points. It cannot use focus points for any reason.

Disabled Hull (pg. 55): Disabling a warjack's hull has no direct effect. However, a disabled hull counts toward the disabled systems limit required to disable a warjack.

Disabled Movement (pg. 55): A warjack with disabled movement has its base Speed (SPD) changed to 1 and its base Defense (DEF) changed to 7. Disabled movement prevents a warjack from charging or making slam power attacks.

Disabled Warjack (pg. 55): A warjack becomes disabled when three of its systems are disabled. Replace a disabled warjack model with a disabled wreck marker corresponding to its base size. A disabled warjack is still a warjack, and hence, a model. It may be attacked, and continuous effects, spells, and animi on it remain in play, so it may continue to suffer damage. A disabled warjack may return to operation if enough of its damage boxes are repaired.

Disabled Weapon System (pg. 55): A disabled weapon system may no longer be used to make attacks. The warjack may no longer use special rules that require the use of this system. If the disabled system contains a shield or buckler, the warjack loses its use, and the warjack's Armor (ARM) reverts to the value listed in its stat bar.

Disabled Wreck Marker (pg. 55): Replace a disabled warjack model with a disabled warjack wreck marker corresponding to its base size. A disabled warjack wreck marker counts as rough terrain for movement and provides cover to models within 1" whose bases are partially obscured from the attacker by the wreck. Models at least partially within the area of the wreck also gain cover.

Disengage (pg. 38): A model disengages from melee by moving out of its opponent's melee range. A model disengaging from melee is usually subject to a free strike by its opponent.

Double-Hand Throw (pg. 43): A type of power attack. A successful double-hand throw attack allows the attacker to throw the defender directly at another model.

Dragoon (pg. 60): A type of cavalry model that begins the game mounted but may become dismounted during play. For some dragoons the ability to be dismounted is optional.

Elevated Attacker (pg. 33): When drawing line of sight from a model on a higher elevation than its target, ignore all intervening models on lower elevation than the attacking model except those that would normally screen the target. Additionally, you can draw a line of sight through screening models that have equal or smaller-sized bases than the attacking model, but the target still gets +2 DEF for being screened.

Elevated Target (pg. 33): When drawing line of sight from a model on a lower elevation than its target, ignore all intervening models on a lower elevation than the target. A model on higher elevation than its attacker gains +2 DEF against ranged and magic attacks from that opponent. Models on lower elevations than the target do not provide screening.

Engaged (pg. 38): If a model is within an enemy model's melee range, it is engaged in combat and primarily concerned with fighting its nearest threat. An engaged model is in melee and cannot make ranged attacks or channel spells. An engaged model can move freely as long as it stays inside its opponent's melee range.

Glossary

Engaging (pg. 38): A model automatically engages every enemy model in its melee range. Engaging models are in melee and cannot make ranged attacks.

Entryway (pg. 79): An opening in a terrain feature, such as a door, window, or breach, that allows a model to enter or pass through the terrain feature. A small or medium-based warrior model can pass through any entryway, but a non-warrior or large-based model can only pass through doors and breaches that are large enough to accommodate its base.

Epic Warcaster (pg. 70): An epic warcaster is a version of a warcaster character that has evolved in the story arc. An army may include one epic warcaster for each full 750-point increment in the point limit for the game.

Facing (pg. 26): A model's facing is the direction indicated by its head's orientation.

Falling (pg. 52): A model slammed, thrown, pushed, or that otherwise moves off of an elevated surface greater than 1" high is knocked down and suffers a damage roll. A fall of up to 3" causes a POW 10 damage roll. Add an additional die to the damage roll for every additional increment of three inches the model falls, rounded up.

Feat (pg. 64): Each warcaster has a unique feat that can turn the tide of battle if used at the right time. A warcaster may use his feat before or after moving, but not in the middle of his movement. Likewise, he may use his feat before and after each attack, but he cannot interrupt an unresolved attack, nor can he use his feat between the movement and attack portions of a charge. Feats may be used prior to initiating an attack or after completely resolving an attack, including determining hits, damage, and special effects. A warcaster cannot use his feat if he runs. A warcaster's feat can only be used once per game.

Field Allowance (pg. 28): The maximum number of models or units of a given type that may be included for each warcaster in an army.

First Player (pg. 29): The player who deploys his army first and takes the turn first every game round.

Fleeing (pg. 75): A model or unit that flees immediately turns to face directly away from the threat that caused it to flee. A fleeing model activates during its controller's Maintenance Phase. A fleeing model automatically runs away from its nearest threat toward its deployment edge using the most direct route that does not take it through a damaging effect or allow enemies to engage it. A fleeing model cannot perform any actions.

Focus (FOC) (pg. 25): FOC represents a model's arcane power. Focus determines a model's control area and focus points. Only models with the Focus Manipulation ability have a FOC stat.

Focus Cost (pg. 69): The number of focus points a model must spend to cast a spell.

Focus Points (pg. 65): The magical energy manipulated by a warcaster. Each of your warcasters receives a number of focus points equal to his Focus (FOC) stat during your Control Phase. A warcaster may allocate focus points to eligible warjacks in his control area and spend focus points on his spells that require upkeep, or he can keep them to enhance his own abilities and cast spells.

Forest (pg. 78): A terrain feature that hinders movement and makes a model inside it difficult to see. A forest is considered rough terrain but also provides concealment to a model with any part of its base inside its perimeter.

Formation (pg. 35): The arrangement of troopers within a unit. There are three formations available to all troopers: skirmish, open, and tight. Cavalry models may also be in cavalry formation. These formations are not mutually exclusive. For example, a trooper in open formation is also in skirmish formation. Some special rules require that models be in a specific formation to benefit from them.

Free Strike (pg. 38): When a model moves out of an enemy's melee range, the enemy model may immediately make a free strike. The model makes one melee attack with any melee weapon that has sufficient melee range to reach the moving model and gains a +2 bonus to its melee attack roll. If the attack succeeds, add an additional die to the damage roll. The attack and damage rolls of a free strike cannot be boosted.

Front Arc (pg. 26): The 180° arc centered on the direction a model's head faces. A model is in another's front arc if any part of its base is in the other model's front arc.

Game Round (pg. 31): A measurement of game time. Each game round, every player takes a turn in the order established during setup. Once the last player in the turn order completes his turn, the current game round ends. A new game round then begins starting again with the first player. Game rounds continue until one side wins the game. See also Round.

Hazard (pg. 78): A terrain feature that causes adverse effects to a model entering it.

Head-butt (pg. 41): A type of power attack. A successful head-butt causes a damage roll and knocks down its target.

Headlock (pg. 40): A type of power attack. A successful headlock prevents the opposing warjack from using weapons or making power attacks associated with its head.

Heavy Warjack (pg. 23): Generally, a warjack with a large (50 mm) base.

Helljack: A type of heavy warjack used by Cryx.

Hill (pg. 78): A terrain feature that represents a gentle rise or drop in elevation. A hill may be open or rough terrain depending on the ground's nature. Unlike obstacles, hills do not impose any additional movement penalties, nor do they provide cover or concealment. A model can charge up or down a hill in open terrain at no penalty.

Hull (pg. 55): A warjack's hull is represented by all the damage boxes in its damage grid that do not have a letter in them.

Impact Attack (pg. 59): An attack made with a charging cavalry model's mount against a model with which it comes into contact during movement. After resolving its impact attacks, a charging cavalry model may continue its charge movement.

Impassable Terrain (pg. 77): Natural terrain that completely prohibits movement. This includes cliff faces, lava, and deep water. A model cannot move across impassable terrain.

In Formation (pg. 35): The group of troopers in skirmish formation with the unit leader or the group of cavalry troopers in cavalry formation with the unit leader is in formation; other troopers are out of formation. Only troopers that are in formation receive orders. Troopers must begin the game in formation and remain in formation after the unit's movement.

In Melee (pg. 38): A model is in melee if it is engaging an enemy model or if an enemy model engages it. A model in melee cannot make ranged attacks.

Independent Models (pg. 23): An independent model is one that activates individually. Warcasters, warjacks, and solos are independent models.

Initial Attack (pg. 37): An attack granted by a model's chosen option for its combat action, to be distinguished from an additional attack. It is generally the first attack made with each weapon during that combat action.

Inert Warjack (pg. 56): When a warcaster is destroyed or removed from play, the warjacks in his battlegroup become inert and cease to function. An inert warjack has no facing, loses all special abilities, and does not gain an ARM bonus for functioning shields or bucklers. An inert warjack may be reactivated by a friendly warcaster or 'jack marshal of the same faction.

Intervening Model (pg. 33): If any line between the center of an attacking model's base at head height and any part of the target passes over another model's base, that model is an intervening model. A line of sight cannot be drawn across an intervening model's base to models that have equal or smaller-sized bases.

Intervening Terrain (pg. 39): A model with any portion of its base obscured from its attacker by an obstacle or an obstruction gains a +2 DEF bonus against melee attacks.

'Jack Marshal (pg. 58): A soldier trained to command a warjack without the benefit of magical skills. A 'jack marshal may control a number of warjacks listed in parentheses beside the 'Jack Marshal special ability in his description.

Knocked Down (pg. 52): Mark a knocked down model with a token. A knocked down model is stationary until it stands up. It does not count as an intervening model, has no facing, and has no back arc. Its front arc extends 360°. A knocked down model cannot be slammed or locked, but it can be pushed. To stand up, a model must forfeit either its movement or its action for that activation.

Large Base (pg. 26): A 50mm base.

Leader (pg. 23): Usually one trooper in a unit is trained as a leader and is generally represented by a model with a different stat profile and possibly different weaponry. A leader can rally and issue orders to his troopers in formation. While its leader is in play, a unit uses his CMD stat for all command checks.

Light Warjack (pg. 23): Generally, a warjack with a medium (40 mm) base.

Linear Obstacle (pg. 78): An obstacle up to one inch tall but less than one inch thick. Linear obstacles can be crossed, but models may not stop on top of them.

Line of sight (LOS) (pg. 32): A model has line of sight to a target if you can draw a straight, unobstructed line from the center of its base at head height through its front arc to any part of the target model, including its base.

Living Model (pg. 23): A non-warjack model is a living model unless stated otherwise. A living model has a soul and will generate a soul token when destroyed.

Glossary

Magic Attack (pg. 67): A magic attack follows all the rules for ranged attacks including targeting, concealment, cover, and all other applicable rules. A warcaster can cast spells, including ranged spells, at models with which he is in melee.

Magic Attack Roll (pg. 67): Determine a magic attack's success by making a magic attack roll. Roll 2d6 and add the attacking model's FOC. An attack hits directly if the attack roll equals or exceeds the target's Defense (DEF).

Maintenance Phase (pg. 31): The first phase of a player's turn. During the Maintenance Phase, remove markers and effects that expire this turn, remove all focus points from your models, and resolve any compulsory effects on your models. Activate fleeing models and units under your control at the end of this phase.

Marshaling Range (pg. 58): A 'jack marshal has a marshaling range equal to his CMD stat in inches.

Massive Casualties (pg. 74): A unit suffers massive casualties when it loses 50% or more of the models in it at the beginning of the current turn. The unit must immediately pass a command check or flee. A unit will only make up to one command check a turn due to massive casualties.

Medium Base (pg. 26): A 40mm base.

Melee Attack (pg. 38): An attack with a melee weapon. A melee attack can be made against any target in melee range of the weapon being used, but it may not be made across another model's base regardless of base size.

Melee Attack (MAT) (pg. 24): MAT represents a model's skill with melee weapons such as swords and hammers or natural weapons like fists and teeth. Add a model's MAT value to its melee attack rolls.

Melee Attack Roll (pg. 39): Determine a melee attack's success by making a melee attack roll. Roll 2d6 and add the attacking model's Melee Attack (MAT). An attack hits directly if the attack roll equals or exceeds the target's Defense (DEF).

Melee Range (pg. 38): A model can make melee attacks against any target in melee range. A weapon's melee range extends 1/2" beyond the model's front arc. A reach weapon has a melee range of 2". A model's melee range is the longest melee range of its usable melee weapons. A non-warjack model with no usable melee weapons has no melee range. Warjacks always have a 1/2" melee range.

Melee Weapons (pg. 38): Melee weapons include such implements as spears, swords, hammers, flails, saws, and axes. A warjack can also use its body as a melee weapon for attacks such as bashes, head-butts, and slams. A melee weapon's damage roll is 2d6+POW+STR.

Mercenary (pg. 60): A model that does not belong to any faction. Mercenaries may be included in the army of any faction for which they will work or in an army consisting entirely of mercenaries using a mercenary contract. A mercenary warjack may only be controlled by a mercenary warcaster or 'jack marshal. Similarly, a mercenary warcaster or 'jack marshal can only control mercenary warjacks. A mercenary model with the Commander ability may only rally or give orders to other mercenaries. Similarly, only mercenaries may use the CMD of a mercenary model with the Commander ability.

Mercenary Contract (pg. 61): A set of rules that allow you to build an all-mercenary army. There are several such contracts from which to choose. A contract may contain special rules beyond those for army construction.

Model (pg. 23): The highly detailed and dramatically posed miniature figurine representing a WARMACHINE combatant.

Model Statistic (Stat) (pg. 24): One of the numeric representations of a model's basic combat qualities. The higher the value, the better the stat.

Model Type (pg. 23): One of the categories of models that defines its game function. There are several basic model types: warcaster, warjack, trooper, and solo.

Mount (pg. 59): A cavalry model's mount is a special type of melee weapon. A mount is indicated by a horseshoe icon in its stat bar.

Movement (pg. 33): The first part of a model's activation, also called its normal movement. A model must use or forfeit its movement before performing an action. There are three types of movement: advancing, charging, and running.

Obstacle (pg. 77): Any terrain feature up to one inch tall. Obstacles can be climbed.

Obstruction (pg. 78): A terrain feature greater than one inch tall. Treat obstructions as impassable terrain.

Offensive Spell (pg. 67): An offensive spell requires a successful magic attack roll to take effect. If the attack roll fails, the attack misses. A failed attack roll for a spell with an area of effect deviates according to deviation rules.

Officer (pg. 58): Some unit attachments include an officer. While the officer is on the table, he is the unit's leader, and the normal unit leader loses his Leader ability.

Open Fists (pg. 39): In addition to functioning as melee weapons, open fists can be used to perform certain power attacks.

Open Formation (pg. 35): Troopers up to one inch apart are in open formation. Troopers in open formation are close enough to coordinate attacks and provide each other mutual support.

Open Terrain (pg. 77): Smooth, even ground. Examples include grassy plains, barren fields, dirt roads, and paved surfaces. A model moves across open terrain without penalty.

Orders (pg. 26): An order lets a model or unit perform a specialized combat maneuver during its activation. A unit may be given an order from a model with the Commander ability prior to its activation or from its leader at the beginning of its activation. (See also Issuing Orders, pg. 76)

Origin of Damage (pg. 53): Some effects and abilities are dependent on the origin of damage. Damage that is the direct result of an attack originates from the origin of the attack. This is also the origin of the damage for a spray attack or a Strafe attack. If the damage is being done directly by some effect without an attack, the origin of the damage is the effect's origin. The origin of damage for a direct hit by an AOE attack is the attack's origin, but the origin of damage for any other damage caused by the AOE attack is the AOE's point of impact. Finally, some non-AOE attacks have special rules that can damage other models besides the target. The origin of damage is the model or point from which you measure the range to other affected models.

Out of Formation (pg. 35): A trooper is out of formation if it is further than 3" (5" for a cavalry trooper) from the nearest member of its unit that is in formation. An out of formation trooper must attempt to get back into formation. Out-of-formation troopers cannot receive orders.

Overboost Power Field (pg. 66): Each of a warcaster's unspent focus points gives him +1 Armor (ARM) against all attacks. This bonus stays in effect until the focus points are no longer on the warcaster.

Point Cost (pg. 28): A model's point cost indicates how many army points you must spend to include one of these models (or in the case of units, one basic unit) in your army. Some entries also include options to spend additional points for upgrades typically in the form of adding more troopers to a unit.

Point of Impact (pg. 48): The point over which an area-of effect attack's template is centered. If the target model suffers a direct hit, center the template over that model. If an area-of-effect attack misses, its point of impact deviates.

Power (POW) (pg. 25): POW represents the base amount of damage a weapon inflicts. Add a weapon's POW stat to its damage roll.

Power Attack (pg. 40): A type of special attack that may be made by warjacks. A warjack must spend a focus point to make a power attack. Unlike other special attacks, a warjack cannot make a power attack after charging. A warjack may make additional melee attacks after a power attack, but it must spend focus points to do so. Power attacks are melee attacks with a 1/2" melee range.

Power Field (pg. 65): Warcaster armor creates a magical field that surrounds and protects the warcaster from damage that would rend a normal man to pieces. The warcaster can use focus points to regenerate damage done to the power field. A warcaster's unspent focus points overboost his power field and give him increased protection.

Power plus Strength (P+S) (pg. 25): Melee weapons add both the weapon's POW and the model's STR to the damage roll. For quick reference, the P+S value provides the sum of these two stats.

Push (pg. 41): A type of power attack that forces the target back 1".

Rally (pg. 76): A fleeing model can make a command check at the end of its activation in the Maintenance Phase if it is in formation with its unit leader or if it is within the command range of a friendly faction model with the Commander ability. If it passes the command check, the model or unit rallies and turns to face its nearest enemies. This ends its activation, but it may function normally next turn.

Range (RNG) (pg. 25): RNG represents the maximum distance in inches a model can make ranged attacks with a specific weapon or spell. Measure range from the nearest edge of the attacking model's base to the nearest edge of the target model's base.

Ranged Attack (pg. 44): An attack with a ranged weapon. A ranged attack can be declared against any target in line of sight subject to the targeting rules. A model in melee cannot make ranged attacks.

Glossary

Ranged Attack (RAT) (pg. 24): RAT represents a model's accuracy with ranged weapons such as guns and crossbows or thrown items like spears and knives. Add a model's RAT value to its ranged attack rolls.

Ranged Attack Roll (pg. 45): Determine a ranged attack's success by making a ranged attack roll. Roll 2d6 and add the attacking model's Ranged Attack (RAT). An attack hits directly if the attack roll equals or exceeds the target's Defense (DEF).

Ranged Weapon (pg. 45): A ranged weapon is one that can make an attack at a distance beyond melee range. Examples include bows, rifles, and crossbows. A ranged weapon's damage roll is 2d6+POW.

Rate of Fire (ROF) (pg. 45): The maximum number of ranged attacks a specific weapon can make in one activation. Reloading time limits most ranged weapons to only one attack per activation.

Reach Weapon (pg. 38): A model with a reach weapon has a melee range of 2" for attacks with that weapon. A model that possesses a reach weapon and another melee weapon can engage and attack an opponent up to 2" away with its reach weapon, but its other weapons can only be used to attack models within its normal 1/2" melee range.

Reactivate (pg. 56): A friendly faction warcaster or 'jack marshal in base-to-base contact with an inert warjack may reactivate it. To reactivate the warjack, the reactivating model must forfeit its action this turn but may still cast spells and use special abilities. The warjack must forfeit its activation and cannot channel spells on the turn it is reactivated, but it functions normally next turn.

Regenerate Power Field (pg. 66): A warcaster may spend focus points anytime during his activation to regenerate his power field. Each focus point spent in this manner removes one damage point from him.

Remove from Play (pg. 56): Occasionally models will be outright removed from play, sometimes instead of being destroyed, at other times in addition to being destroyed. A model removed from play cannot return to the table for any reason. When a model is both destroyed and removed from play, effects triggered by its destruction still occur.

Replenish (pg. 65): A model with the Focus Manipulation ability, such as a warcaster, replenishes its focus points during its controller's Control Phase and receives a number of focus points equal to its FOC stat.

Ride-By Attack (pg. 59): A type of attack made by a cavalry model that combines its movement and action. A cavalry model making a ride-by attack can interrupt its movement at any point to perform its combat action. A cavalry solo may always make a ride-by attack, but a cavalry trooper must receive an order to do so.

Rough Terrain (pg. 77): Terrain that can be traversed at a significantly slower pace than open terrain. Examples include thick brush, forests, rocky areas, murky bogs, shallow water, and deep snow. As long as any part of its base is in rough terrain, a model moves at 1/2 normal movement rate. Therefore, a model in rough terrain actually moves only 1/2" for every 1" of its movement used.

Round (pg. 31): A measure of duration for many game effects. A round is measured from the current player's turn to the beginning of the current player's next turn regardless of his location in the turn order. Also see Game Round.

Run (pg. 34): A running model may move up to twice its SPD in inches. A model that runs cannot perform an action, cast spells, or use its feat this activation. A running model's activation ends at the completion of its movement.

Scenario (pg. 29): A game with specific setup instructions and victory conditions.

Screening Model (pg. 33): A screening model is an intervening model that has an equal or larger-sized base than the target model and is within one inch of it. The target model is screened by a screening model and receives a +2 DEF bonus against ranged and magic attacks.

Shallow Water (pg. 79): Shallow water is rough terrain. A warjack knocked down while in shallow water is instantly disabled.

Simultaneous (pg. 54): Attacks that generate multiple attack or damage rolls normally do so simultaneously. Completely resolve all of the attack and damage rolls before applying any of the target's special rules that are triggered by suffering damage, being destroyed, or being removed from play.

Skill Check (pg. 37): A special action may require a skill check to determine its success. Roll 2d6. If the result is equal to or less than the skill value, the special action succeeds and its results are applied immediately. If the roll is greater than the model's skill value, the special action fails.

Skill Value (pg. 37): A model must roll less than or equal to this number on 2d6 in order to use its skill successfully.

Skirmish Formation (pg. 35): The default and most flexible formation which allows troopers to be up to 3" apart. The group of troopers in skirmish formation with the unit's leader is in formation.

Slam (pg. 41): A type of power attack that combines a model's movement and combat action to make a slam attack.

Slam Attack (pg. 41): A model that attempts a slam and ends its movement within 1/2" of its intended target makes a slam attack if it moved at least 3". A slam attack roll suffers a –2 penalty against a target with an equal or smaller-sized base or a –4 penalty against a target with a larger base. If the slam attack hits, the target gets propelled directly away from its attacker, is knocked down, and suffers damage.

Slam Damage (pg. 42): Determine slam damage after moving the slammed model. A slam's damage roll is 2d6 plus a POW equal to the attacker's current STR. Add an additional die to the damage roll if the slammed model contacts an obstacle, obstruction, or a model that has an equal or larger-sized base. Slam damage can be boosted. The slammed model is also knocked down.

Small Base (pg. 26): A 30mm base.

Solo (pg. 23): An independent warrior model that operates alone.

Soul Token (pg. 53): Certain models can claim a model's soul, represented by a soul token, when it is destroyed. Only living models provide soul tokens. A model only has one soul. If more than one model is eligible to claim a soul, the model nearest the destroyed model receives the token. Refer to a model's special rules for how it utilizes soul tokens. Models removed from play but not also destroyed do not generate soul tokens.

Special Action (★Action) (pg. 26): A special action lets a model perform an action normally unavailable to other models. A model can perform a special action instead of its combat action if it meets the specific requirements for its use.

Special Attack (★Attack) (pg. 26): A special attack gives a model an attack option normally unavailable to other models. Warjacks may also make a variety of punishing special attacks called power attacks. A model may make one special attack instead of making initial melee or ranged attacks during its combat action if it meets the specific requirements of the attack.

Special Effect (pg. 56): Many attacks cause special effects in addition to causing damage. There are four categories of effects: automatic effects, critical effects, continuous effects, and cloud effects.

Special Rules (pg. 25): Unique rules pertaining to a model or its weapons which take precedence over the standard rules. Depending on their use, special rules are categorized as abilities, feats, special actions, special attacks, or orders.

Speed (SPD) (pg. 24): A model's normal movement rate. A model moves its SPD stat in inches when advancing.

Spray Attack (pg. 50): An attack or spell that uses the spray template. Such weapons and spells have a range of "SP" in their profiles.

Starting Roll (pg. 29): The die roll made at the beginning of a game to establish setup and turn order.

Stat (pg. 24): Short for statistic. Used in reference to model or weapon statistics.

Stat Bar (pg. 24): The stat bar presents model and weapon statistics in an easy-to-reference format.

Stat Card (pg. 24): A model or unit's stat card provides a quick in-game reference for its profile and special rules.

Stationary (pg. 54): A stationary model is one that has been knocked down or immobilized. A stationary model cannot move, perform actions, make attacks, cast spells, use animi, use feats, or give orders. A stationary model does not have a melee range. A model is never in melee with a stationary model. A melee attack against a stationary model automatically hits it directly. A stationary target has a base Defense (DEF) of 5.

Strength (STR) (pg. 24): STR represents a model's physical strength. STR is used to calculate damage, grab onto or break free from a model, or determine how far a model is thrown.

Structure (pg. 79): Any terrain feature that can be damaged and destroyed.

System Boxes (pg. 26): Some of a warjack's damage boxes are also system boxes labeled with a letter denoting which component of the model they represent.

Terrain (pg. 77): The type of ground: open, rough, or impassable.

Terrain Feature (pg. 77): A natural or man-made object on the battlefield.

Glossary

Terrifying Entity (pg. 74): A terrifying entity is one with either the Terror or Abomination special ability. A model in melee range of an enemy model with Terror, a model/unit with an enemy model with Terror in its melee range, or a model/unit within 3" of an abomination—friendly or enemy—must pass a command check or flee. Make this command check after the active model or unit completes it movement but before it performs any actions.

Throw (pg. 42): A type of power attack that sends its target flying, causes damage, and knocks it down.

Throw Damage (pg. 42): Determine throw damage after moving the thrown model. A thrown model suffers a damage roll with a POW equal to the attacker's current STR. Add an additional die to the damage roll if the model contacts an obstruction or a model with an equal or larger-sized base. Throw damage may be boosted. The thrown model is also knocked down.

Tight Formation (pg. 35): Troopers that form up in ranks are in tight formation. A rank is a row of troopers in base-to-base contact, or as close as the actual models allow, all facing in the same direction perpendicular to the row of models. A tight formation may consist of any number of ranks, but each rank must be at least two troopers wide. Each rank after the front-most must be parallel to it and have at least one trooper in base-to-base contact with a trooper in the rank ahead of it, or as close as the actual models allow. Troopers in contact with the rank ahead must be lined up directly behind the trooper ahead of them.

Totaled Warjack (pg. 56): A warjack is destroyed or totaled when all of its damage boxes are marked. Remove a totaled warjack from the table and replace it with a totaled warjack wreck marker corresponding to its base size. Any effects, spells, and animi on a warjack instantly expire when it is totaled. A totaled warjack cannot be repaired.

Totaled Wreck Marker (pg. 56): Remove a totaled warjack from the table and replace it with a totaled warjack wreck marker corresponding to its base size. A totaled warjack wreck marker counts as rough terrain for movement and provides cover to models within 1" whose bases are partially obscured from the attacker by the wreck. Models at least partially within the area of the wreck also gain cover.

Turn Order (pg. 29): The order in which players take their turns each game round, starting with the first player.

Trooper (pg. 23): A warrior model that is part of a unit.

Unit (pg. 23): A unit is a group of similarly trained and equipped trooper models that operate together as a single force. A unit usually contains one leader and two or more additional troopers.

Upkeep Spell (pg. 67): A type of spell that remains in play for an indefinite length of time. An upkeep spell remains in play if the warcaster who cast it spends a focus point to maintain it during his controller's Control Phase.

Warcaster (pg. 23): A warcaster is a tremendously powerful sorcerer, warpriest, or battlemage with the ability to control a group of warjacks telepathically.

Warjack (pg. 23): A warjack is a steamjack—a mechanical construct given the ability to reason by a cortex housed within its hull—built expressly to wage war.

Warriors (pg. 23): Warcasters, troopers, and solos are collectively referred to as warriors.

Weapon Crew (pg. 61): A small unit that operates a large or cumbersome weapon. A weapon crew is made up of a gunner and one or more crewmen but does not have a leader.

Wound (pg. 26): An unmarked damage box.

Victory Points (pg. 30): Every model and unit is worth a set number of victory points. Victory points are generally used to determine the winner of a game.

WARMACHINE Errata & Clarifications

The following material includes errata to WARMACHINE models presented in other WARMACHINE books such as *Escalation*, *Apotheosis*, and *Superiority* and also includes clarifications meant to help resolve rules queries as they come up in games. The errata included herein represents the correct current language, so treat stat cards as if they contain this language as well. This section is organized first by book and then by page number.

Escalation

Commander Adept Sebastian Nemo (pg. 23)

Q: Does Nemo gain power tokens from a Greylord or a Skarlock Thrall casting a spell? What about Stormsmiths?

A: Both the Greylords and Skarlock Thralls cast spells, so Nemo will receive power tokens. Stormcall, however, will not grant a power token since it is not a spell.

Q: Does Nemo gain power tokens from spells channeled in his control area?

A: Only if the caster is also within Nemo's control area.

Q: Does Voltaic Snare affect a warjack that moves within 3" of the targeted model or only if it was within 3" at the time of casting?

A: Any time a warjack finds itself within 3" of the target, it is affected.

Q: Does a warjack benefit from a shield when it suffers damage from Electrical Storm?

A: Yes, unless Nemo is in the model's back arc. The point of origin of Electrical Storm is Nemo.

Q: When a model is forced to move directly toward another model by the effects of Voltaic Snare, does the affected model have to end its movement facing the model toward which it moved?

A: No.

Q: When Voltaic Snare affects a model under the effects of Scramble, does the affected model run toward the snared warjack?

A: Yes.

Stormclad (pg. 24)

Q: If a Stormblade is positioned within 3" of more than one Stormclad, will the closest non-Stormblade model within 4" suffer a POW 10 chain reaction damage roll from every Stormclad, or just one?

A: The extra damage roll does not come from the Stormclad. Rather, if a Stormblade is close enough to a friendly Stormclad, the Stormblade's ranged attack arcs to another target. Therefore, an attacking Stormblade only benefits from Chain Reaction once regardless of the number of Stormclads in the vicinity.

Gun Mage Captain Adept (pg. 26)

ERRATUM: LONG SHOT. REPLACE TEXT OF LONG SHOT WITH THE FOLLOWING:
The Magelock Pistol gains +6 RNG for this ranged attack.

Q: Does Snipe affect Long Shot?

A: Yes. The range bonuses from Long Shot and Snipe are cumulative. For example, a Gun Mage Captain Adept has a range of 24" when making a Long Shot while under the effects of a 6" Snipe spell.

Stormblade Officer & Standard Bearer (pg. 27)

ERRATUM: CONDUIT. REPLACE TEXT OF CONDUIT WITH THE FOLLOWING:
Stormblades in an open formation group with the Standard Bearer gain +1 RNG and +1 POW to their weapons.

ERRATUM: LIGHTNING STRIKE. REPLACE TEXT OF LIGHTNING STRIKE WITH THE FOLLOWING:
Once per game, the Standard Bearer may use Lightning Strike during his activation. As part of a charge, after moving but before performing his combat action, each Stormblade who received this order must, if possible, make a single ranged attack targeting the model charged. Stormblades are not considered to be in melee when resolving the Lightning Strike ranged attacks, nor are the targets of those attacks considered to be in melee with them. If the target is not in melee range after moving, the Lightning Strike's ranged attack must still be made before the Stormblade's activation ends. A Stormblade cannot target a model with which he was in melee at the start of his activation with the Lightning Strike's ranged attack.

ERRATUM: UNIT STANDARD. REPLACE FIRST SENTENCE OF UNIT STANDARD WITH THE FOLLOWING:
If the Standard Bearer is destroyed or removed from play, a Knight in this unit within 1" can take the Standard Bearer's place immediately and become the new Standard Bearer.

Q: Do all models in the Stormblade unit have to participate in the Controlled Fire order?

A: No. The order does not require Stormblades to combine their attacks.

Q: Does fielding one Stormblade unit attachment mean that any unit of Stormblades in open formation can benefit from the Conduit ability of the Standard Bearer?

A: No. A Stormblade must be in an open formation group with the Standard Bearer to benefit from Conduit, so other Stormblade units will not benefit.

Stormsmiths [pg. 28]

Q: Does a Stormcall targeting a model with Stealth or Invisibility automatically miss?

A: No. Stormcall is not an attack. It is a skill check and therefore can hit models with Stealth or Invisibility.

Q: What happens if the target of a Stormcall is out of range?

A: The Stormcall automatically fails.

Q: Does Stormcall affect Incorporeal models?

A: No. It is neither a magic attack nor a feat.

Q: Can a Stormsmith use Stormcall while in melee?

A: Yes.

Q: Does a model targeted by a Stormcall benefit from a shield?

A: Yes, unless the Stormsmith is in the model's back arc. The point of origin of Stormcall is the Stormsmith.

Q: If three Stormsmiths use the Triangulation ability, how many lightning strikes occur?

A: Each Stormsmith would generate three lightning strikes for a total of nine. Each one requires a separate skill check to hit.

Trencher Chain Gun Crew [pg. 30]

ERRATUM: ADD THE FOLLOWING ABILITY TO THE TRENCHER CHAIN GUN CREW:

Automatic Fire - The Gunner gains +2 on additional Strafe attack rolls.

ERRATUM: WEAPON CREW. REPLACE FIFTH SENTENCE OF WEAPON CREW WITH THE FOLLOWING:

If the gunner is destroyed or removed from play, a crewman in this unit within 1" can take the destroyed gunner's place immediately and become the new gunner. Remove the crewman from the table instead of the gunner.

Hunter [pg. 31]

ERRATUM: ALL TERRAIN. REPLACE TEXT OF ALL TERRAIN WITH THE FOLLOWING:

During its activation, the Hunter ignores movement penalties from, and may charge and slam across, rough terrain and obstacles.

ERRATUM: PRESSURIZED RESERVE TANK. REPLACE SECOND SENTENCE OF PRESSURIZED RESERVE TANK WITH THE FOLLOWING:

After completing its normal activation, the Hunter may move a number of inches equal to its current SPD. The Hunter ignores movement penalties from rough terrain and obstacles during this movement. The Hunter cannot be targeted by free strikes during this movement.

Q: Can a Hunter with disabled movement use its Pressurized Reserve Tank? If yes, how far can it move?

A: Yes. The Pressurized Reserve Tank allows the Hunter to move its current SPD, so it would move 1".

Q: Can a Hunter use its Pressurized Reserve Tank after running?

A: Yes.

Q: When my Hunter shoots a target with a medium-sized or larger base with the Long Arm, do I round ARM up or down?

A: Always round up in WARMACHINE.

Q: How is Armor Piercing resolved when damaging a model in Shield Wall?

A: First halve the ARM value of the model, rounding up, and then add its Shield Wall ARM bonus.

Q: How is Armor Piercing resolved when damaging a warjack with a shield?

A: Remember that a warjack's shield does not provide a bonus to its ARM. It provides an alternate ARM stat. Assuming the warjack was not hit by an attack from its back arc, halve the ARM value with the shield.

Q: How does the Hunter's Extended Control Range interact with Nemo's Overpower?

A: First double the control range and then add the extra range from Overpower.

Errata & Clarifications

Centurion [pg. 32]

ERRATUM: POLARITY FIELD. REPLACE TEXT OF POLARITY FIELD WITH THE FOLLOWING:

The Centurion cannot be targeted by charges and slam power attacks by a model that began the charge or slam in the Centurion's front arc.

Q: Does Electro-Lock require the expenditure of a focus point?

A: No.

Q: Does an Electro-Lock attack suffer a −2 to hit like a standard arm lock power attack?

A: No.

Q: Can a Devastator be targeted by an Electro-Lock attack?

A: Yes. However, since the Devastator's arms cannot be locked, the Centurion would have to use Electro-Lock to lock the Devastator's head.

Q: Does Polarity Field prevent a Marauder's Combo Slam?

A: No. Polarity Field only affects slam power attacks. The Marauder's Combo Slam is not a power attack.

Q: Can a Centurion be slammed from non-power attack effects like Thunder Strike, a Seneschal's Smite, or a Kovnik or Bokur's special attack?

A: Yes to all. The Magno Shield only stops power attack slams.

Feora, Priestess of the Flame [pg. 36]

Q: If Feora were the Protectorate player's last warcaster, is Death Pyre resolved before the end of the game?

A: Yes. Feora's controller earns victory points for enemy models destroyed by Death Pyre. However, if Death Pyre destroys the opponent's last warcaster in a game where warcaster destruction determines the winner, Feora loses.

Q: Does Inspiration affect Flameguard Cleansers?

A: Yes. Inspiration affects all friendly Flameguard units, not just Temple Flameguard.

Guardian [pg. 38]

Q: Does Ward of Retribution work exactly as the spell Retribution?

A: No. Ward of Retribution is only triggered by melee attack damage rolls.

Q: Does the Guardian need to succeed at an opposed STR roll to throw a model with Critical Pitch?

A: No.

Deliverer Sunburst Crew [pg. 40]

ERRATUM: ADDITIONAL BLASTS. REPLACE LAST SENTENCE OF ADDITIONAL BLASTS WITH THE FOLLOWING:

Additional blasts have a 3" AOE and models in the AOE suffer a POW 6 blast damage roll.

ERRATUM: WEAPON CREW. REPLACE FIFTH SENTENCE OF WEAPON CREW WITH THE FOLLOWING:

If the gunner is destroyed or removed from play, a crewman in this unit within 1" can take the destroyed gunner's place immediately and become the new gunner. Remove the crewman from the table instead of the gunner.

Exemplar Seneschal [pg. 41]

ERRATUM: CHAIN ATTACK — SMITE. REPLACE TEXT OF CHAIN ATTACK — SMITE WITH THE FOLLOWING:

If the Exemplar Seneschal hits the same target with both his initial Relic Blade attacks during the same activation, after resolving the attacks he may immediately make an additional melee attack against the target. If the attack succeeds, the target is slammed d6" directly away from the Seneschal with the same effect as a slam and suffers a damage roll equal to the Seneschal's current STR plus the POW of a Relic Blade. If the slammed model collides with another model, that model suffers a collateral damage roll equal to the Seneschal's current STR plus the POW of a Relic Blade. Do not roll an additional damage die for Weapon Master on successful Smite attacks.

Q: If two friendly Seneschals are within each other's command ranges, and both have zero wound points during the Maintenance Phase, does Restoration restore either of them to one wound?

A: No. Both are simultaneously destroyed.

Q: Does the Seneschal get a +2 STR and ARM bonus for each model destroyed near him?

A: No. The bonus is for one or more models.

Q: If a Seneschal is damaged by an AOE attack and the attack destroys other friendly Protectorate models, does Restoration remove the damage suffered?

A: Yes. Since the damage to all the models is simultaneous, the Seneschal suffers damage from the attack and then removes damage due to Restoration.

Q: Does the Exemplar Seneschal's Field Officer ability allow me to field an extra unit of Exemplars Errant?

A: Yes. Because a unit of Exemplars Errant is a Knights Exemplar unit, you may field either one additional unit of Knights Exemplar or one additional unit of Exemplars Errant above normal Field Allowances for each Seneschal in your army.

Monolith Bearer (pg. 42)

Q: If the Monolith Bearer is the first model in the unit destroyed, do the other models in the unit get the +4 bonus to ARM and DEF from Holy Monolith?

A: No.

Q: If the High Reclaimer uses Resurrection to return a Monolith Bearer to play, and the Monolith Bearer already used Greater Destiny, can he use it again?

A: No.

Q: If a priest in a unit under the effect of Fiery Assault runs, can he perform a Prayer of Menoth special action?

A: No. Models under the effect of Fiery Assault can only perform a combat action after running, but Prayers of Menoth is a special action. However, since the Zealots can run without an order, the Priest can advance and recite a prayer. The rest of the unit must stay in formation with him, of course.

Q: Can you draw LOS to a Monolith Bearer if all you can see is the monolith?

A: No. See page 32: "Unlike warjack models, items held in the hands of warrior models—such as their weapons or banner poles—do not count as part of the model for determining line of sight."

Flameguard Cleansers (pg. 43)

ERRATUM: INCINERATION. REPLACE TEXT OF INCINERATION WITH THE FOLLOWING:

Instead of making ranged attacks separately, every Flameguard Cleanser who received this order may combine his fire at the same target within 5". In order to participate in an Incineration attack, a Flameguard Cleanser must be able to declare a ranged attack against the intended target and be in a single open formation group with the other participants. Incineration requires at least three Flameguard Cleansers. The Flameguard Cleanser with the highest RAT in the attacking group makes one ranged attack roll for the group and gains +1 to the attack roll for each Flameguard Cleanser, including himself, participating in the attack. Incineration is a POW 12 attack with a 4" AOE. Increase the POW by 1 for each Flameguard Cleanser participating in the attack. The Incineration AOE remains in play for one round as a cloud effect. Models entering or ending their activations in the cloud suffer a POW 12 damage roll. Incinerate cannot target a model in melee. Flameguard Cleansers may make one Incineration attack per activation.

ERRATUM: IRREGULAR ARMOR. REPLACE TEXT OF IRREGULAR ARMOR WITH THE FOLLOWING:

Flameguard Cleansers have ARM 14 except against attacks and damage originating in their back arcs. Flameguard Cleansers have ARM 11 against attacks and damage originating in their back arcs.

Q: When two Flameguard Cleansers are destroyed by an AOE originating in their back arcs, how is Explosive resolved?

A: When Cleansers are hit by an AOE attack, do not apply the Cleansers' special rules until after all the damage has been resolved. After you determine that the two Cleansers are destroyed, they explode simultaneously.

Q: What if there were an Exemplar Seneschal standing in the Explosive AOE? Does he remove one damage point due to Restoration before or after he suffers damage from the blast?

A: The Exemplar Seneschal removes one damage point due to Restoration after he suffers damage from the blast.

Errata & Clarifications

Q: Can damage from Explosive cause additional Flameguard Cleansers to explode? What if a model affected by Necrophage explodes in the rear arc of a Flameguard Cleanser? Does Explosive trigger? What about being caught in the blast of Shatter Storm?

A: No in all cases. Explosive is only triggered by attacks, and these effects are not attacks.

The Wrack [pg. 44]

ERRATUM: SUFFERING'S PRAYER. REPLACE TEXT OF SUFFERING'S PRAYER WITH THE FOLLOWING:

The Wrack begins the game with one focus point. It receives one focus point during its controller's Control Phase if it does not currently have a focus point. The Wrack may only have up to one focus point at any time. While a focus point remains on the Wrack, ranged attacks targeting it automatically miss. During a friendly Protectorate warcaster's activation, he may remove one focus point from a Wrack in his control area and add it to his current total. A warcaster may only gain one focus point from any number of Wracks each turn. Any time a focus point is removed from the Wrack, roll a d6. On a roll of 1-3 the Wrack explodes with the same effect as Soulburst and is removed from play.

Q: If my Wrack explodes when my warcaster takes a focus point from it, does he still get the focus point?

A: Yes.

Q: Can I get a soul token from a Wrack when it explodes?

A: No. It is removed from play instead of being destroyed, and models removed from play without being destroyed do not generate soul tokens.

Devout [pg. 45]

ERRATUM: SHIELD GUARD. REPLACE LAST SENTENCE OF SHIELD GUARD WITH THE FOLLOWING:

If the Devout is Incorporeal or denied its full movement, it cannot use Shield Guard.

Q: If an enemy model charges into melee with a Devout and ends its movement within the Devout's melee range, when does the Devout make its Defensive Strike?

A: The Devout makes its Defensive Strike after the charging model completes its movement but before it makes its charge attack.

Q: If a model starts its activation in melee range of a Devout and either forfeits its movement or ends its movement within the Devout's melee range, does the Devout get another Defensive Strike?

A: Yes.

Q: An enemy Wrack activates within melee range of the Devout. Since the Wrack has a movement portion of its activation, would the Devout be able to make a Defensive Strike against it?

A: Yes it would.

Q: Can a Devout use Defensive Strike during its controller's turn if an enemy model affected by Hallowed Avenger ends its movement in the Devout's melee range?

A: Yes.

Q: Can a Devout under the effects of Safe Passage (Choir of Menoth) intercept a ranged attack with Shield Guard?

A: Yes. Safe Passage prevents the Devout from being targeted by a ranged attack, but it does not prevent it from being hit by one.

Q: Can the Devout use Shield Guard if it is affected by Stealth?

A: If the Devout has Stealth, it may still use Shield Guard even if the model making the attack is more than 5" away.

Q: Are the effects of the Shield Guard ability and the Bodyguard warjack bond cumulative?

A: Yes.

Q: What happens if the Devout uses Shield Guard to intercept a spray attack that hits both itself and the warcaster?

A: It can be hit by both attacks.

Reckoner [pg. 46]

ERRATUM: ASSAULT. REPLACE TEXT OF ASSAULT WITH THE FOLLOWING:

As part of a charge, after moving but before performing its combat action, the Reckoner may assault. When making an Assault, the Reckoner makes a single ranged attack targeting the model charged. The Reckoner is not considered to be in melee when making the Assault ranged attack, nor is the target considered to be in melee with the Reckoner. If the target is not in melee range after moving, the Reckoner must still make the Assault ranged attack before its activation ends. The Reckoner cannot target a model with which it was in melee at the start of its activation with an Assault ranged attack.

ERRATUM: CRITICAL SPLASH. REPLACE TEXT OF CRITICAL SPLASH WITH THE FOLLOWING:

On a critical hit, before marking normal damage, target warjack suffers one damage point to each column of its damage grid and target warbeast suffers one damage point to each branch of its life spiral. If a warjack damage column is full then apply the damage to the next column to the right. If a warbeast branch is full then apply the damage to the next branch in order.

Kommandant Irusk (pg. 52)

ERRATUM: UNDYING LOYALTY. REPLACE TEXT OF UNDYING LOYALTY WITH THE FOLLOWING:

For one round, friendly Khadoran warrior models/units currently in Irusk's control area become Fearless, gain +2 on attack rolls, and if they suffer sufficient damage to be destroyed, their controller rolls a d6. On a 4–6, the model remains in play but is reduced to one wound.

ERRATUM: ASSAULT. REPLACE TEXT OF ASSAULT WITH THE FOLLOWING:

As part of a charge, after moving but before performing his combat action, Irusk may assault. When making an Assault, Irusk makes a single ranged attack targeting the model charged. Irusk is not considered to be in melee when making the Assault ranged attack, nor is the target considered to be in melee with Irusk. If the target is not in melee range after moving, Irusk must still make the Assault ranged attack before his activation ends. Irusk cannot target a model with which he was in melee at the start of his activation with an Assault ranged attack.

Q: Does Irusk benefit from Undying Loyalty?

A: Yes. A warcaster is a warrior model and is within his own control area.

Q: Does a model affected by Undying Loyalty make a roll to avoid being destroyed each time it suffers sufficient damage to be destroyed?

A: Yes.

Q: When making Slaughter special attacks, does the second damage roll benefit from spells such as Fury or Battle Lust?

A: No. The second damage roll is not a melee damage roll.

Q: Are shields effective against Airburst?

A: Yes, unless the origin of the damage is entirely within the rear arc of the target. For a model directly hit by Airburst, the origin of the spell is the origin of the damage. For other models damaged by Airburst, the spell's point of impact is the origin of the damage.

Q: When a model or unit is hit by Confusion and uses another model's CMD for the command check, is the check resolved with the −2 penalty?

A: Yes.

Q: If a warjack is under the effects of Superiority and Vladimir's Forced March feat, what is its SPD?

A: Double the SPD for Forced March then add two for Superiority.

Kodiak (pg. 54)

ERRATUM: ALL TERRAIN. REPLACE TEXT OF ALL TERRAIN WITH THE FOLLOWING:

During its activation, the Kodiak ignores movement penalties from, and may charge and slam across, rough terrain and obstacles.

ERRATUM: VENT STEAM. REPLACE TEXT OF VENT STEAM WITH THE FOLLOWING:

The Kodiak creates a cloud effect with a 3" AOE centered on itself that remains in play for one round. The cloud remains at the spot placed even if the Kodiak moves. Warrior models in the AOE when the cloud is put in play suffer a POW 12 damage roll. Damage rolls must be boosted separately. Vent Steam is not a melee attack but may be made after a charge. The Kodiak does not roll an additional damage die when it charges and makes a Vent Steam attack, but the damage roll may be boosted normally. The Kodiak may spend focus points to make additional melee attacks after a Vent Steam attack. A Vent Steam special attack does not need a target.

Q: What kind of attack is Vent Steam?

A: It is a special attack that is neither a melee, ranged, or magic attack.

Greylord Ternion (pg. 56)

ERRATUM: MAGIC ABILITY. ADD TO THE TEXT OF MAGIC ABILITY:

The Greylord cannot make additional attacks after making a magic attack.

Q: Do Greylords benefit from Vladimir's Signs & Portents or Irusk's Undying Loyalty when making magic attacks?

Errata & Clarifications

A: Yes. Both affect all attack rolls.

Q: Do Greylord magic attacks affect Incorporeal models?

A: Yes. They are magic attacks.

Q: Can a Greylord make a magic attack after charging?

A: No. At the end of charge movement, the charging model has to make a melee attack. Casting a spell is a magic attack.

Q: Does Blizzard affect a model using Leap?

A: A model cannot leap if it would begin its Leap

movement within a Blizzard AOE, but otherwise a leaping model is unaffected by Blizzard.

Iron Fang Officer & Standard Bearer [pg. 57]

ERRATUM: UNIT STANDARD. REPLACE SECOND SENTENCE OF UNIT STANDARD WITH THE FOLLOWING:

If the Standard Bearer is destroyed or removed from play, a Pikeman in this unit within 1" can take the Standard Bearer's place immediately and become the new Standard Bearer.

Q: While under the effect of Furious Charge, can affected models charge through rough terrain? If so, do they move at half speed?

A: Yes and yes.

Q: Can you use Defensive Formation after a run or a failed charge?

A: Yes.

Q: When moving into Shield Wall after using Defensive Formation, can the Pikemen be targeted by free strikes?

A: Yes.

Kossite Woodsmen [pg. 58]

ERRATUM: PATHFINDER. REPLACE TEXT OF PATHFINDER WITH THE FOLLOWING:

During his activation, a Kossite Woodsman ignores movement penalties from, and may charge across, rough terrain and obstacles.

Q: Does a model have to stay within 3" of a Kossite during its entire movement to gain the benefit of Trail Blazer?

A: No. However, once a model moves more than 3" away from a Kossite Woodsman, it starts paying normal movement costs again until it is within 3" of a Kossite Woodsman once more. Basically, a Kossite Woodsman continuously negates the rough terrain 3" around him for friendly models.

Man-O-War Kovnik [pg. 59]

Q: If the Kovnik fails his Drive check, can the marshaled warjack still run/boost/charge?

A: No. If the Drive fails, the 'jack gets no benefits at all from being marshaled. However, it can activate normally.

Q: How does the Kovnik's Slam special attack work?

A: The Kovnik's Slam is resolved like a warjack's slam power attack except that he does not have to spend a focus point to perform it.

Q: Will the Man-O-War Kovnik's Field Officer ability allow me to field an additional unit of Man-O-War Demolition Corps?

A: No. The Kovnik's Field Officer only allows you to field an additional unit of Man-O-War Shocktroopers.

Winter Guard Mortar Crew [pg. 60]

ERRATUM: WEAPON CREW. REPLACE FIFTH SENTENCE OF WEAPON CREW WITH THE FOLLOWING:

If the gunner is destroyed or removed from play, a crewman in this unit within 1" can take the destroyed gunner's place immediately and become the new gunner. Remove the crewman from the table instead of the gunner.

Q: Does the Gunner get to choose another target for a Mortar attack if its initial target is less than 8" away?

A: Yes. The original model was not a legal target.

Berserker (pg. 61)

Q: Does a Berserker have to roll for Unstable when marshaled?

A: No. A Berserker only rolls for Unstable after spending focus points.

Q: Is the Berserker's Decayed Cortex box already filled in?

A: Yes.

Devastator (pg. 62)

ERRATUM: ARMORED SHELL. REPLACE FOURTH SENTENCE OF ARMORED SHELL WITH THE FOLLOWING:

A Devastator's arms cannot be locked.

ERRATUM: BULLDOZE. ADD THE FOLLOWING TEXT TO BULLDOZE:

Bulldoze has no effect when the Devastator makes a trample power attack.

ERRATUM: RAIN OF DEATH. REPLACE TEXT OF RAIN OF DEATH WITH THE FOLLOWING:

Models in base-to-base contact with the Devastator suffer a POW 18 damage roll. Other models within 3" of the Devastator suffer a POW 9 damage roll. Damage rolls must be boosted separately. Rain of Death is not a melee attack but may be made after a charge. The Devastator does not roll an additional damage die when it charges and makes a Rain of Death attack, but the damage roll may be boosted normally. The Devastator may spend focus points to make additional melee attacks after a Rain of Death attack. A Rain of Death special attack does not need a target.

Q: When a Devastator is hit by an attack with Armor Piercing, is its Armored Shell ARM halved?

A: Yes.

Q: Can a Devastator Bulldoze a model it charges?

A: Yes.

Q: Can a Devastator use Bulldoze to move other models in its way while charging?

A: Yes.

Q: Is the Devastator's ARM lowered while it maintains an arm lock or headlock?

A: Yes.

Q: What kind of attack is Rain of Death?

A: It is a special attack that is neither a melee, ranged, or magic attack.

Q: When the Devastator charges, when is its ARM reduced?

A: When it makes its first attack.

Q: When a Devastator tries to break a headlock, is its ARM reduced?

A: No.

Goreshade the Bastard (pg. 67)

ERRATUM: CLOAK OF SHADOWS. ADD THE FOLLOWING TEXT TO CLOAK OF SHADOWS:

If Goreshade is greater than 5" away from an attacker, he does not count as an intervening model this round.

ERRATUM: DEATH WALK. ADD THE FOLLOWING TEXT TO DEATH WALK:

A living model destroyed by Bloodcleaver does not generate a soul or corpse token.

Q: When creating my army, do I have to pay the points for Bane Thralls summoned by Dark Summons?

A: No. In addition, Bane Thralls put in play by Dark Summons do not count against the Bane Thralls' Field Allowance.

Q: Can Goreshade use Dark Summons if there is not enough room for all 6 models?

A: Yes, but any models that cannot be placed are lost.

Q: If Deathwalker has been kept from destruction by Death Rage and Goreshade then suffers sufficient damage to be destroyed, can she use Dark Restoration?

A: No. A model affected by Death Rage cannot be destroyed for the turn after Death Rage takes effect, but the Deathwalker must be destroyed to make Dark Restoration work.

Q: What happens when a model recasts an upkeep spell affected by The Claiming?

A: The first version expires and the caster suffers no damage.

Errata & Clarifications

Q: Goreshade casts The Claiming on a unit under the effects of Dark Seduction. Does the new target of the spell have to make a command check?

A: Yes. If the unit passes its command check, Dark Seduction expires. If the unit fails its command check, Deneghra takes control of the unit.

Q: Can damage from Consumption be boosted?

A: No. It is not a damage roll.

Q: Can a living warcaster channel a spell through a warjack in Goreshade's control area during a round in which he casts Mage Blight?

A: Yes, provided the warcaster is outside Goreshade's control area.

Q: If a warjack is placed in another model's back arc using Soul Gate and the warjack activates later during the same turn, does it get a back strike?

A: Yes.

Seether (pg. 70)

ERRATUM: SOUL DRIVE. REPLACE TEXT OF SOUL DRIVE WITH THE FOLLOWING:

The Seether automatically receives one focus point during its controller's Control Phase and it may be allocated up to two additional focus points by its controlling warcaster. The Seether still receives one focus point from the Soul Drive even if it suffers Disruption, but it does not receive the focus point if its cortex is destroyed. If the Seether's controlling warcaster is destroyed or removed from play, the helljack remains active and does not become inert.

ERRATUM: UNCONTROLLED RAGE. REPLACE TEXT OF UNCONTROLLED RAGE WITH THE FOLLOWING:

The Seether's controlling warcaster must pass a command check at the start of the Seether's activation to maintain control over the Seether and may spend a focus point to re-roll a failed test. If the test fails or if the Seether is outside its controlling warcaster's command range, the helljack charges without spending a focus point at the nearest non-incorporeal model in LOS, friendly or enemy, unless the helljack is already engaged. If Uncontrolled Rage forces the Seether to charge a friendly model, its controlling player cannot choose a path that would cause the Seether to contact another model or an obstacle so that the charge fails if there is a clear path. If the Seether cannot charge the nearest non-incorporeal model or there are no

non-incorporeal models within LOS, the Seether advances toward and attempts to attack the nearest non-incorporeal model. Uncontrolled Seethers always make Combo Strike special attacks if possible and must spend all their focus points for additional attacks.

Q: Can a warcaster keep spending focus points until he makes a successful command check for Uncontrolled Rage, or is only one retry allowed?

A: Yes. A warcaster can spend focus points until he runs out of focus.

Q: A Seether is assigned to the Witch Coven of Garlghast's battlegroup. When the Coven makes a command check for Uncontrolled Rage to maintain control over the Seether, is it a single check for the Coven or one check per witch?

A: One check for the entire Coven. You may use any witch's CMD for the check.

Bloat Thrall (pg. 72)

Q: If a Despoiler attack destroys half or more of a unit, does it have to make two command checks?

A: Yes.

Q: Do models hit by a Despoiler attack that fail their command checks flee from the point of impact of the attack or from the Bloat Thrall?

A: They flee from the Bloat Thrall.

Machine Wraith (pg. 73)

ERRATUM: INCORPOREAL. REPLACE SIXTH SENTENCE OF INCORPOREAL WITH THE FOLLOWING:

The Machine Wraith only suffers damage and effects from magic attacks, animi, spells, and feats and is not affected by continuous effects.

ERRATUM: MACHINE MELD. REPLACE FIRST TWO SENTENCES OF MACHINE MELD WITH THE FOLLOWING:

The Machine Wraith may possess an inert or enemy warjack with a functional cortex.

Q: If a Machine Wraith is expelled from a warjack, when can the warjack be activated?

A: Anytime during the warjack's controller's turn.

Q: If the game ends with a warjack under the control of a Machine Wraith, does the controlling Cryx player score victory points for it?

A: No.

Q: How many times can a warcaster try to eject a Machine Wraith from his warjack?

A: As many times as the warcaster has focus points to spend.

Q: The rules for Machine Meld say a warcaster may spend one focus point to make a magic attack roll to eject the wraith. Black Oil's effects (Gorman di Wulfe) state that it prevents magic attacks. Does Black Oil prevent a warcaster from spending a focus point to attempt to eject the wraith?

A: No. Although they use magic attack rolls, attempts to eject a Machine Wraith are not magic attacks and are therefore not prevented by Black Oil.

Q: A Machine Wraith possesses a warjack. During the Cryx player's next turn, the warjack activates. Is this also the Machine Wraith's activation?

A: No. The Machine Wraith is not on the table and therefore does not get an activation.

Necrosurgeon & Stitch Thralls (pg. 74)

Q: Does the Necrosurgeon lose its corpse tokens if it fails a Reanimate skill check?

A: No.

Pistol Wraith (pg. 75)

ERRATUM: CHAIN ATTACK – DEATH CHILL. REPLACE FIRST SENTENCE OF CHAIN ATTACK – DEATH CHILL WITH THE FOLLOWING:

If the Pistol Wraith hits the same target with both of its initial Wraithlock Pistol attacks during the same activation, after resolving the attacks it may immediately make an additional ranged attack against the target.

ERRATUM: INCORPOREAL. REPLACE SIXTH SENTENCE OF INCORPOREAL WITH THE FOLLOWING:

The Wraith only suffers damage and effects from magic attacks, animi, spells, and feats and is not affected by continuous effects.

Q: If the Pistol Wraith is in melee range of an enemy model while Incorporeal, can it fire its Wraithlock Pistols?

A: Yes, it can fire once. After making that attack it loses Incorporeal, becomes engaged, and can no longer make ranged attacks.

Q: What happens when the Pistol Wraith shoots at targets in melee and misses with both attacks but happens to hit another model with both of them?

A: It may make its chain attack against the model that was hit by both of its initial attacks even if that model was not the declared target of those attacks.

Q: What happens if the chain attack misses a model in melee?

A: Nothing. The attack cannot target a model that was not hit by both initial attacks.

Revenant Crew (pg. 76)

Q: A pirate uses Death Stroke while under the effects of Skarre's feat Blood Magic. Do you double the model's STR and then add the modifier for Blood Magic?

A: Yes.

Q: If the Quartermaster has Death Rage cast on it and suffers enough damage to be destroyed, is Death Rage triggered or does it roll for Tough first?

A: Roll for Tough first. If Tough fails, Death Rage is triggered.

Q: The Quartermaster is under the effect of Death Rage and suffers sufficient damage to be destroyed. Which comes first next turn, the expiration of Death Rage (and the subsequent destruction of the Quartermaster) or the return of the pirates?

A: Death Rage expires first. The Quartermaster is destroyed before any pirates can return to play.

Stalker (pg. 77)

ERRATUM: ALL TERRAIN. REPLACE TEXT OF ALL TERRAIN WITH THE FOLLOWING:

During its activation, the Stalker ignores movement penalties from, and may charge and slam across, rough terrain and obstacles.

Q: Does the Power Sink ability mean the Stalker can have more than 3 focus points on it?

A: Yes. Only 3 focus points may be allocated to it by a warcaster, but this is in addition to the focus generated by Power Sink (unlike the focus generated by a Seether, for example).

Q: Is the number of power tokens gained limited by the amount of focus a warcaster has to lose? (For example when attacking with several Stalkers)

A: No. There is no upper limit.

Q: Is Leap considered to be part of the Stalker's normal movement?

Errata & Clarifications

A: No. It is additional movement separate from the Stalker's normal movement.

Q: Can a Stalker still leap after being Soul Gated by Goreshade?

A: No. Leap is additional movement, and Soul Gate forbids movement that turn.

Q: What happens when a Stalker leaps through a Wall of Fire?

A: It suffers damage as it moves through the Wall of Fire.

Leviathan (pg. 78)

ERRATUM: ALL TERRAIN. REPLACE TEXT OF ALL TERRAIN WITH THE FOLLOWING:

During its activation, the Leviathan ignores movement penalties from, and may charge and slam across, rough terrain and obstacles.

ERRATUM: AMPHIBIOUS: ADD THE FOLLOWING TEXT TO AMPHIBIOUS:

An Amphibious model may voluntarily enter deep water without penalty.

Gorten Grundback (pg. 83)

ERRATUM: LANDSLIDE. REPLACE TEXT OF LANDSLIDE WITH THE FOLLOWING:

Enemy models currently in Gorten's control area are moved up to 8" directly toward a table edge selected by Gorten's controlling player. All models must be moved the same distance. A model stops moving if it contacts rough terrain, an obstacle, an obstruction, or another model. Gorten's controlling player chooses the order in which the models are moved. Models moved by Landslide cannot be targeted by free strikes during this movement. Models affected by Landslide cannot give or receive orders and suffer −3 SPD, RAT, and DEF for one round.

Q: Are all models moved by Landslide moved in the same direction?

A: Yes. All models in Gorten's control area must be moved the same distance directly toward the same table edge.

Q: What if I want to use his feat on a table that is not square or has no clear table edges?

A: There are only 4 possible directions of movement for Landslide. If you consider the side where you started as south, Landslide may move models in any one of the cardinal directions (north, south, east, or west).

Q: Can Landslide be used to move the models at an angle toward a table edge?

A: No. They must be moved directly toward the edge.

Q: Can Landslide move models off the table?

A: No. A model that reaches the table's edge stops there.

Q: Can a model be moved off a cliff by Landslide?

A: Yes.

Q: Can the wall of stone created by Rock Wall be targeted like a structure?

A: No. Structures have damage capacity and ARM stats. The wall of stone has neither.

Magnus the Traitor (pg. 86)

Q: How exactly does Hit & Run work?

A: When you use the feat during Magnus' activation, check which of his warjacks are within his control area. Finish the rest of your turn. Then, Magnus and those warjacks advance or run. They may not be targeted by free strikes during this additional movement.

Q: Does Magnus receive his extra Backstab damage against Deneghra?

A: No. Deneghra's Witch Barbs prevent all back strike bonuses.

Q: Does the Backstab ability work on ranged and magic attacks as well?

A: Yes.

Renegade (pg. 88)

Q: If the target suffers damage from an additional attack granted by Shred, do I get another attack?

A: Yes.

Q: If a target suffers damage from a free strike made with the Shredder, do I get another attack?

A: Yes. However, these additional attacks will not get free strike bonuses.

Q: Do all the attacks granted by Shred count as a single attack?

A: No. Each is a separate attack. Resolve each one completely before making the next one.

Mangler (pg. 90)

ERRATUM: CIRCULAR STRIKE. REPLACE TEXT OF CIRCULAR STRIKE WITH THE FOLLOWING:

The Mangler may make one melee attack with the Wrecker against every model within melee range. Completely resolve each attack individually and apply the targets' special rules immediately as each attack is resolved. When performing a Circular Strike, the Mangler's front arc extends 360°. A model is ineligible to be hit if it has a special rule preventing it from being targeted or if the attacker's line of sight is completely blocked by terrain.

Captain Sam and the Devil Dogs (pg. 92)

ERRATUM: ENTANGLE. ADD THE FOLLOWING SENTENCE TO ENTANGLE:

A model's melee range is only increased to 2" for the purposes of resolving this melee attack.

Q: Can Sam participate in a Combined Ranged Attack?

A: No. She's not a Devil Dog.

Q: Can the Devil Dogs use their Entangle ability after a charge?

A: Yes, if they are within melee range of their target after the charge. If they are further away, it is a failed charge despite the range of Entangle.

Rhupert Carvolo, Piper of Ord (pg. 96)

ERRATUM: MARCH. REPLACE LAST TWO LINES OF MARCH WITH THE FOLLOWING:

During its activation, a model with Pathfinder ignores movement penalties from, and may charge across, rough terrain and obstacles.

Q: Can Carvolo play a song without a unit to target?

A: Yes.

Q: Can the Piper play March before moving?

A: No. Carvolo's Songs are special actions, and actions are performed after movement.

Q: The Piper of Ord targets a unit with Dirge of Mists. That unit is within melee range of enemy models. When does the enemy unit make a command check?

A: Immediately.

Q: Carvolo's March ability grants an additional attack. If a unit affected by Carvolo's song runs, what happens?

A: A running model's activation ends at the completion of its movement, so the unit will not be able to use the attacks granted by March.

Kings, Nations, and Gods Campaign

ERRATUM P.141: BATTLE FOR RIVERSMET SCENARIO - SPECIAL RULES AND SET UP. ADD THE FOLLOWING SENTENCE:

The river running through the table is deep water.

ERRATUM P.170: DIRTY DEEDS SCENARIO - SPECIAL RULES AND SET UP. ADD THE FOLLOWING TEXT TO THE END OF THE SECTION:

Cygnar models never flee in this scenario.

Apotheosis

Captain E. Dominic Darius (pg. 32)

ERRATUM: 'JACK HAMMER. ADD THE FOLLOWING TEXT TO END OF 'JACK HAMMER:

While making a special attack, a warjack only benefits from 'Jack Hammer once regardless of the number of attacks generated or the number of models damaged by the special attack. 'Jack Hammer is not triggered by power attacks.

ERRATUM: FORTIFY. REPLACE TEXT OF FORTIFY WITH THE FOLLOWING:

Target warjack in Darius' battlegroup gains +2 ARM. The affected model and any friendly model in base-to-base contact with it cannot be knocked down and can only move or be moved during its activation.

Errata & Clarifications

ERRATUM: TREMOR. REPLACE TEXT OF TREMOR WITH THE FOLLOWING:

Roll 2d6 and add the weapon's POW. This roll cannot be boosted. Compare the result to the DEF of every model within 2". These models are knocked down if the total equals or exceeds their DEF. This effect causes no damage. A Tremor special attack cannot be made after a charge. A Tremor special attack does not need a target.

Q: When Meltdown causes a model to explode, can it damage Incorporeal models?

A: Yes. The damage is caused by a spell.

Q: A warjack is stationary, then disabled, then repaired by Darius' feat. Is it still stationary?

A: Yes. Effects, spells, and animi on a warjack remain on it when it becomes a disabled wreck. However, since such effects expire upon destruction, if the warjack were stationary, then destroyed, then repaired by Darius' feat, the warjack would no longer be stationary.

Q: Is there a maximum to the number of knocked down models that Darius can help up?

A: No.

Q: Can Darius use Crane to help up a model that has been pinned by the Scrapjack's chain attack?

A: Yes.

Q: Does your opponent get a free strike if you use Darius' crane to pull a model from combat?

A: No.

Q: The rules say that a knocked down model cannot be slammed. Why does Dead Lift say it slams a knocked down model?

A: Since Dead Lift specifically says it can target knocked down models with a slam effect, it becomes an exception to the normal restriction.

Q: Darius' Halfjack uses Patch to turn a disabled wreck marker into a functional warjack again. Can that warjack immediately activate?

A: Yes.

Q: Darius' 'Jack Hammer spell and chain attacks both have triggers of "immediately." Which comes first?

A: The chain attack comes first.

Major Markus 'Siege' Brisbane [pg. 36]

ERRATUM: BREACH. ADD THE FOLLOWING TO THE TEXT OF BREACH:

Breach is not cumulative with other effects that halve a model's ARM.

ERRATUM: ILLUMINATION. ADD THE FOLLOWING TO THE TEXT OF ILLUMINATION:

Illumination lasts for one round.

Q: How does Explosivo affect special attacks such as Energy Pulse, Strafe, or Ground Pounder that generate extra attacks?

A: Only the first attack benefits from Explosivo.

Q: How do Explosivo and Darius' Pressure Cooker interact?

A: Damage caused by Pressure Cooker is not caused by a ranged attack, so Explosivo has no effect on it.

Q: Are the ranged attacks granted by Ground Pounder simultaneous?

A: Yes.

Q: Can Siege use his Command Authority ability to issue an Arcane Inferno order to a unit of Gun Mages if the unit's lieutenant is not available?

A: Yes he can. However, the unit cannot follow the order because the order requires the unit's lieutenant to be a participant.

Q: Are the effects of Fox Hole and Higher Ground cumulative?

A: Yes.

Q: Can the range of Siege's Ground Pounder special attack be increased by Snipe?

A: No.

Q: Goreshade is under the effect of Cloak of Shadows. Can Brisbane target him with attacks generated by Ground Pounder?

A: No. Cloak of Shadows prevents Goreshade from being targeted by ranged attacks, and the attacks generated by Ground Pounder are ranged attacks.

Major Victoria Haley [pg. 38]

ERRATUM: DOMINATION. REPLACE 2ND SENTENCE OF DOMINATION WITH THE FOLLOWING:

During this movement and attack, the model is a friendly Cygnar model.

Q: How does Replication work with a spell that names a specific model?

A: Make the appropriate substitutions to the spell's text. For example, if Major Haley replicates Vladimir Tzepesci's spell Ruination, treat the first sentence of the spell's description as if it said "If target model is hit, Major Haley may make magic attack rolls against the nearest d6 enemy models within 3" of the original target."

Q: Can Major Haley replicate a spell cast by a Greylord?

A: No. Major Haley may only replicate spells that required the expenditure of focus points to be cast.

Q: Can Major Haley use an arc node when replicating the Harbinger's spells?

A: Yes, Major Haley can channel spells she copies from the Harbinger.

Q: If Major Haley replicates Cataclysm through an arc node, how do you determine the spell's POW?

A: Measure the distance from the target to Major Haley to determine Cataclysm's POW even if the spell is channeled.

Q: Can Major Haley replicate a non-offensive spell that was cast offensively?

A: Yes, and she may cast it non-offensively.

Q: Can Major Haley use a Faulty Arc Node or Arcantrik Relay with Backfire?

A: No. She can only use Arc Nodes as the spell specifies.

Q: Can Major Haley gain soul tokens when replicating Terminus' Annihilation?

A: Yes.

Q: Can Major Haley use Backfire to channel a spell through a Protectorate player's arc node inside the effect of Castigate?

A: Yes she can. Backfire does not make the channeler an enemy model to the Protectorate player. The model itself is still under the Protectorate player's control.

Q: Major Haley uses her feat Temporal Shift. If one trooper of an enemy unit is affected, does the whole unit have to activate at the same time?

A: Yes.

Lord Commander Stryker (pg. 40)

ERRATUM: ROLLING THUNDER. ADD THE FOLLOWING TO THE END OF ROLLING THUNDER:

Affected models may spend focus points to boost attack and damage rolls when resolving these additional attacks.

ERRATUM: ARCANE STORM. IN LAST SENTENCE OF ARCANE STORM, REPLACE "MODELS MOVING INTO THE AOE" WITH "MODELS ENTERING THE AOE"

ERRATUM: ARCANE STORM. ADD THE FOLLOWING TEXT TO ARCANE STORM:

Completely resolve each damage roll individually and apply the targets' special rules immediately as each damage roll is resolved.

Thunderhead (pg. 42)

ERRATUM: DISRUPTOR FIELD. REPLACE TEXT OF DISRUPTOR FIELD WITH THE FOLLOWING:

A warjack hitting the Thunderhead with a melee attack suffers Disruption. A warjack suffering Disruption loses any unused focus points and cannot be allocated focus points or channel spells for one round.

ERRATUM: ENERGY PULSE. DELETE "ROLL" FROM FIRST SENTENCE OF ENERGY PULSE.

ERRATUM: SUSTAINED ATTACK. REPLACE TEXT OF SUSTAINED ATTACK WITH THE FOLLOWING:

Once the Thunderhead hits a target with the Lightning Coil, additional attacks with it against the same target within the attack's range automatically hit this turn. No additional attack rolls are necessary.

Harbinger of Menoth (pg. 50)

ERRATUM: WORD OF LAW. REPLACE "CTRL" WITH "✶" IN THE SPELL STAT LINE.

The supporting text is correct.

Q: Does each model participating in a combined ranged attack have to check against her Awe ability?

A: Make one command check for the model making the attack roll. If it fails, all participating models are considered to have failed the check.

Q: A model wants to charge the Harbinger. When do you make the command check against Awe?

A: Make the check after movement but before the first attack.

Q: Are there any restrictions on the use of focus forcibly assigned to a warcaster due to the effects of Foresight?

A: Focus forcibly assigned to the warcaster because of the Harbinger's Foresight spell can be used normally. The spell only determines how focus must be allocated, not what a model can do with that focus.

Errata & Clarifications

Q: Do I need to declare what I'm using my focus for when I allocate it due to Foresight?

A: No. The spell only requires you to state how focus will be allocated, not what a model will do with that focus.

Q: The Harbinger's spell Martyrdom and Seneschal's Restoration are both triggered when the model suffers sufficient damage to be destroyed. Which occurs first?

A: Restoration will go off first. Then the Harbinger may use Martyrdom.

Q: Would Martyrdom take effect before Lich Lord Asphyxious' Excarnate spell, or vice versa?

A: When multiple special rules with contradictory effects are triggered at the same time, the attacker's special rule takes precedence. Therefore, Excarnate would take effect first.

Q: Can a model under the effect of Temporal Acceleration activate during its next turn if it is in the AOE of Purification? Does a model under the effects of Boundless Charge still have to charge if it is in the AOE of Purification? If Skarre is in the AOE of Purification, does she still gain focus from Sacrificial Lamb this turn?

A: When cast, Purification nullifies all continuous and spell effects in its area. This includes any ongoing effects of non-upkeep spells. So, a model that was affected by Temporal Acceleration will be able to activate during its next turn, a model that was affected by Boundless Charge is not required to charge, Skarre does not gain focus from Sacrificial Lamb, and so on.

Q: What happens to a model within the AOE of Purification under the effects of Death Rage after the spell has expired?

A: The Death Rage spell effect expires and the model is immediately destroyed.

Q: Are soul tokens gained from casting Annihilation lost if Terminus is within the AOE of Purification?

A: Yes. The effects of Annihilation are not complete until the soul tokens become focus points.

Q: A model is hit by a critical Stygian Abyss roll. If that model is in the Purification AOE, does Blind expire?

A: Yes.

High Allegiant Amon Ad-Raza [pg. 52]

ERRATUM: CIRCULAR STRIKE. REPLACE TEXT OF CIRCULAR STRIKE WITH THE FOLLOWING:

Amon may make one melee attack with Oblivion against every model within melee range. Completely resolve each attack individually and apply the targets' special rules immediately as each attack is resolved. When performing a Circular Strike, Amon's front arc extends 360°. A model is ineligible to be hit if it has a special rule preventing it from being targeted or if the attacker's line of sight is completely blocked by terrain.

ERRATUM: PATHFINDER. REPLACE TEXT OF PATHFINDER WITH THE FOLLOWING:

During his activation, Amon ignores movement penalties from, and may charge across, rough terrain and obstacles.

ERRATUM: SAND BLAST. REPLACE FIRST SENTENCE OF SAND BLAST WITH THE FOLLOWING:

Completely resolve each attack roll individually and apply the targets' special rules immediately as each attack roll is resolved. On a critical hit, instead of suffering a normal damage roll, a non-incorporeal model hit is immediately slammed d6" directly away from the spell's point of origin and suffers a POW 12 damage roll.

Q: Amon is both stationary (e.g., because of Icy Gaze) and knocked down. Can he stand up with his Perfect Balance ability?

A: Yes, but he would still be stationary after standing up.

Q: While using Meditative Stance, can Amon allocate any number of focus points or only the two focus points he receives from that ability?

A: Only the two focus points received from Meditative Stance may be allocated.

Q: Does Synergy affect the damage roll of the first successful attack a model makes?

A: Yes.

Q: Do you get the bonus for attacks made that turn before Synergy was cast?

A: No.

Q: If Amon uses his feat Union, can a warjack that has its movement disabled move more than an inch?

A: Yes. It uses Amon's SPD.

Q: If a warjack in Amon's battlegroup has disabled movement but is then affected by Union, can the warjack charge?

A: No.

Grand Exemplar Kreoss (pg. 54)

ERRATUM: SACROSANCT. REPLACE LAST SENTENCE OF SACROSANCT WITH THE FOLLOWING:

Any enemy model destroying a sacrosanct model with an attack must forfeit its action during its next activation.

Q: Is the Thrust special attack cumulative with the Hallowed Vengeance spell?

A: Yes. Hallowed Vengeance modifies the next normal damage roll, but Thrust only modifies the target's ARM value.

The Testament of Menoth (pg. 56)

ERRATUM: ESSENCE OF DUST. REPLACE TEXT OF ESSENCE OF DUST WITH THE FOLLOWING:

While moving, friendly Protectorate models currently in the Testament's control area may ignore movement penalties from, and charge across, rough terrain and obstacles, may move through other models if they have enough movement to move completely past the model's base, and cannot be targeted by free strikes. When declaring charges and slams, an affected model may ignore other models when determing LOS. Essence of Dust lasts for one turn.

ERRATUM: OATH OF SILENCE. REPLACE 2ND SENTENCE OF OATH OF SILENCE WITH THE FOLLOWING:

Other models/units cannot use the Testament's CMD stat when making command checks.

ERRATUM: SOULSTORM. REPLACE FIRST SENTENCE OF SOULSTORM WITH THE FOLLOWING:

Enemy models that enter the area within 4" of the Testament immediately suffer one damage point.

Q: Does the Omegus also remove warjacks from play without leaving wreck markers when they are destroyed?

A: Yes.

Q: When an enemy model is destroyed in the Testament's control area, the Omegus removes it from play. When removed from play, are effects triggered by the model's destruction triggered?

A: Yes. The model is still destroyed.

Q: A model in the Testament's army destroys an enemy Protectorate model in range of both the Omegus and an unfriendly High Reclaimer. Does the enemy High Reclaimer get a soul token?

A: No. The Omegus keeps the models from generating soul tokens.

The Avatar of Menoth (pg. 58)

ERRATUM: INCINERATE: REPLACE FIRST SENTENCE OF INCINERATE WITH THE FOLLOWING:

Enemy models within 3" of a warjack disabled or destroyed by an attack from the Burning Wrath suffer Fire.

ERRATUM: MENOTH'S GAZE. REPLACE TEXT OF MENOTH'S GAZE WITH THE FOLLOWING:

During its activation, the Avatar of Menoth may spend a focus point to activate Menoth's Gaze. Enemy models within 8" of the Avatar of Menoth beginning their activation with the Avatar of Menoth within their LOS cannot end their movement farther from the Avatar of Menoth than they started. Affected models within 8" of the Avatar of Menoth cannot give or receive orders. Menoth's Gaze lasts for one round.

Q: Can the Avatar of Menoth use Blessing of Menoth to re-roll a Holy Vessel focus roll?

A: No. The roll does not result from an action taken by the Avatar.

Karchev the Terrible (pg. 66)

ERRATUM: ERUPTION. IN SECOND SENTENCE OF ERUPTION, REPLACE "A MODEL MOVING INTO" WITH "A MODEL ENTERING"

ERRATUM: IRON CURTAIN. REPLACE LAST SENTENCE OF IRON CURTAIN WITH THE FOLLOWING:

Errata & Clarifications

A model may only suffer the effects of Iron Curtain once per round. These damage rolls cannot be boosted.

ERRATUM: MAN IN THE MACHINE. ADD THE FOLLOWING TEXT TO MAN IN THE MACHINE:

Karchev may make bash attacks. When in deep water, treat Karchev as a warrior model. Apply damage he suffers from deep water to his Body system only.

Q: When Karchev is hit by an attack that allows the attacker to choose which column takes the damage when damaging a warjack, how is it resolved?

A: The attacker deals damage to the column of his choice just as with a warjack.

Q: Does Eiryss' activation end because of her Technological Intolerance if she ends her movement within 5" of Karchev?

A: No.

Q: Can a Sword Knight that hits Karchev with an attack use Penetrating Strike to inflict an automatic damage point instead of making a damage roll?

A: Yes

Q: When Karchev makes a Fissure attack, does a model benefit from Stealth?

A: No.

Q: What exactly does "cross" mean in Iron Curtain?

A: A model is subject to Iron Curtain's effect if any portion of its base touches any line between the two warjacks' bases.

Zevanna Agha, Old Witch of Khador (pg. 68)

ERRATUM: FIELD OF TALONS. REPLACE SECOND SENTENCE OF FIELD OF TALONS WITH THE FOLLOWING:

Enemy models currently within twice the Old Witch's current FOC stat in inches of the target model cannot run, charge, or make special attacks.

ERRATUM: FIELD OF TALONS. ADD THE FOLLOWING BEFORE THE LAST SENTENCE OF FIELD OF TALONS:

Apply the damage as each model moves.

ERRATUM: MURDER OF CROWS. IN 3RD SENTENCE, REPLACE "MOVING INTO" WITH "ENTERING".

ERRATUM: PATHFINDER. REPLACE TEXT OF PATHFINDER WITH THE FOLLOWING:

During her activation, the Old Witch ignores movement penalties from, and may charge across, rough terrain and obstacles.

ERRATUM: WEALD SECRETS. REPLACE TEXT OF WEALD SECRETS WITH THE FOLLOWING:

Target model/unit gains Camouflage and Pathfinder. A model with camouflage gains an additional +2 DEF when benefiting from concealment or cover. During its activation, a model with Pathfinder ignores movement penalties from, and may charge across, rough terrain and obstacles.

Q: In the text of Field of Talons, does "moving within the area for any reason" include being moved by such things as Gorten's Landslide or the Old Witch's Strangling Chains?

A: Yes. If the model moves in any way at all it suffers damage. Models "placed" do not move, so they are not affected (e.g. Unseen Path and Soul Gate).

Q: The Old Witch casts Murder of Crows. Would an enemy Old Witch or enemy Scrapjack be damaged if it moved into or ended its activation in the AOE?

A: No.

Q: Can you target an enemy Old Witch or enemy Scrapjack with Unseen Path or Field of Talons?

A: Yes.

Q: Can a model affected by Unseen Path be placed in a different part of the same forest or cloud effect it is currently in?

A: No. The model must be placed in a different forest or cloud effect.

Q: If the Old Witch casts Unseen Path and is in a cloud effect or forest that is overlapped by Fog of War, can she move to another location within the Fog of War AOE?

A: Yes.

Scrapjack (pg. 70)

ERRATUM: ALL TERRAIN. REPLACE TEXT OF ALL TERRAIN WITH THE FOLLOWING:

During its activation, the Scrapjack ignores movement penalties from, and may charge and slam across, rough terrain and obstacles.

Q: Do the Scrapjack's Mechanikal Talons have a corresponding location in the Scrapjack's damage grid?

A: No.

Forward Kommander Sorscha Kratikoff (pg. 72)

Q: Can Forward Kommander Sorscha Kratikoff use Reinholdt's Reload ability to add an additional Multi Fire special attack?

A: No. Reload does not allow a model to make an additional special attack.

Q: Do Desperate Pace and Elite Cadre affect Winter Guard Mortar Crews?

A: Yes. Desperate Pace and Elite Cadre affect any model with "Winter Guard" in its name or subtitle.

Q: Does the −2 DEF penalty from Desperate Pace only affect my Winter Guard if I choose the extra blunderbuss attack?

A: No. The −2 DEF penalty applies to both the extra attack and the additional 3" movement.

Q: When Desperate Pace affects a unit, do all models gain the same benefit or can the unit's controller choose to affect each model with either benefit?

A: Either all models in the unit gain +3" of movement or all models in the unit may make an additional blunderbuss attack. Either way, all models in the unit will suffer the −2 DEF penalty.

Q: Sorscha casts Shatter Storm on a unit of Greylords. Does each attack roll from the Frost Bite spray count as a direct hit?

A: Yes.

Q: Does the explosion caused by Shatter Storm affect Incorporeal models?

A: Yes.

Q: While benefiting from Shatter Storm, do models with the Sniper ability choose where to deal AOE damage to warjacks and warbeasts caused by their attacks?

A: No. Models with the Sniper ability only choose where to apply the damage they deal directly. The damage from Shatter Storm is dealt by the spell's effect.

Vladimir Tzepesci, the Dark Champion (pg. 74)

ERRATUM: MARTIAL PARAGON. ADD THE FOLLOWING TEXT TO MARTIAL PARAGON:
Martial Paragon lasts for one turn.

ERRATUM: MARTIAL PARAGON. REMOVE "ROLL" FROM SECOND SENTENCE OF MARTIAL PARAGON.

ERRATUM: RUINATION. REPLACE TEXT OF RUINATION WITH THE FOLLOWING:
If target model is hit, Vladimir may make magic attack rolls against the nearest d6 enemy models within 3" of the original target, regardless of LOS. Each model hit suffers a POW 12 damage roll. When making these additional

attacks, Vladimir ignores Camouflage, concealment, cover, elevation, Invisibility, screening, and Stealth.

Q: Does a Marauder under the effects of Assail gain +2" of distance on Combo Slam attacks?

A: Yes.

Q: Can a model that has special rules preventing it from being targeted by spells be hit by additional Ruination rolls?

A: Yes. The additional Ruination rolls do not target the nearest d6 models.

Behemoth (pg. 76)

ERRATUM: BRAWLER. REPLACE TEXT OF BRAWLER WITH THE FOLLOWING:
The Behemoth gains +2 STR on power attacks and rolls for breaking and maintaining locks.

ERRATUM: SUB CORTEX. REPLACE LAST SENTENCE OF SUB CORTEX WITH THE FOLLOWING:
The Behemoth suffers −2 to Bombard attack rolls while engaged or during any activation it runs, charges, slams, or tramples.

Lich Lord Terminus (pg. 84)

ERRATUM: ANNIHILATION. REPLACE SECOND SENTENCE OF ANNIHILATION WITH THE FOLLOWING:
Terminus gains a soul token for each living model destroyed by Annihilation regardless of his or any other model's location in relation to the model destroyed.

ERRATUM: SACRIFICIAL PAWN. REPLACE FIRST SENTENCE OF SACRIFICIAL PAWN WITH THE FOLLOWING:
Whenever Terminus is directly hit by an enemy ranged attack, his controller may choose to have a friendly non-incorporeal undead model within 3" of Terminus and in his front arc directly hit instead.

Q: Does Terminus get soul tokens for models destroyed during a turn he uses Dragon's Call but before he uses the feat?

A: No.

Q: Can Terminus use Dying Breath after a free strike?

A: Yes.

Q: What happens if Terminus is directly hit by an AOE and uses Sacrificial Pawn?

A: Center the AOE over the model that is hit instead of Terminus.

Errata & Clarifications

Q: Terminus and a friendly non-incorporeal undead model are both hit by a spray attack. Can Terminus use Sacrificial Pawn to have the other model hit twice to avoid being hit himself?

A: Yes.

Q: Does Tattered Wings allow Terminus to charge a target, move past it, and then turn around to face it?

A: No. A charging model must end its charge movement while it engages the target of the charge. In order for Terminus to fly over his charge target, he would have to engage and then disengage it.

Q: How does Demoniac interact with cavalry impact attacks?

A: After destroying a model with an impact attack, an affected cavalry model must make an additional melee attack for Demoniac. This additional melee attack cannot be an impact attack. Once all impact and Demoniac attacks have been resolved, the cavalry model continues its charge movement.

The Witch Coven of Garlghast (pg. 86)

ERRATUM: GHOST WALK. REPLACE FIRST SENTENCE OF GHOST WALK WITH THE FOLLOWING:

During its activation this turn target model/unit may move through any terrain without penalty.

Q: Can each Witch issue an order per activation?

A: Yes.

Q: Each Witch is a warcaster. Does that mean each witch can perform Nightfall once a game?

A: No. The Witch Coven's feat can only be used once per game.

Q: Suppose a model with Stealth crosses the line connecting two Witches and is more than 5" away from both. Does it count as an intervening model when determining if the Witch Coven has a Perfect Conjunction?

A: Yes. The relationship between Stealth and LOS is limited to combat resolution.

Q: A Witch in the Witch Coven of Garlghast targets a model with Stealth with a spell. Which of the models in the Coven has to be within the 5" of the target in order to ignore Stealth?

A: The Witch casting the spell because according to Arcane Nexus, "all modifiers are based on the Witch."

Q: Two models are in base-to-base contact. Is it possible to cast Imprison so that only one of those two is in the perimeter?

A: No.

Q: Can you leave the area of Imprison using a "placing" effect (Flash, Unseen Path, etc.)?

A: Yes.

Q: A warjack affected by Infernal Machine is in melee with a model. The model makes a command check against Terror. Infernal Machine is then cast on another warjack and cast again on the original warjack. Does the model have to make a command check against Terror again?

A: Yes.

Q: A unit under the effects of Necrophage is hit by an AOE or other attack that damages the models simultaneously. How do you determine the first model destroyed in order to resolve the explosion from Necrophage?

A: The attacker chooses which model explodes.

Q: Does the explosion from Necrophage affect incorporeal models?

A: Yes.

Q: Which Witch suffers the damage if a warjack in the Witch Coven's battlegroup is affected by Backlash (Skarre) or Feedback (Satyxis Raiders)?

A: The Witch Coven's controller chooses which of the three Witches will suffer the damage. A different Witch may be chosen for each attack.

Egregore (pg. 88)

ERRATUM: PATHFINDER. REPLACE TEXT OF PATHFINDER WITH THE FOLLOWING:

During its activation, the Egregore ignores movement penalties from, and may charge across, rough terrain and obstacles.

Lich Lord Asphyxious (pg. 90)

ERRATUM: CAUSTIC MIST. IN SECOND SENTENCE OF CAUSTIC MIST, REPLACE "A MODEL MOVING INTO" WITH "A MODEL ENTERING"

ERRATUM: DEATH KNELL. REPLACE TEXT OF DEATH KNELL WITH THE FOLLOWING:

Before dealing damage, count the number of models in the AOE. Subtract one. Add the result to each Death Knell damage roll.

ERRATUM: EXCARNATE. REPLACE TEXT OF EXCARNATE WITH THE FOLLOWING:

Target living non-warcaster, non-warlock warrior model suffering sufficient damage to be destroyed by Excarnate is removed from play. Replace the model with an independent undead Cryx model with one wound under your control. The Cryx player may choose the Excarnate model's facing when it is put in play. The model has the stats, abilities, weapons, and base size of the model removed from play by this spell. If Excarnate leaves play or if the model is destroyed, the model is immediately removed from play.

Q: When using Spectral Legion, what can a returned model do if it cannot charge? What if it can charge but does not have any targets?

A: A returned model that cannot charge at all does nothing. If it can charge but has no target, the model activates but does nothing (pg. 34).

Q: Can Lich Lord Asphyxious use Convocation to cast Puppet Strings or Demoniac offensively?

A: Yes.

Q: A spell cast by means of Convocation cannot be cast by the original caster that turn. Does this also mean that if a caster has already cast the spell this turn before Asphyxious' activation, then Asphyxious cannot use it?

A: Yes.

Q: How does Excarnate and abilities such as the Seneschal's Restoration, Croe's Nine Lives, The Harbinger's Martyrdom, and Weapon Crew interact?

A: Excarnate takes effect first and prevents these abilities from taking effect.

Q: If a model destroyed by Excarnate is knocked down, stationary, has a continuous effect on it, etc., does the Excarnate model inherit these effects?

A: No. It is a new model replacing the one that was destroyed. All spells, effects, and animi on the replaced model expired when it was destroyed by Excarnate.

Wraith Witch Deneghra (pg. 92)

ERRATUM: DARK BANISHMENT. REPLACE TEXT OF DARK BANISHMENT WITH THE FOLLOWING:
After damaging an enemy model with Eclipse, Deneghra's controller may immediately place the model up to d6 inches away from Deneghra plus 1" for each unspent focus point on Deneghra. During this movement the model cannot be targeted by free strikes. There must be enough space to place the models' base. Deneghra's controller chooses the model's new location and facing. If a model is affected by Dark Banishment during its activation, its activation ends immediately after it is placed.

ERRATUM: HARROWING. REPLACE FIRST SENTENCE OF HARROWING WITH THE FOLLOWING:
Models in the target model's unit must move directly toward it during their activation unless they are fleeing.

ERRATUM: INCORPOREAL. REPLACE SIXTH SENTENCE OF INCORPOREAL WITH THE FOLLOWING:
An Incorporeal model only suffers damage and effects from magic attacks, animi, spells, and feats and is not affected by continuous effects.

ERRATUM: MARKED FOR DEATH. REPLACE FIRST SENTENCE OF MARKED FOR DEATH WITH THE FOLLOWING:
Target non-warcaster, non-warlock model loses Incorporeal, Invisible, and Stealth and cannot be affected by effects that prevent it from being targeted.

ERRATUM: TENEBROUS EXILE. REPLACE FIRST SENTENCE OF TENEBROUS EXILE WITH THE FOLLOWING:
Target enemy non-warcaster, non-warlock model/unit becomes Incorporeal and cannot charge, slam, or make melee or ranged attacks for one round.

Errata & Clarifications

Q: If Deneghra is Incorporeal due to Wraith Walker, do continuous effects on her expire before she loses Incorporeal?

A: No. She loses Incorporeal in step 1 of the Maintenance Phase, and continuous effects are resolved in step 4.

Q: Can a model be placed in deep water by Dark Banishment?

A: Yes.

Q: Can Dark Banishment move a model under the effects of Fortify?

A: Yes. Fortify does not offer protection against being placed.

Q: Wraith Witch Deneghra casts Marked for Death on a Khador model within 7" inches of a Winter Guard Mortar Crew. The Mortar has a minimum Range and cannot target within 8". When the Gunner fires the Mortar, what happens?

A: The Gunner must target the marked model when making a ranged attack, so he cannot fire the Mortar at all.

Q: If a model charges or slams a model but a model affected by Marked for Death is also within melee range, what happens?

A: Resolve the attack normally against the original target. Any additional attacks must target the marked model, however.

Q: What happens if Lieutenant Allister Caine uses Maelstrom and there is a model affected by Marked for Death in his control area?

A: Each time Caine makes a Maelstrom attack against a model, the attack is resolved against the marked model instead. Caine must continue to redirect his Maelstrom attacks until the marked model is destroyed.

Deathjack [pg. 94]

ERRATUM: NECROVENT. REPLACE TEXT OF NECROVENT WITH THE FOLLOWING:

Deathjack vents a necrotic ash cloud effect with a 5" AOE centered on itself that remains in play for one round. The cloud remains on the spot placed even if Deathjack moves. Models in the AOE when the cloud is put in play suffer a POW 12 damage roll. Damage rolls must be boosted separately. Necrovent is not a melee attack but may be made after a charge. Deathjack does not roll an additional damage die when it charges and makes a Necrovent attack, but the damage may be boosted normally. The Deathjack may spend focus points to make additional melee attacks after a Necrovent attack. A model entering or ending its activation in the cloud suffers one damage point. Deathjack never suffers damage from Necrovent. A Necrovent special attack does not need a target.

ERRATUM: UNBOUND. REPLACE FIRST SENTENCE OF UNBOUND WITH THE FOLLOWING:

At the start of its activation, without spending a focus point Deathjack immediately charges its controlling warcaster unless it has at least three focus points or a friendly warrior model within 3" of Deathjack is sacrificed and removed from play. If there is a clear path to its controlling warcaster, Deathjack cannot choose a path that would cause it to contact another model or an obstacle so that the charge fails.

Q: Will Disruption prevent the Deathjack from gaining focus from Soul Furnace?

A: No.

Q: What happens when Unbound causes the Deathjack to advance or charge toward its controlling warcaster but it fails to get into melee with the 'caster?

A: Its activation ends.

Q: If the Deathjack is part of the Coven's battlegroup and it becomes Unbound, which of the witches does it charge?

A: It charges the closest Witch within its LOS. Do not forget that the Deathjack has 360° LOS if it has at least one functional Skull of Hate.

Theater of War Campaign System

ERRATUM P.141: PROTECTORATE STRATEGIC OBJECTIVE SCENARIO ONE - SPECIAL RULES AND SET UP. REPLACE FINAL SENTENCE OF THE SECOND PARAGRAPH WITH THE FOLLOWING:

The attacker must destroy all four necrotite mining rigs before Hammertime ends the battle.

ERRATUM P.141: PROTECTORATE STRATEGIC OBJECTIVE SCENARIO TWO - SPECIAL RULES AND SET UP. REPLACE FIRST SENTENCE WITH THE FOLLOWING:

This scenario utilizes Hammertime: adjacent eight (8), near six (6), and distant five (5).

Superiority

Mercenary Contracts (pg. 15)

ERRATUM: MAGNUS' AGENDA CONTRACT ARMY COMPOSITION. REPLACE SECOND BULLET POINT WITH THE FOLLOWING:

The army may also include Boomhowler & Co., Croe's Cutthroats, Gorman di Wulfe, Kell Bailoch, and Steelhead Halberdiers.

Hammersmith (pg. 29)

ERRATUM: BEAT BACK. REPLACE 2ND SENTENCE OF BEAT BACK WITH THE FOLLOWING:

A pushed model moves at half rate in rough terrain and stops if it comes in contact with an obstacle, obstruction, or a model.

ERRATUM: CHAIN ATTACK – CLOBBER. REPLACE 3RD SENTENCE OF CHAIN ATTACK – CLOBBER WITH THE FOLLOWING:

A pushed model moves at half rate in rough terrain and stops if it comes in contact with an obstacle, obstruction, or a model.

Rangers (pg. 30)

ERRATUM: PATHFINDER. REPLACE TEXT OF PATHFINDER WITH THE FOLLOWING:

During his activation, a Ranger ignores movement penalties from, and may charge across, rough terrain and obstacles.

Long Gunner Officer & Standard Bearer (pg. 33)

ERRATUM: SUPPRESSING FIRE. IN SECOND TO LAST SENTENCE OF SUPPRESSING FIRE, REPLACE "WHEN AN ENEMY MODEL MOVES INTO" WITH "WHEN AN ENEMY MODEL ENTERS"

ERRATUM: UNIT STANDARD. REPLACE SECOND SENTENCE OF UNIT STANDARD WITH THE FOLLOWING:

If the Standard Bearer is destroyed or removed from play, a Gunner in this unit within 1" can take the Standard Bearer's place immediately and become the new Standard Bearer.

Trencher Officer & Sharpshooter (pg. 34)

ERRATUM: DAMAGE. CHANGE "DAMAGE" TO "LIEUTENANT'S DAMAGE" BELOW THE STAT BAR.

The Sharpshooter has one damage point.

Errata & Clarifications (right column)

ERRATUM: BAYONET CHARGE. REPLACE TEXT OF BAYONET CHARGE WITH THE FOLLOWING:

Every Trencher who received this order must either charge or run. As part of a charge, after moving but before performing his combat action, each Trencher who received this order must, if possible, make a single ranged attack targeting the model charged. Trenchers are not considered to be in melee when resolving the Bayonet Charge ranged attacks, nor are the targets of those attacks considered to be in melee with them. If the target is not in melee range after moving, the Bayonet Charge's ranged attack must still be made before the Trencher's activation ends. A Trencher cannot target a model with which he was in melee at the start of his activation with the Bayonet Charge's ranged attack.

Feora, Protector of the Flame (pg. 62)

ERRATUM: BLAZING AURA. REPLACE FIRST SENTENCE OF BLAZING AURA WITH THE FOLLOWING:

When a model in target friendly Protectorate unit is damaged by an enemy attack, its attacker suffers an equal damage roll.

Q: If two or more models under the affects of Blazing Aura are destroyed from a single spell or attack, such as Chain Lightning, does the attacking model suffer more than one damage roll?

A: Yes.

Castigator (pg. 65)

ERRATUM: COMBUSTION. REPLACE TEXT OF COMBUSTION WITH THE FOLLOWING:

Models within 1" of the Castigator suffer a POW 12 damage roll. Damage rolls must be boosted separately. Combustion is not a melee attack but may be made after a charge. The Castigator does not roll an additional damage die when it charges and makes a Combustion attack, but the damage roll may be boosted normally. The Castigator may spend focus points to make additional melee attacks after a Combustion attack. Combustion lasts for one round. A model entering the area within 1" of the Castigator and/or ending its movement within 1" of the Castigator suffers an unboostable POW 12 damage roll. A Combustion special attack does not need a target.

Exemplar Vengers (pg. 67)

ERRATUM: BLESSED. ADD THE FOLLOWING TEXT TO BLESSED:

An Exemplar Venger may charge incorporeal models.

Errata & Clarifications

Exemplars Errant (pg. 68)

Q: Does Blessed allow Exemplar Errant models to ignore bonuses from terrain created by spells, such as a cover bonus gained by a model behind Gorten Grundback's Wall of Stone?

A: Yes.

Reclaimer (pg. 70)

ERRATUM: GATEKEEPER. REPLACE TEXT OF GATEKEEPER WITH THE FOLLOWING:

The Reclaimer gains a soul token for each friendly living Protectorate model destroyed within 7".

Q: Can the Reclaimer allocate focus to the Avatar?

A: No.

Temple Flameguard Officer & Standard Bearer (pg. 71)

ERRATUM: UNIT STANDARD. REPLACE SECOND SENTENCE OF UNIT STANDARD WITH THE FOLLOWING:

If the Standard Bearer is destroyed or removed from play, a Flameguard in this unit within 1" can take the Standard Bearer's place immediately and become the new Standard Bearer.

High Paladin Dartan Vilmon (pg. 72)

Q: When Vilmon enters Impervious Wall, do continuous effects on him expire?

A: No.

Kommander Orsus Zoktavir (pg. 98)

ERRATUM: FEEL THE HATE. REPLACE TEXT OF FEEL THE HATE WITH THE FOLLOWING:

This turn, Zoktavir gains a rage token for each enemy model destroyed in his control area after using Feel the Hate. After all friendly models have completed their activations, Zoktavir may allocate up to 3 rage tokens to each friendly non-warcaster Khador model in his control area. Rage tokens that are not allocated are removed from Zoktavir. Zoktavir gains no additional rage tokens after this. A model may spend one rage token to move up to its current SPD in inches immediately and make one melee attack. Additional rage tokens may be spent to make additional melee attacks or to boost melee attack or damage rolls. Remove unspent rage tokens at the end of the turn.

Q: While under the effects of Feel the Hate, can a model move out of formation?

A: No.

Spriggan (pg. 100)

Q: While charging, can the Spriggan trample the target of the charge?

A: No. A charging model must stop while its target is in melee range.

Assault Kommandos (pg. 103)

ERRATUM: FUMIGATE. REPLACE FIRST 2 SENTENCES OF FUMIGATE WITH THE FOLLOWING:

As part of a charge, after moving but before performing his combat action, each Kommando who receives this order must, if possible, make a single Strangle Gas Bomb ranged attack targeting the model charged. Kommandos are not considered to be in melee when resolving these Strangle Gas Bomb ranged attacks, nor are the targets of these attacks considered to be in melee with them.

Winter Guard Field Gun Crew (pg. 104)

ERRATUM: WEAPON CREW. REPLACE FIFTH SENTENCE OF WEAPON CREW WITH THE FOLLOWING:

If the gunner is destroyed or removed from play, a crewman in this unit within 1" can take the destroyed gunner's place immediately and become the new gunner. Remove the crewman from the table instead of the gunner.

Winter Guard Officer & Standard Bearer (pg. 105)

ERRATUM: UNIT STANDARD. REPLACE SECOND SENTENCE OF UNIT STANDARD WITH THE FOLLOWING:

If the Standard Bearer is destroyed or removed from play, a Guardsman in this unit within 1" can take the Standard Bearer's place immediately and become the new Standard Bearer.

Kovnik Jozef Grigorovich (pg. 108)

ERRATUM: FOR THE MOTHERLAND. REPLACE TEXT OF FOR THE MOTHERLAND WITH THE FOLLOWING:

When an affected model is destroyed by an enemy attack, before being removed from the table, the destroyed model may immediately make one ranged or melee attack. For the Motherland ranged attacks ignore a weapon's ROF. Models that are stationary at the time of destruction do not benefit from For the Motherland.

Skarre, Queen of the Broken Coast (pg. 135)

ERRATUM: BLACK SPOT. ADD THE FOLLOWING TEXT TO THE END OF BLACK SPOT:

Attacks gained from this spell cannot generate further additional attacks. While making a special attack, a model only benefits from Black Spot once regardless of the number of attacks generated or the number of models destroyed by the special attack.

ERRATUM: LIFE TRADER. REPLACE TEXT OF LIFE TRADER WITH THE FOLLOWING:

After a successful attack with Takkaryx, Skarre may take one damage point to roll an additional damage die.

Q: How many times can Skarre use Precognition during her activation?

A: There is no restriction to the number of times Skarre can use Precognition during a single activation.

Q: How does Black Spot interact with cavalry impact attacks?

A: After destroying a model affected by Black Spot with an impact attack, the cavalry model may immediately make an additional melee attack. This additional attack cannot be an impact attack. Once all impact and Black Spot attacks have been resolved, the cavalry model continues its charge movement.

Harrower (pg. 137)

ERRATUM: ALL TERRAIN. REPLACE TEXT OF ALL TERRAIN WITH THE FOLLOWING:

During its activation, the Harrower ignores movement penalties from, and may charge and slam across, rough terrain and obstacles.

Satyxis Raider Sea Witch (pg. 142)

ERRATUM: BRUME. REPLACE TEXT OF BRUME WITH THE FOLLOWING:

For one round, models in the Sea Witch's unit gain Pathfinder and Camouflage. During its activation, a model with Pathfinder ignores movement penalties from, and may charge across, rough terrain and obstacles. Models with Camouflage gain an additional +2 DEF when benefiting from concealment or cover.

Bane Lord Tartarus (pg. 145)

ERRATUM: THRESHER. ADD THE FOLLOWING TEXT TO END OF THRESHER:

A model is ineligible to be hit if it has a special rule preventing it from being targeted or if the attacker's line of sight is completely blocked by terrain.

Ashlynn D'Elyse (pg. 168)

Q: When using Roulette in combination with Signs & Portents, who gets to remove dice first?

A: Resolve the attacker's effects first.

Q: If Ashlynn is knocked down, can she forfeit her action to stand, cast Flashing Blade, and then move?

A: Yes.

Q: Can a model affected by Feint move out of formation?

A: No.

Q: Do you choose which column suffers damage every time you cast Kiss of Death, or just if the damage roll fails to exceed the target's ARM?

A: You always get to choose the column on a warjack or the branch on a warbeast.

Durgen Madhammer (pg. 171)

ERRATUM: GROUND ZERO. REPLACE FOURTH SENTENCE OF GROUND ZERO WITH THE FOLLOWING:

A pushed model moves at half rate through rough terrain and stops if it comes in contact with an obstacle, obstruction, or model.

Magnus the Warlord (pg. 173)

ERRATUM: MOBILIZE. REPLACE SECOND SENTENCE OF MOBILIZE WITH THE FOLLOWING:

Affected models may charge, slam, or trample across rough terrain and obstacles.

Q: Can a model suffering Stagger declare a charge?

A: Yes. However, the model suffering from Stagger will not be able to make a charge attack at the conclusion of the charge movement.

Vanguard (pg. 175)

ERRATUM: ASSAULT. REPLACE TEXT OF ASSAULT WITH THE FOLLOWING:

As part of a charge, after moving but before performing its combat action, the Vanguard may assault. When making an Assault, the Vanguard makes a single ranged attack targeting the model charged. The Vanguard is not considered to be in melee when making the Assault ranged attack, nor is the target considered to be in melee with the Vanguard. If the target is not in melee range after moving, the Vanguard must still make the Assault ranged attack before its activation ends. The Vanguard

Errata & Clarifications

cannot target a model with which it was in melee at the start of its activation with an Assault ranged attack.

Mule (pg. 177)

Q: Can models thrown by Critical Devastation collide with each other?

A: No.

Q: Is a distance and direction rolled separately for each model caught in Critical Devastation's area?

A: Yes.

Croe's Cutthroats (pg. 178)

ERRATUM: PATHFINDER. REPLACE TEXT OF PATHFINDER WITH THE FOLLOWING:

During his activation, a Cutthroat ignores movement penalties from, and may charge across, rough terrain and obstacles.

Q: If Croe is destroyed by a continuous effect and replaces a Cutthroat with Nine Lives, does the continuous effect remain on him?

A: Yes.

Q: Croe disengages, suffers sufficient damage to be destroyed by the free strike, and uses Nine Lives to prevent his destruction. Can he finish his movement and action?

A: Yes.

Cylena Raefyll & Nyss Hunters (pg. 179)

ERRATUM: PATHFINDER. REPLACE TEXT OF PATHFINDER WITH THE FOLLOWING:

During his activation, a Nyss Hunter ignores movement penalties from, and may charge across, rough terrain and obstacles.

Q: Can the Concentrated Volley affect models that cannot be targeted due to a spell or ability?

A: Yes. The model is not targeted by the attack.

Alexia Ciannor (pg. 182)

ERRATUM: MAGIC ABILITY. ADD TO THE TEXT OF MAGIC ABILITY:

Alexia cannot make additional attacks after making a magic attack.

ERRATUM: STRENGTH OF DEATH. REPLACE TEXT OF STRENGTH OF DEATH WITH THE FOLLOWING:

Friendly Risen models currently in Alexia's command range gain boosted attack and damage rolls this turn.

Q: What happens if both players are fielding Alexia and a model is destroyed within range for both Alexias to use Raise Dead?

A: A model can only generate one Risen. If more than one model is able to create a Risen through the Raise Dead ability, the model nearest the destroyed model receives the Risen.

Q: Do Risen generated during my Risen unit's activation get an action?

A: Yes.

Q: If Alexia and two Risen models are hit by an AOE attack, can she sacrifice the Risen models that were hit by the attack to prevent damage to herself before they are destroyed?

A: No. The damage is dealt simultaneously.

Q: Alexia activates and commands her Risen unit to run or charge. A model is destroyed and a Risen is added to the unit. Does the new Risen model receive the charge order?

A: No. The new Risen model was not around to receive the order, so it cannot charge.

Q: Is Mob a melee attack?

A: Yes.

Ogrun Bokur (pg. 185)

Q: How does the Ogrun Bokur's Slam special attack work?

A: The Bokur's Slam is resolved like a warjack's slam power attack except that he does not have to spend a focus point to perform it.

Q: An Ogrun Bokur has a Machine Wraith for a client. If the Machine Wraith possesses a warjack and its model is removed from the table, is the Bokur still within 6" of its client as long as it is within 6" of the possessed warjack?

A: No. The Machine Wraith is no longer on the table, so the Bokur cannot be within 6" of it.

Q: Can you have two Bokurs assigned to two separate Witches of the Witch Coven of Garlghast?

A: Yes.

Templates

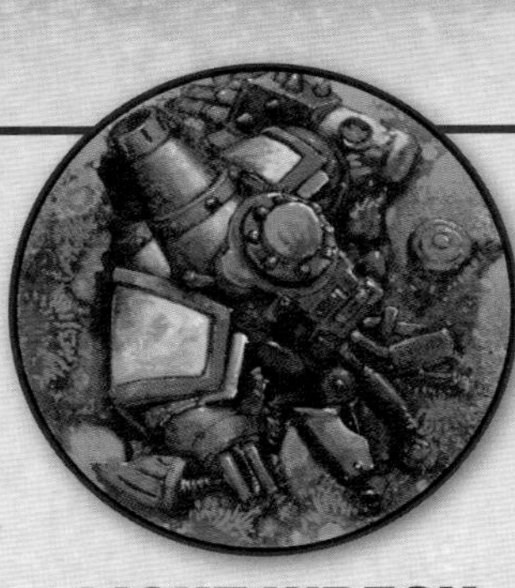

LIGHT WRECK MARKER

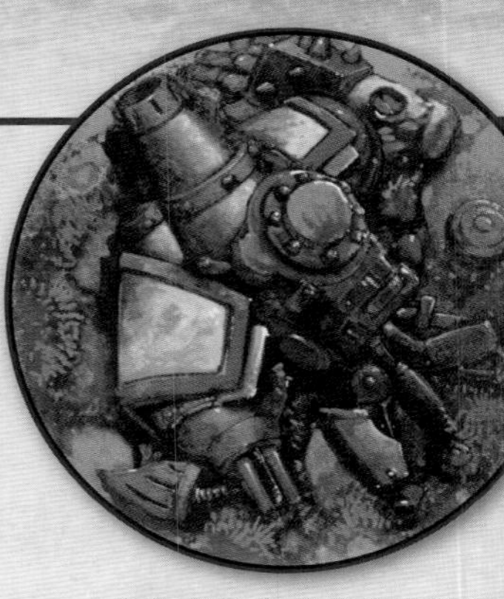

HEAVY WRECK MARKER

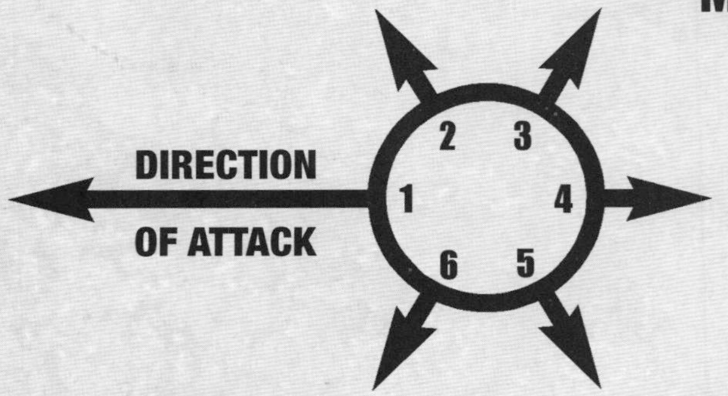

DIRECTION

OF ATTACK

2 3

1 4

6 5

DEVIATION TEMPLATE

3" BLAST

4" BLAST

5" BLAST

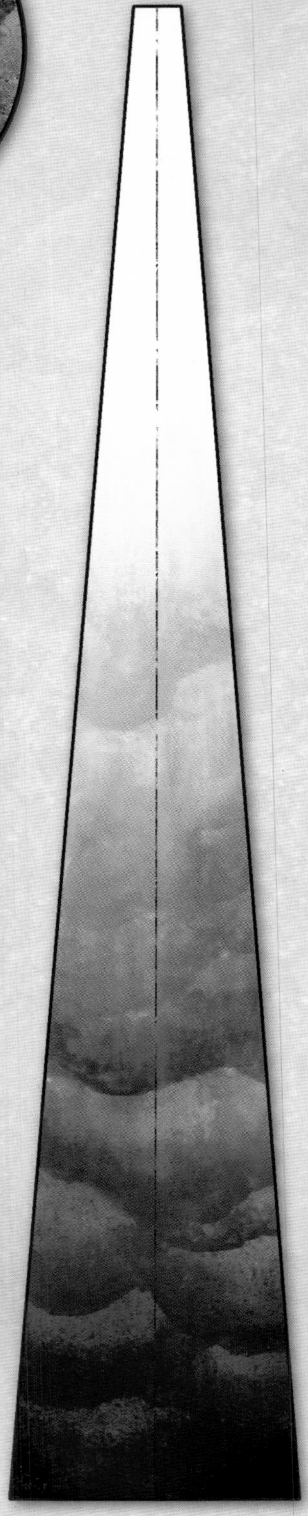

SPRAY TEMPLATE

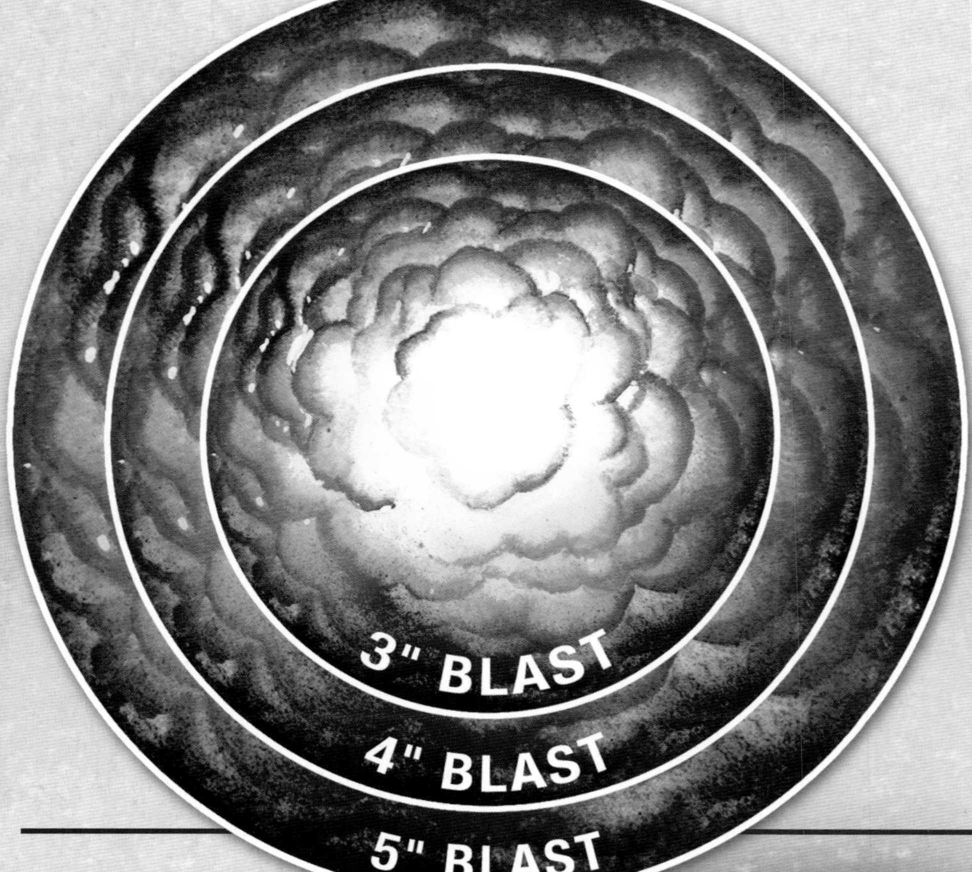